Teachers as Researchers
Qualitative inquiry as a path to empowerment

Second edition

Joe L. Kincheloe

RoutledgeFalmer
Taylor & Francis Group

LONDON AND NEW YORK

First published 2003
by RoutledgeFalmer
11 New Fetter Lane, London EC4P 4EE

Simultaneously published in the USA and Canada
by RoutledgeFalmer
29 West 35th Street, New York, NY 10001

RoutledgeFalmer is an imprint of the Taylor & Francis Group

© 2003 Joe L. Kincheloe

Typeset in 10.5/12pt Bembo by Graphicraft Limited, Hong Kong
Printed and bound in Great Britain by St Edmundsbury Press,
Bury St Edmunds, Suffolk

British Library Cataloguing in Publication Data
A catalogue record for this book is available
from the British Library

Library of Congress Cataloging in Publication Data
Kincheloe, Joe L.
    Teachers as researchers: qualitative inquiry as a path to
empowerment / Joe L. Kincheloe.–2nd ed.
      p. cm. – (Teachers' library)
    1. Education–Research–United States. 2. Teachers–United
States. I. Title. II. Teachers' library (London, England)

LB1028.25.U6 K56 2002
370'.78073–dc21   2002026985

ISBN 0-415-27645-4 (hbk)
ISBN 0-415-27646-2 (pbk)

Contents

Introduction: Positivistic Standards and the Bizarre Educational World of the Twenty-first Century

When I first wrote this book in 1991 I was very concerned with a number of disturbing educational trends operating in the late 1980s and early 1990s. The following is the preface I wrote delineating those concerns and their relationship to *Teachers As Researchers*:

> I am a teacher. I want to do good work. Having attended, worked in, and visited many schools in North America, I believe that at the end of the twentieth century teaching is not good work. As I listen to teachers talk about their jobs or watch hierarchical inter-actions between administrators and teachers, I sense a crisis in the teaching profession. Never sure that I am characterizing the crisis accurately, I listen intensely to the brilliant teachers who talk to me of resigning, to the brilliant teacher education students who can't get hired or who have trouble in student teaching because of their intelligence, and to the great teachers who have worked invisibly for years, rarely rewarded for their dedication.
>
> The crisis seems to have something to do with a *general* lack of consciousness — a garbled sense of purpose, of direction. What I feel in the schools is not simply a failure of schools and school leaders, but a more general inability of Western peoples to conceptualize a system of meaning — i.e., an ethical sense on which they can build humane and evolving institutions. The only social/ educational visions which have gained public attention in the last years of the twentieth century have come from people like Ronald Reagan or William Bennett who offer a misleading vision of a return to a romanticized past, a golden era when teachers enforced rules and students learned the basics. Such an authoritarian vision underlines the crisis I describe; it lays the foundation for educational reform movements that assume that if order can be reestablished, if educational leaders can just lay out what it is teachers should do and teachers just do it, schools may return to their previous glory.
>
> Such a socio-educational vision is naive and dangerous, viewing schools as if they had nothing to do with the world that

surrounds them. It assumes that Western industrial organization
with its bureaucratic, hierarchical structure is the only model available for constructing institutions. In this context it views teachers as
blue collar workers, passive recipients of the dictates of the experts.
In other words, it disregards, as does the industrial organization it
unconsciously emulates, the special knowledge of those who actually
do the everyday work in an organization. It assumes that teachers
cannot take greater responsibility in the administration of a school
and that efforts in such a direction are dangerous. On the basis of
such assumptions it supports forms of teacher education which serve
to deskill teachers, teaching them not to think in self-directed, empowered ways. The professional training which emerges is obsessed
with format over substance, with teaching teachers to be 'supervis-
able' to be team players, to fit into organizational structures.

Teachers understand that something is not right. My conversations with them often touch raw nerves, an anger just below the
surface. Such alienation finds its origins in their perception that
few in the organization respect them, few value their voices, their
knowledge of the educational process. Because of their sensitivity,
I must be careful: I too, am perceived as an outsider, just another
critic who talks at them from afar. I understand such feelings. I
attempt to write this book with that understanding constantly in
mind.

Without romanticizing, patronizing, or denigrating them, I
attempt to engage teachers with some ideas that may be helpful
in their struggle to control their own professional destinies. These
ideas revolve around the notion of teachers as researchers, an old
idea which when reconceptualized in conjunction with a reasonable
system of meaning may provide a starting place for a democratic
reorganization of the way schools work. This democratic reconceptualization of education embraces a vision which takes seriously
notions of social justice, racial, gender, and class equality, and
alternative ways of seeing the world borrowed from people who
have traditionally been ignored. I want students of education to
read this book — but most of all I want teachers to read it. My
hope is that it will serve as an abrasive grain of sand which induces
them to name their discontent, to act on such an articulation. To
embrace hope in this era of cynicism is a revolutionary act. But as
long as we can formulate visions, possibility persists.

My concerns and interests have not changed over the last eleven years
but conditions have. The right-wing deskilling trends I referred to in 1991
have in the ensuing years become institutionalized in the U.S. under the
banner of the standards movement that was just emerging when the first
edition of this book appeared. In this revised context it is important to

discuss this movement and its effects on educational quality and teacher work in particular. A cogent discussion of teachers as researchers, teachers as self-directed scholars cannot take place outside of this context.

The Age of Mediocrity: Top-down Standards and the Desecration of Teachers

We live in an age of mediocrity where dreaming about 'what could be' in the educational, psychological, cultural, economic, and political realm is somehow undervalued and even discouraged. Sometimes when I speak of these matters to groups, they see me as coming from a crack in a time warp. They seem to have never heard such talk in their lives. When we speak of social vision in contemporary Western societies, we seem to stay well within the bounds of the marketplace or neo-fundamentalist religions scarred by their ethnocentrism and disdain of difference. Imagination in this context is domesticated and directed to the realm of escapist entertainment or marketing. Indeed, as a society we don't seem very interested in the complex and deep processes that generate our dreams (defined in multiple ways) and our sense of purpose. After the tragic attacks of September 11, 2001, we speak of unity of purpose but few have taken time to consider what such a concept might mean in a rethinking of the global future.

Education in this globalized age of mediocrity devolves into an effort to make students competitive in the cold new economic order that faces them. The call for high educational standards in a global economy is touted as new and innovative educational policy; but even a cursory survey of twentieth-century educational history will reveal numerous times when 'innovators' instituted such reforms only to watch them fail. When educational purpose is defined as the process of training the types of individuals business and industry say they need, educational quality declines. In this situation reformers attempt to transform schools into venues for ideological indoctrination and social regulation while reducing teachers to deliverers of pre-packaged and homogenized information. Even by traditional canonical modes of evaluation, the sanctity of education is debased.

My purpose in *Teachers as Researchers* both in 1991 and in the present is to argue that these tendencies in educational history and in the present standards movement are not accidental. These technicalizing and deskilling approaches to education are the direct result of particular Western ways of seeing the world, the nature of human beings, the developmental processes of the young, the composition of the mind, and the production of knowledge. This book is based on the contention that Cartesian–Newtonian–Baconian science has produced a very restricted view of humans and their potentials. Indeed, in this framework the definition of a high-functioning student is one with the ability to mirror back the external world described by Western science.

In this reductionistic view the human mind receives information from the body's senses, stores it like a squirrel his nuts in data banks, and at best puts pieces of it together to construct a generalization. Any deviation from this procedure of reproducing 'objective reality' is condemned as a marker of psychological inability or cultural inferiority. In the present era described by many as a knowledge society run by knowledge workers in a knowledge economy, this view of mind and information is woefully inadequate. It is important to understand this view, however, because it has been complicit in all of the truncated perspectives that have historically shaped schooling in general and the lives of teachers in particular. In the contemporary conversation about knowledge workers and their education, understanding the reductionistic view and developing the scholarly and political skills to move beyond it become even more vital to the future of democracy and the pedagogical strategies that support it. Teachers becoming researchers is a necessary component of this important struggle (Grof, 1993; O'Sullivan, 1999).

Technical Standards, Standardization, and Educational Irrationality

The top-down technical standards of the contemporary reform movement are so specific in their prescribed list of 'facts' to be covered that the best teachers are handcuffed in their effort to teach complex concepts and to connect them to the lived experiences of students (Pushkin, 2001). In this irrational context such teachers are victimized by a simplistic and panicky response to social change, youth-in-crisis, or a decline in standardized test scores. Relying on reductionistic measurements of student memorization of unconnected fragments of information, advocates of top-down, imposed content standards have no basis for evaluating more sophisticated aspects of learning and teaching (Bereiter, 2002). Indeed, they cannot measure even the traditional skills of good scholars not to mention the innovative and evolving operations of intellects coming from diverse cultures and counter-Cartesian–Newtonian–Baconian locales. Even the work of Albert Einstein in physics — portions of which such as the Special Theory of Relativity are almost a century old — cannot be taught, learned, or evaluated in the intellectual and pedagogical quagmire of top-down standards (Kincheloe, Steinberg, and Tippins, 1999).

Technical standards demand that teachers in the same subjects and grade levels cover the same content, assign the same importance to the content they cover, and evaluate it in the same way (Marzano and Kendall, 1999). Such standardization ignores the profound differences between diverse schools, school settings, student needs, and so on. As teacher-author Susan Ohanian (1999) puts it: 'a one-size-fits-all curriculum ends up fitting nobody' (p. 43). As it fits nobody, such an educational arrangement subverts the possibility that self-directed teacher professionals might research school atmospheres, the communities surrounding schools, student needs, the disciplinary and counter-disciplinary knowledges constituting the curriculum, and the administrative *modus operandi* of both their districts and their schools. Informed by these understandings, such teachers as researchers could better develop and implement a curriculum connected to the vicissitudes and exigencies of their unique situations.

Such teachers are threats in the eyes of advocates of top-down, technical, and standardized standards. Such teachers seek out diverse perspectives, confront students with conflicting information and different interpretations of the same data. They raise questions in the minds of their students and colleagues — an unappreciated activity in the technicalized status quo. One thing that right-wing advocates of technical standards don't want is for students to question the 'facts.' In this desire they are similar to the educational agents of totalitarian political regimes throughout human history. Democratic educational leaders, simply put, don't repress questions about anything having to do with curriculum or pedagogy. In the contemporary context of top-down, unquestionable standards, the purpose of education becomes based more on the desire for social regulation than for emancipation and freedom. Teachers and students become objects of management, a mode of discipline that serves particular private interests (Weil, 2001b).

In these politico-educational arrangements students — the poor and racially marginalized ones in particular — face the consequences of this pedagogical irrationality: deskilled and dispirited teachers, over-emphasis on standards test preparation, already inadequate educational monies diverted to test preparation materials, and vacuous and fatuous skill and drill exercises (Linne, 2001). Unsurprisingly, many of the more academically talented teachers in this context leave the profession. Such teachers speak with great emotion of the anti-intellectual culture of such schools and the obstacles they faced in their desire to be challenging and inspirational teachers. Again, in this book I attempt to drive home the point that these disastrous realities are not accidental. A diverse set of social, political, and philosophical forces have historically coalesced to shape such situations. For example, the Cartesian–Newtonian–Baconian view of the mind is one of the numerous historical concepts at work in the technical standards fiasco described here. In this conceptualization the mind is not a constructor of reality but merely a filing cabinet into which unproblematized, objective data can be stored.

In this reductionistic modernist perspective not only is the mind a filing cabinet but knowledge is a discrete object that is found in people's brains and reference books. Good teaching, thus, becomes stuffing as much of this knowledge into students' minds as possible. Unfortunately, the Cartesian story goes, some of the students' filing cabinets are much bigger than others and there is nothing educators can do about that (Howley, Pendarvis, and Howley, 1993; Bereiter, 2002). The idea that mind and knowledge are much more complex entities is lost in this context. The notion that understanding this complexity and using it as an embarkation point for future cognitive development and exploration of the cosmos is central to becoming a great scholar and a brilliant teacher is not understood in contemporary schooling. Here is a conceptual window through which we can escape the age of mediocrity and the dumbed-down schools of technical standards. It is the excitement of this venture that drives *Teachers as Researchers*.

Thus, this book opposes reductionistic efforts to construct: (1) education as memory work for objective standards tests; and (2) teaching as a low-skill activity where teachers do only what they are told. In the context of technical standards, teaching for understanding becomes an act of resistance. Advocacy of teaching for understanding would seem unnecessary except for the fact that it is undermined by these reductionistic reforms. In a Socratic vein I fear that forcing critical teachers to drink hemlock will experience a resurgence. Educators who teach for understanding, beware. The remarkable aspect of this contemporary technical reform is that it is actually taking place in the twenty-first century. The only learning that matters is a learning that engages understanding. Mindless memorization of data for standards tests, even from a crass economic perspective, has no value except for performance on the test itself. In a globalized, technological society it is this higher order of understanding that is needed for any type of vocation that involves working with data. Most of the cognitive functions tested on a standards test can now be automated.

But political and educational leaders in the electronic world of the first decade of the twenty-first century don't talk about teaching for understanding or issues of justice and education. Such leaders deal with surface features in a struggle for good public relations. 'I will set high standards for schools,' they tell us, 'and demand strict accountability.' Questions concerning the effect of such standards and accountability procedures are infrequently raised. Public discussion of the purpose of education in a democratic society or inquiries into the relationship between contemporary social problems and schooling are rarely heard in this Disney World of standards.

Even when leaders make grand pronouncements about setting tough new standards, such declarations are rarely accompanied by tangible resources to implement them. This is justified by free market references to the failure of the public space and the elevation of the private realm of business as the proper locale for educational endeavor. In this right-wing ideological context one might argue that standards reforms are set up to fail. In the wake of such failure it will be much easier to justify corporate-run, for-profit schools. In this privatized context the need for scholarly teachers who raise questions about the curriculum will be finally erased. In this cleansed context the work of ideological regulation can continue uncontested (Apple, 1993; Ohanian, 1999; Malewski, 2001b).

In the short run, however, technical standards work to destroy intellectually rigorous educational programs (Fenimore-Smith and Pailliotet, 2001) and undermine concern with the nature and best interests of learners. Studies suggest that once top-down technical standards are imposed, students become progressively disengaged from the process of learning. Curricular standardization particularly subverts the efforts of poor and minority students, as they quickly lose touch with the curriculum and classroom assignments (Novick, 1996). Indeed, technical content standards violate a key pedagogical principle: educational experience should be tied to the psychological and social investments of the learner. This does not mean advocacy of some simplistic effort to be relevant, but a more complex concern with engaging the libidinal energy of students with the pedagogical process.

Brilliant teachers when free from technical constraints work tirelessly to connect disciplinary and counter-disciplinary information with the fears, joys, questions, dreams, aspirations, and interpersonal relationships of their students. Without such connections education can be a supremely empty process. When the real-life experiences and personal investigations of students are no longer germane to curriculum development, the battle for a rigorous intellectual and motivating education is almost lost (Foote and Goodson, 2001; Schubert and Thomas, 2001). Teachers who are researchers study student backgrounds and needs in order to avoid such a pedagogical tragedy. These concerns encompass the basic themes of this book.

Knowledge in Top-down Standards

As we dig deeper into the educational effects of top-down technical standards we begin to realize that many problematic assumptions are hidden within them. One assumption that is central to the focus of this book involves the nature of knowledge. In many ways the technical standards view of knowledge is philosophically impaired. How advocates of technical standards describe knowing, assess what is worthy of being known, and evaluate knowledge exerts profound impact on the nature of classroom teaching (Mayers, 2001b). Technicist educators, John Dewey (1916) argued decades ago, view knowledge as an entity complete in itself unconnected to other forces.

The technicist, positivist tradition of producing knowledge — from which contemporary top-down standards emerge — seeks to provide a timeless body of truth. This so-called 'formal knowledge' is not only unconnected to the world but separate from issues of commitment, emotion, values, and ethical action. The objectivity inscribed in formal knowledge often becomes a signifier for political passivity and elevation to an elite sociopolitical and economic location. Thus, in its lofty position, positivistic formalism refuses to analyze the relationship between knowledge production and educational practices. In technical standards teachers are presented with formal knowledge and expected forthwith to deliver it to their classrooms.

The delivery of such formal knowledge to students involves pronouncements such as: 'after the first Thanksgiving dinner the Pilgrims and the Indians lived happily ever after'; or in its application to practice, 'the research tells us to teach secondary science in this manner.' The problem in the latter example involves formalism's failure to study the complex relationship between professional knowledge and the teaching act. Once again, formalism fails to discern the complexity of teaching, that is, the complicated ways that knowledge, consciousness, everyday life, and professional practice intersect. Without this critical recognition, knowledge production in colleges of education is somewhat irrelevant to teachers. Formal knowledge production too often fails to question the relationship between professional knowledge and indeterminant zones of practice characterized by complexity, conflict, ambiguity, and uniqueness. Such a practical zone exists outside the boundaries of positivism and the formal knowledge it produces. Formalism can't cope with everyday life's and the classroom's ill-formed problems.

The vision of education advocated in this book positions teachers as professionals who produce knowledge about their practice. It is dedicated to transcending the reductionism of formal knowledge. Aware of the complicated nature of curriculum development, the role of power in all aspects of the pedagogical process, and the complexity of educational practice, teachers as researchers understand the flaw of the formalist conception of knowledge. It is simply not possible, I argue throughout this book, to produce objective knowledge that corresponds to and reflects an unchanging, independent world. When advocates of technical standards propose to do this, they are perpetrating a fraud on both the larger society and the educational community. They are arrogantly asserting that they undisputedly possess the one correct interpretation of the world and that the job of teachers is to meekly pass this information along to students.

Knowledge that purports to reflect an independent, external world is ensnared in a web of reductionism. To preserve its sanctity, advocates of formalism must protect knowledge from confrontations with disorderliness and irrationality. In the classroom such epistemological tidiness exhibits itself in the obsession with correctly grasping the author's meaning. Thus, despite what one may see in a text when examined psychoanalytically, epistemologically, politically, culturally, philosophically, and so on, the author's meaning becomes a transcendental object that is the *raison d'être* of the pedagogical task.

The fetishization of the author's meaning is one more part of the puzzle of formalist knowledge. These parts, these things-in-themselves and their relegation to the mental filing cabinet take precedence over conceptual totalities, constellations of ideas and their uses in the world. Indeed, in formalism and the technical standards it supports these totalities and constellations of ideas are deemed irrelevant. In higher education, disciplinary gatekeepers work in concert with advocates of technical standards in elementary and secondary schools to maintain an irrational — although always expressed in the name of rationality — *status quo*. In this context meaning is sacrificed for formalistic order and pseudo-tidiness (Madison, 1988; Schön, 1995; Thomas, 1998).

Reductionism and Technical Standards: The Jail Break to Complexity

This obsession with order and tidiness is one aspect of Cartesian reductionism (Lemke, 1995). In this paradigm — the way of seeing that supports technical standards — scientists assert that the behavior of the whole can be grasped by knowledge of the properties of the parts. In this reductionistic Cartesian analytic the parts of a phenomenon cannot be studied any farther, unless we break them into even smaller parts. On this conceptual foundation Western education has rested. After a series of challenges to the framework in the twentieth century, it has returned with a vengeance in the twenty-first century. Implicit in this Cartesian reductionism is the belief that there are limited and correct meanings to be derived from any phenomenon. And the purpose of schooling is to simply pass on such meanings to students.

Thus, in a reductionistic pedagogical context meanings need to be discovered, rediscovered, and copied. Student analysis and interpretation in this context are an attempt to reconstruct what the scientist produced or, again, the meaning the author intended. These epistemological dynamics tacitly shape the purposes of schooling and the nature of classroom life. A reductionistic paradigm discourages the preparation of inquisitive, knowledge-producing, critical students and teachers; a more complex paradigm encourages more skeptical participants who appreciate the hidden dimensions of knowledge production and the complicity of power in all aspects of the pedagogical process. My argument here is direct: reductionist ways of seeing, teaching, and learning pose a direct threat to education as a practice of democracy (Madison, 1988; Capra, 1996).

Educators who support teacher professionalism look at the reductionistic technical standards with fear and trembling. Because teaching is viewed as a neat and tidy act, it can be standardized and monitored. Susan Ohanian (1999) describes a question–answer session at a Reading Summit in Illinois in 1996. After an advocate of technical standards had spoken on the need for 'highly structured, intense [reading] programs that explicitly teach application of phonologic rules to print,' an educator in the audience raised questions about the desirability and feasibility of controlling a teacher's methods of teaching and individual style. The speaker replied:

> We had careful monitoring of the teachers. First there was thirty hours of training during the summer. Then every teacher was monitored in the classroom every other week — or every day, if necessary. We were breathing down the necks both of raw recruits and veteran teachers. The teacher variable does not contribute significantly above and beyond the curriculum, so what we have here is a powerful mathematical model. My hypothesis is the teacher variable will be less significant within the direct instruction group.
>
> (Ohanian: 49)

This is the language — 'teacher variable' — and mind-set of reductionism. The chilling implication here is that teachers are less important than the standards and techniques employed by the experts. The obvious question that arises in this context is why employ educated teachers if this is the case. Find friendly young people, preferably large for purposes of classroom control, who can read at about the seventh grade level; provide them with scripted material and a six-week training course in teaching techniques and turn them loose in the school. Much money could be saved — hell, we could pay them minimum wages. As soon as the technology is ready, we can replace these functionaries with computer-teachers. No need for teachers as researchers here.

There is something surreal about such perspectives. Proponents of such reductionist, top-down, dehumanized modes of pedagogy and regulation seem to operate at what Ed O'Sullivan refers to as a 'preconscious, non-reflective state' (1999: 34). In this Cartesian trance individuals seem to operate without any consciousness of the contradictions operating in their positions, without an awareness of the anti-democratic strategies they implement, without insight into the way their plans degrade and demoralize the teaching profession. In this reductionistic jailhouse questions involving the educational gaps between the rich and poor are deemed inappropriate. Questions about indoctrination fall on deaf ears. Such problems do not lend themselves to neat reductionistic measurement with handy quantitative results.

Technical standards offer profoundly simplistic answers to difficult socio-educational questions. How is it possible to solve educational problems that are connected to so many social, cultural, historical, political, philosophical, and economic dynamics circulating around them? If the lived world is a complex place, then the lived world of school is a complex place squared. Appreciating the complex and diverse forms of knowing that are needed to deal with the lived world is sobering to even the most brilliant among us. Formal thinking and the formal operations of breaking down phenomena into their smallest parts for analysis fail to raise questions of value to employ the insight of diverse contextualization. Without these more complex dynamics at work we end up with technical-standards-driven schools that stupidify more than they edify (Hinchey, 1998, 2001).

Western Knowledge and Power:
Understanding Ethnocentrism

A central theme of *Teachers as Researchers* involves the understanding of these complex elements of the research and knowledge production process — insights that propel teachers to the status of professional knowledge workers. One of these complex elements involves the ability to identify and trace the effects of ethnocentrism within the Cartesian-Newtonian-Baconian tradition. Over the last few centuries the Western belief in the superiority of such frameworks of knowing has been so assumed and widely accepted in Western societies that it was thought not to deserve comment. Knowledge producers who operated outside the boundaries of Cartesian science were viewed as not only inferior but uncivilized. In the traditions of Western education, Cartesian science is not merely the best way to understand the world, it is the only way. With this broad epistemological brushstroke most of the knowledge production methods and wisdom of human kind is trashed (Grof, 1993).

In this ethnocentric view 'true knowledge' can only be produced by a detached, disinterested, external observer who works to ignore background (contextual) information by developing objective research techniques. In human history most of the great wisdom generated has not been constructed in this manner (Shotter, 1993, 1998). It is not surprising that no institution has carried these Cartesian blinders more zealously than education. As we see so clearly in the contemporary standards movement — a movement that in a socio-political and cultural context might be labeled as part of a broader Cartesian recovery impulse — any historical analysis of what has motivated this mode of pedagogical reform is irrelevant. The concept of a globalized perspective on the standards movement's hyper-Cartesianism cannot even be contemplated by its proponents outside of a crass feeding of the U.S. directed globalized economy. A planetary insight with awareness of and respect for diverse ways of knowing, cultural humility, and an ecologically sustainable and ethical conception of progress is not on the conceptual map.

In 1994 when Lynne Cheney (wife of Vice-President Dick Cheney) was attacking the National History Standards from her post at the conservative think tank, the American Enterprise Institute, she objected to their excessive coverage of women and minorities. The professional historian, she argued, who wrote the 'disastrous' standards were out to destroy Western Civilization and the Enlightenment (i.e., Cartesian) tradition (Wiener, 2000). Even the most minor attempts to include diverse voices in the history curriculum in the U.S. schools are met with vicious objections. Note that the National History Standards were not calling for an inclusion of global, non-Western, and non-Christian information. The call for diverse global understandings and respect for other cultures' epistemologies, as found in this book, are dismissed as an assault on 'all we hold dear.' It is essential that progressive Westerners understand this arrogance, its numerous consequences around the world and within Western societies, and develop the skills to counter its expression and negate its unfortunate consequences (Apple, 1993).

In this cultural context the technical standards movement's call for standardization takes on even more ideological baggage. Not only a manifestation of hyper-rationalization, the standardization of curriculum becomes a means of insuring ethnocentrism in the classroom. Such an ethnocentrism is suspicious of concepts such as diversity, multiple perspectives, criticality, difference, and multiculturalism. Ideologically, it works covertly to promote the interests of the dominant culture over less powerful minority cultures. Such interests involve the power of the privileged to maintain their privilege, as students from economically poorer families, those students whose families possess the least formal education, are transformed into 'test liabilities' (Ohanian, 1999; Vinson and Ross, 2001). In such a category their problems in school can be blamed on their inferiority — 'we tried to teach them the information mandated by the standards but they just didn't have the ability to get it. There's nothing more we can do.'

In this power-centered context dominant European interests and needs are validated while those individuals who fall outside dominant cultural borders are forced to struggle for legitimacy. Technical standards become regulatory forces that limit the professional discretion of teachers while insuring that the individual needs of students in some way alienated from the culture and discourses of schools are rendered irrelevant (Giroux, 1997). In both a macro- and micro-social context we watch the fragmentary influences of Euro-modernism and the ethnocentrism it produces do their 'bad work.' At the macro-level Westerners are alienated from other cultures around the world, as Cartesian ways of seeing and producing knowledge fragment the wholeness that connects us to both each other and the planet in general (Capra, 1996). In a micro-context this Cartesianism separates classroom knowledge from its embeddedness in the lived world and its meaning in our lives, rendering it abstract data to be learned for an absurd standards text.

Positivism and Learning: Certifying Fragmentation

As connections are severed and meanings subverted, Cartesianism's epistemology of positivism takes center stage in education and knowledge production. The detailed delineation of the definition of positivism is a central theme in *Teachers as Researchers*, but for the purpose of situating ourselves, a short description of positivism is in order. Positivism is the prevalent view of knowledge (epistemology) in the history of Western science. Coming into general philosophical usage in the nineteenth century, positivism assumes that nature is orderly and knowable via the scientific method and that all phenomena have natural causes. In a positivistic educational context human-created knowledge is conceptualized as a physical substance handed from one individual to another via the process of teaching. The receiver in this positivistic context is nothing more than a passive recipient who merely accepts the 'physical entity' that has been passed along to him or her (Lee, 1997).

As receivers uncritically take in information in the decontextualized positivistic framework, they are anesthesized into believing that meaning resides in the information fragment itself rather in the network of relationships from which it was retrieved. When educational leaders operate with such a tacit belief embedded in their consciousness, it is much easier for them to fall into an obsession with standards test performance. Losing sight of the complexity of knowledge production and the contextualized nature of teaching for understanding, superintendents, supervisors, and principals focus on the mastery of those factoids included in standardized tests. The stories teachers tell about these obsessions are chilling. As one teacher in Brooklyn described it:

> Our principal has gone nuts. He checks all classrooms to make sure we display charts he made depicting our place in the rankings of school test performance in the city. One teacher had temporarily taken down the chart to put up some student work. The principal screamed at her in front of the students. She was a mess; we thought she was going to get fired. For over two months before students take the test, we are not allowed to do anything but prep them for it: test-taking skills, rote memorization, flash cards, and things like that. He has spies checking up on us to make sure we do nothing else. I can't stay there another year. It'll make me as crazy as he is.

What is so disconcerting in these positivistic, fragmented, and irrational contexts in twenty-first-century schooling is the inability of most observers to view them in a larger analytical context. Too often observers in educational leadership, teachers' unions, political action committees, parental groups, and so on cannot connect these disturbing situations to social, political, philosophical, economic, or cultural forces that rest outside of the immediate perceptions and circumstances of the individuals involved. Critical scholar teachers must understand these ideological and discursive forces and be able to delineate the specific hidden ways that they construct consciousness and everyday educational practice. This is a central concern of critical scholar teachers as researchers.

If we are unable to accomplish this task, positivist education will continue to fragment meaning and mystify reality. Such education will continue to subvert dialogue about the construction of knowledge, view students and teachers as objects of regulation, induce students to ignore the ways their consciousness is produced while isolating them from the world (Zeno, 1998). Indeed, we can see in this panorama the ways that learners are removed from curriculum construction in the technical standards-driven school. And, as always, poor and minority students are the ones hit first and hardest by this positivistic process because of their already existing cultural distance from the workings of schools (Novick, 1996).

In the positivistic context the dumbed-down and inequitable dynamics of education continue to promote their 'bad medicine.' I am amazed when I observe and talk with teachers about life in contemporary standards-driven schools how few questions they are allowed to ask about the process. Authoritarian political/educational leaders know that extensive questioning would constitute a challenge to the *status quo* (Hinchey, 1998, 2001). In the disciplined and sanitized new educational order this is simply not acceptable. 'What is our larger purpose in educating students in a democratic society?' 'Would you hold your questions, please, for a later time?'

Positivistic standards rip through the schools like an Oklahoma tornado, leaving destruction in their wake. Teachers are infuriated when standards-driven district leaders and administrators give them scripts that they must read to their classes in lieu of their own personally devised lessons. The teachers I have interviewed are livid about such disrespectful practices:

> If I had thought I was going to have to read from a script to my students, I would have never, ever gone into teaching. I have master's degrees in both English and education and I am not trusted to prepare a lesson. I am not going to stay in the profession unless this changes. I feel so degraded every day I go to school.

There is no doubt that positivistic deskilling will demoralize our best and brightest teachers. Teaching to a multiple-choice test will undermine the motivation for teachers and students.

Top-down standards ignore the fact that different students are ready to learn different concepts and skills at different times. Brilliant teachers keep tabs on such 'dispositional readiness' and attempt to discern and generate interest before teaching particular lessons. This is a subtle and complex process that becomes an art form when exercised by adept teachers. With one brushstroke positivistic standards destroy it by determining when and how particular lessons will be taught. The theoretical concept here involves the notion of an epistemology of practice. A modernist Cartesian epistemology of practice emphasizes that there are universal steps in formulating the one best practice in pursuing professional activity. Technical top-down standards are based on such an epistemology of practice.

In *Teachers as Researchers* I devote much energy to challenging such positivism. I argue that the realm in which humans live and work is much too multifaceted, complicated, and culturally diverse for the implementation of universal approaches to professional practice. In this context teacher researchers explore their unique situations to generate not a 'correct approach' to practice but a dialogue about the teaching act. Expert-devised systems of practice handed down as positivistic truth to practitioners never work as well as locally produced practice-in-action. Empowered teacher researchers are always engaged in a dialogue with numerous colleagues and scholars about practice and act on their synthetic understandings of a constellation of insights — not by a sequence of rules (Capra, 1996). Devisors of top-down standards have never understood this concept (Apple, 1999; Morris, Doll, and Pinar, 1999; Purpel, 1999; Agnello, 2001).

As a result of this lack of understanding, positivism certifies the fragmentation of the workplace, the undermining of the sanctity of the educational act, and the subversion of education as a practice of democracy. Positivism in its top-down standards disguise tears away at the heart and soul of teacher, sapping energy and dedication. Teachers have to be tough and smart to survive this assault on the profession. Unfortunately, so do students. It is difficult to watch this process unfold, to observe new generations damaged by these positivistic dynamics. The standards frenzy undermines the efforts by smart teachers and administrators to provide lessons in critical and creative thinking, reasoning, and metacognitive understandings of curriculum and knowledge production (Weil, 2001c). In this positivistic briar patch schools intensify their historical functions of social regulation and what Donaldo Macedo (1994) has labeled 'stupidification.' Teachers as scholars and researchers are not welcome in this pedagogical thicket. Indeed, the fragmentation of meaning, purpose, and direction is adeptly accomplished in this context.

Positivism, Standards, and Student Needs

In the rule-orientation, epistemological *naïveté*, and decontextualization of positivist standards, many educational and political leaders maintain that the 'conditions of schools, the material well-being of families, and the dynamics of communities are not even worth thinking about' (Books, 2001). Such contextual features have nothing to do with schooling or its improvement in a positivistic cosmos concerned only with providing the correct data to be learned and the correct rules for teachers to follow in inculcating this eviscerated information. As long as the proper curricular information is clearly delineated and teachers follow the script, advocates of top-down standards assure the public that the economic, social, and psychological well-being of children and young people is a relatively minor variable. Such damnable nonsense is the commonsense of the twenty-first-century discourse of school reform.

If such student needs are not meet, young people will not learn well regardless of the brilliance of the pedagogy. Moreover, teachers who don't know their students well, don't know how their needs are or are not being met, or don't know what moves them, will always have trouble creating meaningful classrooms where learning takes place (Ohanian, 1999; Books, 2001). At this conceptual way station in the pedagogical journey teachers have to pause and carefully observe the ideological terrain around them. They have to wear their night-vision goggles to discern those forces that exist outside of their immediate perceptions and experiences. Schooling, like the culture in general, is a domain of struggle where knowledge and power are always functions of one another.

Positivism is a philosophical/political force of domination. It deftly blinds observers and analysts to the conflicts and interests that covertly shape educational policy and classroom practice. Any force that has the power to convince individuals that student well-being is not a central factor in improving education must be addressed. The exposure and neutralization of such a force must become a central objective of anyone who cares about children, teachers, democracy, justice, and the reform of education. Positivism's capacity to hide itself makes such a process as difficult as flushing terrorists out of remote mountain caves. Democratic educators must develop the capacity to persuade numerous groups and individuals that any pedagogy that dismisses student experience is inadequate for a humane democratic society.

Positivism in the guise of technical standards ignores students in the way it distorts understanding of self and world. Grounded on a reductionistic view of knowledge and curriculum, top-down standards consciously delete multiple perspectives on a topic and teach one ideologically inscribed perspective as truth. Such a perspective usually grants legitimacy to given institutional configurations, prevailing ways of seeing and being, and dominant cultural belief structures. The bloodstains left in the historical political struggle over these ideological positions are hidden, as conflict, oppression, and violence are conveniently erased.

Paulo Freire's (1970b) notion of the banking model of education still has the power to describe twenty-first-century standards curricula. The information transmitted is made only for deposit in mental filing cabinets — no interpretation is necessary. Such positivistic teaching does not encourage rigorous academic analysis; rather, it numbs the mind, producing intellectual passivity and blind rule following. Students and teachers are taught to accept and respect the power of dominant elites. Of course, not all of them will accept such teachings. Many will discern the ideological project confronting them and resist, while others will passively accept such attempts at consciousness construction (Giroux, 1997). Teachers as critical researchers expose this process and insist that it be analyzed and studied by their colleagues and students.

Studying Power: Ideological Consolidation in the Twenty-first Century

It is apparent to many that setting standards is not tantamount to producing a rigorous, challenging, and critical education. Surveying the landscape of standards reform in the first decade of the twenty-first century, one can sense that educational and political leaders have used the opportunity to centralize power over the institution of education. Moreover, standards reform has been deployed specifically to disempower teachers and remove them from the business of curriculum development, constructing educational purpose, and evaluating student performance. While these power plays have taken place under the flag of improving education, proponents of standards have concurrently slashed educational allocations to fund tax cuts for the wealthy (Ohanian, 1999; Thomas and Schubert, 2001). Observing contemporary educational politics in New York City, I am shocked by the degree to which politicians who advocate technical standards have reduced what were already meager schools funds. In this context power blocs are consolidating their capacity for domination, as they tighten their control of knowledge production, media, news programming, and schooling.

The type of critical inquiry and analysis I am advocating for empowered teacher researchers pays close attention to these issues of power (Horn, 2001). Critical teachers as researchers understand the centrality of power in understanding everyday life, knowledge production, curriculum development, and teaching. Power is implicated in all educational visions, it is omnipresent in reform proposals, and it is visible in delineations of what constitutes an educated person. It is the charge of teacher researchers to grasp these dynamics, to study them and to act on the basis of what they find. In such a process teacher researchers raise questions of intent and larger purpose in relation to particular practices. As students forge their way through elementary and secondary schooling, for example, are their experiences designed to adjust them to the existing social and economic order? What school experiences engage students in questioning the justice of that order and the desirability of such adjustment?

Studying the standards movement in numerous macro- and micro-contexts (Horn and Kincheloe, 2001; Kincheloe and Weil, 2001), I am struck by the absence of concern with the duties of democratic citizenship, the need for social change, and issues of justice. The notion of critique of counter-democratic forces, of threats to fragile democratic institutions, and of ideological indoctrination in the guise of education are simply not part of top-down, positivistic standards. Critical teacher researchers are alarmed by these omissions, as they watch state after state mandate authoritarian compliance audits to insure that there is no deviation from the official curriculum, from memorization of the 'approved knowledge of the Party.' The impositional nature of these reforms is a naked form of power that is so confident in its sovereignty it senses little need to mask itself. If such power is not challenged, the education it decrees is little more than an effort to produce social, political, and academic mind control (Nelson, 1998; Norris, 1998; Vinson and Ross, 2001).

The Vision: Teachers as Researchers

In the existing world of schooling and especially in the new educational order being created by technical standards, teachers do not live in the same professional culture as researchers. Knowledge in contemporary education is still something that is produced far away from the school by experts in a rarefied domain. This must change if democratic reform of education is to take place. Teachers must join the culture of researchers if a new level of educational rigor and quality is ever to be achieved. In such a new democratized culture teacher scholars begin to understand the power implications of technical standards. In this context they appreciate the benefits of research, especially as they relate to understanding the forces shaping education that fall outside their immediate experience and perception. As these insights are constructed, teachers begin to understand what they know from experience. With this in mind they gain heightened awareness of how they can contribute to the research on education. Indeed, they realize that they have access to understandings that go far beyond what the expert researchers have produced.

In the new school culture teachers are viewed as learners — not as functionaries who follow top-down orders without question. Teachers are seen as researchers and knowledge workers who reflect on their professional needs and current understandings. They are aware of the complexity of the educational process and how schooling cannot be understood outside of the social, historical, philosophical, cultural, economic, political, and psychological contexts that shape it. Scholar teachers understand that curriculum development responsive to student needs is not possible when it fails to account for these contexts. With this in mind they explore and attempt to interpret the learning processes that take place in their classrooms. What are its psychological, sociological, and ideological effects, they ask. Thus, scholar teachers research their own professional practice (Norris, 1998; Kraft, 2001; Bereiter, 2002).

With empowered scholar teachers prowling the schools, things begin to change. The oppressive culture created by positivistic standards is challenged. In-service staff development no longer takes the form of 'this is what the expert researchers found — now go do it.' Such staff development in the new culture gives way to teachers who analyze and contemplate the power of each other's ideas. Thus, the new critical culture of school takes on the form of a 'think tank that teaches students,' a learning community. School administrators are amazed by what can happen when they support learning activities for both students and teachers. Principals and curriculum developers watch as teachers develop projects that encourage collaboration and shared research. There is an alternative to top-down standards with their deskilling of teachers and the stupidification of students (Novick, 1996; Jardine, 1998; Norris, 1998).

Promoting teachers as researchers is a fundamental way of cleaning up the damage of technical standards. Deskilling of teachers and dumbing-down of the curriculum take place when teachers are seen as receivers not producers of knowledge. A vibrant professional culture depends on a group of practitioners who have the freedom to continuously reinvent themselves via their research and knowledge production. Teachers engaged in complex, critical practice find it difficult to allow positivistic standards and their poisonous effects to go unchallenged. Such teachers cannot abide the deskilling and reduction in professional status that accompany these top-down reforms. It is this concept that generates the subtitle of this book: *Qualitative Inquiry as a Path to Empowerment.* Indeed, teacher empowerment does not occur just because we wish it to. Instead, it takes place when teachers develop the knowledge work skills and pedagogical abilities befitting the calling of teaching.

Technical standards are both based on and promote a reductionistic, truncated view of educational, social, and psychological research. The profound advances in research produced over the last thirty years are virtually ignored by advocates of positivistic standards. What we know or have developed the capacity to know about the complex world of teaching and learning grants educators a far more compelling and diverse view of schooling and its relationship to social, cultural, historical, economic, and psychological forces (Coben, 1998; Symes and Meadmore, 1999; Willinsky, 2001a). It is frustrating to watch these advances in research and knowledge production (Clough, 1998; Denzin and Lincoln, 2000) relegated to the trash heap, while outmoded and destructive modes of inquiry are recovered and legitimated. With their official status, such practices are rendered unquestionable. Teacher researchers have the difficult task of questioning the unquestionable.

Raising the Questions: Teacher Researchers and Educational Rigor

Questioning the unquestionable has never been a picnic in the park. In this complex context critical researchers analyze educational situations with the aim of improving the quality of activity connected to them. In the spirit of complexity, however, teacher researchers move to a new conceptual terrain, as they raise questions about the situation itself so as not to be confined by the assumptions embedded within it. This dynamic raises a central theme within this book: critical teachers as researchers develop the capacity to expose the assumptions behind, the interest served by, and the unarticulated purposes of particular forms of educational activity (Lester, 2001; Raven and Stephenson, 2001). These are key issues within the complex critical form of teacher research presented here. Some forms of action research or practitioner research developed over the last several decades have not conceptualized questions at this level of assumptions, hidden interest, and unarticulated purpose.

In order to produce smarter teachers and higher-quality education, critical teacher researchers push the conceptual envelope. They understand that in some forms of action research issues of historical, sociological, cultural studies and philosophical influences on schooling are irrelevant. Despite the hard work in which teacher researchers might engage, an understanding of forces outside of their immediate experiences was lost. Questions such as the following are not to be found in some action research contexts:

- What is the social role of schooling in a democratic society?

- What discourses shape the form that schooling takes?

- What unseen forces help to construct student performance?

- What are the ideological inscriptions of the curriculum?

- How do epistemological assumptions affect the everyday life of the classroom?

- What is the political impact of particular educational practices?

- Who defines what teacher research takes place?

(Goodson, 1997, 1999)

Efficacious teacher research that leads to more rigorous and just forms of education assumes the importance of these questions and inquiries like them. In such research contextual factors are carefully studied and then classroom practices are analyzed in relation to them. Connections are made, relational links are discerned, and processes and patterns are exposed. Teachers in such a context not only learn about knowledge production, but also learn how to expand their cognitive abilities in relation to inter-connected concepts. Obviously, positivistic standards preclude the need for such sophisticated teacher activity, as meaningful tasks and meaning making itself are subverted. The possibility of the development of rigorous education is undermined. I employ the term 'rigor' here not in its positivistic usage: the careful following of the fixed and predetermined steps of the scientific method. I appropriate and redefine the term as the democratic expression of the best education possible. Throughout this book I will argue that critical teacher research is a pathway to a rigorous education.

Teaching for understanding and democratic social action is a central aspect of this rigorous 'best education possible.' The research process in these contexts is a central aspect of staff development, curricular policy, solving problems that face the school, and classroom activity (Novick, 1996). As we will explore throughout the book, a rigorous and just education demands that teachers research their students (Cannella, 1997; Soto, 1997, 2000; DuBois-Reymond, Sunker, and Kruger, 2001). We need to understand social and psychological conceptions of children and young people, as well as children's and young people's perceptions of themselves. Teachers as researchers explore their students' relationships to the world, the information climate produced by media and popular culture, and new modes of socialization and enculturation in the twenty-first century. Teacher researchers monitor students' reactions to and perceptions of the new rigor and educational experiences in general. The point is simple: a sophisticated pedagogy cannot take place if teachers don't know their students (de Oliveira and Montecinos, 1998; Zeno, 1998).

If teachers don't know their students, what they know and don't know, their fears and their dreams, their failures and successes, they cannot help them construct a compelling and in-depth view of the world and their role in it. Without such insight, teachers cannot help students become knowledge workers in a knowledge-driven world. Students will find it difficult to make sense of existing data while learning to produce their own knowledge. When teacher researchers know their students, become experts in subject matter, and are adept knowledge workers, they are beginning to put together the skills that will help them become great teachers who motivate and inspire their students. As such teachers engage students with the world, they simultaneously make schools more rigorously academic and more practical in the world. This is the vision of teaching on which *Teachers as Researchers* is grounded.

Chapter 2

Teachers as Researchers, Good Work, and Troubled Times

In light of the bizarre educational world shaped by positivistic top-down standards, it is important that we now turn our attention to a careful delineation of those forces that have been shaping the educational cosmos. We will focus on those powerful dynamics that shape education and our consciousness that are typically hidden from everyday experience. In this chapter we will study longer-term processes that create hierarchies which disempower teachers and produce irrational practices. It is extremely important that teacher researchers understand these issues, because such forces undermine their attempts to establish a new culture of the workplace that honors and respects teacher scholars. In such a new culture the needs of students could be better met and students who are now overlooked could gain new access to the benefits of education.

Exploring the Technicalized World: They Might be Experts

Many modern social scientists have observed a world marked by technicalization (and the technicalization of work in particular), a powerful mass communications industry which helps shape human interests and ideological orientations, and an increasing domination of individuals by groups with excessive power. The notion of *knowledge* has become a source of power in this society, as power is often acquired by those who by their economic position or their professional status announce just what is to be considered knowledge. Professionals in various fields determine 'healthy' child-rearing procedures, 'proper' family life, the nature of social deviance, and the form that work will take. Knowledge which must be certified by professionals results in anti-democratic tendencies as it renders individuals dependent upon experts.

Based on these observations, social scientists have become more and more attracted to visions of social research which are grounded in critical theory. These critical social inquirers are interested in questioning the dominant assumptions in modern industrialized societies, rejecting earlier constructions of meaning and value structures, and embarking on a quest for new meanings and practices (Popkewitz, 1981a; Hinchey, 1998). Ever concerned with the centrality of the individual and the powerfulness of individual endeavor, critical researchers refuse to see the individual as a puppet of wider forces. We must protect the creative, active, meaning-seeking aspects of humans; social scientists in particular must see men and women as potentially free and marked by the capacity to set and achieve their own goals. Thus, the forces which preclude this human agency must be exposed and changed. A social science, for example, which deifies the social scientist as expert and purveyor of truth must be confronted (Gibson, 1986; Macedo, 1994; Cannella, 1997).

Personal authority has been undermined by the authority of professional experts who gain unquestioned knowledge through rigorous (methodologically exacting as in the positivistic usage) social scientific research. The family, for example, is subject to state determination of its competence. Parents have little authority over those experts in the legitimized institutions who make pronouncements about normal child-rearing (Steinberg and Kincheloe, 1997). The family's dependence on the professional is representative of a larger pattern of dependence in modern industrialized, bureaucratized societies. Individuals depend on organizations, citizens depend on the state, workers depend on managers, and, of course, parents depend on the 'helping professions.' A professional oligarchy of doctors, psychiatrists, welfare workers, civil servants, and social science researchers exert significant influence on the governance of the state and on the 'knowledge industry.'

The professional assault on the autonomy of the family and its members as well as on other institutions and individuals must be viewed in light of its historical moment. The advent of industrialization and its companion, monopoly or corporate capitalism, set the stage for the rise of the expert (McLaren, 2000). As the family was assaulted by the expert, the advertising industry was persuading people that store-bought goods were superior to home-made items. The growth of scientific management of industry and the expansion of the expert both represent new forms of control within an industrialized, corporate state. The struggle against the destruction of personal authority necessitates a struggle against the general authoritarian trends of the modern industrialized, corporate state.

Taking Matters into Our Own Hands: Critical Practitioners Producing Knowledge

Individuals cannot protect their personal autonomy unless they regain their voice in the workplace and (very important to this work) demand a role in the production of the knowledge on which the modern state and its experts ground their authority. In this context, critical social researchers call for individuals to take the solution of their problems into their own hands. The goal of arresting the erosion of competence will be accomplished, they argue, by ordinary citizens who create their own 'communities of competence.' Thus, teachers, students, and parents must participate in the research act in education. They must help determine what is designated educational knowledge (Lasch, 1979; Carson and Sumara, 1997; Kincheloe, 2001).

In order to create their own knowledge, individuals must understand that such an endeavor is both important and possible. Certain critical theoretical ideas allow for such an understanding. A critical social science is concerned with uncovering the ways by which ideology shapes social relations, for example, in the workplace, in schools, between classes, races, and genders, as well as relations between experts and ordinary citizens (Aronowitz and DeFazio, 1994; Gee, Hull, and Lankshear, 1996). Critical social science is also concerned with extending a human's consciousness of himself or herself as a social being. An individual who had gained such a consciousness would understand how, and why, his or her political opinions, religious beliefs, gender roles, or racial perspectives had been shaped by dominant perspectives (Pinar, 1994, 1998).

Critical social science thus promotes self-reflection which results in attitudinal changes. The basis of these changes rests on insights into causalities in the past. Individuals, as Habermas (1971) argues, thus come to know themselves by bringing to consciousness the process by which their perspectives were formed. Action which is to be taken by individuals to correct social and thus individual pathologies can be *negotiated* once self-reflection has taken place. Prudent action which proceeds only while asking questions of ethics, morality, and politics does not take the form of rules and precise regulations. Critical theory provides a framework of principles around which action can be discussed rather than a set of procedures. Teachers who engage in critical research are never certain of the exact path of action they will take as a result of their inquiry (Popkewitz, 1981a; McLaren, 1995; Giroux, 1997; Hart, 2001).

Thus, critical social science is concerned with the notion of the practical. This implies that it is interested in the relationship of scientific research to society, of theory to practice. Because of this practical concern, critical social science must always examine social relations and social processes historically (Allison, 1995; Kincheloe, 2001). Such an examination reminds the inquirer that our traditions, ceremonies, institutions, and belief systems are constructed by human beings. This human construction is often obscured from our sight as we go about the mundane rituals of teaching, administering, interacting, and relaxing. Thus, the dynamics of social change are lost, the forces which have shaped modern educational institutions are forgotten. History dies as we come to celebrate and attend only to that which exists; indeed, that 'which is' seems as if it could have been no other way. Critical social science moves us to uncover the genesis of those assumptions that shape our lives and institutions and to ask how they can be altered (Popkewitz, 1981a; Lather, 1986, 1991; O'Sullivan, 1999).

The notion that teachers as well as research professors and other 'experts' should engage in critically grounded social inquiry rests on a democratic social theory which assumes that social research is not the province of a small elite minority. John Dewey argued in 1908 and 1932 that though the theoretical knowledge of the sciences is confined to specialists, it affects all persons (Simpson and Jackson, 1997). Its human effect, he continued, is not so much beneficent as it is exploitive, for those who possess the knowledge of the sciences often use it to take advantage of others. Considerations of private profit limit the social usefulness of scientifically based research.

The limitations, Dewey maintained, of the hierarchical workplace prevent the non-elite from gaining access to the methods of social inquiry. Thus, they have little chance to develop their capacities. Aware of the worker-control strategies of his contemporary, Frederick Taylor, and his scientific management strategies, Dewey charged that workers, who in the industrial era were becoming merely operators of machines, found their creative and participatory sensibilities deadened (Kincheloe, 1995, 1999). 'The maldistribution of material goods,' he wrote, 'is reflected in an even greater maldistribution of cultural goods.' 'The greatest form of moral loss which comes from industrialism's worker control,' he argued, is related to the effect of this policy 'upon participation in the higher values of friendship, science, art, taking an active part in public life, in all the variety of forms which these things are capable of assuming.' The democratic ideal is based on the premise that there is an ethical basis on which social institutions are constructed. This conception, as old as Plato, requires that every human counts, regardless of social position. Moreover, whether in the workplace of the factory or the school, leaders must make sure that the wide variety of abilities and interests among individuals must be considered so that the unique potentialities and the contributions of each one may be realized (Dewey, 1908: 408).

Teachers as Researchers Strive to Operate in a Culture of Good Work

On these premises rest the concept of good work. If the schools are to become democratic and offer challenges to the anti-democratic tendencies of the era, they must pursue the concept of good work for teachers and individuals in the society as a whole. Many labor and educational theorists have pondered the key characteristics of democratic work (Aronowitz and DiFazio, 1994; Lakes, 1994a, 1994b). The notion of teachers/workers as researchers certainly fits into any notion of democratic work. Characteristics of good work might include the following principles.

The Principle of Self-direction

Workers/teachers are ultimately their own bosses. Except in unusual circumstances, the worker/teacher should be free from supervisory direction. Teachers operating under this principle would not be subjected to the humiliation of supervision which requires them to submit stylized lesson plans where format takes precedence over purpose. Teachers would be free of control by supervisory forms which use the tyranny of pre-packaged materials, and curriculum guides and supervisors who demand coverage of specific information at specific times, for example, 'I want you on page 30 at 1:30.' Teachers freed from such constraints would need research skills to conceptualize and carry out the goals of their classrooms.

The Principle of the Job as a Place of Learning

Workers/teachers who are encouraged to set their own goals by necessity must view the workplace as a laboratory. Workers are equal partners in research and development, as their 'shop-level' experiences are valued as unique insights to the production process. In schools, teachers with their 'child-level' experiences are viewed similarly. Thus, teachers are encouraged to contribute to our knowledge about the educational act, while at the same time they are challenged (by administrators and one another) to push their knowledge to new levels via new questions involving topics which transcend mere teaching technique. Understandings of psychological theory, socio-economic context, and political outcomes of learning are pursued. The central role of research is apparent.

The Principle of Work Variety

Workers in industrial contexts are plagued by repetitive, boring tasks. In the democratic workplace, workers struggle to provide opportunities for variations of routine which preclude boredom. Teachers who are learners and thus who are involved with the difficulties of research and conceptualization are rarely bored. A school organization which would allow teachers periodically to perform effectively in these varied roles would be grounded in a research facility.

The Principle of Workmate Cooperation

Industrialization has unfortunately produced conditions where it is not in one person's interest to help another; indeed, one person's gain is often another's loss. Teachers are not unaffected by such impulses, as they hoard materials away from one another and rarely exchange ideas about successful practices. The idea of sitting down together and seriously discussing educational purpose and how it might be achieved is not typically found in the teachers' lounge. The democratic workplace transcends this fractured set of relations. Teachers who are researchers share their findings with one another, discuss interpretations of the findings, and work together to implement strategies based on new understandings which emerge.

The Principle of Individual Work as a Contribution to Social Welfare

When workers/teachers employ this principle, they reconceptualize their work so that it serves the social good. If work is not socially ameliorative then it must be made so. Workers in a factory who produce items that are ecologically harmful contribute to the redesign of the product (Bowers, 2001). Teachers who are faced with school policies which limit children's potential and/or reproduce socio-economic inequality change the policies. Teachers who are researchers are much more likely to recognize the socially deleterious effect of certain educational strategies than non-researching teachers (Emery and Thorsrud, 1976).

The Principle that Play is a Virtue which Must be Incorporated into Work

Herbert Marcuse argued that labor in the industrial era has been determined by objectives and functions that are not controlled by individual human beings. The value of protecting the free play of human abilities and human desires is not expected in the rationality which directs the workplace. Individuality in a work context is not a value or end in itself. Play, Marcuse maintained, is basic to human civilization. When such a premise is accepted, labor must be grounded on a commitment to the protection of the free evolution of human potentiality (Marcuse, 1955: 195). Once we overcome our adult-centered bias against play as one of the highest expressions of human endeavor, we may incorporate its principles into our work lives. Play principles which may be utilized as means of democratizing work would include: (a) rules of play are not constructed to repress freedom, but to constrain authoritarianism and thus to promote fairness; (b) the structure of play is dynamic in its relation to the interaction of the players — by necessity this interaction is grounded on the equality of the players; (c) the activity is always viewed as an autonomous expression of self, as care is taken not to subordinate imagination to predetermined outcomes. Thus, in play, exhaustion is not deadening since the activity refreshes the senses and celebrates the person. Research can be viewed as a form of play when the teacher is guided by the play principles (Aronowitz, 1973).

Thus, good work progresses from the pursuit of these democratic principles. The delineation of the democratic principles of good work confronts us with the reality that much of the time in contemporary life, work is not good — it is not in line with these principles. Based on his reading of Freud, Herbert Marcuse set the stage for our understanding of 'bad work' with his notions of surplus repression and the performance principle. Surplus repression involves the additional controls over and above those necessary for civilized human association and species perpetuation. The performance principle is the prevailing historical form of the reality principle. The reality principle is one of the value systems human beings use to govern themselves in order to perpetuate the species.

The principle embraces delayed gratification, the restraint of pleasure, work, and productiveness. The victory of the performance principle and its accompanying surplus repression in the modern industrialized world has ushered in a period where instrumental rationality (the separation of means from ends and the preference for ends; the disconnection of fact and value and the preference for fact; and the removal of human feeling and human concern from disinterested intellect and the preference for intellect) defines our view of work. In a context shaped by the idea of instrumental rationality the argument that work should be guided by the concept of play would appear silly and outrageous (Marcuse, 1955: 12, 35, 37).

Defining Bad Work

If we are to avoid the continuation of the exclusion of teachers from participation in research grounded in the critical social sciences, we must expose and defeat bad work. Teachers must be capable of identifying that instrumental rationality which not only shapes bad work but also influences a form of teacher education which promotes an obsessive concern with means (technique of instruction) over ends (critical examination of educational purpose). Leo Tolstoy anticipated a similar manifestation of instrumental rationality in *Anna Karenina*, as he wrote of the artist, Mihailov. Some art patrons are discussing an artist's work in which Christ is a main figure.

> 'Yes — there's a wonderful mastery!' said Vronsky. . . .'There you have technique.' . . . The sentence about technique sent a pang through Mihailov's heart, and looking angrily at Vronsky he suddenly scowled. He had often heard this word technique, and was utterly unable to understand . . . a mechanical facility for painting or drawing, entirely apart from its subject.
>
> (Tolstoy, 1981: 62)

This concern with means/technique crushes critical attempts to assess the nature of an education which promotes self-direction and blinds us to forms of labor which fall into the categories of bad work.

The concept of 'bad work' in the modern period is based upon a specific set of ideological assumptions, as discussed below.

Social Darwinism

Every human is out for himself or herself. The strongest and the most resourceful will gain the rewards and privileges; the weakest will fall by the wayside into demeaning situations. The position is inherently naive as it fails to question the forces which privilege certain groups and impede others. Success, thus, is founded not simply on one's resourcefulness but on one's initial acquaintance (often attained through socio-economic background) with the forms of knowledge, the attitudes, and the skills required for success, often called 'cultural capital.' Therefore, undemocratic hierarchical work arrangements are viewed not as anti-humanistic but as natural and just.

Nature as Enemy

Ever-increasing material growth requires that nature be viewed as a collection of objects to be acted upon and exploited (Wirth, 1983). Nature is viewed as an object that is to be used, worked upon, and controlled. It is not intrinsically valuable: to hold significance, it must serve the ends of human beings. Scientific research is the human creation which allows for this — the laws of nature can be known and thus manipulated and controlled. Human beings as products of nature can be known in a similar way and, as a result, be manipulated and controlled. Like the ancients with their myths designed to control nature, scientific man attempts a similar goal. The control of men and women in the workplace is simply a natural extension of the 'control impulse' (Held, 1980: 151–6).

Science as 'Fact' Provider

Scientific research provides humans with indisputable knowledge. Values are subjective opinions which have little role in the world of research and work. Operating from this assumption, scientific managers have objectified the workplace, focusing on measurable factors related to the bottom lines of productivity and profit. The examination of human values as represented by Dewey's assertion that good work must be pursued as an ethical imperative does not fit into a view of work based on such a notion of science.

Efficiency as Maximum Productivity

The productivity of humans and their machines can be measured only one way — quantitatively. Only in a social context in which human beings and nature could be viewed in any way other than intrinsically valuable could this assumption exist. The notion of efficiency becomes deified in bad work. Worshipping this false god, school supervisors in the school workplace encourage modes of teaching which answer to the goal of efficiency rather than the goal of human nurturing. Methods of evaluation are developed on the basis of efficiency rather than on an appreciation of the attempt to learn about the learner, the forces which move him or her, and the possible pathways which might be taken to help them realize their potential. The subtle emotional forces which move teachers and other workers to pursue excellence are crushed by the search for efficiency.

The Supremacy of Systems-efficiency and Cost-benefit Analysis Models

Such models assume that work goals are already agreed upon by all parties involved. 'Isn't the omnipresent goal of the workplace to increase profits?', the systems analysts ask. 'Isn't the ultimate goal of schooling to increase test scores?', educational systems analysts ask. The systems researchers view the goal of scientific inquiry as the identification of so-called production functions. These entities refer to the effectiveness of certain inputs in the attempt to reach pre-specified objectives. Effectiveness in this context involves the cost-benefit of the production function, as it is examined in terms of its economic efficiency. Thus, the effectiveness of educational methods could be compared in terms of test score results. When researchers combine this measure of effectiveness with an analysis of cost-benefit factors, decisions could then be made on which educational methods to require teachers to use. All teachers, regardless of context, would thus be expected to teach in the same 'efficient' way. Questions about non-measurable outcomes such as the dignity of the laborer in the workplace or student happiness in the educational workplace are irrelevant in systems analysis. Questions concerning the tacit professional knowledge of teachers and the subtle actions they take to connect learning to life, to ground learning in humane and ethical concerns, or to make students feel secure, are suppressed by this research model. Questions about teacher happiness, control of the conceptualization of their work, and their dignity as professionals are deemed trivial and unscientific. Teaching becomes bad work (House, 1978; Wirth, 1983).

The Purpose of Work as the Promotion of at least Short-term Personal Welfare and at most Short-term National Welfare

Bad work holds no vision of work as an activity which concerns itself with the long-term welfare of other human beings or of subsequent generations. Little effort is made in the workplace to cultivate the notion of the community of human beings past, present, and future. Such a concept would negate tendencies such as dynamic obsolescence, which serves as a symbol of bad work's alienation from human need. Educational researchers too often fail to consider the social and future consequences of educational policy as they examine short-term skill acquisition. The inclusion of concerns with the long-term welfare of the human community into research design is often viewed as frivolous and unscientific. In the rush to conform to the norms of the scientific peer group it is neglected. Labor and teaching and research into them are ethically fragmented; laborers and teachers see little connection between their work lives and the needs and concerns of the human community. Work is further separated from life.

The Contingency of Human Happiness on the Acquisition of Better Consumer Items

Industrial progress is viewed as the result of more centralized, more mechanized work. In a well-administered world better consumer items will result from efficiently managed industries and institutions. Education becomes an arm of the ideology which promotes this view of work. Schools are designed to turn out individuals who fit comfortably into the bad workplace. Students are taught (by a variety of teachers who are found far beyond the classroom, e.g., in television advertising) to embrace an important commandment. In a sense consumption becomes a ritual of salvation for the modern worker as he or she attempts to regain psychic peace after a forty-hour week of mechanized bad work. It is not unsurprising that 'Born to Shop' bumper stickers have achieved so much popularity in recent times, as shopping becomes a *raison d'être*. Social and educational researchers concern themselves with studies of how better consumer goods can be produced, how humans can be convinced that their happiness and self-worth depend on the acquisition of these goods, and how schools can contribute to the production of the labor pool needed to produce these items and even these attitudes (Wirth, 1983).

Bad Work and Deskilling: Dumbing-down the Workplace

No one has to remind us of the psychic, social, economic, and educational effects of bad work — we are confronted with them every day. Bad work produces waste, shoddy products, apathy, hostility, alcohol and drug abuse, nihilism, reliance on 'experts,' and depression. Opinion polls conducted periodically indicate that Americans are alarmed by the poor quality of goods produced in the American workplace. A study published in the *Harvard Business Review* indicates that 20 per cent of all consumer purchases lead to some form of purchaser dissatisfaction — this does not include dissatisfaction based on price. Automobile recalls are legendary; tires explode and kill drivers. Obviously, technological advance by itself does not ensure quality of workmanship. Indeed, we honor the label 'hand-made' as an indication of high quality. It implies a sociological relationship missing in modern industries which operate on the principles of bad work. Products which have been hand-made historically emerged from cultures where producers and consumers were the same individuals or close kin. Men made their own spears; women wove their own baskets. Even when technology advanced, material culture grew more complex, and specialization developed, the relationship between consumer and producer remained intact.

Since World War II mergers in American industry have rendered manufacturing corporations more unwieldy than ever before. Even though products grew shoddier and shoddier, horizontal industrial organization allowed large companies to stay in business. Bureaucratization of labor unions and the contracts which resulted from negotiations in the 1950s and 1960s protected incompetent workers from dismissal. Workers who were understandably alienated, bored, and careless understood their immunity from management threats of dismissal. Management's lack of concern about the quality problems which result from the megacorporation's workplace is well illustrated by the virtual absence of life-cycle data on consumer products.

Life-cycle studies follow products from birth to death under actual conditions of use to learn how an item breaks down, the type of repairs it needs, and how long a consumer can use it. There was no need for such data in industries which profited from planned obsolescence. Add to these factors the fact that the conglomerates which emerged from the mergers are not primarily in the business of producing goods — they are interested in buying and selling companies. Most executives in the United States have never been involved with the manufacturing process. Profit-mad MBAs (holders of Masters of Business Administration degrees) are often primarily interested in building empires and good 'quarterly numbers.' The company's reputation for quality is not the concern of these money managers and marketing specialists — they are interested in immediate profits during their short stays with individual companies.

We have been conditioned in the last few years to believe that work is improving both in terms of job satisfaction for workers and product quality for consumers. Management is aware of bad work, analysts argue, and things are getting better. The service and information-based economy, we are told, with its computerization, is producing more white-collar workers who are less deskilled and more professionalized. Such claims do not meet the test of scrutiny (Aronowitz and DiFazio, 1994). First of all, service and information jobs are primarily low-paying positions. Contrary to popular opinion, even goods-producing jobs demand higher pay than service and information jobs. Second, women hold over half of the service and information jobs, and females have traditionally received less money and less decision-making power in the workplace than males. The feminization of service and information jobs does not bode well for the possibility of improving work unless a dramatic change occurs in the way women are treated in the workplace. Good work demands respect for the dignity of women in the workplace (Harris, 1981).

In response to labor's and the general public's sense that something should be done about bad work and its resulting problems, managers have initiated Quality of Working Life (QWL) programs. The worker-as-decision-maker rhetoric of the programs has found its way into the educational workplace, as principals and supervisors speak of teacher as partner, teacher as decision maker and participant. Such programs are particularly dangerous because they have given the public the impression that workers are full participants in management decision making. In his book *Empty Promises: Quality of Working Life Programs and the Labor Movement*, Donald M. Wells (1987) exposes the true interests of QWL programs. Given the threat from emerging industrial giants such as Japan, American industry must find new ways to remain competitive. Management realizes that such a goal demands massive investment. In order to protect their profit margins (and their substantial salaries) managers must squeeze their workers harder than ever. Thus, companies are desperate to increase labor productivity. To accomplish such an objective, managers have concluded that they need more power over job conceptualization. It is not enough to *make* workers obey — management through QWL programs hopes to induce workers to *want* to obey (Lynd, 1987).

Engaged in programs which ostensibly grant them more decision-making power in the workplace, workers come to trust the pronouncements of management. Through QWL, managers hope to produce enthusiastic workers who will unleash their creative capacities, which managerial control has traditionally squashed. Granted more autonomy to make microcosmic decisions on the shop floors, workers (managers believe) will be less inclined to demand more voice in the larger decisions of production. Workers imbued with a sense of self-direction will be less likely to press collective bargaining demands. In the early 1980s, executives at General Motors circulated a confidential memo encouraging plant managers to use QWL programs to convince workers that their demands were dangerous to the health of the company. Workers must be aware of the way that democratic, participatory rhetoric can be used to secure undemocratic, non-participatory ends. If worker alienation is to be seriously addressed, employees must have genuine input into the control of the workplace. Workers must be true partners in the formulation of policies of personnel selection and training, product design, the use of new technologies, and the scheduling of production (Wells, 1987). The possibility of good work for educators rests on similar concerns as teachers attempt to control the educational workplace.

Teacher Work in the Same Rationalized Context

In the quest for enhanced educational productivity, teachers' work has become increasingly controlled from above. Public perception of teacher incompetence, like public perception of worker incompetence, has provided justification for an increasing teacher-deskilling process by educational managers. Teacher education has often neglected those traditional teacher skills based on a knowledge of academic subject matter, an understanding of a variety of child development theories and their socio-cultural and philosophical assumptions, an appreciation of the social context in which education takes place, an acquaintance with the relationship between educational purpose and the needs of a democratic society, and an overview of the social goals which education has historically been expected to accomplish. Colleges of education have often emphasized the technique of teaching, focusing on the inculcation of the 'best' method to deliver a body of predetermined facts and the familiarization of teachers with the 'proper' format for lesson plans which enhances supervision efficiency and thus allows for stricter accountability.

Just as the technicalization of the workplace deskilled workers by making them an appendage to their machines, teacher deskilling has proceeded by tying teachers to pre-packaged curricular materials. As mentioned in Chapter 1, researchers find that in many of these pre-packaged programs, even the exact words of the teacher are specified. Traditional teaching skills are deemed unnecessary in this situation, for all the conception and planning goes on far away from the school and the unique students it houses. Thus, teachers relinquish control of the teaching act — teaching is rendered bad work.

In a strange sense, the world of teaching and its workplace might possibly be characterized as a Third World culture with hierarchical power structures, scarce resources, traditional values, and teachers as disenfranchised peasants (Oldroyd, 1985). If we accept such a metaphor, the work of Paulo Freire becomes quite relevant to our attempt to make teaching good work. Like their Third World counterparts, teachers are preoccupied with daily survival — time for reflection and analysis seems remote and even quite fatuous given the crisis management atmosphere and the immediate attention that survival necessitates. In such a climate those who would suggest that more time and resources be delegated to reflective and growth-inducing pursuits are viewed as impractical visionaries devoid of common sense. Thus, the status quo is perpetuated, the endless cycle of underdevelopment rolls on with its peasant culture of low morale and teachers as 'reactors' to daily emergencies. I see the contemporary teacher as the plate juggler on the old *Ed Sullivan Show*, frantically running from plate to plate, keeping each one spinning atop each stick, unable to pause long enough to reflect on the purpose of the enterprise. Time to reflect might be dangerous — why juggle the plates in the first place? Academic research seems to avoid such basic questions, researchers prepare their research for other researchers, the teacher is viewed as the aborigine to be studied objectively.

Indeed, when the status of teachers is so low, can the 'natives' gain the 'permission' to conduct their own research? Even though the practitioner may be in the school every day, engaged in an intensely personal relationship with students, he or she is deemed incapable of conducting research in the situation. Research and theory building are the domains of the academic expert — teachers should stick to the execution of their tasks. Such elitism precludes teacher-directed research and the democratization of the workplace; it reinforces authoritarian hierarchical distinctions which disempower teachers and ultimately their students (Altrichter and Posch, 1989; Apple, 1999). Teachers are 'studied down' in the sense that those who control the research use their inquiry to inform themselves about their subordinates (mere practitioners), later using their information to manipulate and control them.

Because of the asymmetrical power relationships, teachers are excluded from inquiring into how those who employ, supervise, judge, and administrate them make their policies (Tripp, 1988). Research loses a liberatory function as it is coopted as a mechanism of domination, as a manifestation of the low esteem in which teachers are held. A vicious circle, a tornado of bad work thus develops. Because of their low status, teachers are excluded from research. Researchers 'study down' the teachers. Uninformed by the valuable insights of teachers, the resulting research is abstracted from the lived world of school. Outside reforms of education emerge from an ungrounded knowledge base, and as such reforms are imposed teachers are further disenfranchised and alienated.

At the same time, ironically, that calls to increase the autonomy and self-direction of teachers are becoming common, state boards and even local districts have been imposing policy after restrictive policy. The standards movement ups the ante, as it mandates new, more draconian controls of teacher work. Protected from public concern with centralized control of education because they emanate from state and local agencies, such reform measures specify what is to be taught, how it is to be taught, and what constitutes student and teacher competence. As a result of such specification, the task of teaching becomes more technical and less autonomous, that is, more deskilled. Such hierarchical domination can occur only when teachers are viewed as low-status executors, members of a craft culture, not a profession.

The logic of such reforms posits that the intuitive knowledge of these 'teachers as craftspeople' must be replaced with research-based algorithmic teaching strategies (Porter, 1988; Elliott, 1989a). One of the many flaws in the logic of such hierarchical reform involves the genesis of the so-called research base. Such knowledge is often produced via a snapshot of the complex, highly contextualized classroom. Professional researchers observe for brief moments and administer problem-riddled tests to measure student progress. The focus is far too simple, much too narrow, the observation much too short and devoid of context to understand the dynamics of the classroom, not to mention prescribing generalizable procedures for effective teaching.

Teacher Research in an Over-managed Educational Cosmos

Schools and teachers have fallen prey to the bad work syndrome of over-management. School leaders fail to see educational problems as teachers see them, resulting in policies far removed from the daily world of teaching and learning. Such policies are notoriously insensitive to the reasons that teachers under-achieve, or why they withdraw from engagement with students. Typical of such a situation is the implementation of time-on-task research in schools in the United States. Empirical research showed, not surprisingly, that when student time spent on a particular subject increases, student standardized test scores increase. Accordingly, principals and supervisors in some systems have sought to control teacher work-time to insure that they teach directly to specific objectives. Teachers were not included in the process of negotiating the policy implications, or the meaning of such research. Teacher perspectives on the loss of classroom autonomy, the loss of a practitioner's freedom to assess the level of student understanding and to adjust the pace of instruction accordingly were not relevant in policy making. Policy and the lived world of the classroom were bifurcated by over-management (McCutcheon, 1981).

The concept of teacher as researcher in a democratic, critical context is incompatible with such a form of institutional management (neo-Taylorism) (Wallace, 1987; Hinchey, 1998). Teacher research, much like the Quality of Working Life programs in industry, is vulnerable to cooption by uncritical educational managers. John Elliott argues that teacher research has already been hijacked by the leaders of technocratic educational reform. Teachers are being trained to view action research in schools as a form of inquiry into the best techniques to produce pre-specified curriculum objectives or increases in standardized test scores. The socio-political and ethical dimensions of teaching and learning are not a part of the teacher research envisioned by these educational managers. It is only a matter of time, Elliott concludes, before action research will be promoted as the newest strategy to help teachers improve pupil achievement in order to meet national curriculum targets (Elliott, 1989a).

But those of us committed to democratic education and democratic workplaces for teachers can take heart. Hope rises from the ruins of mandated change imposed from above — reform coming from outside the school doesn't work. The school is a unique socio-cultural system marked by complexities rarely recognized by external agents. The teacher-as-researcher movement, especially the critical democratic conception of it, is gaining in popularity because of the recognition of the failure of positivistic, technocratic, teacher-proof reform. The plethora of small changes made by critical teacher researchers around the world in individual classrooms may bring about far more authentic educational reform than the grandiose policies formulated in state or national capitals (Oldroyd and Tiller, 1987; McKernan, 1988; Chattin-McNichols and Loeffler, 1989; Carson and Sumara, 1997). But our optimism must be tempered; merely granting teachers more power will not, at this historical juncture, make education democratic and teaching good work.

The teaching corps is large and heterogeneous. As Michel Foucault (1980) repeatedly pointed out, knowledge is power; and though it may be difficult for many of the proponents of action research to admit, part of the reason why teachers don't appropriate more authority involves the fact that they are insufficiently educated to take this step. Teachers with weak academic and pedagogical backgrounds must, out of necessity, defer to the judgments of their administrators, the certified experts (Maeroff, 1988; Porter, 1988; Raven and Stephenson, 2001). Theoretical understandings are necessary to the teacher's appropriation of authority — to his or her empowerment. The culture of teacher education, however, has tacitly instructed teachers across the generations to undervalue the domain of theory while avoiding basic questions of the ideological, psychological and pedagogical assumptions underlying their practice (Tripp, 1988; Pinar, 1994).

Even when teachers have taken research courses, which are often offered at the graduate level, few ever recognize the relationship between their research experience and their lives as teachers. Most of the research courses taken involve a survey of quantitative, statistical techniques of data analysis. Neither the on-the-job socializing forces of schooling nor in-service education are committed to the cultivation of the teacher's role as researcher. Evidence seems to indicate that if students are not introduced to the power of practitioner research during initial teacher training, chances are they will never be involved in it. Too much teacher education focuses student attention on short-term survival skills that do not offer the prospective teachers frames for examining their own teaching or subjecting their own and their school's practices to questions of educational purpose or social vision (Chattin-McNichols and Loeffler, 1989; Ruddick, 1989; Allison, 1995; Quinn, 2001).

Teacher education has failed to connect teacher education coursework with the teaching workplace in more than an obvious, technical way. Devoid of theoretical and analytical frames, young teachers fall easy prey to an unceremonialized initiation into the alienation and disillusionment of the bad teaching workplace. Donald Schön (1987) argues that if teacher education is to produce reflective, ethical practitioners who are equipped

to resist the demoralization of bad work, colleges of education must connect teachers' ways-of-knowing to social and educational theory. One of
the most important aspects of teacher education might involve the study
of the processes by which teachers acquire the practical knowledge, the
artistry that makes them more or less effective as professionals. When
such inquiry is pushed into a critical dimension, teacher educators address
the process of how professional consciousness is formed, how ideology
contributes to the teacher's definition of self. Without such inquiry and analysis, teachers remain technicians, and teaching remains bad work (Noblit,
1984, 1999; Oldroyd and Tiller, 1987; Denzin and Lincoln, 2000).

Teacher Scholars Developing the Skills to Reform Schools

Teaching can be good work. To make it so, teachers and teachers' organizations must be aware of the nature of good work and the forces which
serve to preclude it. Teachers who understand the guiding democratic
social theory of Dewey, the purposes of a critical social science, and the
issues which confront all social researchers as they attempt to produce
'knowledge' will be better prepared to avoid the bad work of teaching.
If teachers are to control their work lives, they must control the conceptualization of the teaching act. To control their teaching they must not
allow 'educational experts' to control knowledge production. To insure
good work, teachers must become researchers. It is important to explore
what exactly it means for teachers to become researchers.

The very basis of teacher research involves the cultivation of restless,
curious attitudes that lead to more systematic inquiries. Such attitudes
preclude unreflective orientations which fail to subject school practices
and life in general to criticism. All educational acts become problematic to
the teacher as researcher. This critical consciousness sees all educational activity as historically located. The perspective cannot view the educational
act separately from a social vision, that is, a view of a desirable future.
Educational acts, the researcher comes to understand, imply certain purposes, political positions, teaching strategies (recitation, simulation, dialogue,
rote-based exercise, etc.), forms of knowledge (subject matter content,
skills, competencies, conceptualization, tacit understanding, etc.), and
relationships between participants, for example, students and teachers.

John Dewey well understood the relationship between teaching as
democratic work and the teacher as researcher. In *The Sources of a Science
of Education* (1929) he argued that one of the most important roles of a
teacher was to investigate pedagogical problems through inquiry. Writing
of the 'teacher as investigator,' Dewey saw teachers as the most important
inquirers into the successes and failures of the school — he did not see
how viable educational research could be produced in any other way. Not
only did Dewey's teacher investigations lead to knowledge about the school,

but they led to good teaching (Dewey, 1929: 46–8). Indeed, the ultimate benefit of teacher research over seven decades later continues to be good teaching, defined not simply as effective ways of getting facts across but as understanding the significance of ideas and their effect on humans (McCutcheon, 1981; Duckworth, 1987; Kincheloe, Steinberg, and Hinchey, 1999).

One of the quickest ways to apply teacher research to the pursuit of good teaching involves, simply, teachers listening to students. This 'research on students' is a cardinal tenet of good teaching, as the teacher details his or her observations of the student as well as his or her reaction to the learner. These observations must be contextualized by an examination of the social context in which student *and teacher* consciousness are formed and education takes place. As teachers come to understand how they themselves and their students construct understandings of the educational process, they can move themselves and in turn their students into unknown territory, new frontiers of thinking. In this way teacher research revolutionizes traditional conceptions of staff development, making it a democratic, teacher-directed activity rather than a manifestation of the hierarchicalized imposition of the bad workplace. It promotes good work by assuming that teachers are knowledgeable and entitled to make decisions about their profession (Wood, 1988; Diamond and Mullin, 1999).

In many ways this conception of teacher research is little more than a common-sense explanation of what good teachers already do; but by making teacher research a central point of the conversation about good teaching we can extend the value of the concept. When Patricia Wood (1988) began her work with teacher research, like many of us, her impression was that she already incorporated the basic elements of the action research model: planning, acting, observing, and reflecting. By focusing her attention on the process, she sharpened her observation skills and began to reflect in a more textured, conscious manner. A more textured reflection on one's teaching involves a teacher's self-understanding of his or her practices, especially the ambiguities, contradictions, and tensions implicit in them. When the teacher as researcher connects with other teachers as researchers and with faculty interested in these ambiguities, contradictions, and tensions, a dynamic process ensues. This is the basis of educational change, of critical pedagogy, of a democratic workplace (Torney-Purta, 1985; Elliott, 1989b).

Teacher education which neglects these aspects of teacher research misses the point — it misses the distinct demands of the teaching workplace, the implications of democracy for educational theory, the ambiguity of practitioner ways of knowing. Piaget (1973) argued that teacher educators must acquaint teachers with the nature of research as quickly as possible. The notion of teacher research cannot be separated from any single component of teacher education. Research is an act which engages teachers in the dynamics of the educational process, as it brings to consciousness the creative tension between social and educational theory and classroom practice. What exactly does this creative tension mean? Although many readings are possible, it involves a form of thinking which moves into a 'post-formal' realm of *problem discovering* — it has transcended the Piagetian formal stage of *problem solving*.

In this context the teacher travels into a realm of analysis which forces him or her to confront the relationship between social vision and its concern with the nature of justice (social theory), educational purpose and its concern with the effects of the way we define education (educational theory), and how we as educational leaders and teachers conduct our daily professional lives. A teacher education which confronts this three-dimensional relationship cannot be simplistically technocratic, it cannot help but connect theory and practice, by necessity it must view teachers as self-directed agents, sophisticated thinkers, active researchers in a never-static, ambiguous context. Here, teachers are encouraged to construct their own views of their practice; they do not implement the constructs of others or act in response to the officially-certified knowledge base. They discover the asymmetries and contradictions created by the pursuit of harmony between critical conceptions of justice and the untidy world of learners and schools.

A recurrent theme here is teacher education's history of ineffective incorporation of research into professional education programs. Teachers involved in on-site action research projects often have difficulty adapting their teacher education-inculcated notion of research in education into the context created by the teacher research proponents. Even after their involvement in educational action research, teachers are reluctant to say that they really did research; even if they admit to having done research they maintain that it was unscholarly or of low quality (Ross, 1984). Their college of education-generated definition of research as a positivistic, controlled experimental design, replete with systematic statistical analysis, seems to undermine their ability to reconceptualize what form research might take or how it might be connected to their lives as practitioners.

The Inseparability of Research and Conceptual Analysis: The Historical Evolution of Action Research

It seems apparent that teacher education has to do more than *train* teachers in quantitative research methods. When critical teacher research is incorporated into teacher education, research methodology cannot be separated from conceptual analysis. Teachers as researchers in a democratic workplace are capable of meta-theoretical thinking. The assumption perpetuated in many graduate research courses that the analysis of pre-theoretical assumptions has little to do with the research act will have to be challenged

(Van Hesteren, 1986; Kincheloe and McLaren, 2000). Transformation of the educational workplace is impossible without a concurrent transformation of teacher education.

In the good workplace of the democratic school, educational improvement occurs when the practitioner learns to think more precisely and conceptually. In educational or workplace reforms in bad work situations, the idea of improving practitioner thinking and self-direction simply does not appear — the external imposition of rules on the practitioner brings about the desired change. Thus, the primary purpose of critical research activity for teachers is teacher empowerment. This empowerment involves teachers providing themselves with the skills and resources that enable them to reflect on educational practice. The purpose of educational research, therefore, is not merely to turn out better theories about education or more effective practices. Democratic educational research performed by teachers renders teaching practice more theoretical in that it is supported by reflection and grounded in cultural and socio-historical context. Teachers as researchers gain the skill to interrogate their own practices, question their own assumptions, and to understand contextually their own situations (Carr and Kemmis, 1986; Steinberg and Kincheloe, 1998).

Some scholars have termed this research by participants (or practitioners) action research. Researchers in the 1940s (Lewin, 1946) called for such forms of research, and such approaches have been discussed in Britain and Australia in particular for several years. Drawing upon several traditions mid-century, action research was praised as an important innovation in social inquiry. Kurt Lewin in social psychology probably did the most to popularize the term, but the method was utilized in a variety of contexts from industry to American Indian affairs. During the post-World War II era Stephen Corey at Teachers College led the action research movement in education. Corey argued that action research could reform curriculum practice, as teachers applied the results of their own inquiry. There was considerable enthusiasm for the movement in the post-war period, but by the late 1950s action research became the target of serious criticism and started to decline. Analysts have posited that the decline was precipitated by the bifurcation of science and practice which resulted from the growth of the cult of the expert. As policy makers came to rely more and more on expert educational research and developmental laboratories, the development of curriculum and pedagogical practices was dictated from the top down. Thus, the production of research was separated from the world of the practitioner (McKernan, 1988).

By the 1970s action research was rediscovered and by the 1980s had aligned itself with the attempt to redefine teacher professionalism. Many teacher educators have expressed concerns over the foundations of much of what passes for action research. Theorists interested in democratic conceptions of education and the teaching workplace have raised ideological questions about neo-action research. Reflecting John Elliott's fear of the technocratic cooption of action research, Patti Lather (1986) warns teachers that much of what has been called action research has not been critically grounded. Much of it is ahistorical and apolitical and thus lends itself to subversion by educational leaders who are tempted to employ the technical form of action research as a means of engineering practitioner 'improvements.' To avoid such appropriation of action research it must be carefully conceptualized and defined. Critically grounded action researchers must promote a self-reflective form of analysis which improves the rationality and justice of their own practices.

For action research or any type of research to be considered 'critical' it must meet five requirements:

1   It must reject positivistic perspectives of rationality, objectivity, and truth. Critical research will reject the positivistic notion that all educational issues are technical and not political or ethical in character.

2   It must be aware of the interpretations of educational practices held by those who perform educational acts. The self-understandings of educational practitioners who are reflective will lead them to be conscious of their own value-commitments, the value-commitments of others, and the values promoted by the dominant culture. Such consciousness will dramatically affect the way the practitioner interprets his or her professional activities. Teachers who become critical researchers will hold this consciousness of the relationship between personal values and practice as a goal of inquiry.

3   Critical research must attempt to distinguish between ideologically distorted interpretations and those which transcend ideological distortion. When practitioners seek to become aware of the interpretations they place on their practice, they always face a danger. Their interpretations, their consciousness of their own values and other values in the society may be distorted by illusory beliefs which sustain contradictions in the life of the society. Critical research, therefore, attempts to unveil this false consciousness while providing methods for overcoming its effects.

4   Critical research must reveal those aspects of the dominant social order which block our attempt to pursue rational goals. Often the goals that teachers work toward are not the result of their personal choice but are dictated by the social structure and the educational bureaucracy which it creates.

5   Critical research is always guided by an awareness of how it relates to practice. Its purpose is to help guide the work lives of teachers by discovering possible actions they might take if they are to overcome the obstacles social structures place in their way.

(Carr and Kemmis, 1986)

The Complexity of Critical Teacher Research:
Moving to the Level of Praxis

Critical research is praxis. Praxis involves the inseparability of theory and practice — that is, informed practice. We must understand theoretical notions in terms of their relationship to the lived world, not simply as objects of abstract contemplation. The truth of research must be proved in practice. Approaching truth, Max Horkheimer (1971) argued, is an active process where human beings apply it and 'bring it to power.' Verification of ideas, he continued, does not consist in mere laboratory experiments or the search for historical documents, but in historical struggle. Truth, Horkheimer concluded, is found in and is a moment of correct practice. Viewing research as praxis, we use our research to help participants (ourselves included) understand and change their situations (Held, 1980; Hinchey, 1998; Kincheloe, 2001).

It is important to note that teachers are not the only educational actors who engage in research. If we are serious about Dewey's notion of a democratic community where all parties have a voice in the formulation of policy, then parents and community members must be participants in the public conversation about education. These people will also be empowered by an understanding of critical research. One of the most democratic roles a public educator might play involves sharing critical research skills with the public, especially the disempowered public. This is a radical action on a number of levels. First, it negates the cult of the expert. It helps destroy the myth that men and women should seek guidance from those blessed with society's credentials to direct them. In this way it celebrates human self-direction. Second, it expands the role of the teacher. The teacher moves from classroom technician to active political agent, as he or she views education as a vehicle to build an egalitarian community. And third, it sees the school as an agent of democracy which is dedicated to an ethic of inclusion and negotiation. As a democratic agent, the school seeks to uncover those forces which thwart participation.

Critical research, of course, involves the production of new knowledge. Ira Shor and Paulo Freire (1987) write of a critical theory of knowing, arguing that there are two moments of knowing: (1) the production of new knowledge; and (2) when one knows the existing knowledge. What typically happens is that we separate these two moments. Critical research insists that they be brought together. Knowledge is produced far from the teacher and the students. Knowing is thus reduced to taking existing knowledge and transferring it. The teacher is not an inquirer who researches existing knowledge; he or she is merely a specialist in knowledge transference.

Teachers in this situation lose the indispensable qualities that are mandated by knowledge production: critical reflection, a desire to act, discomfort, uncertainty, restless inquiry, and so on. When such qualities disappear from teachers, schools become places where knowledge which supports dominant interests is stored and delivered. Knowledge is produced by official researchers, scholars, textbook writers, and sanctioned curriculum committees — it is not created and re-created by teachers and their students in the daily life of the school. Teaching and researching, the official story goes, are separate entities. Critical teaching is not viewed as a form of inquiry. The symbiotic ties between teaching and research are not seen.

There are countless examples of the way teachers act on their research abilities. They develop curricula for their schools, they research problems and share their findings with other teachers during in-service education meetings, they devise methods grounded on their research to bring dignity and intelligence to self-evaluation procedures. Stephen Kemmis (1982) describes the critical research of a group of junior high school teachers on ways of improving remedial reading in their school. They began by exploring various strategies which had been used by remedial reading teachers around the world and by examining a variety of problems associated with remedial reading. Different teachers examined different reading strategies and used the information to improve the remedial reading teaching. Based on their work they implemented programs which involved more teachers in the attempt to help children with reading problems, altered the school day to devote more time to the development of reading, and formed teams of classroom teachers and specialist remedial teachers to tie remediation into the regular classroom.

Teachers involved in this project gained sophisticated understandings of remedial reading based on their own research, not the research and pronouncements of 'experts.' They learned how some techniques for teaching remedial reading worked to separate reading skills from the learning situations which necessitated them. Some of the methods utilized often served to perpetuate the status of students labeled remedial rather than allowing them to break away from the stigma. Other strategies resulted in student deskilling by removing remedial students from the learning context of the classroom, with the result that their poor classroom performance was maintained. Several techniques created situations where teachers found it hard to work together to develop reading skills in various curricular contexts. Teachers were becoming conceptualizers, not mere executors of someone else's plans (Carr and Kemmis, 1986). Examples of teachers as researchers are numerous and can be found in a variety of recent publications (Kemmis *et al.*, 1982; Carson and Sumara, 1997).

One of the most important examples of the liberating possibilities offered by teachers as researchers is presented by Paulo Freire and Ira Shor. Teachers, they argue, must research their own students. It is a research which focuses on the spoken and written words of students in order that the teacher may understand what they know, their goals, and the texture of their lived worlds. I can teach effectively, Ira Shor asserts, only if I have researched my students' levels of thought, their skills, and their feelings. I conduct this research in the classroom, he continues. Success is possible only if the teacher creates a situation where students feel comfortable to open up and express what they are authentically feeling. To accomplish such openness, teachers must exercise restraint. They must avoid monopolization of classroom conversation in order to encourage student talk — talk which reveals their idiom and their consciousness. The words of students are the ore of teacher research. From this ore the teacher as researcher extracts valuable insights into the students' cognitive levels, their pedagogical intuitions, their political predispositions, and the themes they consider urgent.

Shor and Freire are desperately concerned that teachers understand student experience. They read what their students read, watch TV, listen to the radio, and go to popular movies in order to stay in touch with student reality. Teachers may not prefer Nine Inch Nails; but if they are to understand their students, part of their research activity may involve listening to their musical act enough to understand the basis of their appeal. Critical teachers might juxtapose an understanding of the popular culture which forms the terrain on which student values are often negotiated with the dominant school script. The interaction between the two worlds and the enculturation process accompanying them may provide important insights into student *and teacher* behaviors in school settings.

Shor and Freire (1987) advise teachers as researchers not to be submissive to school texts. Fight with the text, rewrite it as a form of research. Resist the demand of the official curriculum for deference to the texts — a demand predicated on the dominant culture's requirement to condition students to the industrial world's need for submission to authority, to reliance on the expert. One of the first research acts I undertake in my role as teacher is the effort to expose the assumptions of the texts. 'What is not said here?', I ask myself and my students. What does the tacit message tell us about the beliefs and goals of the textbook writer? Do these goals conflict with the overt goals of our school? If so, why does the conflict exist? How does this conflict affect your role as student, citizen or potential worker? Or my role as a teacher?

Indeed, the outcomes of teacher research can be dramatic. Critical research by teachers is not a technique for bringing about democracy; it is an embodiment of democratic principles as it allows teachers to help determine the conditions of their own work. It leads to group decision making, a basic principle of democracy. Critical action research allows teachers to organize themselves as communities of researchers dedicated to the achievement of their own and ultimately their students' enlightenment. As we see so clearly with Shor and Freire, critical research improves educational practice, curriculum, and school organization. When teachers and parents come together in research projects, no single activity better serves to improve school and community relations (Carr and Kemmis,

1986). Teachers, parents, and members of the community when engaged in such a process come to ask serious questions about what is taught, how it is taught, and what should constitute the larger goals of education (Giroux and Aronowitz, 1985; Giroux, 1997).

Teacher Research as a Political Struggle

As long as teacher work is bad work political activities are unthinkable. In a context where labor is divided to the point that teachers have little influence in shaping the conditions of their work, such visions of the possibilities of the role of teacher may be disregarded with ridicule of the visionary. To become critical researchers teachers face a political struggle. As in any political struggle, organization is a key. Teachers must organize groups to investigate school policy, government education policies, the terms of employment of teachers, and strategies to educate the community (Kincheloe, 1999; Willinsky, 2001b).

In other words, critical teachers as researchers cannot avoid the political role of promoting critical self-reflection in the society. Undoubtedly, there will be critics who will argue that such a role politicizes the school. The school should remain neutral, they will argue. Such a position reflects a common *naïveté* which fails to recognize dominant definitions of neutrality as problematic. The role of teacher as transmitter of prearranged and often isolated fact bits, is not understood as a politicized role (McLaren, 1995). The question of 'what could be' is submerged to the 'what is,' as the *status quo* is rendered natural. The implicit message of such teaching is that knowledge is already known, the information worthy of being known has already been discovered, and that the student role is ultimately a passive role. If schools are to be places which promote self and social empowerment, teacher work will have to be redefined. Teachers will find it necessary to develop knowledge and skills that allow them to connect educational practice with larger social visions. When they inevitably pass such knowledge and skills along to students and community members, they will be providing the tools which will allow them to become leaders rather than simply managers or civil servants.

In their political role as critical researchers, teachers must form alliances with social groups which share their concerns and social visions. An essential aspect of these alliances will involve research networks which connect teachers with laborers, theologians, social workers, lawyers, doctors, politicians, environmental activists, and so on. Not only will such alliances further the goals of democratic empowerment, but they will help bring about the conditions which allow teaching to become good work and teachers to become scholars. Society does not at present view elementary, junior high, and high school teachers as scholars. The public does not hold an image of teachers which is characterized by individuals engaged in reflection, research, sharing their work with others, constructing their workplace, producing curriculum materials, and publishing their research for other teachers and community members in general. To destroy dominant images, teachers will have to confront engrained values of competition, individualism, and patriarchy which inhibit most attempts at change (Giroux and Aronowitz, 1985; Leistyna, Woodrum, and Sherblom, 1996).

Change is a fundamental goal of the teacher as critical researcher. Henry Giroux develops this idea with the conception of what he calls the transformative intellectual. Transformative intellectuals treat students as active agents, render knowledge problematic, utilize dialogical methods of teaching, and seek to make learning a process where self-understanding and emancipation is possible. Giroux interprets this to mean that transformative teachers 'give students the opportunity to become agents of civic courage, and therefore citizens who have the knowledge and courage to take seriously the need to make despair unconvincing and hope practical' (Giroux and Aronowitz, 1985).

Such teachers hold a vision and act through their research to achieve that vision. These critical researchers come to understand and then transform the bureaucratization which wipes out our memory of what educational institutions might be. With their memory of educational possibility intact, transformative teachers work to relate student experience, popular culture, and the effects of dominant modes of thinking in the attempt to help students and community members make sense of their relationship to the world which surrounds them. When such concerns are informed by the academic perspectives of disciplines such as history, literature, sociology, cultural studies, anthropology, political science, philosophy, and others, the possibility of critical thinking and self-direction is enhanced. The cultivation of teaching as good work leads to creative, research-grounded, motivated teachers. Research ability provides the vehicle by which teachers reach the emancipatory goal of learning to teach themselves. Our purpose now is to explore in more detail the nature of this critical research and the debate it elicits about the nature of educational research in general.

Chapter 3

Connecting Knower and Known: Constructing an Emancipating System of Meaning

To begin our exploration of the debate about educational research, let us briefly examine a few basic premises of the philosophy of science. We will explore the relationship of the knower to the known (i.e., the researcher to their research) and from this understanding begin an attempt to construct a system of meaning, a foundation on which to ground an ethical, democratic orientation toward the research act. Using the principles of good work in conjunction with our system of meaning, we will theorize a research/pedagogical orientation called critical constructivism.

Defining Critical Constructivism: Grounding Teacher Research

A critical constructivist position assumes that there is no knowledge without a knower (Fenstermacher, 1994). Before we say anything else, the knower is a living human being. As a living human, a perceiving instrument, the perspective of the researcher must be granted the same seriousness of attention as is typically accorded the research design and the research methods in traditional forms of inquiry (Lowe, 1982; Gordon, Miller and Rollock, 1990; Hankins, 1998). Like knowledge, the knower also belongs to a particular, ever-changing historical world, a web of reality. The human being as a part of history is a reflexive subject, that is, an entity who is conscious of the constant interaction between humans and their world. This reflexivity recognizes that all knowledge is a fusion of subject and object. In other words, the knower personally participates in all acts of understanding. Moreover, the world in general, the social and educational world in particular, is not an objective structure, but a constructed, dynamic interaction of men and women organized and shaped by their race, class and gender. Thus, it is impossible from the critical constructivist perspective to conceive knowledge without thinking of the knower (Reinharz, 1979; Lowe, 1982; Lytle and Cochran-Smith, 1992; Hursch, 1997).

But the constructivist notion of knower–known inseparability has not been the dominant position in educational research. Teacher researchers need to understand that the myth of Archimedes, the belief in an objective body of knowledge unconnected to the mind of the knower, has helped formulate how educators have conceptualized the research act. Such an assumption tacitly constructs not only what counts as research but, via the shaping of educational research, formulates what we 'know' about education. The myth assumes that the human perceiver occupies no space in the known world; operating outside of history, the knower knows the world of education and its students, teachers, and leaders objectively. This separation of the knower and the known is a cardinal tenet of the Cartesian–Newtonian paradigm. The impact of this 'way of seeing' on the theory and practice of Western science has been profound. René Descartes' analytical method of reasoning, often termed reductionism, has formed the foundation of modern scientific research. Cartesian reductionism asserts that all aspects of complex phenomena can be best appreciated by reducing them to their constituent parts and then piecing these elements together according to causal laws (Mahoney and Lyddon, 1988).

All of this took place within Descartes' bifurcation of the mind and matter/body. Known as Cartesian dualism, human experience was divided into two different realms: (1) an internal world of sensation; and (2) an objective world composed of natural phenomena. Drawing on this dualism, scientists asserted that the laws of physical and social systems could be uncovered objectively; the systems operated apart from human perception, with no connection to the act of perceiving. Descartes theorized that the internal world and the natural world were forever separate and one could never be shown to be a form of the other. Constructivism rejects such a dualism and posits an alternative to the Western traditions of realism and rationalism (Lowe, 1982; Lavine, 1984; Mahoney and Lyddon, 1988). Briefly, realism presumes a singular, stable, external reality that can be perceived by one's senses; rationalism argues that thought is superior to sense and is most important in shaping experience. Our notion of constructivism contends that reality, contrary to the arguments made by proponents of realism, is not external and unchanging. In contrast to rationalism, constructivism maintains that human thought cannot be meaningfully separated from human feeling and action. Knowledge, constructivists assert, is constrained by the structure and function of the mind and can thus be known only indirectly. The knower and the known are Siamese twins connected at the point of perception.

Constructivism draws upon an anti-Cartesian tradition emerging from the New Science of Giambattista Vico in the early 1700s and extending to the phenomenology, critical theory, and women's epistemology of the twentieth century. Vico insisted to the consternation of the Cartesians that a different conceptual apparatus was necessary for the analysis of social and cultural phenomena from that which might be used to study the structure of the physical world. The tradition that Vico established insisted that human beings were more than objects; when conceived as such, the uniqueness of men and women is lost — they are reduced to things, to 'its.' When people are seen as objects serious ethical questions arise. For example: is manipulation acceptable? Is self-determination a basic human right? Is the purpose of research the improvement of the human condition? Should democracy be considered in the conceptualization of the research act?

The point is clear: the objectivism, the separation of the knower and the known implicit in the Cartesian tradition deny the spatio-temporal location of the knower in the world. This results in the estrangement of human beings from the rhythms of life, the natural world (White, 1978; Lowe, 1982; Mahoney and Lyddon, 1988; Noffke and Stevenson, 1995). Alvin Gouldner extends the counter-Cartesian critique, arguing that the social sciences promote a form of inquiry suitable for an alienated age and an alienated people. The dominant expressions of the social sciences serve to accommodate researchers to socio-cultural alienation rather than work to overcome it (Reinharz, 1979). Descartes argued that knowledge should be empirical, mathematical, and certain, and the orientation toward research which emerged worked to exploit the forces of nature in a way which transformed the landscape of the Earth. As a result of this objectivist epistemology and the positivism which emerged from it, we now inhabit a human-made, artificial environment. Emerging from the tradition was a behavioral science which set out to manipulate people and an educational system which utilized the behavioral sciences to mold students and their consciousness in a way which would foster efficiency and economic productivity, often at the expense of creativity, social justice, and good work.

Drawing on the Counter-Cartesian Tradition: Capitalizing on the Unique Abilities of Human Beings

The counter-Cartesian recognition of such alienation sets the stage for our attempt to develop an emancipatory system of meaning to ground ourselves as teacher researchers. If knowledge is the prerequisite for social action, and if social action transforms knowledge, then knowledge cannot be conceived as static and certain — the foundation is laid for the social construction of reality. Donald Lowe theorizes that there are first- and second-degree constructs of social reality. First-degree constructs involve knowledge in the world, direct experiences and the understanding derived from them which helps shape the behavior of men and women. Second-degree constructs involve the social scientific interpretations of first-degree constructs — that is, outsider constructs of the insider, first-degree constructs made by the actors on the social scene. The central concern of educational research, it would follow, is the relationship between first-degree construction of the lived world of education and the second-degree explanation of that reality by the educational researcher. Does the second-degree explanation expand our consciousness and appreciation or reduce and simplify our understanding of the meaning of first-degree reality? Critical constructivism argues that the traditional methods of educational science have often reduced our understanding of educational reality. It attempts to develop new ways for educational researchers, teacher researchers in particular, to approach the study of first-order educational reality (Lowe, 1982).

The first step in such a process, as you might guess, is to understand the relationship between researchers and what they are researching. Where do we start such a process? I would argue that an awareness of self and the forces which shape the self is a prerequisite for the formulation of more effective methods of research. Knowledge of self allows researchers to understand how social forces and research conventions shape their definitions of knowledge, of inquiry, of effective educational practice. Knowledge of the self allows them consciousness to choose between research traditions which depersonalize the process of knowing in hopes of gaining certainty, pure objective knowledge, and research orientations which assert that since the mind of the observer is always involved, it should be utilized as a valuable tool. Humans possess a tacit knowledge which can be drawn upon to make sense of social and educational situations. Such tacit, intuitive knowledge guides researchers as they conduct interviews, observations, document analyses, and so on. A primary purpose of the critical constructivist approach to teacher research is to connect teachers to the nature and formation of such a form of knowledge and, in turn, to learn how to employ it for maximum benefit. Let us examine some of the dimensions of this tacit knowledge which makes humans the most valuable of all research instruments.

To begin with, humans are sensitive to subtle, hard-to-categorize dimensions of social life. Because of such sensitivity the human inquirer can interact with a situation in such a way that the unspoken, the hidden, can be made explicit. The empirical research instruments which are capable of assessing particular factors are inappropriate for assessing other factors. Such is not the case with human instruments — they are almost unlimited in their adaptability. Researchers as agents freed from reliance on particular instruments of inquiry are capable of simultaneously collecting information about a variety of factors at a variety of levels. Humans, unlike research instruments, can perceive holistically. In the maelstrom of confusion which constitutes the socio-educational world, only humans can see connections between the disparate parts; only humans can grasp and perceive dominant themes in the ostensibly unrelated remnants of the socio-educational fabric. Human inquirers can extend knowing to a higher level through their capacity to grasp the realm of the felt, the emotional, the unconscious. Those unexamined usages, those unintended meanings which reveal insights that open windows into the significance of experience, are the type of understanding that only humans are capable of grasping. These are the insights that allow us to comprehend the actual educational and ideological effects of schools and other institutions.

Unlike empirical instruments, humans can synthesize information, generate interpretations, and revise and make those interpretations more complex at the site the inquiry takes place. In the process, the human as research instrument can explore the unusual, the idiosyncratic situation, whereas the traditional empirical research instrument may have no use for the atypical situation because it does not fit the categories delineated. Such idiosyncrasy may serve as the path to a new level of understanding of the effect of a curriculum on a student or a community. While such dimensions of research are quite valuable and very sophisticated, we can look at them merely as extensions of everyday human activities: listening, watching, speaking, reading, and so on. The cult of the expert will undoubtedly be uncomfortable with such research populism, but our understanding of social and educational life will be enhanced in the application of such a perspective (Lincoln and Guba, 1985; Richardson, 1994; Denzin and Lincoln, 2000). Teacher researchers can revolutionize professional practice by viewing themselves as potentially the most sophisticated research instruments available.

In order to improve our abilities as teacher researchers we need to appreciate the value of comprehending the relationship between the knower and the known. To accomplish such a task teacher researchers must understand more fully the insidious ways that traditional Cartesian research orientations have worked to restrict our understanding of that relationship. Feminist theory provides an excellent analytical tradition from which to begin such an exploration. Feminist scholars start with the counter-Cartesian assumption that researchers and the researched are always historically situated and assert that researchers should take this as a given and build it into their methodological and theoretical strategies. The claim of traditional researchers that objective knowledge exists independent of the researcher's historical location is false (Smith, 1974; Reinharz, 1982; Aronowitz, 1988, 1993). Feminist theory or women's ways of knowing radically transform traditional research, forcing us to conceptualize new relationships between the knower and the known. Research must be considered from a new perspective that attacks the traditional deference to authority and exposes science as a form of regulatory power (Semali and Kincheloe, 1999). The androcentric principle of a neutral, hierarchical, non-reciprocal interaction between researcher and researched is transcended via feminist theory, as feminist researchers attempt to reconnect the knower with the known (Fee, 1982; Mies, 1982; Hicks, 1999; Kohli, 2000).

No longer can emancipatory-oriented researchers allow Cartesian science to blind the knower intentionally, thus restricting what science can 'see' in the world of education. By revealing what can be learned from the everyday, the mundane, feminist scholars have opened a whole new area of inquiry and insight. They have uncovered the existence of silences and absences where traditional scholars had seen only 'what was there.' Women scholars were able to uncover such absences by applying their own lived experience to the research process, thus connecting knower and known (Belenky, Clinchy, Goldberger, and Tarule, 1986). Traditional Cartesian researchers had weeded out the self, denied their intuitions and inner voices, in the process producing restricted and object-like interpretations of socio-educational events. Using the traditional definitions, these object-like interpretations were certain and scientific; feminist self-grounded inquirers were inferior, merely impressionistic, and journalistic (Reinharz, 1979, 1982; Rosenau, 1992; Clough, 1998).

Feminist theorists realized that the objective science of the Western tradition was released from any social or ethical responsibility. Objectivity in this sense became a signifier for ideological passivity and an acceptance of a privileged socio-economic position. Thus, scientific objectivity came to demand separation of thought and feeling, the devaluation of any perspective maintained with emotional conviction. Feeling is designated as an inferior form of human consciousness — those who rely on thought or logic operating within this framework can justify their repression of those associated with emotion or feeling. Feminist theorists have pointed out that the thought–feeling hierarchy is one of the structures historically used by men to oppress women. In intimate heterosexual relationships if a man is able to present his position in an argument as the rational viewpoint and the woman's position as an emotional perspective, then he has won the argument — his is the voice worth hearing.

The power dynamics of this relationship are projected onto a larger scale in the domain of educational research: the research experts occupy a male role, while the researched, and even the consumers of the research, occupy a female role. On a variety of levels research is not a value-free, non-ideological activity. Traditional science reproduces particular power relations which lead to the production of specific forms of knowledge. In this context certain questions are asked, while others are deemed irrelevant. Presuppositions, try as traditional Cartesian researchers might, cannot be eliminated. They can be brought to consciousness, confronted, and transformed over time, but they cannot be discarded (Reinharz, 1979, 1992; Fee, 1982; Britzman, 1991). The methodologies of scientific research emerge from these dominant presuppositions. Revered as sacred, traditional methodologies are rarely questioned even when they separate research technique from research purpose. To initiate inquiry with a question of method rather than with a question of purpose, feminist researchers alert us, is irrational. It is irrational in the sense that it bifurcates the way we obtain knowledge and make judgments. Flannery O'Connor argues that 'judgment is implicit in seeing,' that is, constructing judgments is not an isolated process and when it is it is so diluted that the insights derived are bland and trivial (Westkoff, 1982).

Our notion of critical constructivist teacher research maintains that inquirers connect knower and known, purpose and technique by utilizing the human as instrument. From this counter-Cartesian perspective inquiry begins with researchers drawing upon their own experience. Since the educational researcher is a human being studying other human beings he or she is privy to the inner world of experience. Utilizing his or her own empathetic understandings, the observer can watch educational phenomena from within — that is, they can know directly, they can watch and experience. The gap between experience and traditional scientific description begins to close. On a variety of levels the private is made public. Not only do we get closer to the private experience of our students, other teachers, and administrators and the effect of these experiences on the public domain; but we also gain access to the private experience of the researcher and the effect of that experience on the public descriptions he or she presents of the phenomena observed. In our situation as teacher researchers, of course, *we* are the researchers, and it is our private experience and its relation to our public descriptions (and our public actions as teachers) that are being analyzed. Thus not only do we learn about the educational world surrounding us, but we gain new insights into the private world within us — the world of our constructed consciousness (Reinharz, 1979, 1982; Clandinin and Connelly, 1995; Quinn, 2001).

Learning to Produce Knowledge from Feminist Researchers

These ideas do not have to remain in the isolated world of academia, the subject of discussions between educational researchers in academic journals or educational conferences. They are important understandings for teachers who are contemplating ways of improving their everyday professional practice. Not only does feminist theory help us to formulate the purpose of research in general, but it also provides a model for how action research can be implemented in various contexts — action research which is grounded on a counter-Cartesian fusion of knower and known. Maria Mies theorized a women-as-researchers project which set out to empower women to make their own history, to take control of the social changes to which they had been subjected. To accomplish this task Mies and her researchers set four goals.

First, the women set out to document their life histories. Such a project allowed the action researchers to achieve a critical distance from their own subjective biographies. As a result, they were paroled from the incarceration of their own pasts, using the knowledge of their imprisonment to liberate their futures. Second, the researchers wrote their biographies and in the process gained a form of objective documentation that enabled them to recognize their lives. Third, the women analyzed their

biographiles in a historical and sociological manner which took i
not only their individual stories but explored the relationsh
their stories and larger historical forces of race, class, gender an
Individual lives were viewed as intrinsically important but also as manifestations of the social contradictions and fissures of contemporary life.

Fourth, the women used their biographical and ideological knowledge to formulate strategies of individual and collective political action.
The purpose of such action was to create a collective critical consciousness
among women which would move them to fight oppression in their own
lives and social contexts. The women staged plays and made videos, showed
them to women's groups, and initiated discussions of the productions. In
the discussions they began to move beyond their isolated lived experiences
as they realized that women as a group have a collective social destiny.
Teacher researchers, both female and male, have much to learn from such a
process. Like the women action researchers, teachers can also come to understand the forces which constrict them and the ways they become victimized
by historical constructions of what constitutes an effective, efficient workplace. Through such understandings teachers can formulate strategies of
resistance — political action which helps them take charge of their professional lives (Mies, 1982: 127–35).

Renate Duelli Klein extends our notion of feminist-based action
research by elaborating on the connection between the researcher and the
researched, the knower and the known. She describes a research project
involving battered women. The researched, the battered women, were
never looked upon as research objects but as subjects who were sisters,
mirrors of self. Researchers approached the project with the assumptions
that the battered women were co-researchers; as such, the researchers and
the researched compared their own experiences as women and negotiated
the findings of the project in a way whereby the experience of each group
was extended by interaction with the other. Our notion of critical teacher
research is informed by such experiences (Klein, 1982). As the researcher
and the researched interact — in our case teachers and students, teachers
and teachers, teachers and administrators, teachers and community members
— experiences can be compared, insight can be gained through interaction, and democratic perspectives toward the teaching act can be fostered.

Establishing a Critical System of Meaning:
Grounding Teacher Research

Before we continue our discussion of critical action research, we need to
establish clearly the system of meaning, the way of seeing which underpins
our approach to research. Throughout the book we will expand our system,
but at this point we need to delineate the assumptions which guide our
notions of the role of teacher and the purpose of education, and how

action research fits into such visions. Henry Giroux is extremely helpful in our attempt to develop an emancipatory system of meaning. In *Schooling and the Struggle for Public Life*, Giroux (1988) theorized a reconceptualization of the meaning of a democratic education which we will use as a starting point in our attempt to empower teachers via action research. The most innovative aspect of Giroux's book involved his attempt to integrate his understanding of critical theory, semiological/textual analysis, feminist theory, Deweyan educational philosophy, and liberation theology into a critical educational/curriculum theory.

Giroux's educational perspective views teaching as an act of deconstructing knowledge for the purpose of understanding more critically oneself and one's relation to the larger culture. Instead of fitting the marginalized into the dominant culture, for example, to train workers for jobs that require 'functional' reading and writing, Giroux's view of schooling emphasizes the importance of naming and changing social situations which thwart the development of a democratic community. Informed by Paulo Freire, Giroux theorizes that critical literacy involves the development of the capacity for self-criticism of the historically constituted nature of one's consciousness. Giroux's pedagogy never detaches context or history from the teaching act; on the contrary, teaching and culture are binary stars revolving around one another in a reflexive relationship that includes community, difference, remembrance, and historical consciousness as orbiting planets in their solar system. Without this capacity for historical consciousness and self-criticism, Giroux fears that teachers are in danger of assuming the role of passive followers of administrative directives — regardless of the ethical issues at stake.

Extending Giroux's work into the realm of action research, we can argue that teachers are obligated to become researchers of themselves, revealing the interests implicit in their own teaching. Our emancipatory system of meaning will alert teachers to the need to cultivate and listen to the voices of students, understanding from the beginning that student voices encompass complex and contradictory relationships between students and the world. Teachers operating on the basis of an emancipatory system of meaning will find the need to incorporate a variety of qualitative research strategies into their teaching repertoire. Making use of such strategies, teachers can uncover those concealed social constructions that shape curriculum structures, curriculum materials, and the consciousness of students, teachers, administrators, and community members.

Thus, teachers as researchers become active producers of meanings, not simply consumers. Conservative leaders tell teachers and the public that the basis of the crisis in modern education revolves around the loss of authority in the modern socio-educational world. Rejecting the conservative attempt to reconstruct an undemocratic, patriarchal, obedience-based theory of authority, Giroux argues that authority must be redefined in a democratic context. In Giroux's attempt to define a progressive, democratic,

inclusive notion of authority, we find an important base to l
struction of an emancipatory system of meaning. This syst
must be grounded on our notion of good work, an inclusiv
citizen-to-citizen solidarity, and hope. Applied to the context of education,
this critical system of meaning helps us to visualize schools as places where
students learn and work together to establish the socio-economic conditions that make possible individual freedom and social empowerment
(Giroux, 1988).

Such a theoretical orientation requires that teachers critique those right-
wing notions of authority that establish hierarchical divisions of labor
that serve to disempower both students and teachers. Our emancipatory
system of meaning rests on a rejection of hierarchical social relations.
On this principle it grounds a view of teacher professionalism which uses
action research as a vehicle for empowerment via a more sophisticated
appreciation of the tacit outcomes of schooling, the inner world of students, the ideological effects of the structure of schools and school reform,
and the forces which shape teacher self-image. Let us now extend these
basic principles and explore in more detail the ideas which form the foundation of an emancipatory form of action research in education.

Critical Theory and Teachers as Researchers

No emancipatory system of meaning can be contemplated outside of the
Frankfurt School's formulation of critical theory, in particular, its attempt
to explore how consciousness is tied to history. A critical democratic
approach to teacher research would always be mindful of the relationship
between teachers', students', and administrators' consciousness and the
socio-historical contexts in which they operate. In this way the critical theory of feminism helps us open the door to the analysis of the personal —
how our private selves have been shaped by historical forces (Haraway,
1991; Kincheloe and Steinberg, 1997). Guided by feminism in our action
research, we expose those buried parts of ourselves which we hold in
common with our brothers and sisters — such solidarity allows us to overcome impediments to self-direction together. To study the links between
women's history and modern women's education, for example, is to open
the possibility for discovering how one's lived experiences are connected to
those of other women or, for that matter, other men. The bonds between
consciousness and history reveal a new form of knowledge to the teacher
inquirer: the self-understanding and possible empowerment which come
from the uncovering of the ways that one's psyche has been constructed
by historical gender roles (Westkoff, 1982; Kincheloe, 2001).

Guided by such concerns, teacher researchers inspired by critical theory
seek to expose what constitutes reality for themselves and for the participants in educational situations (Hinchey, 1998; Kincheloe and McLaren,

2000; McLaren, 2000). How do these participants, critical teachers as researchers ask, come to construct their views of educational reality? Critical constructivist action researchers see a socially constructed world and ask what are the forces which construct the consciousness, the ways of seeing of the actors who live in it? Uncritical action researchers attempt to provide accurate portrayals of educational reality, but they stop short of analyzing the origins of the forces which construct actor consciousness. Without such information, critical constructivist teacher researchers maintain, emancipatory action is impossible. Descriptions of educational reality outside the boundaries of the socio-economic cultural context hold little meaning for educators concerned with social justice and ethical action.

Why are some constructions of educational reality embraced and officially legitimized by the dominant culture while others are repressed (Lincoln and Guba, 1985; McLaren, 1989; Denzin and Lincoln, 2000)? This is the type of question that critical action researchers seek to answer. Indeed, the essence of critical constructivism concerns the attempt to move beyond the formal style of thinking which emerged from empiricism and rationalism, a form of cognition which solves problems framed by the dominant paradigm, the conventional way of seeing. Like Einstein's physics, critical constructivist action researchers attempt to use their understanding of the social construction of reality to rethink and reconceptualize the types of questions we ask about the educational enterprise (Noblit, 1984, 1999; Yeakey, 1987; Kincheloe, Steinberg, and Tippins, 1999; Willinsky, 2001b).

A central theme of these reconceptualized questions involves the inquiry into whose constructions of reality prevail and whose ought to prevail. Michael Young (1971) argues that the dominant definitions, the official ways of seeing in schools, are constructed realities which benefit some groups and not others. The ways that schools distinguish bright from stupid, good citizenship from bad, model behavior from disruptions, good work from bad work, are constructions which emanate from those in a position to induce less privileged actors to grant their consent to the dominant definitions. Much of the inquiry into education commences without an attempt to construct a system of meaning on which to ground analysis of the questions it pursues — it merely accepts the unproblematized assumptions of mainstream research. Even when we do attempt to construct a system of meaning to ground our inquiry, it may be intellectually immature if we neglect an analysis of the hidden ideological forces which define our methodology, shape our logic, anesthetize our ethical sense, and select our questions. Without attention to such concerns, our inquiries lapse into an irrelevancy and a myopia which constrain the educational possibilities offered by empowered, insightful teachers (Yeakey, 1987; Cochran-Smith and Lytle, 1993, 1998).

Teacher researchers informed by critical theory seek a system of meaning which grants a new angle, a unique insight into the social consequences of different ways of knowing, different forms of knowledge, and different approaches to research. Inquiry and the knowledge it produces are never neutral but constructed in specific ways that privilege particular logics and voices while silencing others. Why do science and math curricula in the United States, for example, receive more attention and prestige in public schools than liberal arts (Barton and Osborne, 2001; Brown, 2001; Roth, Tobin, and Ritchie, 2001)? Critical researchers searching for the way power helps shape individual and social consciousness uncover links between the need of large corporations to enhance worker productivity and the goals of contemporary educational reform and standards movements to reestablish 'excellent' schools (Horn and Kincheloe, 2001). They discover relationships between the interest of business and the exclusion of the study of labor history in Western schools (Kincheloe, 1995, 1999). They expose the connections between the patriarchal, Eurocentrism of educational leadership and definitions of classics which exclude the contributions of women, minorities, and non-Westerners to the literature, art, and music curricula (Powell, 2001).

Power regulates discourses; discursive practices are defined as a set of tacit rules that regulate what can and cannot be said, who can speak with the blessing of authority and who must listen, whose socio-educational constructions are scientific and valid and whose are unlearned and unimportant (Lemke, 1995). In the everyday world of teachers, legitimized discourses insidiously tell teachers what books may be read by students, what instructional methods may be utilized (Madeleine Hunter, Success for All, etc.), and what belief systems, definitions of citizenship, and views of success may be taught. Schools may identify, often unconsciously, conceptions of what it means to be educated with upper-middle-class white culture; expressions of working-class or non-white culture may be viewed as uneducated and inferior. In this context teachers are expected to sever student identification with their minority group or working-class backgrounds, as a result alienating such students through the degradation of their culture. The culture of schooling privileges particular practices and certain methods of discerning truth. Foucault argues that truth is not relative (i.e., all world views embraced by different researchers, cultures, and individuals are of equal worth), but is relational (constructions considered true are contingent upon the power relations and historical context in which they are formulated and acted upon). The question which grounds our attempt to formulate a system of meaning for our action research asks: If what we designate as truth is relational and not certain, then what set of assumptions can we use to guide our activities as professionals, to inform our questions as teacher researchers (McLaren, 1989; Pinar, 1994; Rasberry, 2001)?

This is why our system of emancipatory meaning is so important. This is why liberation theology is so important to our attempt to develop an emancipatory system of meaning. Liberation theology, with its roots deep in the Latin American struggle against poverty and colonialism, morally situates our attempt to formulate an explicit set of assumptions, an ethical starting line from which to begin our formulation of educational questions. Liberation theology makes no apology for its identification with the perspective of those who are excluded and subjugated. Proclaiming their solidarity with the marginalized, liberation theologians work along-side them in their attempt to expose the existing social order as oppressive and unethical. All aspects of our emancipatory system of meaning and teacher research which grows out of it rest on this notion of identification with the perspective of the oppressed. Accordingly, one of the main goals of critical teacher research is to reveal the ways that dominant schooling serves to perpetuate the hopelessness of the subjugated (Welch, 1985). On the basis of this knowledge, of their 'dangerous memory,' strategies for overcoming such oppression can be built.

Questioning Neutrality: The Critical Move from Disinterest to Interest

There is no doubt that our emancipatory system of meaning and the action research which it fosters will elicit charges of educational politi-cization, of tainted, unobjective research with predetermined outcomes. Critical constructivism asserts that such forms of pious pseudo-objectivity must be confronted. If critical educators cave in to such objectivist critics, the possibility of taking a moral stand in education, of seeing education as something more than a technical act, will be destroyed. As they argue that we must keep politics out of education and avoid emancipatory action research, Cartesian objectivists misrepresent the basic tenets of emancipat-ory action research and critical pedagogy in general. Critics miss the point that research is never neutral — alas, when we attempt to remain neutral, like Pilate, we support the prevailing power structure. A recognition of the ideological nature of research implies that researchers by necessity must take a position and make it explicit to their readers and to those they are researching. They do not impose their positions or their interpretations as the truth — of course, readers, co-workers, and the researched have the right to reject everything asserted.

Along with other advocates of critical pedagogy and critical research, I would maintain that non-critical, mainstream researchers are every bit as guilty of value-laden research as any critical inquirer. To assume a posi-tion which refuses to seek the structural sources of human suffering and exploitation is to support oppression and the power relations which sustain it (Freire, 1970b, 1985; Perry, 2001). The arguments of traditional objectiv-ist researchers that any inquiry grounded on explicit value assumptions is subjective to the point of worthlessness is similar to the nineteenth-century ruling-class idea that engaging in social criticism violated a 'gentlemanly'

code of civility. It is similar to a twentieth-century notion ᴏ̣̄__
thinking (cf. Dale Carnegie) which views overt oppositional behavior aᵤ
a form of negativity which is not only politically incorrect but distasteful
as well. Indeed, the difference between critical constructivist research and
objective traditional educational research rests on the willingness of critical constructivist researchers to reveal their allegiances, to admit their
solidarities, their value structures, and the ways such orientations affect
their inquiries (Carlson, 1997; Carlson and Apple, 1998; Cary, 1998; Coben,
1998).

Revealing their solidarities, critical teacher researchers operate on
the counter-Cartesian assumption that knower and known are inseparable.
Learning from the liberation theologian, critical researchers embrace
subjugated knowledges, in the process disallowing an objectivist subject–
object dualism. When researchers respect subjugated knowledges and the
unique perspective of the oppressed, they, as a matter of course, begin to
subvert the relationship of domination that permeates traditional objectivist research. It is a relationship of domination which allows for both the
manipulation of natural processes to serve the logic of capital (the needs
for profit-making) and the manipulation of human beings as the passive
objects of social engineering (McGinty, 2001). This separation of knower
and known, this epistemological distancing, produces a tacit logic of
domination between researcher–researched and knower and known; not
content to occupy only the terrain of inquiry, this logic trespasses into
the domain of race, class, and gender relations (Fee, 1982). Indeed, it is the
logic of hierarchy and authoritarianism, not democracy — it is the logic of
bad work.

Operating within this domain of Cartesian logic, educational research
has often served the interests of power elites. Critical constructivist action
research, with its commitment to the perspective of the oppressed, seeks
to confront such consequences. The view from above of the traditional
paradigm gives way to views from below. Emerging from an understanding and respect for subjugated knowledge, such an epistemological position not only boasts of ethical assets but holds scientific benefits as well.
The scientific dimension revolves around the hierarchical relationship of
researcher and researched; much of the information gathered by traditional
methods is irrelevant because the subordinate researched, realizing their
inferior position, often develop a profound distrust of the researchers
interrogating them. Oppressed groups interviewed by researchers from
a higher social stratum often provide expected information rather than
authentic data. Respect for subjugated knowledge helps construct a research
situation where the experience of the marginalized is viewed as an important way of seeing the socio-educational whole, not simply as a curiosity to
be reported. Such a research perspective is counter-hegemonic (i.e., a threat
to entrenched power), and radically democratic as it uses the voice of
the subjugated to formulate a reconstruction of the dominant educational

structure. It is a radical reconstruction in the sense that it attempts to empower those who are presently powerless (Mies, 1982; Connell, 1989; Kincheloe, Steinberg, and Villaverde, 1999).

Critical Research Questions: Exposing Elitist Assumptions

With this reconstructive imperative in mind, one of the central tasks of a critical constructivist researcher is to formulate questions which expose the conditions which promote social and educational advantage and disadvantage (Brosio, 1994, 2000). For example, it is obvious to many that when the methods of evaluation of advocates of the competitive, top down standards curriculum are employed, non-white and working-class students do not generally do well — their performance is interpreted as a manifestation of slowness, of inferior ability (Kincheloe, Steinberg, and Gresson, 1996). Researchers devise tests to evaluate school, student, and teacher performance, forgetting throughout the process that evaluation is based on uncritically grounded definitions of intelligence and performance (Owen and Doerr, 1999).

The definitions of intelligence and performance employed are not generated by the marginalized. When liberals attempt, for example, to develop curricula or initiate research based on a recognition of the existence of marginalized experiences, they miss the lessons provided by an understanding of subjugated knowledge. A common liberal reform involves the inclusion of women or blacks in a history curriculum which has traditionally emphasized the contributions of famous (especially military) men. In a traditional curricular framework this simply adds a few new facts to be committed to memory: it is a tokenism which perpetuates the power relations of the *status quo* (Kincheloe and Steinberg, 1997). Another such reform might involve making sure that respondents to a survey include a percentage of women and minorities (Connell, 1989).

The advantage of subjugated perspectives, the view from below, involves what has been termed the 'double consciousness' of the oppressed (King and Mitchell, 1995; Brown and Davis, 2000; Steinberg, 2001). If they are to survive, subjugated groups develop an understanding of those who control them (e.g., slaves' insight into the manners, eccentricities, and fears of their masters); at the same time they are cognizant of the everyday mechanisms of oppression and the way such technologies shape their consciousness, their lived realities. Because of their class, race, and gender positions, many educational researchers are insulated from the benefits of the double consciousness of the subjugated and are estranged from a visceral appreciation of suffering (Zappulla, 1997). Contemporary social organization, thus, is viewed through a lens which portrays it as acceptable.

Why would such researchers challenge research metho of interpretation which justify the prevailing system or (Ellis, 1998; Jardine, 1998; Malewski, 2001a; Mayers, 2001a, 2001b)? What lived experience would create an ethical dissonance within the minds of such researchers that would make them uncomfortable with the *status quo*? The oppressed — while often manipulated by mechanisms of power to accept injustice and to deny their own oppression — often use their pain as a motivation to find out what is not right and to discover altern- ative ways of constructing social and educational reality (Mies, 1982; Jaggar, 1983). Women's ways of knowing as a subjugated form of knowledge have initiated a virtual revolution in our conception of what we know and how we come to know it. Serious consideration of such subjugated ways of knowing transforms forever our conceptions of the relation of the knower to the known and the conceptualization and execu- tion of the research act — our system of meaning is intimately tied to these different ways of knowing. The research questions we ask as critical teacher researchers often find their source in these subjugated epistemologies.

By the first decade of the twenty-first century we have come to recognize and accept that there is a connection between gender and ways of knowing. Machismo inquiry as reflected in Cartesian science is charac- terized as cold, hard, rational, and certain; feminine inquiry is characterized as humane, deep, tactile, and concerned with the world of consciousness. Rational 'man' is a gender-specific concept in that it refers to the style of knowing and discovering characteristic of traditional males. The rational man is rational as opposed to emotional; he is objective as opposed to subjective; immersed in the public realm instead of the private (see my dis- cussion of patriarchy in Chapter 17 of *Getting Beyond the Facts: Teaching Social Studies/Social Sciences in the Twenty-First Century*, 2001).

Rational men love truth, women beauty; rational men are active, women passive. Rational man is the maker of history, while woman maintains closeness with nature, that is, the body, sexuality, passion, and human interaction. The way of knowing ascribed to rational man defines abstraction as the highest level of thought — symbolic logic, mathematics, signifiers far removed from their organic function. Women's modes of inquiring and knowing are grounded in identification with organic life and its preservation. Rational man contends that emotions are dangerous as they exert a disorganizing effect on the progress of science (Reinharz, 1979; Fee, 1982; Clatterbaugh, 1997; Pinar, 1999). Informed by feminist perspectives, critical constructivist teacher researchers admit that, indeed, emotions do exert a disorganizing effect on traditional logocentric (reason- centered) ways of knowing and inquiring. But such disorganization is a positive step in the attempt to accommodate and integrate (in a Piagetian sense) our perceptions of ourselves and the world around us. Emotions thus become powerful knowing mechanisms that extend our ability to make sense of the universe (Mahoney and Lyddon, 1988; Kincheloe, Steinberg, and Hinchey, 1999).

Madeleine Grumet extends our understanding of the feminist attempt to transcend logocentrism by connecting the language of the body, of feeling, with inquiry. Social science, she argues, whether guided by right-wing or left-wing impulses, has been enmeshed in a male-dominated snare of abstraction. Grumet has sought new methods of inquiry which were capable of drawing the body and feeling into the public conversation about education. Making use of qualitative methodologies such as history, theater, autobiography, and phenomenology, she confronts androcentric abstraction with the uncertainty, specificity, and contradiction of the private, the corporeal, the feminine (Grumet, 1988). From the perspective of the guardians of the Cartesian tradition such epistemological confrontations constitute overt subversion. After exposure to such theorizing, inquiry can no longer be viewed as a cold, rational process. As feeling, empathy, the body, are injected into the research process, as the distinction between knower and known is blurred, as truth is viewed as a *process* of construction in which knowers play an active role, passion is injected into inquiry. Critical constructivist teacher researchers see themselves as passionate scholars who connect themselves emotionally to that which they are seeking to know and understand.

Personal Knowledges, Passionate Knowing, and Empathetic Research: Learning from Diverse Sources

Several decades ago Michael Polanyi wrote about personal knowledge — that is, a way of knowing which involves the passionate participation of the knower in the act of knowing. Guided by such notions, critical constructivist action researchers embrace a passionate scholarship, a reconceptualized counter-Cartesian science which is grounded upon and motivated by our values and solidarities (Belenky, Clinchy, Goldberger, and Tarule, 1986; Quinn, 2001). Passionate knowers use the self as an instrument of understanding, searching, as Madeleine Grumet has, for new methods to improve the way the self is used in research. Søren Kierkegaard anticipated this notion of feminist passion, arguing in the first half of the nineteenth century that there *is* an intimate connection between commitment and knowing. Subjectivity, he maintained, is not simply arbitrary — instead, it reflects the most profound connection between an individual thinker and the world.

As inquirers grow passionate about what they know, they develop a deeper relationship with themselves. Such a relationship produces a self-knowledge that initiates a synergistic cycle — a cycle which grants them more insight into the issue being investigated. Soon, Kierkegaard argued, a form of personal knowledge is developed which orients the mind to see social life as more than a set of fixed laws. Social life is better characterized as a process of being, a dialectic where the knower's personal participation in events and the emotional insight gained from such participation move us to a new dimension of knowing. Not only did Kierkegaard anticipate feminist theory's concept of passionate knowing and Polanyi's personal knowledge, but he also foreshadowed a post-Piagetian, post-formal mode of thinking which forms a central tenet of our notion of critical constructivism (Reinharz, 1979, 1992).

Another precursor of the feminist notion of passionate scholarship which shapes our system of meaning (and which should serve to humble Eurocentric academicians) concerns the ways that indigenous peoples have defined knowing (Semali and Kincheloe, 1999). Afro-centric and American Indian ways of knowing are similar to the counter-Cartesian perspectives of Kierkegaard, Polanyi, and contemporary feminists. To such peoples reality has never been dichotomized into spiritual and material segments. Self-knowledge lays the foundation for all knowledge in the African and Native American epistemologies. Great importance has traditionally been placed on interpersonal relationships (solidarity), and a connected, unfragmented form of logic has moved these traditions to appreciate the continuum of spirit and matter, individual and world.

Indeed, indigenous ways of knowing and the European Cartesian tradition come into direct conflict over the epistemological issues of mind and body, individuals and nature, self and other, spirit and matter, and knower and known — a conflict which has generated serious historical consequences. It is only in the last forty years that some Eurocentric people have come to recognize the epistemological sophistication of the indigenous paradigm, which recognizes a unity in all things and a connected spiritual energy embedded in both human and natural elements. That deemed primitive by traditional Western scholars becomes, from the perspective of critical constructivist researchers, a valuable source of insight into our attempt to reconceptualize an emancipatory system of meaning (Nyang and Vandi, 1980; Myers, 1987; Mosha, 2000).

Antonio Gramsci well understood some of these epistemological concepts as he wrote from Mussolini's prisons in the late 1920s and 1930s. The intellectual's error, he wrote, consists of believing that one can know without 'feeling and being impassioned' (Gramsci, 1988: 349). The role of intellectuals and researchers, from Gramsci's perspective, revolved around their attempt to connect logic and emotion in order for them to 'feel' the elementary passions of the people. Such an emotional connection would allow the inquirer to facilitate the struggle of men and women to locate their lived worlds in history. Finding themselves in history, they would be empowered by a consciousness constructed by a critically distanced view of the ways that the structural forces of history shape lives (Kincheloe, 2001). One cannot make history without this passion, without this connection of feeling and knowing, since without it the relationship between the people and intellectuals is reduced to a hierarchical formality. The logic of bureaucracy prevails, as intellectuals move to the higher rungs of the organizational ladder, assuming the privileges of a superior caste, a modern Egyptian priesthood (Gramsci, 1988). The essence of action research rests on an appreciation of Gramsci's exposure of the power relations between intellectuals and non-intellectuals (Coben, 1998).

Peter McLaren grounds this analysis of passionate knowing educationally with an insightful analysis of the difference between the ways of knowing in the street-corner world of Toronto's Jane-Finch Corridor and the world of classroom knowledge. In the streets students gained a 'felt' knowledge which made use of the body, organic symbols, and intuition. Classroom knowledge was abstracted from the lived world, objectified, and corrupted by a Cartesian rationalism. To the students the abstracted knowledge of the classroom was light years away from their everyday experience. Students resisted what seemed to them to be useless ways of knowing in a variety of creative and often disconcerting ways. They struggled for creative control of knowledge production, viewing experience as open to question rather than something simply to be taken for granted.

In other words, McLaren argues that street-corner epistemology challenged the school's tendency to present knowledge as unproblematic, not open to emotional negotiation. Students from such subjugated cultures questioned the school view of them as passive recipients of concrete facts. Teachers themselves have assumed the same passive position in relation to expert educational researchers. Teachers have become the passive recipients of the objectified, abstracted knowledge handed down to them. Even though they formulate their own understanding of classroom life and teaching on both an emotional and logical base, practitioners are induced to improve their understandings of the educational process by consuming and incorporating the distanced scientific knowledge of the experts into their professional labors (McLaren, 1989; see also Mayers, 2001a).

By synthesizing feminist notions of passionate knowing, indigenous people's epistemology, subjugated knowledges, and liberation theological ethics, we are constructing a critical system of meaning. From this base we are able to critique the existing knowledge base of education and to formulate methods and questions for our own work as teacher researchers. In essence, we are moving ourselves into another socio-educational dimension, a land of uncertainty where the traditional rules of knowing no longer apply. We are beginning an exploration of a new universe — a world where the distortions of the Cartesian dualism are exposed, where multiple ways of knowing are sought and valued. Of course, what we are doing is taking a step into the uncharted world of postmodernism, a land where the Cartesian rationalistic voice is no longer a universal one (Poster, 1989).

Negotiating the Counter-Cartesian Landscape of Uncertainty: Making Use of Critical Constructivism and Postformalism

Postmodern analysis, though diverse in the ways it is conceptualized, has consistently laid bare the assumptions of Cartesian logic by illustrating the ways that the structure of traditional science constructs imaginary worlds. Like a novel, science is 'written'; both the novel and science operate according to the arbitrary rules of a language game. Such postmodern understandings confront us with a dramatic socio-educational dilemma: how do we function in the midst of such uncertainty? Critical constructivism offers us aid in our dilemma — not salvation, just help. Using our system of emancipatory meaning, tempering it with a dose of postmodern self-analysis and epistemological humility, we take our notion of critical constructivism one more step. In this stride we employ our emancipatory system of meaning as a basis for conceptualizing a democratic form of action research which leads to a new way of seeing, a post-formal way of perceiving the educational world (Kincheloe and Steinberg, 1993; Kincheloe, Steinberg, and Hinchey, 1999; Horn, 2000).

What are the limits of human ways of knowing? Where might we go from here? Such questions have both research and pedagogical implications — as do our emancipatory system of meaning and our notion of critical constructivism. Drawing upon our system of meaning, we cannot help but anticipate ways of knowing and levels of cognition which move beyond Cartesian convention and Piagetian formalism. Adults do not reach a final cognitive equilibrium beyond which no new levels of thought can emerge; there have to be modes of thinking which transcend the formal operational ability to formulate abstract conclusions, understand cause–effect relationships, and employ the traditional scientific method to explain reality. We know too much to define formality as the zenith of human cognitive ability (Arlin, 1975). The qualitative path to empowerment on which our critical constructivist research hikes leads to these exciting new ways of inquiring and knowing (Kincheloe, Steinberg, and Villaverde, 1999; Kincheloe, 2001).

Formalism implies an acceptance of a Cartesian–Newtonian mechanistic worldview which is trapped within a cause–effect, hypothetico-deductive system of reasoning. The formal operational thinker/researcher employs a science which divides a social or educational system into its basic parts in order to understand the way it works (Aronowitz, 1988, 1996). Emphasizing certainty and prediction, formal operational thinking/researching organizes verified facts into a theory. The facts which do not fit into the theory are eliminated, and the theory developed is the one best suited to eliminate contradictions in knowledge. Thus, formal operational thought and its attendant mode of inquiry operate on the assumption that contradiction resolution is an important objective (Kramer, 1983). Schools and standardized test-makers, assuming that formal operational thought represents the highest level of human cognition, focus their efforts on its cultivation and measurement (though sometimes they fail to get too far beyond concrete forms of thinking) (Owen and Doerr, 1999). Students who have moved beyond formality are rarely rewarded and sometimes even punished in educational contexts. Researchers who transcend formality have been severely criticized for their lack of rigor, their subjectivism (Sternberg, 1985).

Postformal thinkers/researchers are comfortable with the uncertain, tentative nature of knowledge emerging from critical constructivist research. They are tolerant of complexity and contradiction, and value the attempt to integrate ostensibly dissimilar phenomena into new, revealing syntheses. In other words, postformal thinkers/researchers escape the confines of Cartesian–Newtonian modernity and venture into the post-modern realm. Postformalism underpins a form of inquiry suitable for a postmodern world: only a postformal thinker is cognitively and conceptually equipped to handle the uncertainty of postmodernism. Where the formal operational orientation functions on the basis of the Cartesian assumptions of linear causality and determinism, the postformal perspective assumes reciprocity and holism (the complex, non-linear interconnection of events) (Kramer, 1983; Van Hesteran, 1986; Capra, 1996; O'Sullivan, 1999).

Simple, privileged vantage points from which to view socio-educational phenomena are rejected by postformal thinkers, as they come to realize that there are many ways of approaching an event. Researchers will see multiple depictions of the phenomenon depending both on the context from which it emanates and the system of meaning they employ to help formulate their questions and research strategies — for example, do they adopt a view from above or a view from below? Traditional Marxism argued in its own deterministic way that humans see only what their conceptual lenses allowed them to see, and that they understood what the context for understanding permitted. In the spirit of hope, possibility, and anti-determinism, critical constructivist researchers seek to liberate themselves from such determinism by taking control of our perceptual abilities, by transcending what the context permits. In this way we emancipate ourselves from the constraints of the Cartesian dualism and the structural forces which limit our ability to see the world from outside our restricted vantage point. In its logocentrism Cartesian modernity discounted the terrain of private inner reality (Pinar, 1994). What good was such a landscape in the process of industrialization, material progress, and the conquest of nature? As postmodernism rediscovers the sensuous, postformalism incorporates such notions into new ways of exploring and perceiving the social, educational, and even physical world (Kramer, 1983; Slaughter, 1989; Gordon, Miller, and Rollock, 1990; Kincheloe, Steinberg, and Tippins, 1999).

Postformal Inquirers as Researchers of Themselves

Such new modes of thinking and researching incorporate sensual know-ledge and self-knowledge in interesting ways. Researchers who do not understand themselves tend to misconstrue the pronouncements and feelings of others. The complexity and multiple readings characteristic of postmodern analysis are remote to formal thinkers, as they seek comfort in the prescribed methods, the objectivity, the depersonalization of traditional social scientific, educational research (Van Hesteran, 1986; Lemke, 1995). In a sense, the Cartesian objectivist tradition provides a shelter in which the self can hide from the deeply personal issues which permeate all socio-educational phenomena. Such personal issues would, if it were not for the depersonalization of traditional inquiry, force an uncomfortable element of researcher self-revelation (Schneider and Laihua, 2000; Rasberry, 2001). Postformal thinkers/inquirers seek insight into how their own assumptions (as well as those of the individuals they research) came to be constructed. They transcend formalism's concern with problem-solving by seeking to determine the etiology of the problem — in other words, they seek to learn to think about their own thinking (Romano, 2000).

In his effort to explore post-Piagetian thinking, Robert Kegan (1982) theorizes that an essential characteristic of postformalism involves the individual's attempt to disengage himself or herself from socio-interpersonal norms and ideological expectations. This postformal concern with questions of meaning, emancipation via ideological disembedding, and attention to the process of self-production rises above the formal operational level of thought/inquiry and its devotion to proper procedure. Postformalism grapples with purpose, devoting attention to issues of human dignity, free-dom, authority, and social responsibility. Many conceptions of postformalism contend that an appreciation of multiple perspectives necessitates an ethical relativism which paralyzes social action. Our conception of postformal perceiving and inquiring is tied to the construction of a system of meaning which is used to guide the research/cognitive act. Never content with what they have constructed, never certain of the system's appropriateness, always concerned with the expansion of self-awareness and consciousness, the postformal thinker/researcher engages in a running meta-dialogue, a constant conversation with self, a perpetual reconceptualization of his or her system of meaning.

Such a dialogue focuses the postformal thinker/researcher's attention on the process of question formulation, as opposed to formalism's concern with question answering or problem solving. This question-formulating, problem-posing stage, Einstein argued, is more important than the answer to the question or the solution to the problem. Critical constructivist teacher researchers are postformal question formulators, problem posers. When teacher researchers set up a problem, they select and name those things they will notice. Thus, problem posing is a form of world making — how we select the problems and construct our worlds is based on the system of meaning we employ. Without a system of meaning, teachers and administrators learn how to construct schools but not how to determine what types of schools to construct. In other words, teachers, school leaders, and teacher educators need to realize that school and classroom problems are not generic or innate. They are constructed and uncovered by insightful educators who possess the ability to ask questions never before asked, questions that lead to innovations that promote student insight, sophisticated thinking, and social justice (Pozoni, 1985; Schön, 1987).

If the genius of, say, an Einstein revolved around his ability to see problems in the physical universe which no one else had ever seen, then the genius of a teacher researcher revolves around his or her ability to see educational problems that no one else has ever seen. The application of such skills by action researchers moves inquiry to a level unimagined by researchers trapped within the Cartesian tradition. Not only is such a research orientation grounded on a democratic conception of teacher empowerment, it also serves to expose previously hidden forces which shape the consequences of the educational process. It is a testimony to what can happen, to what can be revealed, when researchers transcend the limitations of traditional definitions of research and explore the relationships between the knower and the known. Let us now turn our attention to the prevalent ways that educational research has been conducted in the Western world and the unfortunate effects it has engendered; we will begin our analysis with an examination of positivism.

Chapter 4

Exploring Assumptions Behind Educational Research: Defining Positivism in a Neo-Positivist Era

Equipped with an understanding of the Cartesian tradition, we are prepared to understand its epistemological extension — positivism. Few epistemological orientations have exerted so much influence or have been so little understood. An historical overview is in order to begin our exploration of positivism. The Enlightenment (Age of Reason) of the seventeenth and eighteenth centuries realized its rational self-fulfillment with the advent of modern science. True reality, the Enlightenment thinkers posited, was founded upon scientific understanding — the world could be comprehended only via science and scientific methodology. This form of science was universal in the sense that it applied to all subjects of study and was based on mathematics. With the realization of this type of scientific enterprise during the Enlightenment, Western thought was prepared for the advent of what many have called 'the era of positivism' (Held, 1980; Giroux, 1997; Kincheloe, 2001).

The History of Positivism

The label, positivism, was popularized by Auguste Comte, the nineteenth-century French philosopher, who argued that human thought had progressed through three stages: the theological stage, the metaphysical stage, and the scientific or positivistic stage. One could only designate scientific findings as certain in the scientific stage. Comte sought to discredit the legitimacy of thinking which did not take sense experience into account, that is, *a priori* modes of thought. Advocating such a position, Comte extended the scientific orientation of the Enlightenment (J. Smith, 1983; Kneller, 1984).

Comte did not see a distinction between the methods used for research in the physical and the human sciences. Thus, from Comte's perspective, sociology was a reflection of biology. Society came to be viewed as a body of neutral facts governed by immutable laws. These facts and laws could be researched in the same manner as any physical object could be researched.

Like nature, society is governed by natural necessity. It therefore followed that social movements would proceed with law-like predictability (Held, 1980).

The Vienna Circle cadre of philosophers of the 1920s extended the work of Comte. Coming from a variety of backgrounds, the members of the Vienna Circle (or the logical positivists) enumerated several positivistic axioms:

1 *The separation of science from metaphysics.* It was certainly true that European metaphysics in the 1920s was marked by an intellectual pomposity and inbreeding which had choked the life out of philosophy. As they expunged metaphysics (the branch of philosophy that studies the nature of things such as being, time, identity, causation, etc.) from philosophy, the logical positivists attempted to remove it from science as well. Thus, metaphysical questions, with the discomforting uncertainty and abstraction which surrounded them, were not appropriate for *scientific* inquiry.

2 *The importance of the verifiability principle of meaning.* The verifiability principle implied that something is meaningful only if it can be supported empirically (observation via the senses) or is a tautology (an expression whose truth is known merely by understanding the meaning of the statement, e.g., 'today is tomorrow's yesterday') of mathematics or logic.

3 *The significance of observation statements.* As the logical positivists promoted the verifiability principle, they had to confront the questions: 'What is the proper process for the verification of scientific statements?' and 'What will count as verification?' The positivists responded to such queries by referring to what they called the necessity of 'observation statements.' Verifiability, they contended, had to take place in terms of simple and direct descriptions of sense experience. We proceed from these observation statements, the most epistemologically primary form of knowledge (i.e., the given). These statements form the basic elements of our constructional system of scientific knowledge. The universe, thus, is reduced to a set of observation statements that are forged into the smallest possible number of axioms. That which fell outside these observation statements was suspect. To the Vienna Circle, the idea that thought might encompass knowing more about the universe than that which could be expressed in observation statements was not a viable possibility (Giroux, 1983; Philips, 1983).

Many educational researchers emphasize the point that Comte's positivism and the Vienna Circle's logical positivism died long ago. Indeed, one of the leading proponents of logical positivism, A. J. Ayer, proclaimed shortly before his death that the biggest problem with logical positivism was that it was fundamentally wrong. Why then do we speak of the great debate over positivism in educational research? The answer to that question is quite simple. While the formal systems of positivism died in the 1950s, 1960s, and 1970s, some of the main themes of the tradition lived on. For convenience, let us call this new form of positivism, neo-positivism. It is this neo-positivism which often sets the parameters of the modern debate over educational research (Shweder and Fiske, 1986). It is neo-positivism which continues to inform a good portion of the work conducted in educational research and is reflected in the training of young researchers in teacher education. Indeed, since the first edition of *Teachers as Researchers* was published in 1991, neo-positivism has experienced a resurgence, rearing its head under different names in a variety of educational venues. Chapter 1 documented one example of this positivistic reassertion in the contemporary educational standards movement.

Fred Kerlinger (whose textbook, *Foundations of Behavioral Research*, has been a leading seller in colleges of education for decades) provides numerous examples of neo-positivistic thinking in educational research. He argues in the first chapter of his 'bible' for students of educational research that educational scientists, as they attempt to explain relations between the phenomena they have observed, must exclude 'metaphysical explanations.' He defines a metaphysical explanation as a 'proposition that cannot be tested.' Science is not concerned with questions of value, Kerlinger continues, for they are not publicly observable or testable. If questions cannot be publicly observed or tested, he concludes, 'they are not scientific questions' (Kerlinger, 1973: 5).

Describing Neo-positivism

Positivism has never been a neat, easily categorized system. During the heyday of logical positivism in the 1920s and 1930s, it was marked by ambiguity and argument among its principal proponents. In the attempt for clarity, I will try to delineate the main themes of what is referred to as neo-positivism in contemporary social science parlance (Frankel, 1986). Such a delineation, I believe, will help lay the foundation for our understanding of the complex web of ideas associated with modernist research on human beings, particularly the research on the education of these humans. The four main themes of neo-positivism include: scientism, the positivist conception of science, the doctrine of scientific politics, and value freedom.

Scientism

This positivistic doctrine insists that only science should be regarded as an authentic form of human knowledge. Science here is not merely one form of knowledge; knowledge must be identified with science. Non-science is thus held in disdain, as ways of knowing such as religion, metaphysics, and ideological analysis, are dismissed as unverifiable nonsense. The second positivistic doctrine clarifies scientism by specifying the nature of scientific knowledge.

The Positivist Conception of Science

Here positivists maintain that science should be concerned with the explanation and prediction of observable events. The ability to predict is founded upon the fact that observable phenomena are micro-expressions of universal laws that are appropriate in all contexts. The positivistic conception of science must be protected from the intrusion of metaphysics. The elimination of the unobservable from the scientific reality serves to exclude metaphysics from the exclusive fraternity of scientific knowledge.

The Doctrine of Scientific Politics

The knowledge of the social sciences, positivistic advocates argue, should provide the basis for political decision making. Arguments in politics should be settled in the same way that disagreements in engineering or medicine are resolved. Engineering and medical arguments are settled not on the basis of personal values, nor on the basis of the status of the proponents and opponents, nor as a result of the oratorical prowess of a disputant; indeed, the positivists argue, they are settled on the basis of objective aspects of the subject in question. The issues are objective because they are measurable and empirically testable, and as such the subjective, emotional, and conjectural ingredients which characterize political discussions would disappear once approached scientifically. Scientifically-based political arguments would allow for testable conclusions and, as a result, fulfill the promise of a correct solution to a specific problem. Unsubstantiated opinion would be eliminated from the political sphere and scientifically grounded, 'rational' solutions would improve the social world.

Value Freedom

Positivists contend that values should not play a role in scientific investigation. Research has focused not on the ends that it serves but the means of achievement. The knowledge which emerges from inquiry should be value-free. Indeed, values are the nemesis of facts and are viewed as potentially irrational responses. Scientific knowledge, the positivists conclude, should be objective. Methodological choice should proceed outside the realm of values, and the researcher should aspire to value-free inquiry. Values in positivistic research are discomforting because they do not lend themselves to true or false judgments, that is, verifiability (Keat, 1981; Giroux, 1981, 1997).

The Critical Exposé: The False Promises of Positivism

These positivistic doctrines evoke great emotion from many different analysts for many different reasons. Henry Giroux attacks neo-positivism in the spirit of the critical theorists from the Frankfurt School. Drawing upon the earlier critiques of positivism presented by Max Horkheimer, Theodor Adorno, and Herbert Marcuse, Giroux accuses positivistic thought of crushing the traditional desire of scholarship to improve the human condition, substituting in its place an inclination to pursue only that perceived to be technically possible. This characteristic commits positivism to specific political positions and thus uncovers new dimensions of complexity in the debate over educational research. To say the least, Giroux and the critical theorists are unimpressed by the positivistic claims to value freedom and political neutrality; on the contrary, they argue, positivism has become an important prop for the dominant ideology. There is a profound difference, anti-positivists argue, between claiming objectivity and the actual conduct of research. When analysts study the ways researchers design their research, collect their data, and proclaim their findings, they find that subjective choices are made throughout the process (Allen, 2000; Denzin and Lincoln, 2000).

Denis Phillips strongly disagrees with Giroux and the critical theorists, arguing that they use the word, positivism, as a blanket to cover any position contrary to their ideology, regardless of whether or not the position is positivistic or not (Phillips, 1983). Indeed, Giroux's critical use of the term, positivism, does transcend strict philosophical definitions of the position. But, Giroux argues, this transcendence is precisely his point — positivism has taken on a life of its own. To illustrate this point, Giroux employs the phrase, 'the culture of positivism.' In this culture the traditional epistemological position known as positivism affects not only inquiry but moves into the realm of ideology and social practice. As a result, it supports a frame of mind which views the world without the benefit of an understanding of the social-political context which gives reality its meaning. Let us examine the critical perspective on positivism in more detail.

Giroux argues that since the assumptions of positivism are drawn from the logic and methods of investigation associated with the natural sciences, the hermeneutical principles of interpretation hold little status (Madison, 1988; Giroux, 1997; D. Smith, 1999). What is important in the culture of positivism involves explanation, prediction, and technical control. How we decide what constitutes a desirable state of affairs is of little consequence, he contends. This is a retreat from the Western humanistic tradition, for the Greeks viewed scholarship as a means of freeing oneself from uninformed opinion in order better to pursue ethical action. Theory and research, from the classical perspective, played the role of extending ethics and contributing to the search for truth and justice. Prevailing positivist consciousness, Giroux maintains, has forgotten this valuable role.

Knowledge to the positivist, Giroux continues, is worthwhile to the extent that it describes objectified data. Questions concerning the social construction of knowledge (this would involve the codes, media, ideologies, and socio-economic structures which shape facts (Scholes, 1982; Kellner, 1995; Kincheloe, 2002) and the political interests which direct the selection and evaluation of data) are irrelevant when knowledge is assumed to be objective and value-free. The information gleaned from the subjective realm of intuition, insight, philosophy, and non-scientific theoretical frameworks is not considered important.

This objectivity, this value freedom comes at a great cost to those of us interested in the pursuit of truth, Giroux claims. To most people the pursuit of value-free knowledge through objective research is a worthwhile goal. The quest hides more than it uncovers, however. Those who challenge the goals of value freedom and objectivity are often perceived to be advocating bias and unfairness in research. The point that what is designated as objective research is socially agreed upon by communities of scholars — and thus not 'objective' in any real sense — is missed by many scholars and by the public at large. Value-free research is an impossible goal, Giroux tells us, and the attempt to separate value from social research is tantamount to an attempt to draw a map that portrays every detail of a specific part of the earth. Such an attempt is a value-laden activity, as the mapmaker uses his or her judgment and values to decide what to include and what not to include on the map.

Since the hidden values of knowledge are unexamined by the positivistic tradition, Giroux argues that this cult of objectivity suppresses political discussion in the public sphere. Since the knowledge has supposedly been arrived upon in a value-free manner, it is immune from political questioning. Thus, the culture of positivism is silent about its own ideology, as it is incapable of gaining insight into how oppression hides in the language and lived experience of everyday life (Lemke, 1995). Since it is incapable of reflecting on its own assumptions, it ultimately offers uncritical support for the *status quo*.

Positivism glorifies the present, Giroux continues, and in the process rejects the future. By focusing on 'what is' rather than 'what should be,' positivism ignores ethics as a category of research. This process promotes the idea that society has a life of its own, and no matter what human beings might do they cannot interfere with this social determinism. If human beings cannot see beyond the 'what is,' they are incapable of formulating an alternative vision to the *status quo*. Research in the positivistic model merely examines the details of the *status quo*, maintaining a calculated disinterest in a questioning of the power interests and assumptions which support them.

Positivistic culture, Giroux asserts, presents a view of research, knowledge, and ethics that has no use for a world where humans decide their own meaning, order their own experiences, or fight against the social forces which crush their efforts to do so. By downgrading the importance of such efforts at self-direction, the culture of positivism ignores how humans ought to live with one another and tacitly supports forms of domination, hierarchy, and control.

Knowledge collected by positivistic researchers is often treated as an external body of information, independent of human beings. This objectified information is temporally and spatially independent, existing outside of an historical context. Since it is expressed in a language that is technical it is supposedly value-free and context-free (Giroux, 1981). This means that it is separated from the political and cultural traditions that provide its meaning. Knowledge becomes a body of isolated facts to be committed to memory by overwhelmed and baffled students. Stanley Aronowitz (1973) argues that the factual memorization characteristic of schooling is so pervasive that students have enormous difficulties when they are asked to undertake conceptual learning.

The 'facts' of the curriculum appear to be value-free, devoid of any underlying set of assumptions; after all, they are 'just the facts' as Sergeant Joe Friday once put it. For the positivists, research appears to be liberated from any theoretical pre-assumptions. This appearance of theory freedom renders positivism the great deceiver, wrapping itself in the cloak of objectivity while often unconsciously promoting specific values, world views, and assumptions about what constitutes an educated person. Any teacher who wants to engage in research or familiarize himself or herself with the work which exists might want to analyze how hypotheses are generated. Such an exercise might be especially valuable when a practitioner wanted to examine the origins of the research which produced the knowledge base on which modern educational reforms are based. What, for example, in the 1970s and 1980s were the assumptions behind Madeleine Hunter's research on lesson organization? In the twenty-first century what are the assumptions on knowledge production and teaching in Success for All (Astman, 1984; Yeakey, 1987; Kincheloe and Weil, 2001)?

To engage in empirical research without understanding the need for philosophical analysis of the assumptions behind it, John Goodlad argues, is to guarantee its irrelevance. In the positivistic research which has dominated education, empirical inquiry has preceded our conceptual/philosophical analysis. Without such analysis we fail to understand that positivistic science examines only portions of the world — to the positivist the world is only what science says it is (Yeakey, 1987; McNay, 1988). Conceptual analysis helps us deconstruct the values implicit in such a worldview and such a view of research. Positivistic research, we discover, can operate only on the basis of the researcher's prior theory, interest, and insight — it is tainted with subjectivity from the beginning. Beginning with a question that is of interest to them, educational researchers formulate a hypothesis and a research question which are derived from a theoretical construct. The inquiry is then conducted in a prescribed manner which stays carefully within the boundaries of the established research tradition (Lincoln and Guba, 1985; Jardine, 1998; Denzin and Lincoln, 2000; Kincheloe and McLaren, 2000).

The tradition dictates that the hypotheses and the research procedure must not be altered even if the field experiences encountered suggest that changes are needed. All in the name of objective procedure, the results of the empirical research are examined in light of the original theory which generated the hypothesis; the research is confirmed or falsified on the basis of its congruence with the hypothesis. This hypothetico-deductive research procedure, as it is called, posits a discrete sequence of steps with each step influencing the following one — for example, formulation of hypothesis, data collection, data analysis, and so on. Since the procedure does not allow for the adaptation of research procedures to the circumstances encountered in the observation, the inquirer must not look at anything not explicitly anticipated in the original design of the research (Altrichter and Posch, 1989). For the positivistic researcher to attend to the 'extraneous noise' of the research site is to risk turning into a pillar of salt, that is, to risk the invalidation of the entire project. Of course, the noise of the research consistently turns out to be the source of the clues which grant insight into the mystery, the data which yield the subtle insight into the significance of an educational or social situation.

Shulamit Reinharz (1979) writes of her research experience in a study of teachers in Washington, D.C. It is impossible to know, she contends, which questions will facilitate understanding a situation until data has been obtained from other questions. The positivistic project of which she was a part was flawed, she concluded, because the researchers had no philosophical, conceptual basis from which to formulate their research questions — with no grounding, relevance could not be judged. Reinharz reports that without grounding, without on-site time to rethink and fine tune the project in light of deeper understandings, the inquiry came to reflect stereotypical thinking. On these stereotypes their eventual analysis was constructed and, accordingly, was well within the regime of truth, the prevailing conception of 'what is' in the public schools. The *status quo* was thus reified (made to appear natural) through the project, as no alternative way of viewing the teachers' realities was uncovered.

Reinharz's experience is not uncommon. Without the researchers even knowing it, their work is mechanized, their findings are predestined given the research design. Without a familiarity with a conceptual critique of positivism, researchers fail to think about their own thinking, to research their own research. Reinharz's co-researchers accepted everything at face value, never examined their own motivations, and never posed meaningful questions. They never asked the Washington teachers to help them re-formulate their questions, they never made use of the teachers' knowledge of their own situations. Teachers, Reinharz reflects, were not human beings but objects of the research project. As a result, those leaders who had commissioned the research found out what they already knew and used the information to 'stay the course.' Teachers saw the project for what it was — an expensive waste of time. The 'facts' of the project were not simply facts — they were facts that assumed a variety of notions about research and values relating to how we regard human beings.

Educational Research in the Culture of Positivism

Isolated contextually, educational research reproduces the fundamental assumptions of the positivist paradigm. Researchers who fail to question the assumptions of educational institutions accept definitions of school reality provided by school professionals in leadership positions. Unexamined definitions of, say, intelligence are accepted without subjecting them to political and cultural interrogation. Definitions which reflect very specific political orientations or cultural backgrounds are allowed to pass as objective descriptions. Consumers of the research which emerges from this situation are unaware of the spate of assumptions on which it rests. This is another example of the insidious nature of the culture of positivism, Giroux (1997) concludes.

How can the culture of positivism continue to exert such a profound effect on the nature of educational research? If teachers are to be researchers they need to understand from a critical perspective the assumptions the culture makes about the nature of the world and its inhabitants, that is, the ontology of positivism. Only then will teachers understand positivistic research and be empowered to act in opposition to the policy implications which come from it. One of the first characteristics of positivism which teachers as researchers need to grasp is its simplistic view of human behavior. Positivism assumes that the personal histories of individuals and the social histories of their contexts are not germane to an appreciation of an educational setting and its significance. Such contextual information is invariably ambiguous and thus complicates the reductionism, the attempt to simplify the cause and effect relationships so important to a positivistic study (Astman, 1984). But the rub is that human activities such as education are rarely free of ambiguity, and to miss their complexity is to miss the point.

When positivist researchers examine the social and educational world using the methods of the physical sciences, they adopt a dehumanizing view of such a world; they look at education as if it were a concrete structure. As they manipulate (think of the use of this term in a human

context) data via multivariate statistical analysis, such researchers are trying
to freeze the world as if it were made of concrete and were structurally
immobile (Bogdan and Biklen, 1982). Humans are thus reduced to mere
pawns trapped in the immobilized structure, ever subject to the influence
of the predetermined forces emanating from it.

Thus, the researchers assume that the objects they study will remain
constant. Our experience as teachers tells us, however, that such is not the
case — students do not remain stable, they change as we teach and/or
study them. The researchers from a positivist background fancy that the
environment of the objects they study will stay constant. We know as
teachers that the learning environment of children is constantly changing. To attempt a study of educational influence of a particular learning
environment is quite an ambitious task, for the situation changes from day
to day in a multitude of ways. A laboratory situation in chemistry is very
different from a laboratory school. To study both phenomena in the same
way constitutes a basic conceptual mistake.

Indeed, a physical scientist knows at what temperature water freezes,
but an educational researcher cannot measure at what temperature a child's
imagination freezes. The questions are very different and involve different
conceptual and analytical strategies. In the same vein physical scientists
assume that any quartz crystal they study will be identical, that different
crystals will behave the same. Obviously, this is not the case in education,
for no two children are identical and cannot be expected to behave the
same. The positivistic educational research that examines categories of
children as if they were categories of crystals is inherently flawed (Besag,
1986b). Even though two children may both be Hispanic, female, upper
middle-class, and visually handicapped, they will not 'crystalize' at the
same time (Bullough and Gitlin, 1995; Clandinin and Connelly, 1995; Beyer
and Liston, 1996).

It seems safe to argue that human and educational research differs
from research in the physical sciences in some basic ways. Human contexts are so contingency-laden that the attempt to generalize cause–effect
and make predictions is unrealistic. Non-positivistic educational research
is less ambitious than its positivistic counterpart — it seeks understanding
and interpretation of these human contexts (Mayers, 2001a). Educational
contexts involve moral considerations at practically every level of action.
There is no doubt that physical science-oriented positivistic research involves
moral elements. Issues such as what questions to ask about the physical
world or how to make use of the knowledge produced are inescapably
moral in nature. The moral dimension, however, of a question involving
the temperature at which oxygen freezes is quite different from an inquiry
into what constitutes a socially just way of providing equal educational
opportunity to the children of the poor.

Teachers, administrators, and educational policy makers must make
daily moral decisions about the 'right' thing to do. Positivistic research is

of little help to such practitioners because it assumes that research exists only to describe and help make predictions and, of course, has no value dimensions. It is unequipped to evaluate educational purposes or to assess various strategies for improving schooling (Culbertson, 1981; Hinchey, 1998). Educational knowledge obtained through the use of physical science methods, then, is not simply unhelpful to practitioners, but potentially very misleading because of its attempt to erase the moral dimension of human life. When the morality of an educational act is removed as a research consideration, the data produced inevitably reproduce the inequity of the *status quo*, for it has no mechanism to question and to visualize what might be a just situation.

Positivistic process-product researchers, for example, have shown that most teachers react to student responses, whether correct or incorrect, in very much the same way. Researchers have counted and categorized teacher responses to student answers in class; one study reported that in over three out of four incorrect student responses teachers made positive comments. Researchers labeled such statistics as irrational and bizarre and indicative of teacher inconsistency and weakness. When one abandons the physical scientific, positivistic interest in counting long enough to examine contextual and ethical factors, a very different picture of this teacher behavior emerges. The multi-dimensionality of classroom life demands particular forms of coping strategies from teachers. Teacher communication with students has to do with many more factors than simply supplying praise for correct answers and corrective responses for incorrect answers. The teacher has to juggle a myriad of concerns simultaneously, ranging from factual consistency on the part of students, to interpersonal sensitivity, to teacher accountability in regard to bureaucratic demands, to maintenance of a viable learning environment. Upon deeper analysis the so-called inconsistency of providing positive responses to incorrect answers is not so bizarre after all (Doyle, 1977; Ohanian, 1999).

Avoiding Positivistic Simplicity: From Complexity to Justice

Feminist educational researchers are painfully aware of the 'quick and dirty' nature of physical science-oriented, positivistic research and its simplistic view of human behavior and education. The most illustrative examples involve studies which ignore gender differences or look at gender as simply a causal factor, not taking into account the existence of other variables in the situation. When positivistic research ignores the wider context and the presence of a multitude of other variables, the conclusions drawn from such studies typically suggest innate differences (often hierarchical) between the sexes. Studies, for instance, that look only at gender differences in math achievement might discover (accurately) that boys do better than girls on particular standardized math tests. By not examining the results contextually, by not pursuing explanatory factors, positivistic researchers fail to consider the panoply of reasons for the different scores. Appealing to the accuracy of their statistics as authority, researchers fail to confront the quick and dirty simplicity of their research design. Thus, 'what is' appears to be only what has to be; the public is provided with further 'proof' that boys are naturally better than girls in math (Jayaratne, 1982).

Non-positivistic, critical, qualitative educational researchers might describe their approach to inquiry as methodological humility. As opposed to the quick and dirty positivist who seeks concrete structures and validated data which can be used to make predictions, the humble researcher practices a form of inquiry which is humble in the sense that it respects the complexity of the socio-educational world. Humility in this context is not self-depreciating nor does it involve the silencing of one's voice; humility implies a sense of the unpredictability of the educational microcosm and the capriciousness of the consequences of one's inquiry. Methodological humility is an inescapable characteristic of a postmodern world marked by a loss of faith in scientific salvation and the possibility of a single frame of reference, a common vantage point from which we might all view the world. Methodological humility eschews the positivistic impulse to dominate the world through knowledge of it. Though it was on the lam for a long time, positivistic science can no longer escape the creeping skepticism that dominates our postmodern conversations about almost everything else (Ruddick, 1980; Aronowitz, 1983; Macedo, 1994; Bartolome, 1998; Beyer, 2000).

Schulamit Reinharz is always helpful in analyzing the failure of positivism in educational research. The use of questionnaires, she contends, which force a 'yes,' 'no,' or 'no opinion' is an example of the positivistic distortion of the socio-educational lived world. Using such instruments, positivistic researchers substitute a controlled reality, a social situation with its own conventions and rules, for the ambiguity of the world of schools. They make a serious conceptual error when they correlate respondents' answers to questionnaires (responses peculiar to the controlled situation of being questioned about their attitudes) to their attitudes in another, completely different social situation, the lived world of their workplace, their teaching situation. Reinharz appreciated the limitations of such questionnaires when she tried to answer the questions herself. She could not answer the questions seriously, for her feelings and thoughts were not capable of being translated into simple, binary responses. Like the educational lived world, her attitudes were subtle, often ill-defined, and capable of being discovered and articulated only in dialogue with friends or during silent introspection (Reinharz, 1979).

Positivistic research is inappropriate in a practitioner field such as education — it simply does not produce insights relevant to the professional life of the teacher (Carson and Sumara, 1997). Positivistic educational research is limited in the sense that its language, the language of propositions, does not speak to the practitioner. Propositional language is concerned with the specification of the criteria by which statements about the world can be verified or refuted. The needs of a teacher transcend the language of propositions, for they revolve around the particularity of certain entities: the creativity of *one* child, the 'feel' of a child's anger or affection, the ambiance of a classroom full of students captivated by a lesson. This is the material of teacher knowledge; and this is precisely the type of complex knowledge that positivistic propositional language cannot address. It is irrelevant in such contexts, for it cannot capture the subtleties of interpersonal emotion — those subtleties which expose the intricacies of the teaching act (Eisner, 1984; Kincheloe and Steinberg, 1998; Steinberg and Kincheloe, 1998). Simply put, positivistic measurements or frequency studies cannot convey a nuanced understanding or feeling for the individuals and social contexts under observation. In its quest for propositional generalization, positivistic research misses an essential point: for the practitioner it is often the infrequent behaviors, the deviations from the general tendency that are most important to pedagogy (Doyle, 1977; Mies, 1982; Pinar, 1994; Jipson and Paley, 1997).

Positivistic research is also inappropriate in educational contexts since teachers do not 'own' such inquiry. The positivistic impulse renders research inaccessible to teachers in that it prevents teachers from conducting their own research. The practicalities of school life preclude teachers from collecting the number of samples that the method requires, not to mention the time it takes to process the copious data demanded. Only trained professional researchers have the time or interest to engage in such research. Because of their status-superiority relative to the practitioner, the professional researcher sets the research agenda, formulating questions primarily of interest to him or her. Thus, the practitioner is excluded; the professional researcher is the real proprietor of the inquiry — indeed, the professional researcher becomes both producer and consumer of the knowledge gleaned. Practitioners are the passive objects that are acted upon; they are invalidated as reflective teachers (Tripp, 1988; Van den Berg and Nicholson, 1989; Sumara, 1996). This is one of the many obvious reasons why the concept of teachers as researchers is so valuable.

Not only is the teacher excluded from ownership of research in a positivistic context, but such an orientation dictates our idea of what constitutes a professional in education (Raven and Stephenson, 2001). We are left with a notion of the professional teacher as technician — the hard-to-qualify concept of professional wisdom or artistry does not fit into the schema (Kincheloe, 1995). As a result, teacher education programs retreat into a vicious circle of technical rationality focusing on a 'how-to' curriculum which promotes general, universal methods of teaching. Practicing teachers are judged along the lines of technical criteria — a procedure which tends to erode their professional autonomy as they scramble in the name of accountability to meet their superiors' expectations of competence. In such a context the idea of a self-regulating professional who conducts research into his or her own practice is quite out of place. Why should teachers engage in such activities, the positivists ask, when educational science has produced a knowledge base and researchers know which procedures work (Schön, 1987)? But the positivists are wrong. Qualitative research in education over the last couple of decades has challenged the efficacy of research designed to uncover the generic features of effective classrooms. What works in one classroom may not be effective in another (Strickland, 1988; Kincheloe and Weil, 2001). The development of particular learning skills is situation-specific. Indeed, the entire attempt of positivism to develop verified, generalizable knowledge about educational practice may be inappropriate.

The Centrality of the Unobservable: The Blindfolds of Positivism

When positivists argue that nothing which is not practically demonstrable can be regarded as truth, we are forced to assume that a truth's practical demonstrability revolves around the ability to generalize it. Any particular human behavior is motivated by a panoply of unobservable factors (Odi, 1981). If the positivists' goal is to make generic statements about what constitutes an effective educational practice, then even within their own microcosm of logic such an attempt is misguided. There is no way in human situations to control the unobservable factors. If such factors are uncontrollable, then generalization is impossible. The implications here are frightening. If positivistic generalization in human situations is impossible, then what forces shape the generalizations that are made by positivistic educational researchers? This is where the Frankfurt School of critical theory has historically had so much to offer educational researchers. It is the Frankfurt School's notion of ideology which informs our understanding of the political interests of positivism — ideology involving worldviews unknown even to researchers themselves, which shape the assumptions they bring to the inquiry (Habermas, 1970; Grady and Wells, 1985–86; Kincheloe and McLaren, 2000). Werner Heisenberg had a similar idea when he maintained that 'what we observe is not nature itself, but nature exposed to our method of questioning' (Lincoln and Guba, 1985: 98). The questions emerge from the ideological preconceptions of the researcher. When researchers are unaware of the very presence of ideology, then they cannot be aware of the ways it shapes their research.

The last couple of decades have witnessed valuable work by critical theorists in education who have argued that the attempt to dispense with values, historical circumstance, and political considerations in educational research is misguided. Our understanding of an educational situation depends on the context within which we encounter it and the theoretical frames which the researcher brings to the observation. These ideological frames are the glasses through which we see the world — they are not subject to empirical verification. Positivism tells us that as researchers we must be non-partisan, we must serve no particular cause; but we have come to realize that every historical period produces particular rules that dictate what counts as a scientific fact. Different rules privilege different causes — facts are generated, they are not just 'out there' waiting to be discovered (Aronowitz, 1983, 1988, 1996; Elliott, 1989a). The implicit rules which guide our generation of facts about education are formed by particular world views, values, linguistic conventions, political perspectives, conceptions of race, class, and gender relations, definitions of intelligence — in a word, ideology. Research, then, can never be non-partisan for we must choose the rules which guide us as researchers; critical theory's disclosure of the hidden ideological assumptions within social research marked the end of our innocence.

Positivistic research in the name of rigorous method and a hard realism about the nature of the world fails to recognize the forces which shape research. Not only is the researcher isolated from the forces that shape him or her, but the entity that is researched is isolated from the conditions that grant it meaning. So-called scientific controls help achieve a more perfect isolation of the educational setting being studied. In this controlled context attention to circumstances surrounding the object of the study must be temporarily suspended. This suspension of attention is based on the interesting assumption that these extraneous circumstances will remain static long enough to allow the study to be validated; these extraneous circumstances, of course, never remain static. Research isolated in this way from its context can never be validated (Longstreet, 1982).

Yet research of this type continues to dominate the field of education. Most attempts by educational researchers, even in the first decade of the twenty-first century, to study something as contextually contingent as, say, the growth of human understanding have been made outside of natural settings, such as classrooms. Researchers have followed the rules of research laid down by positivism and opted for controlled settings, for example, laboratories, clinics, or research institutes. It seems obvious that such settings could not allow for a textured picture of the growth of human understanding. Any research strategy that locks the subject of the study within the confines of the laboratory, or is satisfied with partial photographs of isolated events at a particular point in time, insults the subject by denying its complexity, its multi-dimensionality. The laboratory upsets the educational environment so dramatically that the outcomes observed in a controlled setting may have meaning only in the confines of another laboratory. Are we to be surprised when the results of such studies are so often replicated in one laboratory setting after another? In the positivistic isolation of the laboratory, researchers learn about situations that are short-lived and would rarely appear in a natural educational setting (Armstrong, 1981; Lincoln and Guba, 1985; Denzin and Lincoln, 2000). What exactly have we learned? Not much about education as it occurs in the lived world, I'm afraid. Couldn't teachers have told us this about research a long time ago?

Reduce and Control: The Regulatory Mission of Positivism

But we must remember the origins of positivism in order to explain the absurdity of its application in education. Comte and the founders of positivism believed that through the process of reductionism general laws could be reduced to propositions that could then be verified through empirical research. The goal of such knowledge was to predict and control both natural and human phenomena. In education, positivism has attempted to predict the relationship between educational objects (students) and educational events (teaching). Invariably, particular rules of the research act will focus our attention on certain aspects of education and away from others — in the case of positivism our attention is focused on education as a technical act. When we measure certain portions of education to determine how well school systems, or particular schools, or particular teachers are doing, we cannot separate this question from the political issue of what schools should be doing.

Therefore, if positivist researchers can establish the criteria via their research instruments that measure how well we are doing in education, they have also established what schools *should* be doing. Positivism thus becomes a political instrument of social control while its adherents are all the while proclaiming their neutrality, their disinterestedness, their disdain of mixing politics and education. And they are telling the truth — they do not even know that they are positivists! When teachers are unequipped to see beneath the surface of these claims of neutrality, they are rendered powerless. They are encouraged by the positivists in the name of professionalism to deskill themselves (Apple, 1999). They are not encouraged to acquire the wisdom to evaluate their own teaching in terms of its relationship to larger visions of educational purpose or social justice. Instead, they are expected to implement scientifically validated, and thus uncontestable, criteria of educational quality. In their and their pupils' conformity to such criteria, positivism accomplishes its insidious social control.

Any scientific orientation which seeks to control human beings cannot view humans as sacred, as very different from other, non-living objects of scientific research. Thus, the human is viewed as an entity to be tailored to fit the proper social order. People are subordinated to a controlled environment where values are seen as non-rational, as outside the realm of science. Teachers can observe this positivistic ideology of social control with its minimization of the human in school practices such as label-ing, homogeneous grouping, tracking, positive reinforcement, behavioral management systems, content standards, and so on (Dobson, Dobson, and Koetting, 1987; Noblit and Eaker, 1987; Noblit, 1999; Porter, 1988; Van den Berg and Nicholson, 1989; Benson, Glasberg, and Griffith, 1998).

In all of these practices complex human processes are reduced to a technical calculation of means and ends — human intentions are unimport-ant. Humans do not simply respond to the social world. Human beings actively contribute to the creation of the world, they construct it (Lincoln and Guba, 1985). They base their constructions on their experiences, but positivism devalues the experience of both the subjects and objects of research. By definition, when human experience is devalued, social aliena-tion sets in. In other words, educational and social scientists have fashioned their own alienation from the world and from themselves (Reinharz, 1979, 1992; Yeakey, 1987; Paley and Jipson, 2000). As they devalue the role of the human, positivist researchers become educational voyeurs, peering at the school through binoculars, never experiencing the situation themselves, never knowing what it really feels like.

But these voyeurs are the experts. Our happy model of teachers doing research on their practices and the world of the school does not fit into the positivistic microcosm of authoritarianism, hierarchy, and top-down standards. The culture of positivism fosters the notion of the researcher as expert — an expert anointed by the holiness of science. The cult of the expert succeeds because it is blessed by 'scientific neo-divinity.' With such blessing the positivist researcher enters the school with little need for interpersonal skills. Indeed, such skills may be an impediment; inter-personal distance is important in the pursuit of objectivity. The researcher has been brought to the school by the school administration and uses that relationship to define his or her interaction with the teachers. Thus, the social relations between outside researcher and teachers at the research site are well defined in terms of a patron–client framework. The researcher is the client of the patron sponsor (the administrative staff). He or she must show deference and fidelity to the administrators during the contract negotiations in order to gain access to the schools and to maintain power and credibility during the final processes of conclusions and recommenda-tions (Noblit and Eaker, 1987; Van den Berg and Nicholson, 1989; Brosio, 2000).

The framework represents the 'top-down' approaches to educational change and to workplace reform that characterized positivistic scientific management strategies of the twentieth century and now characterize the standards movement of the twenty-first century. In this framework teachers are seen as the targets of research and often as the research problem to be solved. Such a set-up inevitably results in exploitative relations between the researcher and the teachers. Before the researcher comes, administrators often coach teachers on how to answer questions. Teacher guilt is tapped by administrative announcements that the data derived from the study will be used to improve the school. The conception of school improvement utilized in this context is disturbing in its paternalism: if something needs improvement we do not draw upon the strengths of our own staff for the solution, we hire an outside researcher to question the participants and make recommendations. Change will thus be imposed; it will not be based on the experiences of those who actually teach the children. As a result, teachers are delegated to a secondary position, reduced to the role of respondents to a researcher's questionnaire. Peering in from their voyeuristic perspective, the researchers use their 'instruments' to collect data that will be employed to change the workplace for teachers (Reinharz, 1979; Jayaratne, 1982).

Such exploitive relationships between researchers and teachers are possible only in a social context where science has enjoyed the status of the sacred. The more obscure its propositional, mathematical language becomes to the layperson, the more it is seen as something holy, something authoritative. We are shocked when we stop and examine how much scientific authority shapes our daily lives. Late industrial culture teaches us to revere science and the scientific method unscientifically. The authoritative voice of positivist science silences our natural language — the way *we* talk about schools and our professional lives as teachers. The worth of such language is undermined by a view of positivistic science which regards it as soft, effeminate, impressionistic, and non-scientific. Cowed by the authority of positivistic science, we accede to its demands and humbly allow it to define our role as mere practitioner (Koller, 1981; Aronowitz, 1983, 1988; Eisner, 1984; Hinchey, 1998).

Positivism Is More than a Way of Producing Knowledge — It Is a Force That Shapes Lives

The salient point here is that empowered teachers as researchers need to understand that research is not simply a way of gathering data. A society's or a profession's orientation toward research makes more of a cultural impact than we might at one time have imagined (Aronowitz, 1983; Carspecken, 1996, 1999; Clough, 1998). There is a direct connection between the shape of our professional lives as teachers, our schools, and how we consider the research act. Such a connection pushes the topic of research to the center of our discourse about a democratic transformation of schooling. This is the importance of positivism to our exploration of the teacher as researcher — its centrality, invisible though it may be, to making schools what they are in the first decade of the twenty-first century. Even though much progress has been made in schools and workplaces around the world in theorizing alternatives to positivist research, schools are still directed by positivist assumptions.

Teachers are subjected to positivist empirical expectations. Student scores on standards tests are used to measure the performances of teachers. The number of graduate courses amassed determine teacher pay. I.Q.s and grades categorize students. Student knowledge is based on the notion of replication rather than interpretation, as students are deemed 'to know' only when they can display a fragment of data at a test's bidding. Schools reflect positivist assumptions when they affirm that the most significant aspects of school can be measured. In their positivist tunnel-vision, object- ive tests deny students a chance to transcend the reductionism of measur- ability. Learners cannot in this context interpret subject matter as does a rigorous scholar, respond creatively, develop a relationship between their lived experience and the information, or learn intrapersonally by establish- ing a personal position on the issue.

Such an approach encourages a stimulus–response reflex, erasing the totality of the person from the learning process. In the positivistically defined school, student subjectivity is viewed with suspicion if not hostility. Students seeking self-definition and clarification of their identity are injected into a context that is externally oriented, rewarding efficiency and economic expedience (McMahon, 1970). The process of self-discovery, emancipation, creative consciousness, nuanced scholarship can no more be objectively measured than can a child's curiosity. The teacher who understands the learning process, the field being taught, the students involved, the social context in which learning takes place, and who acts as a self-directed, reflective professional is often in danger of administrative rebuke (Horn and Kincheloe, 2001).

One finds little challenge to the authority of the culture of positivism in contemporary schools. The traditional conservative–liberal dichotomy in political analysis does not help (it actually impedes) our attempt to analyze and address the power of positivism in education. Both conservat- ives and liberals have been uncritical of the culture of positivism. The failure of late twentieth-century liberalism was directly connected to its inability to understand the underside of scientific hyper-rationality (Giroux, 1988; Grossberg, 1992, 1995). Indeed, the cult of the expert has grown in a liberal soil. Social engineering finds some of its most important historical roots in university departments of sociology with their liberal visions of the good life (Bourricaud, 1979).

In the past forty years this liberal vision has fallen into disrepute around the world. The brief challenge to professional authority of the late 1960s was as much anti-liberal as it was anti-conservative. One of the keys to understanding the success of right-wing movements of the 1970s and 1980s was the right-wing cooption of the anti-authority rhetoric of the 1960s counterculture, translating it into the anti-government rhetoric of Reagan, Bush and Thatcher and the anti-educational expert rhetoric of William Bennett. They were able to portray the domain of the expert as a liberal domain. If we are to be successful in our attempt to critique positivism and those positivists who hide behind misleading labels, we will have to move beyond liberalism. Its blindness to the various ways that the poor, the non-white, and women are dominated and its concurrent blindness to the underside of Western science do not provide us with an acceptable alternative to the *status quo*.

The critically grounded teacher-as-researcher movement is designed to provide teachers with the analytical tools to overcome such conservative and liberal weaknesses. Researching teachers possess the ability to challenge the culture of positivism, exposing the origins of many of the constraints which obstruct their ability to implement educational strategies that respond to the experiences and lived worlds of students from all backgrounds. But even the action research projects which have been established are not always free from the blindness of modern conservatism and modern liberalism and the culture of positivism. Many of the conceptions of teachers as researchers are informed by a form of liberalism which supposes that teachers can bring about change without recognition of the historical, social, and epistemological dimensions of educational development (Tripp, 1988; Van den Berg and Nicholson, 1989). Critical theory's critique of power relations and modernity's conception of science is an invaluable tool in formulating our view of teacher empowerment through practitioner research. In subsequent portions of this work we will explore in greater detail the implications of the critical perspective on research. The challenge of critical analysis is extremely valuable to practicing educational researchers. Critical theorists dare us to look beyond common sense, to challenge accepted definitions, to uncover manifestations of hidden power, to break the tacit codes of human meaning, and to search for new and more appropriate methods of researching the lived world of education.

Chapter 5

What Constitutes Knowledge?

What we refer to as knowledge is problematic. Human knowledge, knowledge about humans, and knowledge derived from research about human education are constituted by a variety of forces. In this section let us contemplate the nature of this complex notion in light of its effect on educational research. We might start with the idea that any research strategy presupposes an epistemological stance. It is our charge to interrogate that stance.

Epistemological Crisis or Epistemological Opportunity?

One task of epistemology is to provide theories of the nature of knowledge, of its genesis and its justification. Traditionally, scholars have assumed that once we were conversant with theories of knowledge we would be better prepared to proceed with our research. These diverse theories of knowledge, of course, conflict with one another over the definition of true knowledge; indeed, some epistemologies deny even the possibility of true knowledge. Nevertheless, different epistemologies promote different forms of knowledge along with different methodologies and ways of knowing. Thus, we accept religious knowledge and ways of knowing, ethical knowledge and ways of knowing, and linguistic knowledge and ways of knowing.

In the social sciences and in educational studies scholars in the last three or more decades have been confronted with an epistemological crisis. The crisis has produced some difficult questions for researchers: What is the proper method of pursuing social and educational knowledge? What constitutes knowledge in these domains? Social scientists and educational researchers have grown more and more dissatisfied with the positivistic definitions of knowledge — though the discomfort is not by any means universal. Among the uncomfortable, no consensus has been reached on a new definition of social knowledge.

As students of metatheory in social science have in the last couple of decades become more and more aware of the social construction of what we call knowledge, they have begun to realize that research findings are largely specific to the method or methods utilized. The uniqueness of the data obtained from each method of inquiry has led to the existence of separate bodies of knowledge in the social sciences. Even when the same event is studied via a variety of methods, the information obtained often has little covariation. In other words, researchers using different methodologies share so little common ground that they have no way to relate their disparate findings.

When a particular intelligence test, for example, is examined by a critical sociologist and an educational statistician, divergent analyses emerge. To the critical sociologist the test reflects an unexamined set of socioeconomic assumptions about the nature of intelligence. To the statistician the test may suffer from internal inconsistency, that is, its rank order of individuals relative to their intelligence differs from other intelligence tests. Thus, it is a flawed instrument. The point, of course, is that depending on the paradigm and the purpose of the researcher, what constitutes our 'knowledge' about this test may vary widely. The possibility for covariation or the recognition of interrelation by the scholars operating from the diverse paradigms is, unfortunately, limited.

Critical analysts argue that social science will continue to develop many diverse bodies of knowledge in the future. It thus becomes the task of the educational researcher to understand both the various ways this knowledge is produced and the specific forces which contribute to its production. The *Zeitgeist* (spirit of the times) influences knowledge production as it directs our attention to certain problems and potentialities. Such dynamics might include questions of equity emerging from the civil rights movement, of the nature of fundamentalism coming from the rise of the New Right, of gender bias growing out of the women's movement, and of colonial domination arising from postcolonial rebellions. The new insights arising from these epistemological questions, critical analysts believe, offer compelling opportunities to develop new epistemologies, new angles from which to view the world (Kincheloe, 2001).

As the *Zeitgeist* changes, some bodies of knowledge go out of fashion and are forgotten for the time being. Other bodies of knowledge are shelved because they seem to be tied to one particular methodology and/or are not amenable to extension into different contexts. Of course, other bodies of knowledge persist, transcending the concerns of a particular *Zeitgeist* as they influence educational analysis in some way or another, generation after generation. Thus, social knowledge is vulnerable to the ebb and flow of time with the changing concerns and emotional swings of the eras. This vulnerability to the temporal will probably continue, for social science shows no signs of developing consistent universal strategies for evaluating the validity of these various forms of knowledge. Indeed, such a unified strategy would probably be positivistic in scope (Fiske, 1986).

Fickle Knowledge and Subtle Interests

To put the point simply, what we designate as knowledge is fickle, subject to change given our contexts and interests. Jürgen Habermas illustrated this concept in his theory of cognitive interests (or knowledge-constitutive interests). The premise on which a theory rests involves the idea that knowledge cannot be separated from human interests. Knowledge, he argued, over the last couple of centuries has become a product of an empirical-analytic methodology — the impact of the positivistic tradition. 'Where did this methodology arise?' he asks. Did it just emerge from trial and error? Habermas bases his theory on the answer to these questions.

There are three forms of knowledge, Habermas maintains, and all three exist as a result of specific historical circumstances. As humans struggle to survive and confront the problems which challenge them, they develop particular concerns (interests) which determine their definition of knowledge. The three forms of knowledge are based on: (1) the technical interest — data which increase the human power of technical control; (2) the practical interest — information which allows for people to be understood symbolically; and (3) the emancipatory interest — information which helps bring about human autonomy by the analysis of distorted communication activities (critical knowledge) (MacDonald, 1975; Keat, 1981). Let us examine these interests in a little more detail. The understanding of the implicit interests which help humans define the nature of what is called knowledge is an important step in making sense of *how* research is conducted in education and *what* it tells us.

The Technical Interest

This interest is based on an understanding of the human's role as a tool-making animal who survives via his or her use of the natural world. Thus, humans have a need for knowledge which contributes to the control of natural processes — technically useful knowledge. In this empirical-analytic mode of knowing, particular phenomena are classified under general categories. When one examines phenomena with these categories in mind, knowledge is produced which enables researchers to duplicate conditions and to reproduce results. The technical interest is served as empirical-analytic knowledge is used to predict patterns of events. Such predictability allows for a measure of control. Thus, positivism is a child of the technical interest. It is not inappropriate, Habermas concludes, to study phenomena (even social phenomena) in this manner. The point is that researchers who are tied *exclusively* to this procedure are incapable of comprehending the social world.

The Practical Interest

This interest is based on an understanding of humans as language-using beings. Human beings need a form of knowledge which would allow them to communicate with their fellows through the employment of mutually understood symbols. Such communication allows for the development of common traditions and the practical action which would emerge from such commonality. Thus, the hermeneutical sciences are an outgrowth of the practical interest. Habermas argues that the hermeneutical study of language fails at times to comprehend the ways that language hides the conditions of social life — Hans-Georg Gadamer disagrees. Indeed, Habermas argues that language sometimes serves as a force for domination and as a means of legitimizing power interests. The attempt to expose such ideological characteristics of language, he concludes, is not a concern of the practical interest.

The Emancipatory Interest

This interest goes beyond the technical interest of controlling objects in the environment and the practical interest of fostering intersubjective understanding. The emancipatory interest, Habermas argues, is concerned with a form of knowledge which leads to freedom from dominant forces and distorted communication. Assuming that history is marked by domination and repression, Habermas tells us that emancipation and self-knowledge are restricted by often unrecognized conditions. If humans are to unleash their rational capacities, a special form of knowledge is necessary to abolish these hidden impediments. The emancipatory interest promotes a relationship between knowledge and interest that is quite different from the ones promoted by the technical and practical. Unlike the other two interests, the emancipatory interest connects the act of knowing with the immediate utilization of knowledge. The act of knowing is a form of self-reflection that allows an individual to gain an awareness of the connection between knowledge and interest. If we are to understand research, Habermas contends, we must pursue the emancipatory nature of critical theory which dissolves the dominant forces separating humans from an understanding of their own histories and contexts. In this context critical analysts also document the forces which limit the self-understanding and social awareness of those who conduct research (Held, 1980; Cannella, 1997; Kincheloe and Steinberg, 1997; Benson, Glasberg, and Griffith, 1998; Lester, 2001).

How has this technical interest (the form of knowledge which lays the basis for Giroux's culture of positivism) come to exert such an important influence on the ways we define knowledge and the ways we conduct social and educational research? Habermas attempts to answer the question by outlining what he calls the dissolution of epistemology. Post-Enlightenment thought, with its emphasis on the technical interest of knowledge, turned away from the examination of the conditions informing our definitions of knowledge. Positivist epistemology dissolved into a restricted examination of questions about the technique of research. The scientific idealist concern with the role of the knower (often called the epistemic subject) in the process faded away. Epistemology could not question the meaning or social role of science because there was no recognized form of knowledge independent of science which could be used to analyze and criticize scientific endeavor. Habermas contends that his theory of the interests which determine the forms of knowledge will help reestablish the critical dimension of epistemology.

Epistemological Introspection: The Rocky Road to Criticality

What does Habermas's reassertion of critical epistemology imply for the ways we define knowledge and conduct educational research? Hopefully, the attempt of this present work to examine the relationship between teachers and research in education is an extension of Habermas's hope for epistemological introspection. Teachers as researchers who are familiar with the philosophical, historical, and political context in which inquiry takes place, will, I believe be better able to understand their roles as producers of knowledge. Hopefully, consumers of educational research who understand this context will be better equipped to evaluate the various assumptions which underlie the research they read. In addition, both producers and consumers of research will be more familiar with the impact exerted on the lives of teachers, students, and the public when the 'knowledge' derived from research seeps into our world view and our practice. Further discussion may help illustrate the value of Habermas's conception of epistemological self-analysis on the part of the researcher.

A research orientation resulting from the absence of epistemological reflection is sometimes called methodological unitarianism. Advocates of such a stance would argue that all research calling itself scientific must utilize the classical method of the natural sciences. Knowledge here is scientific knowledge. Many students of research epistemology would argue that such a position is marked by a philosophical flaw. The flaw would result from the fact that in social research utilizing an empirical physical science methodology, the unobservable and mental are eliminated from consideration. Moreover, it is argued that this unobservable and mental dimension (the non-empirical) is possibly the most important aspect of social and educational research. We return to our notion that teacher researchers may find that the most important elements of their work involve unseen forces shaping their everyday experiences (Held, 1980; Eisner, 1983; Howe, 1985; Frankel, 1986; Fenstermacher, 1994; Macedo, 1994).

This methodological unitarianism has supported positivism in theory and practice as social and educational researchers have emulated the methods of physical science research. When researchers fail to reflect on the interests and assumptions behind knowledge, inquiry becomes a means of acquiring information that can be used for social engineering. The capacity of researchers to think beyond the technical interest is severely impaired. Problems are reduced to the cause–effect rationality of empirical science. As this takes place, social knowledge is viewed as a tool to control not nature but people themselves. Thus, humans might be understood, used, and controlled just like any other *thing*.

The objects of social research, humans, possess a special complexity which sets them apart from other objects of study (Capra, 1996; O'Sullivan, 1999). This complexity precludes the possibility of research neatness desired by physical scientists. The variables with which the social researcher is forced to contend dispel any illusions of methodological simplicity of outcome and applicability (Popkewitz, 1981b; Eisner, 1983; Soltis, 1984; Baldwin, 1987; Denzin and Lincoln, 2000). To the positivist this lack of a precise, simple outcome is not precipitated by the special nature of the subjects of social research but is caused by a deficiency or a lack of rigor in particular social science research methods. When educational research is marked by ambiguity and disagreement, the positivists blame the research strategy. To the positivist the untidiness of social knowledge is a fatal flaw (Shweder and Fiske, 1986). Here rests the foundations of scientific reductionism. A critically reflective epistemology attempts to move beyond such simplification and its resulting distortion.

If social researchers are blind in their application of physical scientific methods to complex social phenomena, they stand to miss the meaning of the social world. These epistemologically unreflective researchers will fail to recognize that in the natural sciences, observations are imposed on the objects being observed. Natural scientists do not have to consider the thoughts of their objects of study or their history and socio-cultural context. Such a situation requires a research methodology which differs from the classical method of the physical sciences. Critical social researchers will choose strategies of inquiry which recognize the ambiguity of the human condition, the nature of knowledge, and the importance of context. In this context they understand that the outcomes of the inquiry may not be quantifiable or replicable and that they may produce knowledge which promotes specific conceptions of human beings and certain value orientations. The task is complex, the road is rocky, but because of the complications of the social, psychological, and educational worlds, critical researchers have no choice (Zuss, 1999; Willinsky, 2001a).

Science and scientific methodology are cultural artifacts. Though most people fail to understand it, the techniques of science affect most institutions, especially education, in some way or another. The techniques seep into our thinking process, covertly dictating our perceptions of reality and knowledge (Popkewitz, 1981b; Smyth, 2001). Dominant conceptions of science influence the questions we ask about education, our definitions of intelligence, the phenomena we deem worthy or unworthy of study, and ultimately the very fabric of school life. In the 1970s and 1980s the discourse of 'basics education' permeated educational conversations. Since the early 1990s the standards conversation has dominated. Such discussions have often been tacitly informed by a positivistic epistemology with its accompanying set of assumptions, cultural inscriptions, concerns, and *way of knowing*. The everyday use of the terms 'basics' or 'content standards' implies a view of knowledge grounded in scientific realism. Knowledge is out there, quantifiable, measurable, and capable of being purchased, distributed, and acquired. 'Basics talk' and 'standards talk' assume the desire of educators to be efficient, objective, dispassionate, business-like, and accountable.

The basics/standards mind-set promotes a technical view of knowledge — that is, information which is essential, neutral, and detached from the knower and cultural context. There is a specific body of knowledge to be learned, the technical view asserts, and there are specific methods of teaching and learning it. The conversation about the basics is impatient with uncertainty, the concern with the genesis of knowledge, epistemological quibbling, and the complex interaction between knower and known. The positivistic search for certainty and knowledge rooted in Habermas's technical interest (which in this case serves the imperative of technological progress) lays the foundation on which the house of basics/standards talk has been constructed. In other words, basics/standards talk is legitimized by the positivistic conception of scientific methodology (van Manen, 1978: 56–7).

Knowledge and Research Methods as Historical Artifacts: Alice Rivlin and the Emergence of Educational Accountability

An historical example of the positivistic view of educational knowledge as physical scientific knowledge may be helpful at this point. The immediate origin of many of the research-based reforms of the past thirty-five years can be traced to the Great Society education programs of the Johnson administration in the U.S. Before they would appropriate the funds to implement compensatory programs for disadvantaged students, Congress demanded a rigid system of accountability. Thus, evaluation of some form was deemed essential.

The system of evaluation adopted reflected the ideological assumptions of systems analysis and cost-benefit analysis which gained popularity in the Pentagon in the mid-1960s. The positivistic epistemology of the systems analysts imposed a physical scientific view of knowledge on educational research that continues to help define the parameters of educational inquiry. The identification of efficient educational programs became a central concern of the federal leaders in education at the time (House, 1978).

Senator Robert Kennedy was in part responsible for the accountability features which would accompany compensatory programs. Kennedy demanded a scientific system of reporting the effects of the new programs. Economically disadvantaged parents, especially poor black parents, he argued, deserved access to the statistics on how their children were doing. The Senator reasoned that these statistics (in the form of standardized test scores) would hold school officials accountable to their constituents. With its faith in the validity of test scores, Kennedy's plan was undoubtedly flawed. But his purpose was to help parents of children in need of compensatory education become informed participants in the educational process.

Kennedy's intentions were lost, however, when President Johnson announced in August 1965 that he was introducing the Planning, Programming, and Budgeting System (PPBS) throughout the federal bureaucracies. In the Department of Health, Education, and Welfare (HEW) a new office was created, entitled the Assistant Secretary for Program Evaluation. It was filled by William Gorham who had helped implement PPBS in the Department of Defense. Along with his assistants Alice Rivlin (who would later take Gorham's place) and Robert Grosse, Gorham attempted to 'develop goals that could be stated, measured, and evaluated in cost-benefit terms.' Gorham, Rivlin, and Grosse were not interested in Senator Kennedy's attempt to make the schools responsive to local parents. They viewed the evaluation problem as a research effort to identify efficient approaches to educating disadvantaged children (House, 1978).

Congress passed the Elementary and Secondary Education Act with all of its accountability provisions. Gorham, Rivlin, and Grosse saw Title I which emerged from it as a 'natural experiment' which would facilitate the identification of the most effective methods of teaching. These 'best methods' would be passed on to teachers and administrators so that resources would ultimately be allocated in an efficient manner. They would remedy teachers' ignorance of what works — scientific research would provide the positive knowledge needed to improve teaching practice.

Problems emerged, however. Even though the systems analysts had won the battle to require an evaluation stipulation for all subsequent social and educational legislation, they came to find out that educators were not equipped to provide the uniform data necessary to complete the cost-benefit analysis procedures necessary to determine which programs were efficient. Programs, the systems analysts argued, would have to be arranged in a manner that would facilitate evaluation. This attempt spread to other levels of government in the following years. Educational research was thus profoundly affected. Indeed, educational practice was affected. State after state initiated reform movements incorporating positivistic systems of analysis-based assumptions about educational evaluation, knowledge, and research. A closer examination of these assumptions is in order.

Alice Rivlin soon emerged as the most important theoretician and spokesperson for the systems analysts. In 1971 she laid out her assumptions about social and educational research quite explicitly in *Systematic Thinking for Social Action*. Before any policy-producing research can take place, Rivlin argued, educational experts must identify the objectives of education. Such a pronouncement is reminiscent of the accountant's advice on how to become a millionaire who pays no taxes — first, get a million dollars. Neither task is deemed problematic. The deep differences over educational goals which divide the public and educators are ignored. Rivlin is guided by the assumption that educational experts can dictate educational objectives because of the social consensus over what schools should do. 'I believe there is a wide measure of agreement in the nation . . . about desirable directions of change' (pp. 46–7), Rivlin wrote. Differences between the right, the middle, and the left over social and educational policies do not involve the objectives of such policies. Rivlin and her systems analysts soul mates did not see a world where different groups competed for power and resources. The educational interests of rich and poor, management and labor, black and white, and men and women were basically the same. The historical and contextual nature of social scientific knowledge was not understood by Rivlin.

The important goals of education are not only easily identified, Rivlin continued, but they are capable of being measured. Reading proficiency, mathematical competencies, and the mastery of acquired knowledge of certain subjects can be illustrated by standardized test scores. Thus, she reasoned, we need to 'focus on these measurable outcomes' and how best to produce them. Goals are already determined; let us turn our attention to the identification of the most efficient methods of improving our scores (Rivlin, 1971: 69–70). When faced with the failure of her evaluation studies in 1968 and 1969 to detect a cause–effect relationship between educational policies and test score improvement, Rivlin did not abandon her attempt to identify efficient methods. The problem, she argued, was that social services and education were not organized to properly answer questions of methodological efficiency. That, she concluded, would have to change (House, 1978).

Indeed, the goals of evaluation began to change. Once evaluations were designed to measure the success of programs; now the programs were designed to insure the success of the evaluations. In the process, Rivlin called for more governmental control of all aspects of the programs — design through evaluation. Teachers, she reasoned, did not possess the expertise to produce efficient and effective products. Ignorance of productive techniques and methodologies was the basis of the problem of delivering good education, Rivlin maintained. Experts were charged with the task of establishing a 'production function,' that is, the identification of a functional relationship between resources employed and results produced. 'Stable relationships,' Rivlin wrote, 'exist between these outcomes and the "inputs" to the educational process: different types of teachers, facilities, equipment, curriculum, and teaching methods' (p. 70). Just as the engineer sought regular relationships between inputs and outputs, Rivlin's social researcher would seek similar associations in the world of education. The knowledge of education produced would be certain — it would be verifiable.

Rivlin's use of physical scientific and manufacturing analogies is noteworthy. Educational methods and children were viewed in the same way as raw materials in manufacturing. The analyst would arrange the methods and the children in various combinations in order to ascertain the grouping that would provide the best output. The best output in the manufacturing process was the product; in education it was the test score. The Pentagon origins of the systems analysis methods were highlighted by the phrase heard frequently in Department of Health, Education, and Welfare during the late 1960s: 'We want the biggest bang for the buck.' What was good for missile systems and manufacturing was also good for social services and education.

Immersed in the positivistic view of knowledge of the 'Pentagon boys,' Rivlin was hard pressed to understand the mind of the educator. Some of the educators she encountered were 'frightened by words like "input" and "output" production function.' School people simply do not understand the necessity of good record-keeping, she complained. Without good record-keeping it is impossible to make sense of standardized test results. Her effort to institute national standardized testing met with 'illogical' resistance. 'National testing,' she reported in frustration, 'is a bugaboo of school people.' She appealed to 'commonsense.' Surely, we can measure our success in a logical way, she wrote. We can take into account changes in test scores, drop-out rates, attitudes, and so forth and use our data to determine connections between success and the methods employed. 'It seemed logical,' Rivlin recollected. Most people agreed (Rivlin, 1971: 80–2).

Rivlin applied this mind-set to the study of the Title I programs, but the data provided by the schools, she lamented, proved to be too scanty and imprecise. It was not merely that the programs were not designed to allow for evaluation, but, as Ernest House argues, the '"*world*" was not organized properly to yield information about production functions.' It was too complex, too messy, to allow for precise identification of cause–effect relationships; it was too ambiguous, too contradictory to allow for positive knowledge. Such realities, however, did not deter Rivlin. The problem, she argued, was not with the paradigm, not with the epistemological foundations on which her research and evaluation studies were built — the problem was with the design of the Title I programs. Even with more rigorous evaluation methods, Rivlin maintained, experts would still face limitations on what they could learn about the programs. To yield information for evaluation, the programs would have to be designed more scientifically. 'There was no experimental design. There were no control groups.' School people, Rivlin continued, made 'no attempt to define promising methods or approaches and try them out in enough places to test their operation under different conditions.' School people would have to learn the techniques of the physical scientific laboratory (Rivlin, 1971: 83–4).

We have no choice, Rivlin argued, we must design social and educational programs as laboratory experiments — this is the *only* way to gather the information necessary to improve the effectiveness of social and educational service. The physical science approach will work, she maintained. All we have to do is delineate the treatment precisely and then control all extraneous influences. Habermas's notion of the technical interest is pervasive in this context. The knowledge which Rivlin hoped to produce would enable social scientists to duplicate conditions and to reproduce results. Thus, educational events could be predicted and controlled (Rivlin, 1971: 108).

Control would be centralized in the hands of federal bureaucratic agencies. Educational laboratory experiments (Rivlin called them systematic innovations) would not happen spontaneously. An experimental strategy would take careful planning, research-based organization, and adequate funding formulas devised by a cadre of federal experts. Worshipping the cult of the expert, Rivlin wanted empirically trained bureaucrats to design curricula, teacher training methods, and teacher recruitment policies. The voices of individual teachers were to be silenced. It will work, Rivlin proclaimed. The implementation of such policies requires centralization of decision-making, and Rivlin believed that in the last half of the twentieth century America was achieving that goal. State governments are achieving more and more control over local schools, she observed. Big-city school systems are sufficiently centralized to carry out systematic innovation on a major scale. It would take little prodding, Rivlin wrote, to encourage a success-oriented school superintendent to engage in systematic innovation. Once he was provided with the 'best new ideas in curriculum and approaches' the leader would 'map out a plan for trying the most promising ideas in a systematic way in his own system . . . Why does it not happen this way?' the perplexed Rivlin wanted to know (Rivlin, 1971: 92–3).

Rivlin admitted that such centralization could possibly result in bureaucratic red tape and rigidity. But there was a way to avoid such outcomes, she asserted. Accountability procedures must not focus on compliance with inputs, for example, teaching methods, curricular arrangement, and detailed guidelines. Evaluators must focus their research on outputs, for example, standardized test scores, drop-out rates, and school attendance statistics. Federal grant monies could be used to reward those systems which improved measurements of outcomes. School leaders would be rewarded, Rivlin maintained, just like plant managers in large corporations who are 'promoted according to sales and profits.'

The Legacy of Rivlin's Positivistic Accountability in the Production of Educational Knowledge

Rivlin's faith in positivistic research methods and conceptions of knowledge has profound implications for those of us concerned with making teaching good work. Educational experts from the systems analysis school seek to impose research-based techniques on teachers in the place of the knowledge of teaching derived from experience, apprenticeship, and study of educational context and purpose. Such context-stripped research-based knowledge cannot substitute for professional knowledge — especially when teachers are researchers. Much of this professional knowledge is tacit rather than overt and can only be acquired through years of practice. Rivlin's positivistic vision of knowledge, many would argue, confuses Michael Polanyi's notion of tacit knowledge with scientific generalizations and methodological rules. If teaching could proceed only on the basis of scientific rules, teachers would be paralyzed (Hinchey, 1998). Teaching is like speaking, for if a speaker were to rely on research-based, formalized rules he or she would be mute (Rivlin, 1971; House, 1978; Raven and Stephenson, 2001).

The centralization of decision-making power in the hands of educational experts results in the reduction of teachers to mere executors of the experts' conceptualization of the teaching act. Teacher power and self-direction are thus undermined. Rivlin and her colleagues have expressed little embarrassment over the autocratic, controlling features of their social science. Systems analyst Charles Schultze, who would become Head of the Council of Economic Advisors in the Carter administration, openly wrote of the need to control local administrators and practitioners in order to secure their allegiance to the goals set by the experts. Fidelity to the goals would be insured by building in a set of incentives for those who comply and 'penalties [for those] who thwart social objectives' (Rivlin, 1971).

Arthur Wirth (1983) is not comfortable with such views of knowledge, research, and humanity itself. The positivist physical science tradition is not adequate for the study of human affairs, he argues. It treats human problems as if they can be solved only by 'one right way' — provided by rigorous application of physical science techniques. When positivism and its view of knowledge are combined with inquiry into human life, the main interest becomes the identification of the natural universal laws of human behavior. Once identified, these laws are used to predict and control. The result of Alice Rivlin's research orientation, he reasons, is to 'translate the life world into a mathematical form.' 'Is there not something about human life that is violated deeply by such efforts?', Wirth asks (Wirth, 1983: 113).

Henry Giroux (1981, 1997) picks up where Arthur Wirth leaves off. Arguing that knowledge is an entity which must be constantly challenged, redefined, and negotiated by all participants in social and educational settings, Giroux counsels teachers to resist the domination of the educational experts. In order to resist, teachers (and their students) must gain the ability to unveil the truth claims of the experts and to uncover the genesis of knowledge which has become official. To be critical, teachers must analyze how knowledge conceals or distorts the social, political, and economic *status quo*. Here Giroux draws upon Habermas and his notion of the emancipatory interest of knowledge which leads to an understanding of dominant forces and distorted communication.

Stanley Aronowitz and Giroux use Chester Finn as a example of an educational researcher who is caught in Habermas's technical interest and the use of physical scientific, positivistic definitions of social knowledge (Aronowitz and Giroux, 1985). Finn (1982) argues that educators must use testing as a method to insure quality in American schools. 'Hesitant to pass judgment on lifestyles, cultures, and forms of behavior,' Finn writes, 'we have invited relativism into the curriculum and pedagogy' (p. 32). Finn accepts the existence of a set of absolute standards which lay the foundation for a form of objective measurement of progress. As he promotes the positivistic standards movement in the first decade of the twenty-first century, Finn is the contemporary bearer of Rivlin and Schultze's legacy: let the experts determine the definition of quality and the goals of schooling. The cult of the expert is alive and well as teachers continue to search for their voice in the standards-driven educational workplace. Knowledge of teaching practice is commodified, packaged, and distributed to teachers. Teachers, in turn, are expected to take the pre-packaged knowledge of the various subjects and 'dish it out' to their passive students. If successful, students will become 'culturally literate' and 'vocationally competent.'

Renouncing the Critical Intent of Knowledge Production

The educational results of the application of physical scientific views of social and educational knowledge are often quite unfortunate. Aronowitz and Giroux charge that Finn and his soul mates have renounced the critical intent of knowledge acquisition and education in general (Aronowitz and Giroux, 1985: 9). This critical intent involves an understanding of who we are and the forces which have shaped us. It concerns the ability to connect the formal knowledge of schooling with the ever-changing conditions under which everyday life takes place. The ability *to connect* is central to the critical intent of education. The evaluation techniques required by Rivlin's experimental programs are incapable of measuring the student's or the teacher's ability to make these connections. The only knowledge they are capable of measuring are the fragments of data which by themselves grant us little insight into the nature of reality. In order to compare educational techniques efficiently, curricula must be standardized and focused on the measurable. By definition, the critical intent of knowledge acquisition cannot be included — it is much too imprecise, too much subject to individual variation. The wisdom of Dewey and his speculations on the nature of school knowledge are rendered irrelevant by Rivlin and Finn. Consider a few of Dewey's speculations on school knowledge and their incompatibility with the schooling-as-manufacturing metaphors we have investigated.

Dewey on the Nature of Knowledge: Making Connections

Dewey was uncomfortable with what school reformers over the past thirty years have called knowledge of the basics and content standards — forms of knowledge we referred to previously as essential, neutral, and detached from the knower. It is something external, Dewey wrote in 1916, a body of data an individual might store in a warehouse. Operating under this view of knowledge, academic study becomes a process by which one draws on what is in storage. Such a perspective misses an important point, Dewey argued. 'The function of knowledge,' he said, 'was to make one experience freely available in other experiences.' At this point Dewey distinguished between knowledge and habit. His distinction is valuable, for Dewey's description of habit sharpens our understanding of the type of 'knowledge' taught in schools tacitly managed by physical scientific, positivistic research models.

When a learner has formed a habit, he or she has gained the ability to use an experience so that effective action can be taken when he or she faces a similar situation in the future. This is valuable, Dewey argued, for everyone will face similar situations in the process of living. A child who learns to solve long division problems will certainly be faced with such problems again and again. But habit is not enough; it makes no allowance for a change of conditions, for novelty. An individual who has learned a habit is not prepared for change and thus is vulnerable to confusion when faced with an unencountered problem. The habituated skill of the mechanic will desert him, Dewey wrote, 'when something unexpected occurs in the running of the machine.' The man, on the other hand, who *understands* the machine is the man 'who knows what he is about.' This mechanic understands the conditions which allow a certain habit to work, and is capable of initiating action which will adapt the habit to new conditions. The type of teaching and the type of schools which engender such types of thought are far distanced from the standards-driven schools which view all knowledge as empirically measurable.

Dewey provides another example of the difference between habit and his definition of knowledge. A prehistoric group of humans watch a flaming comet streak across the sky. Frightened by the spectacle, they react to it in the same way they react to other events which threaten their security. They try to scare it away as if it were a wild animal. They scream, beat gongs, and brandish weapons — reactions which to moderns seem absurd. The actions are so ridiculous to modern observers that they fail to comprehend the fact that the primitives are 'falling back upon a habit in a way which exhibits its limitations.' Contemporary observers do not act the same way since they see the comet not as an isolated event but as part of a process. They see its connections with the astronomical system and, based on their *knowledge,* respond to its *connections* and not simply to its immediate occurrence. Knowledge based on connections, then, would view an experience as a vantage point from which a problem presented by a new experience could be considered (Dewey, 1916: 335–41).

To Dewey the *content* of knowledge is what has happened, that is, what is considered finished and settled. But the *reference* of knowledge, he argued, is the future. Knowledge in the Deweyan sense provides the means for understanding what is happening in the present and what is to be done about it. It is this aspect of Dewey's theory of knowledge which informs Aronowitz and Giroux's notion of the critical intent of education — in their words, 'the ability to connect contemporary experience to the received information that others have gained through their generalized experience' (Aronowitz and Giroux, 1985: 9).

Basics proponents, standards devisors and positivistic systems analysts intent on precisely measuring the 'output' of education continue to misunderstand the inexact and ever-changing nature of knowledge based on connections. Many educational thinkers, Dewey contended, deny the future reference of knowledge. These thinkers regard knowledge as an entity complete in itself. Dewey's Hegelian background, with its emphasis on the dialectic, helped move his view of knowledge beyond the 'knowledge in isolation' format. The dialectical notion of process was omnipresent in his view of the nature of knowledge. Knowledge from this perspective could never be viewed outside the context of its etymology and its relationship to other information. We only have to call to mind, Dewey wrote, what passes in our schools as acquisition of knowledge to understand how it lacks any meaningful connection with the experience of students. A person, he concluded, is reasonable in the degree to which he or she sees an event not as something isolated 'but in its connection with the common experience of mankind' (Dewey, 1916: 342–3). Alice Rivlin, the systems analysts, Chester Finn, the basics proponents, and standards advocates have been hard pressed to measure such a form of knowledge. Here, again, positivism fails in an educational context.

Knowledge in Action Research

When action research was rediscovered in the United Kingdom in the 1970s, the motivation for its resuscitation involved the growing acceptance of the positivistic view of knowledge with its emphasis on pre-specified measurable learning outcomes and its degradation of the role of teacher as a self-directed professional. Teachers were beginning to question the usefulness of positivism's abstract generalizations in the concrete and ambiguous situations in which they operated on a daily basis. The teachers and researchers who conceptualized this teacher-as-researcher movement began to reformulate the notion of educational research, which, they maintained, is different from empirical research just as practitioner knowledge is different from traditional scientific knowledge (Elliott, 1989a).

Educational action research is ongoing in conception rather than aimed toward the achievement of generalizable conclusions. The conclusions of the teacher researcher would never be more than tentative generalizations, always subject to revision because of their recognition of continuous contextual change and the divergence of differing teaching situations. Such research would differ from positivistic research in that it would not seek traditional methods of verification or replication — teacher research would find itself in a never-ending state of revision. In the traditional positivistic framework, the action researchers argued, too much evidence vital to the appreciation of the complexity and ambiguity of human learning situations is abandoned in the attempt to meet scientific requirements of verifiable knowledge. The knowledge produced by teacher researchers is significantly different from positivistic findings (Elliott, 1981; Longstreet, 1982; Carson and Sumara, 1997; Willinsky, 1997, 2001a).

In the traditional positivistic paradigm, the need for replicable generalization constricts all other purposes to which educational research might be applied. Educational research, the action researchers argue in the spirit of Dewey, must be judged afresh in new situations. General rules are not substitutes for actual experience, but guides to reflection gleaned from experience. What constitutes an appropriate teacher action is not preordained by an education deity — it is a matter of personal judgment in a particular situation. 'Generalization' takes on a different meaning for the teacher researcher from what it does for the empirical researcher. Constantly confronting the idiosyncrasy of one unique situation after another, the teacher researcher would be guilty of a crude and impractical reductionism if he or she claimed to have sorted out cause and effect relationships in the classroom (Lincoln and Guba, 1985; Elliott, 1989a; Kincheloe, 1993).

The goals of teacher research do not involve the identification of cause–effect relationships between classroom variables. From the teachers-as-researchers' perspective teaching itself is thought of as a form of research which attempts to understand the process of translating larger educational values into modes of daily practice and knowledge production about such practice. Such a process requires that a teacher develop an understanding of educational purpose, preferably one aware of its dependence upon a vision of larger social purpose. The teacher researcher thus attempts to continuously evaluate his or her strategies for implementing those educational values deemed of worth. In the process such action research hopefully helps to redefine the crude forms of teacher evaluation presently employed by administrators and supervisors. The structure of bad work cannot hold when critical teacher research becomes common — it is simply out of philosophical alignment with the democratic grounding of teachers as researchers critically conceived.

'Theory' as a Form of Positivistic Knowledge: Reconceptualizing Theory

It should come as no surprise to teacher educators that teachers often react quite negatively to attempts to feed them theory. Theory, in the eyes of many teachers, represents their disenfranchisement in the educational workplace, it signifies the power of researchers to define what counts as valid knowledge. Theory is threatening to teachers because it is generated by a group of status-superior outside experts who use a set of certified, official procedures to inquire into teacher practices. From these procedures generalizations are produced which often serve to delegitimize the experience of teachers.

Here theory is used in a technical context — theory about teaching as a technical act, teaching as practical skills. These practical skills of teaching cannot be ignored; indeed, they are essential to successful practice. Many educators have argued that theoretical knowledge of practical skills can be useful only after a practitioner has a set of lived classroom experiences to build on. Teachers do not gain initial knowledge of practical skills by devoting themselves to a study of the theoretical domain — one does not grasp a theoretical principle about education and then put it to use in his or her classroom. Teacher educators might want to keep these ideas in mind in designing their curricula (Torney-Purta, 1985; Elliott, 1989a).

Critical teacher research must walk very carefully around this problem of theory. Critical teacher research does not view teaching as simply a technical act, and as a result does not seek theoretical generalizations about the proper techniques to employ in the classroom. Thus, it certainly rejects positivistic attempts to produce generalizable theory about proper classroom practice. Critical teacher research especially rejects the attempt to use action research in education to produce generalizable theory. Nevertheless, critical teacher research is very concerned with the notion of the theoretical at the level of social vision and its connection to educational purpose — social theoretical questions of ethics, justice, and democracy are very important to critical researchers. William Pinar and Madeleine Grumet have written of a reconceptualized notion of theorizing, viewing it as a contemplative activity which does not seek an immediate translation into practice. Reconceptualized theory, they write, interrupts taken-for-granted understandings of our work. It allows the demands of the practical to assume a depth and complexity that respect the human condition (Pinar and Grumet, 1988: 98–9). Freed from positivism, liberated from its capture by the domain of the expert, theory in critical teacher research aids practitioners in their attempt to contemplate and appreciate the complexity of their task.

But obviously not all that passes as action research in education has escaped the clutches of positivism; much has not considered the democratic implications of the research act. Many school projects have viewed teacher researchers as implementors of theoretical strategies devised by research experts or administrators. Teachers test how well particular strategies work through analysis of particular techniques in their own classrooms. Promoted as teacher-friendly, these projects in the name of good work actually promote a very restricted view of the role of teachers. Teachers are supporting actors, they are not capable of playing lead roles, that is, in developing critical perspectives at the level of ideas (Connelly and Ben-Peretz, 1980). Practitioners, in this context, are still seen as mere executors. Advocates of teacher research who support this implementation orientation are quite naive when it comes to the realm of ideology. They do not realize that the act of selecting problems for teachers to research is an ideological act, an act that trivializes the role of teacher. When administrators select problems for teacher researchers to explore, they negate the critical dimension of action research.

When the critical dimension of teacher research is negated, the teacher-as-researcher movement can become quite a trivial enterprise. Uncritical educational action research seeks direct applications of information gleaned to specific situations — a cookbook style of technical thinking is encouraged, characterized by recipe-following teachers. Such thinking does not allow for complex reconceptualizations of knowledge and as a result fails to understand the ambiguities and the ideological structures of the classroom. Teachers, in this context, retreat to cause–effect analysis, failing to grasp the interactive intricacy of a classroom. The point that educational problems are better understood when considered in a relational way that transcends simple linearity is missed. Thus, teacher research becomes a reifying institutional function, as teachers, like their administrators and supervisors, fail to reveal the ways that the educational bureaucracy and the assumptions which support it constrain one's ability to devise new and more emancipatory understandings of how schools work (Orteza Y Miranda, 1988; McKernan, 1988; Apple, 1999).

Teacher research is coopted, its democratic edge is blunted. Action research becomes a popular grassroots movement that can be supported by the power hierarchy — it does not threaten, nor is it threatened. Asking trivial questions, the movement presents no substantive challenge or offers no transformative vision of educational purpose. It ignores deep structures of schooling such as the positivistic view of educational knowledge. Teachers are assumed to be couriers, that is, information deliverers, and are accorded a corresponding lack of status in the workplace (Ponzio, 1985; Ruddick, 1989). Uncritical educational action research fails to recognize that inquiry must always subject its findings to assessment and some form of critical analysis — and critical analysis is always dangerous in its unpredictability and transformative character.

This data analysis aspect of critical teacher research must always be directed toward an understanding of self (Kincheloe, Steinberg, and Hinchey, 1999). In this critical context it must analyze the ideological forces which frame our views of ourselves as teachers and democratic agents (Giroux, 1997; McLaren, 2000). How does ideology, for instance, work to define our relationship with the teaching workplace? Teacher researchers as critical analysts search for patterns and underlying themes. As previously argued, a system of meaning is developed which helps us separate the significant from the insignificant. This system of meaning in critical educational action research is, of course, derived from critical ways of knowing — feminist theory is a prime example. Feminist epistemology has taught us that we cannot grant dominance either to subject or context in educational research. Traditional androcentric ways of knowing such as positivism have denigrated the importance of context, thus allowing for a decontextualized research which produces a dissociated body of information and theory about education. Traditional Marxism denigrated the importance of the subject, granting dominance to context (i.e., economic base) thus producing a form of economic determinism. The feminist system of meaning grants us an analytic device which allows us to expose such ideological influences in our schools, our classrooms, our consciousnesses. Through critical action research we thus come to understand the insidious ways that ideology shapes our self-images, our definitions of professionalism.

Chapter 6

Purposes of Research: The Concept of Instrumental Rationality

In a democratic context teachers decide what needs to be learned in their classes, how such experiences might contribute to sophisticated thinking necessary to democratic citizenship, how to help children learn it, and how such learning might then be assessed. In a positivistic system we know that the quality of our teaching and student learning will be tested and measured even if it is never clearly specified what exactly constitutes the purpose of testing. Even if the tests serve to fragment, narrow, deflect, and trivialize the curriculum, we still must use them because accurate scientific measurement takes precedence over curricular considerations. This positivistic obsession with measurement, exemplified by the basics talk and the discourse of top-down standards, forces us to assume for the sake of testing efficiency that there is a specific body of knowledge to be learned, and there are correct methods of teaching and learning it.

Such an assumption forces us to unquestioningly accept the validity of the specific body of knowledge to be learned and that such truth belongs in our classrooms. Teachers and educational researchers need not trouble themselves with inquiry about the constituent interests of this knowledge. Educational researchers need only concern themselves with empirical investigations of how best to teach this information. If we manipulate this variable in this specific way, do students acquire more or less of the knowledge? Thus, many would argue, educational issues in this positivistic framework are reduced to technical issues. Questions of ends or purposes are subservient to questions of means or techniques. Critical theorists have labeled this tendency 'instrumental rationality.' Advocates of critical qualitative approaches to educational research argue that the purpose of educational activity must always be an integral aspect of the research process.

Teacher Researchers Overcome Instrumental Rationality with a Vision of Educational Purpose

One of the most profound failures of the twenty-first-century conversation about teaching and education involves the inability to construct a democratic vision of educational purpose. Devoid of such a vision, educators are unable to imagine what kinds of students they want to produce, what kinds of skills and abilities they would possess, or what kind of world they would want to build. Operating in such a vacuum, teachers, students, and educational leaders often find themselves discouraged, unable to find an incentive to push the scholarly envelope, incapable of providing meaningful answers to questions concerning 'why do we have to do this?' or 'when would I ever need to know this?' Any rigorous and socially worthwhile education must not only reflect the complexity of studying the world around us but must also be developed in concordance with an exciting vision of schooling. Such a vision respects the untapped capacities of human beings and the role that education can play in producing a just, inclusive, democratic, and imaginative future.

Schools that are connected to such a vision help us discern those qualities that characterize an educated person both in the present and far into the future. Such forms of pedagogical thinking connect educational purpose with social need and individual possibility (Theobold and Mills, 1995; Smyth, 2001). As we consider these interconnecting concepts, questions about civics, ethical activity, social justice, compassion, equality, and democracy seep into the public discourse about education. When such questions are raised, advocates of instrumental rationality find it difficult to subvert the scholarly and democratic goals of schooling. When expressions of hyperrationality manifest themselves in top-down edicts, teacherproof scripted lessons, and standardized test-driven curricula, teacher researchers who possess a well-developed sense of purpose and a compelling educational vision will expose them.

As they escape the grasp of instrumental rationality, scholar teachers study different purposes of education held by peoples in different places and time periods. When we grapple with positions different from our own we emerge with a more sophisticated understanding of an issue. Instead of hiding differing conceptions of educational purpose from students, scholarly teachers and administrators encourage forums where students can listen to debates about such issues. In classroom practice teachers can illustrate to students the diverse ways different groups might choose for particular academic topics to be taught or not taught. This is the antithesis of instrumental rationality with its narrow view of 'the right way, the correct perspective.'

In a complex critical context, lessons are grounded on the ways different values and world views shape the form school takes. What a provocative lesson for students learning to make meaning about themselves *vis-à-vis* the world, to make sense of their relation to school, and to ascertain their own social and educational goals. Central to the development of such a democratic education is the necessity for scholar educators at all levels to help students understand that the curriculum taught is just one of countless ways of approaching a particular subject matter. Such educators would research the ways other curricula may be grounded on different values and assumptions. These teachers would demonstrate how these divergent curricula would require students to engage in a very different set of activities, develop a different set of skills, confront a different body of knowledge about the subject in question.

Teaching that fails to escape instrumental rationality and as a result does not explore alternative ways of approaching issues, is not ironical about its own assumptions, is not reflective and self-critical, and will tend to produce lower-level cognitive activity and a limited view of the phenomena under study. All curricula come from somewhere. The 'somewhere' subject matter and modes of teaching come from is marked by particular understandings, philosophical assumptions, interpretations of information, cultural inscriptions. It is a subjective place where some interests are included and others excluded. A self-conscious curriculum, therefore, is aware of the power relations that shape it. In the contemporary educational debate advocates of top-down content standards fail to take this form of reflective and research-grounded understanding of curriculum into account, as they promote the memorization of dominant Western cultural knowledges and ways of knowing. Traditions of understanding that fall outside of the narrow rationalistic confines are excluded without deliberation. Such cultural, analytical, and philosophical narrowness provides society with a profound educational disservice (Apple, 1993, 1999; Zuss, 1999). With these understandings in mind, it is important to carefully delineate what exactly is meant by the term, instrumental rationality, and how it affects the educational process.

The Fragmentation and Rigidity of Instrumental Rationality: Separating Execution from Conceptualization

When teacher researchers separate purpose from educational research, the tendency to break learning into discrete pieces considered in isolation is perpetuated. In the instrumental rationality of James Mill's 'mental mechanics,' through Edward Tichener's structuralism, to behavioral objectives and top-down content standards, educators have assumed that the whole was never more than merely the sum of the parts. Houses from this perspective are no more than the nails and lumber that go into them, and education is no more than the average number of objectives mastered. Many educators have referred to this fragmentation process as 'bitting.' It is not hard to imagine a classroom caught in the bitting process. Students copy information from chalkboards and overhead projectors and skim textbooks to find information fragments that would answer the questions in the study guides and the multiple-choice tests. Children listen (when they're not talking); they respond when called upon; they read fragments of the textbook; they write short responses to questions provided on worksheets. They rarely plan or initiate anything of length or conceptualize their own projects. They rarely even write essays. In New York City in the twenty-first century, I have taught masters level students who have never engaged in primary research or secondary research. They are learning to be deskilled, to be passive, to be citizens who are governed, not citizens who govern. They are being taught not to seek deep structures which move events, but to examine only the surface level of appearance. They will not understand the concept of consciousness construction or the subtlety of the process of hegemony. Ideology will remain a foreign abstraction in their eyes. Students who will transcend such blindnesses will make their emancipatory journey in spite of their classroom experiences, finding analytic inspiration outside the school context. Instrumentally rational research serves to perpetuate the most pernicious effects of bureaucratized school practices (Bracy, 1987).

Just as positivism negates our view of how instruction and evaluation might take place in a natural setting, it also shapes our view of how teachers might naturally relate to the research act. In a positivistic, instrumentally rational context we know that research produces theories which are applied to achieve specific goals. Positivistic research sets up a context whereby the factory model division of labor is reproduced: the researcher conceptualizes the teaching act and produces theory; the practitioner executes the directives of the researcher and applies theory. The teacher is alerted to some weak component of his or her theory of education by the researcher's comparison of it to a research-grounded scientific theory. The researcher provides the teacher with scientifically validated teaching strategies. The teacher applies, and then practices the validated strategy in a supervised training session where contextual variables have been controlled.

All phases of such a process depend on an instrumentally rational concern with the measurable results of particular strategies. Does the strategy serve to raise test scores? No questions are asked of issues such as the worth of raising the scores, the tacit view of intelligence embedded in them, the educational and political side effects of viewing their improvement as the primary goal of teaching. Value dimensions, ideological dimensions of human practice escape the vision of instrumental rationality. No room for uncertainty or spontaneous innovation exists; instrumental rationality demands that research cannot begin until agreement exists on all definitions and that a well-formed problem has been established. Research and thus teaching will proceed in line with the dictates of the well-formed problem — in contemporary schools the improvement of test scores often constitutes the problem. Research is reduced to the attempt to find relationships between specific teaching skills and test score improvement. We make 'remarkable' findings which are passed along to teacher education students — for example, the more time students study a particular subject, the greater the possibility that they will raise their test scores in that subject. Such logocentrism, an embrace of reason accompanied by the exclusion of the affective, the emotional aspects of learning and knowing, forces us to focus on the least important aspects of the educational process — aspects which are inevitably the most measurable (Eisner, 1984; Schön, 1987; Kroath, 1989; Raven and Stephenson, 2001).

A medical analogy might be in order. In the instrumentally rational world of positivistic medicine doctors are subjected to some of the same forces as teachers. Technological innovation in medicine has produced machines which inexorably fix the attention of both doctor and patient to those aspects of an illness which are measurable. Human dimensions of the illness which are at least of equal importance are neglected. Doctors must rebel if they are to serve their patients effectively. They must not allow a science of measurability to dictate what techniques they use, no matter how effective the techniques might be in addressing the particular variable measured by the high-tech equipment purchased at great cost by the hospital administrators. The doctor must never lose sight of the patient as a human being with unmeasurable but nevertheless important feelings, insights, pains, and anxieties (Wiggins, 1989). In education the technology of the standardized tests often moves us to forget that students are human beings with unmeasurable but nevertheless important characteristics.

Instrumental Rationality and the Lust for Technique, Control, Order, and Method

We cannot suppress the concept that science is more than merely a method. Indeed, it is a philosophy. Moreover, reason embraces a corpus of qualities transcending mere calculation — it cannot, in other words, be reduced to a formula for problem-solving. Positivistic researchers, their opponents argue, focus on the rigor (defined in this context as commitment to the established rules for conducting inquiry) of research at the expense of touching reality. William James captured this idea almost one hundred years ago when he chided scientists of his day about their excessive love of method. Science, he wrote, 'has fallen so deeply in love with method that . . . she has ceased to care for truth by itself at all.' Anticipating one of the central tenets in the critique of instrumental rationality, James argued that scientists pursued their technically verifiable truth with such a vengeance that they forgot their 'duty to mankind' — that is, technical means took precedence over human ends. Human passions, he concluded, are more powerful than technical rules, as the heart understands that which reason cannot comprehend.

Technical elegance for research is insufficient in our struggle to understand. The positivistic concept of technical elegance has redefined the very way we look at reason and what it means to be reasonable. Reason has as much to do with *what* we think as with *how* we think. It is as concerned with the substance of our thought as it is with its form. Habermas and Marcuse maintained that positivistic instrumental rationality has focused our research strategies on the how and the form to the neglect of the what and the meaning. Thus, the science of education becomes a technology focused on moving us to educational outcomes that we take for granted. These outcomes typically maintain existing power relationships, Habermas and Marcuse argue, as they disregard the ways in which current forms of schooling affect human life (W. James, 1956; Marcuse, 1964; Habermas, 1971, 1973; Hinchey, 1998; Kincheloe, 2001).

Research based on instrumental rationality fails to comprehend the importance of the existential conditions in which problems take shape. As a result, the information emerging from such inquiry loses a significant portion of its meaning. By focusing on the technical, research is fragmented and thus loses sight of any holistic sense (Giarelli and Chambliss, 1984). By spending more time on tasks and by identifying beforehand the competencies students will master during class, teachers may indeed increase the amount of knowledge inserted into each student's mind. Questions concerning the worth of such knowledge and whose interests it serves, however, are irrelevant to the process. Instrumentally rational researchers focusing on a quantitative measurement of the knowledge component of such a classroom might ignore the very meaning of the educational experience. The relationship of the knowledge to the existential worlds of the students is a question infrequently asked in an instrumentally rational research context.

When they overlook the content of teaching, positivistic researchers acquire a very thin view of the nature of the educational process. In asking a question about, say, the causes of student learning in a classroom, a far more in-depth understanding would be necessary if the researchers were to suggest policy changes on the basis of the understanding gained through research. This use of thin knowledge of education to support policy changes and methodological changes often reflects modern educational practice. Modern empirical investigations often eventuate in a set of rules for pedagogical planning and management of a classroom. These rules are often cited as inviolate because of their hard scientific basis. Not only are there research methodological questions about the efficacy of such rules, but there are also questions about the general relationship between research findings and the process by which rules for practice are developed. If we fail to ask these questions, positivistic researchers may transform value-laden issues of policy into merely technical issues which can be resolved empirically (Macmillan and Garrison, 1984; Donmoyer, 1985).

The effect, then, of educational research based on instrumental rationality, Edith Baldwin (1987) writes, is educational policy marked by an emphasis on control and conformity. Researchers strive to understand systems of causal laws and the ways the variables relate to one another. Such understanding, Baldwin contends, lead to a perspective which assumes that certain variables may be manipulated to achieve certain outcomes. Control and thus conformity are deemed desirable and rendered possible by such research orientations.

Instrumental Rationality and Regulation: Covertly Controlling the Work of Teachers

Teachers are profoundly affected by such attitudes. They are taught to accept passively and to apply empirical knowledge gathered by professional researchers. Manageable bits of facts are the building blocks of knowledge, and these pieces of knowledge can be efficiently transmitted to students. Contemporary reform movements are often grounded in instrumentally rational research. Teachers have curricular choices only when their decisions contribute to a more efficient and controllable system. Positivistic, instrumentally rational science is geared toward the administration of human beings. The moral implications of goals such as control and efficiency are eliminated from consideration. Educational practitioners, grounding their actions on the research base, act upon the belief that the laws of social life are well-known and devoid of ambiguity (Popkewitz, 1981b; Baldwin, 1987; O'Sullivan, 1999).

For example, modern educational reform movements are often justified by curricular research which accepts without question the goals of certain programs. The primary task of such research is to help explain how the teaching techniques which are employed contributed to the accomplishment of the predetermined objectives. Questions on which inquiry is based might include: Was the course material learned or not? Did teachers consider the pre-packaged teaching material clear and easily useable? Did students understand the course goals? How well did students achieve the course goals? By assuming the validity of the course goals, researchers tacitly promoted an *ad hoc* curriculum theory which supported the ideological and pedagogical assumptions of the designers of curriculum materials (Popkewitz, 1981b; Pinar, Reynolds, Slattery, and Taubman, 1995; Quinn, 2001).

The instrumentally rational, positivistic researcher must be able to measure precisely whether or not predetermined objectives have been met. Maxine Greene (1985) writes of the instrumental rationality of reform movements which emerged from the National Commission on Excellence in Education's *A Nation at Risk*. Teachers, the report argues, should be evaluated in light of the knowledge provided by the research base on teacher effectiveness. Decisions on teacher salary, promotion, tenure, and retention should be based on these evaluations. Greene maintains that the governing definition of effectiveness was so closely linked to the researchers' use of test scores and *measurable* achievement that discussion about the complex nature of effectiveness was discouraged.

Moral aspects of effectiveness were removed from the evaluation procedure. Questions about justice, humanity, compassion, and their relationship to effective teaching were deemed out of place when judging a teacher's worth. The effective teacher, or master teacher, is a master of means; he or she is not to be concerned with moral or ethical ends. In other words, Greene argues, efficiency takes precedence over moral vision. Concern for 'should' or 'ought' disappears, as 'effective' teachers properly organize their materials, devise their pre-operational sets, incorporate their mnemonic devices, and apply their innovative monitoring procedures (Greene, 1985).

Who are we to question the research which has identified the good teacher as one who is prompt and orderly, reviews materials, asks specific questions, expresses enthusiasm and uses body behavior (smiles and gestures) which display interest, and spends more time on tasks? Who are we to question the research instruments which have been devised to measure precisely the degree to which teachers' behavior matches the verified 'effective teacher' behavior? Robert Sherman (1985) in an assessment of Florida's master teacher plan argues that single-minded focus on these isolated components of effective teaching diverts our attention from the forest to the trees. In his studies of great teachers in history and literature, Sherman points out that almost every one of these criteria of effective teaching is violated by one great teacher or another. The failure of instrumentally rational educational researchers to focus on ends and purposes has undermined the value and applicability of much of our effort to understand the educational process.

Instrumental Rationality in Historical Context: Frederick W. Taylor and Scientific Management

In the latter portion of the nineteenth century American society was reeling from the socio-economic changes wrought by industrialization. Factory work had changed the lives of millions of Americans, the fabric of economic life with its mass markets had altered the existence of almost everyone, and labor unrest and violence on the part of the new industrial workers had struck fear into the hearts of the well-to-do. Frederick W. Taylor, the industrial engineer, argued that his scientific methods could bring about a rational society, an efficient workplace, higher productivity, and more docile workers (Fay, 1975).

Using a rigorous methodology, Taylor conducted empirical inquiry to identify inefficient aspects of the production process. Time-and-motion studies used a stop-watch to isolate all the moves and procedures in a specific task. After he identified all the possible time-saving changes, he tried them out with groups he had designated as first-class workers. Testing his procedures with the first-class workers, Taylor refined the specifics. Once satisfied with the steps, the procedure was standardized and taught to other workers. Each worker was provided with an instruction card describing in detail the job, how it was to be accomplished, and the exact time he had to do it. There was only one way to do a job, Taylor argued, and that could be determined only through scientific research on the job by experts. One type of man, therefore, was required to analyze and plan the work, another entirely different type was needed to execute it. As Taylor told a mechanic working under him: '[you're] not supposed to think; there are other people paid for thinking around here' (Wirth, 1983: 12).

This is an excellent example of instrumental rationality: the *means* of improving worker efficiency and productivity take precedence over the *end* of respect for human dignity. Taylor's perspective on the uses of social research was enthusiastically received not only by industrial leaders but by educational leaders as well. It was in the first decades of the twentieth century that the goals of schools and the goals of business and industry began to merge. Reports commissioned by business organizations indicated that students who did not stay in school did not make good workers. Since most schools held on to the classical curriculum while neglecting so-called 'practical' vocational studies, the business reports argued that even children who possessed a formal education were not being supplied with 'industrial intelligence.' Students who acquired this industrial intelligence would gain certain technical skills and social attitudes such as the desire to contribute to the good of the community, the ability to take orders, respect for authority, the disposition to follow directions, and the desire to be productive workers. Workers holding such attitudes would contribute to an orderly and stable workplace, free from the unhealthy consequences of labor–management disputes. Working toward the same goals, business and education adopted organizational strategies grounded on instrumental rationality. The positivistic principles of scientific management were beginning to be seen as the panacea not only for business but also for education (Church and Sedlak, 1976).

Taylor's research was implemented in industry and was then transferred directly to American schools as it became the prototype for educational administration. An examination of the application of Taylorism's impact on American schools illustrates the manner in which instrumentally rational science became the guiding light in American educational policy. First, we will examine Taylor's system of scientific management and then we will survey its educational expression.

Taylor's research indicated that a new role for management was needed. Under his system, industrial managers would plan and control every aspect of the manufacturing process in detail. Controlling the process involved the reduction of the role of the laborer to the point that he had only one basic responsibility — to do what he or she was told. The need for the judgment of the worker, Taylor claimed, would be eliminated in his system. Thus, a deskilling process was rationalized; the conception of work was separated from its execution. Human beings were viewed as components of a larger system; men and women were simply factors in a physical scientific system. The notion of human dignity or that humans are conscious beings were not considered by Taylor's research and the policies emerging from it.

Taylor's Principles of Scientific Management and their Impact on Education

Taylor divided his system of scientific management into several components. From these components educational-administration theorists devised the basic principles behind what came to be known as scientific education. The first component of the Taylor system concerned the development of a means of measuring the quality of an employee's work — 'management based on measurement,' he called it. In education this component shows up in the need for the school to measure the achievement of all students and teachers. In order to make this possible, the goals and outcomes of schooling must be conceived in measurable terms. In the process, the instrumental rationality of scientific management comes to dictate educational purpose and teacher role. One can clearly see the influence of this perspective in contemporary educational reform.

The second component involved standardization. Once the efficiency researcher determined the *best* way a particular job was performed, then all workers would perform the job that way. Everyone would gain, Taylor claimed, as workers would perform their tasks with more efficiency and less frustration, productivity would be increased, and management would experience higher profits. In education this component emerges in the standardization of curriculum and teacher method seen by many educational leaders as necessary to an efficient school system. Teachers whose jobs are standardized can be monitored far more closely. Incompetence, it is argued, can be quickly identified, for when a supervisor walks into a standardized classroom he or she knows precisely what *should* be occurring. Again, teacher control of the conceptualization of the teaching act is diminished.

The third element of his plan Taylor called the 'task idea.' It was necessary, Taylor argued, for management to set specific measurable tasks for each worker every day. Standardized and measurable, these precisely stated work objectives would keep workers on task, as they would always know what was expected of them. Management by object-ives would emerge decades later as a more sophisticated expression of the task idea. When the language of behavioral psychology was added to the idea, behavioral objectives would be the result (Callahan, 1962).

Taylor's notion of the task idea seems like a prototype of Madeline Hunter's research-based teaching/supervision model which became so popu-lar in American schools in the 1980s and 1990s. Hunter's self-described 'scientific' model assumed a predetermined, prescribed version of teaching based on 'seven essential steps.' Hunter-oriented teachers, no matter what their subject, would follow these specific, measurable steps in every lesson. Supervisor evaluation would be simplified and streamlined, as administrat-ive personnel came to define quality instruction as that which conformed to Hunter's model and, her supporters argued, thereby facilitated account-ability. Teachers, proponents contended, 'will know what behaviors are expected of them, and they will be able to perform accordingly.'

Hunter's model was important because it was the forerunner of so many strategies circulating in the first decade of the twenty-first century (Kincheloe and Weil, 2001). The range of behaviors deemed good teaching are considerably narrowed under Hunter's plan. Supervisors admit that creative lessons failing to follow the model must be evaluated as unsatisfac-tory. Thus, rewards for teaching are not based on well-conceived notions of competence and creativity but on adherence to format, that is, teacher compliance. Like the workers in Taylor's efficient factory, the Hunter system strips teachers of their role in the conceptualization of the teaching act. Teachers become executors of managerial plans. Managers concern themselves with devising strategies to keep teachers on task. This instrumentally rational system is justified on its scientific basis and is thus shielded from interrogation because of its *objective* status (Garman and Hazi, 1988).

Taylor labeled the fourth element of his plan 'functional foreman-ship.' After standardization of the job had occurred, it was necessary that workers be supervised to insure that they carried out the standardized method. The traditional arrangement of one foreman keeping watch over a shop-full of employees was insufficient, Taylor argued. Under functional foremanship one foreman was replaced by 'eight different bosses.' If the conception of the job was to be controlled by management, then employers had to make sure that their drone workers were controlled at every point in their work. In education one might note the proliferation of supervisory and administrative personnel in recent years. Teachers often feel like the victimized workers in industries managed by Taylor's prin-ciples. As workers' or teachers' control of the conceptualization of their jobs is reduced, the need for more administrators increases.

By 1911 educators all around the United States were calling for the development of educational principles grounded on Taylor's research. At the NEA convention held in Chicago in 1912, the positive response to the call was obvious. Many of the sessions took their themes from the mentality of business efficiency and scientific management: 'By What Standards or Tests Shall the Efficiency of a School or System of Schools Be Measured?'; 'Standards of Measuring the Efficiency of Normal School Students'; 'A Study in Adolescent Efficiency'; 'The Principles of Scientific Management Applied to Teaching Music in the Public Schools.'

As the Taylor system picked up steam in educational institutions, educational aims had to be trivialized in order to be made sufficiently measurable to fit the demands of the new system. Add to this the fact that school leaders spent little time identifying problematic factors. For all his *naïveté*, Taylor devoted great effort to the analysis of the problems of industrial production. The administrators who applied scientific management to education typically did not have Taylor's research background. Nor did they have the time and resources for thorough research. Their efforts produced pitifully naïve programs which terrorized teachers and stifled students.

Taking their inspiration from Taylorite research strategies as they were applied in the study of business and industry, educators began to employ factory metaphors in discussions of the educational process. Pupils were seen as the 'raw material of the business of education.' The school building was termed 'the plant.' The school boards and the teaching staff were the 'directorate and the working force.' Society's expectations of education were called the 'problem of the market.' When the language of business had become the lexicon of the school, the business domination of schools was complete. Instumental rationality had crept in the unlocked back doors of schools and covertly promoted a silent revolution.

Training Efficient Educational Leaders: Instrumental Rationality, Technicism, and Efficiency

In an educational system employing factory language and sharing the ideological assumptions of business, it is not surprising that decisions were made on the basis of quantifiable notions of efficiency. There are so many components of education that research can measure, administrators argued, that it would be silly to worry about those few things that cannot be measured. Decisions in curriculum development were made on the basis of the dollar value of teacher–pupil ratio — not on educational considerations. Because of small class sizes, a subject like Greek could never be described as efficient; it was therefore dropped from most curricula. The outcomes of the so-called educational efficiency experts' research were always the same: increase the number of classes per teacher; increase class size; cut teachers' salaries; and reduce the number of classes offered so that fewer teachers would be needed.

Researchers in business and industry, educational administrators concluded, can best determine the goals of schooling. Thus, the function of educational leaders was not to formulate educational policy but to carry out the desires of business leaders. Soon the argument was made that it was a waste of time for school administrators to study social and cultural contextual questions or history or philosophy. Administration theorist Frank Spaulding summed up this crudely practical, decontextualized view of the education of the administrator: he (*sic*) would not borrow his perspective from 'Hegel or Herbart, Harris or Hall.' The educational leader should be like the great captain of industry who merely 'projects an idea ahead, then works up to it.'

By removing educational administrative research and education from the qualitative realm of social context and surrounding it with the trappings of physical science and business, administration theorists succeeded in improving their own status as well as that of school leaders. Because the public was impressed with the trappings of hard science and business terminology, educational leaders were rewarded for devoting most of their efforts to matters of efficiency and measurement. No matter how hard it may be, administrative theorists argued, it is necessary for educational leaders to establish quantifiable standards in the intangible as well as the more concrete fields of study. In this way educational leaders could improve their public images because it would be possible to report research on educational progress in comparative numerical terminology which everyone could understand. Such language echoes across time in the contemporary standards movement.

By the second and third decades of the twentieth century the training of educational administrators reflected these trends. Administrator education stressed the technical: courses stressed procedures in processing records and reports, finance, cost accounting, child accounting, and general business management. Statistical research methodology was added to the administrators' curriculum and served to provide the profession with a more scientific appearance. Based on the work of Edward Thorndike, school leaders learned statistical research methods allowing them to evaluate the many standardized tests that were beginning to be used at this time. Studies of the textbooks utilized in administration courses in much of the twentieth century indicate that the courses were virtually unconcerned with the larger social and philosophical purposes that educational administration must confront. Topics addressed in the most popular administration textbooks until late in the 1940s included toilet paper, toilet bowl cleaners, roach powders, towel services, and the purpose of painting, to name only a few. Obviously, the emphasis of administrator education (and the policies such administrators often implemented) was on *means* (the achievement of efficiency) rather than on *ends* (an understanding of educational purpose as it relates to political and philosophical questions concerning the nature of a good and just society) (Callahan, 1962).

Such an instrumentally rational system could not have develop___ out a corps of technically trained administrators. An educational culture based on positivistic assumptions had worked to preclude questioning of the goals of educational leadership. The fact that such a technicist orientation could result in large part from the way we have defined the nature of educational science has escaped most educational analysts and certainly the public. The forces working to shape educational and social visions are often shaded from view. It is essential that educators, especially teachers who are researchers, understand such forces.

The Necessity of Teacher Researchers Understanding the Insidious Effects of Instrumental Rationality

It is extremely difficult to understand such ideological forces using a positivistic orientation to educational research. Such a research perspective has attempted to measure ambiguous educational processes by focusing only on unexamined and quantified educational outcomes. The resulting ideological innocence supports the power relations of the *status quo*, the mythology of classlessness, the equality of opportunity, the political neutrality of school, and financial success as a direct consequence of an individual's initiative. When positivistic research focuses on educational outcomes, the importance of cognitive ability is exaggerated and its role in learning is decontextualized and, thus, misunderstood.

This decontextualization, this separation of cognitive processes from situations which give them meaning — why, for example, might we want to develop our cognitive abilities? — produces a simple-minded view of both educational purpose and the actual effect of schools on the lives of its students and teachers. As students and as teachers we are molded by dominant ideology, yet we rarely understand the character of the constraints that ideology enforces on our psyches and our bodies. Indeed, we are too often unaware of the possibility existing for all humans to transcend such limitations and to move in an emancipatory direction. In many ways the democratic critique of educational research as merely outcome measurement is rather simple. How can we possibly assume that schools can maintain a separate identity unaffected by the processes of power, capital accumulation, racial, gender, and class relationships and the impact of instrumentally rational ways of seeing (Kickbusch, 1985)?

Outcome measures tell us a little about a specific condition, but they fail to tell us about the most important aspect of the educational research act — the description of the situation contributing to the creation of the condition. Such a situation must be understood before we can understand or ameliorate the condition. Instrumentally rational outcome measures are like a thermometer which reports body temperature but cannot tell us what has brought about a fever. When we view research as mere outcome measurement and fail to explore just what it is that educational research should do, we are left vulnerable to a bevy of abuses of research data. We assess teacher effectiveness, assign students to curriculum tracks and specific classes, and decide which schools receive excellence awards on the basis of such research data. As a result, we often reward the most conventional teachers, assign creative and highly capable students to non-academic curricula, and celebrate schools which possess a large percentage of upper-middle-class students. In all of these cases research strategies focusing only on outcomes, not processes, are employed. In all cases the outcomes measured only partially reflect the texture, complexity, and quality of the process: what is good teaching?; what makes a good student?; what does a good school do? (Richards, 1988; Elliott, 1989a; Sumara, 1996; Arney, 2000).

When we rely too heavily on traditional outcome research, our view of the educational process is seriously affected. Our ability to theorize purpose, to understand the way our educational goals are socially constructed, is severely limited. We begin to equate talent with the outcomes we have chosen to measure. Our view of ability or intelligence becomes exclusive, as it regards only previously defined skills as worthwhile — a common consequence of instrumental rationality. Adult accomplishments, for example, have been found to be unrelated to test scores, suggesting that there are many kinds of talent related to later success that, although unmeasured by research instruments and thus unaddressed by schools, could be nurtured in educational situations. School knowledge is rendered irrelevant for participation in and preparation for life. Instead it becomes little more than a mode of preparation for instrumentally rational standards tests.

When instruction is directed by outcome measurements, students are denied the opportunity to learn how to interpret, to decode, to organize knowledge in a way which reflects their own passions and experiences — that is, to engage in rigorous scholarship. All learning is reduced to a concern with right or wrong answers. Challenging material cannot be addressed in instrumentally rational schools because it often does not lend itself to an outcome-based, right or wrong answer framework. Students are adapted to the needs of the socio-political and economic system. They quickly recognize that ways of knowing not lending themselves to such an acculturation process are not very important in the everyday life of school (Munday and Davis, 1974; Duke, 1985; Kincheloe, 1995; Apple, 1999; Brosio, 2000). Many of these students come to hold the entire process in disdain.

The outcome measurement of instrumentally rational research leads to a factory-model, Tayloristic view of knowledge. Like work in turn-of-the-twentieth-century factories, central office staffs take apart the curriculum, sequencing knowledge, numbering it, and sub-numbering it — for example, performance objective 1, activity 7, content standard 14c, milestone 6. Teacher lesson plans are required to match an official format and to fit particular objectives and proficiencies. Subjects like English with a diverse range of content are reduced to measurable proficiencies involving reading comprehension and grammar. Social studies and science are reconstructed into fragments of facts (factoids) and arbitrary pieces of jargon. Measurability thus takes precedence over substance and significance. Deeper, more complex, more existentially significant questions are set aside because we cannot control contextual variables.

Critical, Democratic Goals of Education are Squashed by Instrumental Rationality

If the goal of education is to produce a kind of thinking that sees beyond surface appearances, that focuses both on solving problems and imagining unnamed problems to solve, then research centered on outcome measures will not tell us much about our successes and failures. Such a research orientation tends to force teachers to direct their attention to isolated skills and quantifiable entities that render the entire process inauthentic, inert, reductionistic. If teachers, students, and schools, for example, are assessed on the basis of how much homework is assigned, teachers will be leaned upon to increase homework assignments. It doesn't take an astute observer to figure out that if the homework is repetitive memory work, students will learn little and feel more alienated, more uninterested in school.

Outcome-directed research often conveys an inappropriate message to teachers, administrators, and the public, sometimes with dangerous consequences. When researchers, for example, studied airline performance, they asked which airline had the best record for being on time. When such a factor is analyzed outside a variety of contextual factors, for example, safety, serious consequences may result from airlines scrambling to achieve a better on-time record. Along the same line, researchers who evaluate teachers on the basis of particular outcomes may miss the brilliance of their lessons if they do not take into account particular contextual factors. Knowing a student's special needs may move a teacher to abandon a particular content standard in order to provide a pupil with a much needed success experience. Such adept teaching cannot be mandated by rationalistic top-down management structures. The validation of the student's ability may mean far more to both the long-term emotional and learning needs of the child than would a short-term focus on the mandated standard (David, 1988; McNay, 1988; McNeil, 1988; Horn, 2000; Agnello, 2001; Horn and Kincheloe, 2001).

In schools insidiously shaped by instrumental rationality, technicist leaders eliminate efforts to move schools to new levels of scholarship and critical understanding. In light of the contentious debate raging over educational purpose in the first decade of the twenty-first century, critical scholar teachers would use their research abilities to transcend the restrictions of instrumental rationality. Such teachers would make the educational debate an important aspect of any curriculum. Curricular knowledge would take on far more meaning if it were contextualized in the contemporary debate. Indeed, one of the most significant stories of our era involves the conflicting cultural and philosophical values, the different views of the future, the different conceptions of educational purpose held by diverse groups within this society. The debate over education, the standards debate, as much as any other single issue, seems to crystallize these differences and bring them into sharp contrast. Shouldn't students learning about the world understand the values and belief structures that divide contemporary Westerners? Shouldn't students understand that the positions individuals take in these debates shape what should be taught, how it should be taught, and for what purposes education be directed?

In such a critical democratic context a portion of a biology curriculum would analyze the struggle over what should be taught in a biology course. The historical dynamics of the fight between religious fundamentalists and modernist scientific advocates of Darwinian evolution would be studied in relation to the history of biological research and the assumptions of the field. The debate over the biology curriculum could be used to illustrate the ways that social and cultural values shape individuals' relationships with institutions. Students in such a critical science pedagogy would not only emerge with a deeper knowledge of biology, but their sociological understanding and insights into knowledge production would be profoundly enhanced. A pedagogical innovation of this sort would cost nothing, deepen the level of teacher and student understanding, and even grant a sense of inclusion to parties that had traditionally felt excluded from the educational conversation.

Such a critical, researched-based curriculum would induce everyone involved to consider the purposes of education: in the biological context, is the goal in a democratic educational system to indoctrinate students so they unquestioningly accept the truth of Darwinian evolution or fundamentalist Christian creationism? Or is the purpose to engage them in a serious, rigorous, historically and socially contextualized analysis of the traditional and contemporary debate and the chance to develop and offer their own perspectives on it? A key lesson in the counter-rationalistic biology class involves the appreciation that no curriculum is neutral. What we study in school results from a set of subjective choices reflecting the perspectives of those with the power to decide. Unfortunately, like so many other important understandings, this too is left out of the public conversation about education. Unfortunately, it is often left out of the conversation about the social, historical, philosophical, and political forces that shape education. Critical teacher researchers value such emancipatory perspectives and paths to empowerment.

More Regulation: Instrumentally Rational Evaluation as a Technology of Control

Critical teacher researchers understand the negative effects of the types of evaluation produced by an instrumentally rational conception of research. Many times such teachers have to divide their classes into two segments: one which is challenging and thought-provoking and another which teaches simplified, context-stripped information for student use on proficiency and standards tests. High school biology teachers have reported that they teach a textbookish, misleadingly simplified version of photosynthesis for proficiency tests and then a rigorous lesson explaining why their instrumentally rational, test-based description doesn't explain the actual complexity of the process. This form of teacher resistance to the malformations of instrumental rationality teaches students a valuable lesson — the official content of the proficiency test-guided curriculum negates the ambiguity of physical reality and provides only partial and misleading information about the world. In the name of educational reform, state educational agencies unable to see beyond the instrumental rationality of positivistic research establish policies which require teachers to focus on simple skills that are easily tested — not on critical, more sophisticated thinking styles and creative activity. In this manner education is both controlled and dumbed-down.

Thus, outcome-directed research based unwittingly on Taylor's efficiency procedures for pacing assembly lines remakes teaching into a set of generic behaviors. Drawing upon scientific management and a reductionistic cognitive psychology, teacher evaluation based on such a research model devises checklists of behaviors that teachers must exhibit. I was legally required as a student teacher supervisor to use South Carolina's mandated teacher assessment instrument (the Assessment of Performance in Teaching — the APT) to evaluate my practice teachers. The instrument reduces teaching to 51 behavioral performances which must be met to gain teacher certification. Word always circulates among the student teachers that for the APT observation a certain type of lesson is required — a lesson often unlike the student teacher's regular teaching style.

Thus, on APT evaluation day the lesson an observer sees is quite different (and usually less challenging) than the norm. The APT assessors and evaluators in similar evaluation models do not need to possess subject-matter expertise in the classes they observe. Such knowledge would be irrelevant because the teaching skills are generic — verified technical acts emanating from the mandates of the empirical research base. Thus, teachers can achieve perfect scores on the assessment instrument even though their understanding of the subject is weak and their lesson is boring and trivial. Teaching may be judged on the basis of whether: simple-minded activities are consistent with ill-conceived goals; all the materials that are to be used in the lesson (e.g., chalk, chalkboard, overhead projector, etc.) are listed in the lesson plan; or a teacher uses a student's name to illustrate a point in the lesson. These are actually three of the 51 performances mandated by the South Carolina State Department of Education's APT. Thus, teachers and evaluators are reduced to puppets of the tyrannical instrument (McNeil, 1988; Haney and Madaus, 1989). Linda McNeil (1988) writes of the effects of these outcome research-driven evaluations on teachers. On days when they are evaluated, creative teachers often teach very traditional lessons because evaluators would not understand a critical and creative lesson. Because of such demeaning requirements many teachers have for the first time felt the need to engage in political action. They are ready to organize to try to reclaim control of teaching from the technocrats who in the name of instrumental rationality take away teachers' prerogatives to do what they know their students need. In this positivistic context the best practices of teachers are rarely linked with assessment procedures.

McNeil provides an excellent example of teacher frustration and administrative blindness. In a workshop designed to engage students in the role of active, creative workers in the classroom, one teacher questioned how such an effort could be accomplished in light of the instrumentally rational system of assessment used by the school. A principal responded that it would be easy. If students were engaged in a project, the principal assured her, an evaluator would just come back at a more appropriate time. The principal, designers, and implementers of teacher evaluation strategies confuse technique for teaching and management for pedagogy. It is the best teachers who are frustrated by this situation, the best teachers who begin to think about leaving. When a teacher's student proficiency test scores are tied to career advancement and merit pay, creative teachers make up their minds — they have to leave teaching or at least the school district (McNeil, 1988).

In the form of outcome-driven research, instrumental rationality has weakened the voice of teachers, while centralizing the governance of schools. Because it has the blessing of the scientific cult of objectivity, teachers, administrators, and community members often cannot see the positivistic dimensions of educational policy emanating from such research. Teaching that is legitimized by positivistic research is increasingly controlled by centralized agencies far away from the school. Questions such as what is taught, how it is taught, by whom, to whom, and for what purposes are answered less by teachers than by bureaucratic functionaries. Those who define what constitutes educational research will control the purposes of education, the shape of schools, and what is viewed as good teaching. Indeed, one of the greatest dangers of rationalistic schools of the first decade of the twenty-first century involves their support of one narrow view of educational excellence. In such a context the very assumptions on which a pluralistic, egalitarian, democratic education is based are undetermined. Questions of ethics and justice are neglected by policies emanating from a research tradition incapable of addressing them. Such questions are relegated to the fuzzy realm of personal judgment — a realm which must always be subservient to the authority of impartial rationalistic scientific analysis (Salganik, 1985; Porter, 1988; Kincheloe, 1993, 1995, 2001).

In the industrialized workplace of the twentieth century analysts have often found that the evaluation of work has been the primary mechanism through which employers have controlled employees. Thus, the assumptions guiding researchers in their construction of evaluation instruments take on greater importance than many of us might have realized. Teachers who are not being coerced by administrators do not use objective test results or highly technical evaluation instruments to judge their own teaching. Since the advent of technocratic reforms teachers and their workplace supervisors have more and more come to hold different conceptions of the way teaching should be carried out — a situation which opens the door to potential conflicts. Educational leaders tend to emphasize task uniformity, while teachers tend to value task diversity. After the implementation, for example, of Tennessee's Master Teacher Plan in the 1980s, established on an outcome-based model of research, teachers voiced strong displeasure because of the conflicting visions of the teaching task. Tennessee teachers were troubled by their loss of professional autonomy to provide appropriate instruction. The standardized and rationalized procedures and curriculum which were justified by the knowledge base of empirical research moved teacher concerns away from the needs of individual students (Rosenholtz, 1987). The Tennessee master teacher experience illustrates one of the central concerns of critical teacher research and of this book: policy makers in education too often lack an understanding of the assumptions which underlie a research act and the pedagogical and political consequences of particular views of what constitutes research. If educational leaders do not understand these aspects of research, then critical teacher researchers must edify them. The teacher-as-researcher movement may reverse the typical flow of communications in the educational hierarchy — teachers may speak with an authoritative voice to their managers.

Instrumentally Rational Research Methods are Unsuitable to the Culture of the Classroom — Enter Qualitative Methods, Stage Left

As teachers come to speak with a more authoritative voice, they will feel more freedom to express their opinion of the instrumentally rational research they have read. Such research, teachers argue, seems quite irrelevant to their purposes and needs. Positivistic research has contributed neither to the clarification of educational problems nor to the formulation of solutions to them. The precision of positivistic research and its emphasis on prediction have little application in the everyday classroom. Such teacher perspectives lay the foundation for a culture gap between practitioners and positivistic researchers. In the last few decades teachers have increasingly perceived that educational researchers have less and less to say that would be helpful to their everyday life. Research and practice are separate entities — researchers are captives of their epistemologies and their culture's own agenda (Longstreet, 1982; Oldroyd, 1985; Schön, 1987; Aronowitz, 1988; Orteza Y Miranda, 1988; Smyth, 2001).

Researchers are captives in the sense that they have asked only those questions answerable by the empirical methods of hard science. One discipline or paradigm is not adequate to the task of understanding the network of the intricate and ambiguous human relationships making up a classroom. Researchers need a multi-dimensional set of research strategies to understand such classroom interactions and the relationship between the classroom and the deep structures of the larger society. In the instrumental rationality of much educational research, the attempt to translate such intricate relationships into numbers often renders the data gathered meaningless in the eyes of practitioners. Until researchers free themselves from the oppressive culture of positivism, their research will remain irrelevant to teacher practice (David, 1988; McNay, 1988; Orteza Y Miranda, 1988; Giroux, 1997; Apple, 1999).

Many positivistic research studies depend on observation within strictly controlled teaching situations that have little to do with everyday classrooms. What teachers perceive as the irrelevance of such research often relates to what Lee Shulman labeled 'task validity,' that is, the degree to which the environment in a laboratory is analogous to the complex environment of the classroom. Informed by their practical knowledge, teachers have intuitively questioned the generalizability of laboratory research findings to the natural setting of the classroom. Teachers have suspected the inapplicability, but the research establishment was not so insightful. The positivistic mainstream assumed that laboratory research findings were the source of solutions applicable in every classroom setting (Doyle, 1977; Ponzio, 1985; Kincheloe, Steinberg, and Tippins, 1999). Positivistic researchers failed to understand that every classroom possesses a culture of its own — a culture which defines the rules of discourse in classroom situations. Meanings are negotiated around who should talk, and what are the consequences of particular behaviors.

The meanings of specific classroom events depend on a researcher's knowledge of what happened previously — how classroom meanings, codes, and conventions were negotiated. A positivistic researcher simply cannot walk into a classroom without an understanding of the previously negotiated meanings and expect it to make sense. Indeed, it is even more unrealistic for him or her to expect that generalizations applicable to other classrooms can be made from this incomplete and often misleading snapshot of a classroom. To understand the complexity of the classroom, alternative research methods must be employed. This realization has sparked the mushrooming acceptance of qualitative, naturalistic research. Contrary to positivism's attempt to make quick and clean observations devoid of context, this research orientation places a high priority on detailed, long-term observation of behavior in natural settings. Qualitative, naturalistic researchers realize that the space between teaching and learning outcomes is shaped by a cornucopia of variables. Because of this complexity, the attempt to explain divergence in student performance by reference to a few generalizable aspects of teacher action is reductionistic and misleading (Doyle, 1977). Who is in a better position to make long-term, detailed, multi-dimensional observations of the classroom than a teacher researcher?

Research seeking to improve teaching does not fit the instrumentally rational positivist paradigm. Teachers who do research will never approach the act of inquiry without an agenda — they will be prejudiced because they live and work in the schools. These prejudices are not an impediment, however. All researchers possess prejudices and assumptions. These suppositions are part of the germane understandings teachers have acquired from their experience. In conjunction with their classroom inquiry, these understandings when teacher researchers identify their origins can lead to more sophisticated reflection and reflective action. The tenets of critical action research do not allow this teacher reflection to be cannibalized by instrumental rationality. Teacher research assumes that no one has a more intimate knowledge of students than do teachers. The teacher is the individual who hears students speak day after day, monitors their work, listens to their problems, applauds their successes. Who is better equipped to determine the grounds on which students are evaluated (Madaus, 1985; Altrichter and Posch, 1989)?

Teacher Researchers Taking Advantage of their Unique Vantage Point: Defining the Struggle

Even though teachers occupy this unique vantage point and possess special forms of educational knowledge, they are still vulnerable to the demands of an instrumentally rational culture of positivism. The technocratic system of surveillance and workplace hegemony spawned by the culture is very difficult for teachers to resist. I listen to my teacher-graduate students who are excited by an emancipatory vision of the teaching act express despair over the power and ubiquity of the technocratic management model crushing their dreams. To survive, teachers resist the techno-teaching model imposed on them by instrumentally rational reforms; but the form their resistance takes may be emancipatory or it may exacerbate their domination. The practical knowledge teachers extract from their experience is undoubtedly valuable, and it is often used by teachers as an alternative, a form of resistance to the accountability strategies shaped by positivism. But without a mechanism for questioning such knowledge it becomes a reactionary form of resistance, a static, regressive response to the rationalistic attack on teacher integrity. Politicians and the general public perceive it as a manifestation of teacher incompetence. As such, it serves to justify tighter controls and the extension of technical reforms. We have no choice, political leaders contend, these incompetent teachers must be held accountable. In order to insure 'quality education' the reins are tightened — the public, politicians insist, deserve scientific assurances that teachers are teaching the 'basics.' The culture of positivism thus perpetuates itself.

Advocates of critical action research maintain that emancipatory forms of resistance to the malformations of techno-teaching exist. Of course, positivistic administrators and political leaders oppose it and teacher researchers will have to deal with that. In this context their best aid is an action research-based resistance forging alliances with critical democratic groups within the community. Such actions pose an emancipatory alternative to both the static traditional craft culture grounded on an unexamined practical teacher knowledge and the instrumental rationality of the top-down technical reform movement. Teachers operating in this critical action research orientation, which seeks solidarity with democratic social groups, draw upon their notion of subjugated knowledges to develop a system of meaning, a source of authority to which they appeal for professional guidance. While their practical knowledge serves as an invaluable source of insight into the conduct of their professional lives, teachers develop methods of inquiry into their own teaching while collaborating with groups outside of the educational establishment who offer special perspectives on the effects and consequences of schooling. Collaboration with such groups may spur teachers to ask questions of their practices never before considered: Do I unconsciously respond to the children of the dispossessed differently than I do to the children of the privileged? Do I condemn the children of the dispossessed with low expectations? Do I operate with a different set of rules for students from different status backgrounds? Do I respect the form of knowledge (subjugated knowledge) that many of my students bring to school or do I equate education with the eradication of such ways of knowing? Does my classroom encourage an active view of citizenship or does it view citizenship as a passive form of rule-following?

When teachers begin to understand the perspectives and subjugated knowledges of the marginalized and use such frames of reality to formulate research questions in their own practices, the positivistic management of the school workplace cannot survive. The creative forms of resistance emerging from such emancipatory orientations liberate the teacher from the role of obedient functionary of the state to that of a self-directed professional. Teachers will no longer simply follow instrumentally rational definitions of excellence (which usually involve test score improvement) emanating from political and educational leaders. Critical teacher researchers empowered by their solidarity with democratic groups will demand a clarification of educational excellence — excellence for whom. and for what purpose. Is it an excellence based on an economic resurgence spurred by workers who are more productive but less self-directed? Or is it an excellence which revolves around an emancipatory vision of self-directed citizens alert to the way power works to construct our consciousnesses and which is motivated by a well-defined conception of pragmatic social justice? Research models defining school success in terms of a narrow definition of student achievement are not consistent with this teacher-driven reconceptualization of excellence. Teacher research grounded on an emancipatory system of meaning is essential to the realization of this democratic reconception of the teacher workplace (Duke, 1985; Elliott, 1989a; Jipson and Paley, 1997).

Subverting Instrumental Rationality: Producing Virtuoso, Critical Teacher Research

Critical conceptions of the teacher as researcher must avoid the pressure of the positivistic culture of schooling to devise slick packages promoting 'how to do critical action research — ten e-z steps to teacher research.' Advocates of critical action research must walk a tightrope here. While avoiding step-by-step models of the 'proper' methods of educational action research, they must at the same time be sufficiently concrete and specific to provide guidance to teachers who might have no conception of how to begin their lives as practitioner researchers. While I am no tightrope walker, I will attempt to walk that tightrope in the following paragraphs. I do not mean to be glib when I argue that there are as many ways to conduct educational action research as there are creative teachers. Indeed, there are numerous forms of data collection. As we teach we are constantly collecting data from different sources, in different ways, and for different purposes. Critical teacher research brings these data collection techniques to our consciousness. Teachers refine them and extend them through exposure to the ways other teachers and researchers have employed them and act on them in a way that is consistent with the system of meaning we have constructed. As teachers bring their data collection techniques to the front of their consciousness, they learn new dimensions of the research process. Such activities could include recording field-notes and subsequent reflection about them, producing audio and visual recordings of classroom events or of students away from the classroom, and interviewing students about various dimensions of the educational process (Torney-Purta, 1985; Wood, 1988; Carspecken, 1996, 1999; King and Mitchell, 1996).

An important aspect of the teacher research process involves the attempt to discern patterns and insights from such data. Practitioners may conduct this activity alone or in conjunction with other teachers. One of

lt, yet vital, portions of the process revolves around the
: to distinguish what data are significant and what are
which has been regarded as noise by traditional research-
, ɔe heard differently by a practitioner. A public address system,
typically ignored by instrumentally rational research, may take on new
significance to the teacher researcher. A female elementary teacher may
hear a gender-related condescension toward a predominately female staff
coming across in the edicts issued by the male principal over the P.A.
What was once background noise that had to be filtered out of 'real'
educational research becomes an important manifestation of the power
dynamics operating in the elementary school workplace. Before their
acquaintance with critical action research, many teachers may have viewed
their research act as primarily concerned with deriving information about
students and the factors leading to enhanced test performance. After bringing the research process to a critical level, a variety of topics are open to
teacher inquiry. Utilizing a systematized mode of analysis which produces
previously overlooked insights, the teacher perceives deep structures which
shape and grant meaning to classroom events (James and Ebbutt, 1981;
Wood, 1988; Morris, Doll, and Pinar, 1999).

The benefits of critical action research go beyond the effort to escape
the blinders of instrumental rationality and to gain insight into the dynamics of the classrooms. When teachers listen to their students and elicit
their opinions and perspectives, a variety of benefits are derived. Students
who are allowed to express thoughts previously suppressed for fear of
negative judgment or retribution experience a form of catharsis. This
catharsis allows for a healthier, more authentic, teacher–student relationship inevitably leading to better communication and mutual understanding.
The student, and in many cases the teacher, is confirmed, his or her experiences validated. If for no other reason, the student feels a greater sense of
self-worth resulting from the attention and interest displayed by the teacher
researcher. Such teacher-questioning of students induces pupils to organize
previously unfiltered thoughts in order to render them understandable to
the teacher. Thus, an element of interpretation is necessary — an interpretation which is relatively easy to elicit from students because of its
connection to their lived worlds (Reinharz, 1979).

Daniel Duke extends this concept of teachers interviewing students,
labeling the process 'debriefing.' Students are asked questions which
move them to recollect and reconstruct previous experiences. From this
information, Duke argues, teachers can make valuable decisions about
how to improve their courses and develop curriculum in a way that is more
responsive to student needs. Few examples exist in the literature of curriculum research which make use of student perceptions of what they
have learned and what it means to them. Instead of asking students what
they have learned, instrumentally rational research has settled for empirical
observations of student classroom behavior or student responses to

standardized tests or highly-structured survey instruments. Duke lists seven debriefing questions teachers can use for student interviews: (1) What did you learn in the class?; (2) You just told me what you learned. What do you think learning is?; (3) Now that you've defined learning, is there anything you learned in class that you didn't mention in question one?; (4) What do you know as a result of taking the class that you didn't know before taking it?; (5) What can you do as a result of taking the class that you couldn't do before taking it?; (6) What one point did the teacher emphasize the most during the course?; (7) You tell me that you can reduce what you learned in an entire course to a few minutes. Is that all you learned in the course? (Duke, 1977: 157–8). Thus, teacher research becomes a valuable teaching tool. As they reconstruct their own experiences by answering Duke's debriefing questions, students take responsibility for organizing, interpreting, and making sense of their academic lives (Duke, 1985: 674).

Paulo Freire and Teacher Research: Gaining a Sense of Purpose

Paulo Freire (1970b, 1985) is very instructive in our attempt as critical action researchers to involve our students in our research. When we act on Freire's conception of inquiry, teacher research becomes a powerful teaching tool, a learning experience for students. Freire maintains that there are no traditionally defined objects of his educational research — he insists on involving the people he studies as subjects, that is, as partners in the process. He immerses himself in their ways of thinking and levels of perception, encouraging them all along to begin thinking about their own thinking. This method of critical research, which involves the study and criticism of the research process, is also a pedagogical process. Everyone involved, not just the researcher, joins in the process of investigation, examination, criticism, and reinvestigation — everyone learns to see more critically, to think at a higher level, to recognize the forces which subtly work to shape their lives.

Critical action researchers can put Freire's methods to work in their own classrooms. In the process of conducting their own research, they can teach students the research techniques that they have learned. Students may be encouraged to employ fieldwork skills such as observing, interviewing, picture-taking, videoing, tape-recording, note-taking, and life history collecting. In the process students learn and improve upon the traditional skills we value in curriculum: reading, writing, arithmetic, listening, interpreting, and thinking. An excellent example of such student research is the Foxfire approach developed in Georgia thirty-five years ago in which students learned research skills by going into the community and collecting local folklore (Freire, 1972).

As they conduct this type of research, Freire contends, the researchers (be they teachers or students) are educating and being educated along with their students. When we return to the research site to put into practice the results of our inquiry, we are not only educating and being educated, but we are researching again. The teacher research process, thus, is never ending, never complete. When we implement the concepts emerging from the research, we change the consciousness of both our students and ourselves — a change which initiates a new set of questions and a new phase of research. Of course, Freire's critical, democratic concept of research is anathema to the instrumental rationality of positivistic researchers. His invitation to those being examined to participate in the formulation, criticism, and reformulation of research provides a direct challenge to the positivistic cult of the expert. At the same time, it provides critical educational action researchers with a sense of direction, an orientation which transforms our idea of research from mere data gathering into a consciousness-raising, transformative pedagogical technique. In Freire's genius we find a sense of purpose (Freire, 1972).

Starting with Freire, Teacher Researchers Study their Students

Central to this notion of emancipatory action research is an appreciation and a utilization of the student's perception of schooling. Before Freire's approach can work, teachers must understand what is happening in the minds of their students. Such an approach comes directly out of a critical theoretical notion of intersubjectivity which rejects positivistic methods of understanding human behavior. Freire, Habermas, and other critical analysts seek to uncover the social construction of consciousness, focusing on motives, values, and emotions. Operating within this critical context, the teacher researcher studies students as if they were texts to be deciphered. The teacher researcher approaches them with an active imagination and a willingness to view students as socially constructed beings (Grady and Wells, 1985–86).

When teachers have approached action research from this perspective they have uncovered some interesting information. In a British action research project, for example, teachers used student diaries, interviews, dialogues, and shadowing (following pupils as they pursue their daily routines at school) to uncover a student preoccupation with what was labeled a second-order curriculum. This curriculum involved matters of student dress, conforming to school rules, strategies of coping with boredom and failure, and methods of assuming their respective roles in the school pecking order. Teacher researchers found that much of this second-order curriculum worked to contradict the stated aims of the school to respect the individuality of students, to encourage sophisticated thinking, and to engender positive self-concepts. Students often perceived that the daily lessons of teachers (the intentional curriculum) were based on a set of assumptions quite different from those guiding out-of-class teacher interactions with students. Teachers consistently misread the anger and hostility resulting from such inconsistency. Only in an action research context which values the perceptions of students could such student emotions be understood and addressed (Oldroyd, 1985).

One of the most important techniques teacher researchers have used to gain access to student perceptions and their (and their teachers') own understandings of them involves keeping student and teacher journals. As teachers keep track of their practices, understandings, research strategies, and research interpretations, their ability to act on their reflections is enhanced. Michael Armstrong (1981) writes of how as a teacher researcher he would write every evening about what happened in his class that day. He structured his journal writing around the question, 'What were the most significant events of the day?' He followed this description with his own observations, interpretations, and speculations about the events. Typically, he wrote about particular incidents illuminating the nature of the children's learning. To excavate student perceptions that are often hidden from the teacher, often concealed from even the student's own consciousness, teacher researchers may want to read parts of their own journals to students. Such an act of teacher disclosure of self may spark a meta-analytical process initiating student and teacher thinking about their own thinking. As a result, closer, more authentic student–teacher and student–student relationships may develop which allow for more revealing social interactions, more sophisticated learning activities, and more opportunities to connect academic learning with the lived experience of students and teachers. This is one of the ways that teacher researchers lay the conceptual infrastructure for profound improvements in the scholarly quality of schooling.

In such a context classroom change becomes a negotiated process based on the shared perceptions of students and teachers. The positivistic view of change as a means of power coercion is abandoned — such a perspective simply does not fit the culture of a classroom where teachers and students attend to, reflect and act upon the perceptions of one another. In such classrooms empowered teachers released from the control of instrumentally rational administrative surveillance procedures pass more and more responsibility to their students. Along with such responsibility students gain more opportunities to think for themselves, to engage in their own research, and in the process to become educated in a critically defined way. Such an education would allow students to perceive themselves as significant agents in the political life of the society. In such a situation learning is seen as an act of social participation, that is, citizenship (Armstrong, 1981; Oldroyd, 1985; Wood, 1988; Hursh and Ross, 2000; Steinberg, 2000; Kincheloe, 2001).

Tentative Guidelines for Incorporating Critical Action Research into the Classroom

Of course, as an author of a book on the teacher as researcher, I believe that teachers have much to gain from an understanding of action research. But, as I tried to convey in Chapter 3, educational action research conceived outside of a larger system of meaning simply becomes one more educational fad whose popularity, like the child-centeredness and the standards movements, waxes and wanes periodically. When grounded in an emancipatory system of meaning, action research may be one of many strategies employed to empower teachers and to revamp the project of public schooling. It may help us avoid the tendency of teachers to fall prey to the deadening routine of school, the anti-intellectual culture of schools which stifles teacher interaction as professionals, the victimization motif which induces teachers to see themselves as powerless objects of administrative tyranny devoid of a professional decision-making prerogative. Without some form of critical intervention, teachers encounter the same situations over and over again, seeing what they expect to see, and constantly reconstructing the classroom in its own image (Ruddick, 1989).

To avoid a slick step-by-step prescription of quick and easy methods of initiating critical teacher research, here are seven tentative guidelines for teachers interested in incorporating critical action research into their classrooms.

1   *Constructing a system of meaning.* Critical action research begins with the teacher's construction of a tentative system of meaning, a source of authority to which they look for philosophical guidance in considering the purpose not only of their research but of their teaching. From my perspective critical theory, feminist theory, postmodern analysis, liberation theology, Deweyan educational theory, Afrocentric epistemology, and indigenous peoples' knowledges serve as starting points in our construction and ongoing reconstruction of a system of meaning.

2   *Understanding dominant research methods and their effects.* Armed with this emancipatory system of meaning, critical teacher researchers are empowered to expose the assumptions of existing research orientations, to critique the verified knowledge base that emerges from them, and to reveal the ideological effects of such processes on teachers, schools, and the culture's view of education. Once the assumptions and effects of such research strategies are revealed, critical action researchers can begin to see those aspects of education ignored by such approaches. Often critical research will begin its inquiry at the locations invisible to instrumentally rational research.

3   *Selecting what to study.* Guided by their emancipatory system of meaning and their rejection of instrumentally rational research and the educational practices justified by it, critical teacher researchers begin to see their schools and classrooms from unique angles which reveal problems often unperceived by less-prepared practitioners. Teacher decisions about what to study emerge from this ability to see familiar settings from the outside looking in.

4   *Acquiring a variety of research strategies.* Acquaintance with the literature of qualitative inquiry provides the teacher researcher with a diverse battery of inquiry methods. Different methods may be employed for different purposes in divergent situations, thus promoting research flexibility and the potential for unique teacher insight.

5   *Making sense of information collected.* The system of meaning developed by the critical teacher researcher is invaluable to the action research process. In this case the system of meaning allows the teacher researcher to identify previously unrecognized patterns in the data collected in the classroom, school, and community. Bolstered by the emancipatory system of meaning, the teacher researcher is able to uncover relationships among classroom, school, and community which serve to change the focus of one's professional life. Teachers may ask: Why do I react this way to these particular students? Why do I feel that I must cover this body of information? Why did this particular student behavior anger me so?

6   *Gaining awareness of the tacit theories and assumptions which guide practice.* Critical action researchers turn their inquiry on themselves, seeking to uncover the forces that construct their own *consciousnesses*. In this process teachers develop a dialectic of distance which simultaneously puts them closely in touch with their thoughts and feelings about their teaching, while at the same time granting them the analytical ability to see themselves from a critical distance — a distance which allows them a view of their relationship to wider social and ideological forces. As teacher researchers view themselves as part of a wider cultural panorama, relationships are revealed which help them to see how they come to believe and act. Aided by the dialectic of distance, teachers study themselves as they would the students in their classrooms.

7   *Viewing teaching as an emancipatory, praxis-based act.* Critical action research is incompatible with a view of teaching as a technical act of information delivery. The term praxis-based signifies this incompatibility in its concern with informed practice. Critical action research requires a pedagogy of personal and social transformation. The mere act of developing a system of meaning which guides research design, selection of research methods, interpretation of research, action based on research, and personal analysis of

consciousness construction cannot help but alter a teacher's way of seeing, of reading the world. Thus, critical action research cannot claim neutrality. It can never avoid initiating challenges to the undemocratic, scientifically managed, instrumentally rational workplace of teaching. When adopted, critical teacher research enters into the fray. It operates in the struggle to reclaim educational inquiry from the instrumental rationality of much educational research, to redefine knowledge in a way which exposes the political consequences of positivism, and to save the dignity of teaching from the culture of narrow accountability (Bogdan and Biklen, 1982; Longstreet, 1982; Torney-Purta, 1985; Oldroyd and Tiller, 1987; Kroath, 1989; Horn, 2000; Smyth, 2001).

Chapter 7

The Quest for Certainty

Julian Jaynes in his *The Origin of Consciousness in the Breakdown of the Bicameral Mind* (1976) presented a grand theory of the development of human consciousness and its relationship to the development of human history. In Jaynes's theory the bicameral mind began to break down in Western civilization around 12 BC. Prior to the breakdown of this two-sided bicameral mind the right hemisphere of the brain had subconsciously made meaning of everyday life. As a meaning-making entity, the right hemisphere transmitted its perceptions to the whole brain. Individuals interpreted such transmissions as the voices of gods speaking to them. After the breakdown humans were no longer blessed by this divine intervention in their lives. As a result, they were beset by anxieties and tensions resulting from the need for truth about the world and the ability to make conscious decisions. Subsequent Western history, Jaynes maintained, thus became a quest for certainty, a search for new forms of authority.

The Historical Quest for Certainty

The main themes of the last four millennia in Western culture (some of the same themes are present in other cultures but in differing time-frames) emerge when studied in this Jaynesian context. In the late second millennium BC, many stopped hearing the voices of the gods. By the end of the first millennium BC, those men and women (the prophets and the oracles) who still heard the voices were dying away. From the time of Christ until AD 1000, it was the transcripts of the testimonies of the oracles and prophets which provided our authorization and our volition. In the last 1000 years these writings began to lose their authority. During this millennium the Church found itself challenged by science. Contrary to popular belief, the two forces clashed not over the existence of the divine but over the proper path to divine certainty. Indeed, the scientific revolution was driven by a desire to uncover hidden divinity, that is, a divine plan for the universe. With the coming of the Enlightenment and nineteenth-century scientific materialism this search for a divine plan ran into an ironic detour. The romantic search for God's hand was dismissed as scientists began to posit that there was no room for the divine in a cold, rational universe. Darwin's thesis that it was evolution, not divine wisdom, which created nature implied that there was no authorization from the outside. Man (*sic*) had to depend on his own volition.

This breakdown of divine authorization is reminiscent of the breakdown of the bicameral mind at the end of the second millennium BC. We are inundated with substitutes as more and more people have become aware of the breakdown: meditation, sensitivity-training groups, mind control, scientology, neo-mysticism, the rise of fundamentalism in all religions and many others. Indeed, the types of organized religion which have flourished in recent years (e.g., fundamentalism) have ignored the great questions raised by social, cultural, and scientific events of the last few centuries. They have allowed little, if any, inquiry into questions concerning evolution, anthropology of religion, or the psychological quest for certainty.

Furthermore, science itself takes on a quasi-religious role, as it seeks certainty in the ruins of traditional religion. Taking its cue from traditional religion, science has developed an 'infallible dogma.' Science strives to be a force which explains everything, soothes our uncertainty, provides a ritual (a research methodology) which if followed grants a pathway to truth and releases humans from the need for cultivating their own self-direction. Positivistic science has often sought, in the same manner as traditional religion, the Final Answer and the One Truth (Kincheloe *et al.*, 1987).

Critical theorists have argued that these scientific tendencies affect all aspects of a culture. As previously mentioned, Henry Giroux (1997) (drawing upon the work of Horkheimer, Adorno, Marcuse, and Habermas) has contended that when positivistic science is combined with the forces of domination in a society, a 'culture of positivism' is formed (Horkheimer, 1974). This culture of positivism informs the way we approach all problems — both technical and human. Critical analysts maintain that the positivistic culture assumes that certainty exists and that there are final answers in the world of humans. The critical perspective argues that there is no certainty in the world of human affairs and it is high time we abandon the search. The quest for certainty in the social realm often focuses our attention on the trivial — on that which can be easily measured. Rarely do the most significant questions of human affairs lend themselves to quantification and the pseudo-certainty which often accompanies numbers.

If Jaynes's thesis is correct, social and educational researchers find themselves as players in a larger historical context where human beings have searched for certainty in an attempt to regain a lost security. The instrumental rationality that we have analyzed reflects this tendency, as positivistic researchers have searched for a method (a means) which is never-changing, an anchor in a stormy sea of ambiguity. Some analysts would argue that the critique of positivism moves humans and their search for knowledge into a new era. In the post-positivistic age, they argue, human beings will no longer be crippled by the quest for certainty. As a result, humans would find greater comfort with ambiguity. In their pursuit of knowledge, researchers would abandon the search for an Absolute Method, utilizing a wide diversity of research methods to study a wide diversity of topics. Let us examine in more detail the quest for certainty in educational research.

Positivism and the Quest for Certainty: One Way to Universal Truth

Positivistic researchers argue that social research should be designed to accumulate evidence which will allow us to make sense of the social world in a systematic fashion. In this process we will find and modify laws while extending existing ones. Once again we see the physical science model informing social and educational research, as positivistic researchers argue the point that all sciences are unified — that is, the classical method of the physical sciences is applicable in all research contexts, education included (Smith, 1983).

There is great security in this unity of science position. Researchers have been frightened by the prospect of diversified conceptual frameworks and research strategies. When we give credence to a variety of methods of seeking and validating information, many researchers argue that belief, meaning, experience, and knowledge become muddled and confused. Therefore, positivistic researchers have traditionally presented a case for rigorous methodology. Rigor implies conceptual clarity and consistency and the elimination of bias — that is, the human input of the researcher. Most importantly, rigorous research limits the way in which information might be interpreted, *one* way being the ideal. To facilitate rigorous research, proponents have called for a universal language of ideas in which all research problems could be formulated. In this manner debate over linguistic meaning would be eliminated and objectivity would be insured. Thus, the natural order could be described with great accuracy as the problems of observer bias and language imprecision would be solved (Eisner, 1983; Carspecken, 1996, 1999).

This belief in an underlying natural order where there is regularity in the way humans act exerts a profound impact upon the way humans approach research. These regularities or social laws, positivists maintain, are best expressed through quantitative analysis and the language of mathematics. Mathematics plays the role of the universal language of ideas which eliminates human bias and imprecision. The *raison d'être* for educational research within this tradition, therefore, is to develop theories which give coherent expression to human regularities.

The assumptions of social regularity and certainty behind this positivistic research tradition influence social practice. What began as a research method slowly evolves into a view of the world which includes descriptions of how humans should behave, believe, and experience. Educational science which is grounded in positivistic research assumes that the laws of society and the knowledge of human existence have been verified and are ready to be inserted into the minds of children. Educational 'engineers' devise curricula and organizational strategies for schools as if there were no ambiguities or uncertainties in the social and educational world. Children in these circumstances, anti-positivists charge, are controlled and manipulated like animals in a biology laboratory. The sacred rituals (methods) of science grant these practices an aura of legitimacy and sanctity (Popkewitz, 1981; Aronowitz, 1988, 1993).

Anti-positivists argue that the attempt to alleviate anxiety produced by the questioning of scientific unity causes researchers to hold fast to positivistic formats. In the larger Jaynesian historical context marked by the quest for certainty, science has traditionally played the role of the new religion while scientific methodology has been substituted for Church liturgy. In this quest for authorization and certainty humans have often sought rules, orders, and structures. Numerous studies have indicated that positivistic science attracts more 'authoritarian personality types' (Adorno *et al.*, 1950) than do the arts, humanities, and non-positivistic science (Oxtoby and Smith, 1970). That such authoritarian personalities are attracted to the positivistic sciences should not be surprising, as positivism accepts a rationally ordered universe, seeks to discover universal laws and patterns, and attempts to provide absolute explanations of phenomena (Head, 1979).

Abandoning the Quest: Moving toward Pluralism in Research

Elliot Eisner believes that the quest for certainty is hopeless, for if we can learn anything from science it is that our ideas about the world change and that they will continue to change in the coming years. The chance of arriving at some juncture in human history where research will become unnecessary because we will understand the nature of reality is slim. There are no social and educational laws and thus no certainty — and we should get used to it. There is unlikely to be any single research strategy or theoretical view that will allow us to grasp the whole of reality.

Given such prospects, counter-Cartesians and critical analysts tell us, researchers should welcome a proliferation of research paradigms and take advantage of the new angles they provide for viewing the world. This research pluralism or eclecticism, they argue, will take our understanding of the world to previously unexplored dimensions. Those who accept research pluralism will recognize that divergent theoretical systems and research paradigms designate different phenomena as data and that what we consider reality cannot be separated from the methodological procedures employed to produce those conclusions (Eisner, 1983). We will examine this pluralism in more detail in our discussion of the research bricolage.

The path to such eclecticism, however, is beset with obstacles. Indeed, philosophers of social science describe a crisis in contemporary research precipitated by two actions: (1) the fight to free social science from the positivistic quest for certainty; and (2) the struggle by those freed from it to figure out what to do with their freedom — i.e., their efforts to cope with the choices presented by research pluralism.

Evidence of the crisis is manifested by an inability to agree upon standard criteria for judging the progress of a field of study. With so many approaches to research available, social scientists find it increasingly difficult to make evaluations across the wide range of activities undertaken in the name of their discipline. Maybe even more disconcerting is the inability of researchers in social sciences to understand the assumptions, aims, and languages of one another. Yet, what is the alternative? The attempt to bond our studies in a common language with shared assumptions takes us back to a positivistic quest for a universally understood language of research — an Esperanto of inquiry, if you will. Shared aims, anti-positivists maintain, stifle our creativity and research freedom. Much of the great physical and social scientific research seemed aimless to the patriarchs of the disciplines when it was first encountered. In the most healthy scientific situation there is generally little consensus about what the next step should involve, what method should be utilized to pursue the next step, or how exactly success should be measured. The price of our abandonment of the quest for certainty is untidy diversity, but the world itself (especially the social and educational world) is not all that neat (Eisner, 1983; Smith, 1983; Clough, 1998).

Barbara Frankel (1986) states it well, arguing that those who are disturbed by this untidiness are simply lamenting the 'confusion and noise' foisted upon social science by the 'humanness of human beings.' Like the librarian who dreams of the tidiness of a library without patrons, Frankel's neo-positivists fantasize a spick and span social science where researchers are all identical, unbiased, infallible measuring instruments. Research would be so much easier, they dream, if researchers and the researched didn't have to interact through the imprecise medium of verbal language, disagree over standards of success, and find themselves separated by divergent value structures (Shweder and Fiske, 1986; Willinsky, 1999). At this rate, they warn, we will never really 'know' anything.

Can We Deal with the Messiness, the Complexity of the Social, Educational, and Psychological Worlds?

Psychologist Donald Fiske (1986) argues that we can achieve greater certainty than many eclecticists believe and that unification of science is possible.

Indeed, if social science is to progress in its attempt to describe reality, we must focus our attention on its unification. Agreeing that different methods of science research produce different forms of knowledge, Fiske argues that there is no reason that the different forms of knowledge cannot be brought together. We have unrelated bodies of knowledge, Fiske argues, because we have not developed an adequate general theory of social knowledge.

We must search for ways of integrating divergent research methodologies, he says. Researchers must disregard the pessimists who doubt that such integration is possible and develop systems of meta-analysis which provide strategies for pulling together data obtained by different methodologies. Once meta-analysis pulls together diverse data, it must compare and analyze the facts so that researchers can decide their next steps. Thus, Fiske believes that universal scientific aims are possible and necessary in the struggle to overcome the confusion of research eclecticism.

One of the most important ways of escaping the uncertainty of eclectic social science, Fiske argues, is to delimit precisely what it is that social science wants to know. Pointing to physics, Fiske reflects E. P. Wigner's observation (as quoted in Frankel, 1986) that progress in physics has come from the restriction of the discipline's concern to the attempt to explain the 'regularities in the behavior of objects.' Nobel Laureate Wigner argued that this 'specification of the explainable may have been the greatest discovery of physics so far.'

There are obvious implications here for social scientists, Fiske asserts. Social science has simply had too high a level of expectation, as it has attempted to understand broad, vague entities such as intelligence and culture. We must focus our research on the regularities in the behavior of social objects. Strongly disagreeing with anti-positivists such as Frankel and Eisner, Fiske argues that social laws exist and can be discovered. The regularities to which he refers are the building blocks of social laws. In other words, Fiske contends that our search for the laws of society must start small with microscopic methods of investigation. The objects of social inquiry, he says, must be small objects and short temporal periods. Fiske is confident that years and years of such microscopic research will eventuate in an accurate portrayal of social reality (Frankel, 1986: 354–5).

Fiske cannot accept a postmodern conception of disorder. The positivistic discomfort with uncertainty motivates the construction of logocentric designs. Build more jails and get the deviants into them. Reestablish old-fashioned discipline and solve school management problems. Allow administrators to determine what textbooks teachers should use and adopt them. Inquire into what strategies improve test scores, then require teachers to use them. Set contents standards and watch to see if teachers teach them. Give principals and deans more responsibility to fire people. Pass a law or a constitutional amendment which requires citizens to respect the flag. Conduct research that is simple, orderly, and elegant, and produces verifiable data. Devise questionnaires that soothe our quest for certainty by subtly requiring respondents to answer questions in ways that prove that the world is stable and predictable. As a research analyst, assume that the word and the deed are consistent. All of these designs are based on the assumption of common frames of reference. The fact that they are arrived upon in a way which reflects the tacit dominant ideology of a time and place is not considered in the quest for certain knowledge of the world of education. Thus, in its assurance, its refusal to examine the assumptions which guide it, the quest for certainty often obscures more than it uncovers (Gordon, Miller and Rollock, 1990; Horn, 2000; Horn and Kincheloe, 2001).

Jacques Derrida ridicules the certainty with which science makes 'valid' arguments. Such arguments always begin with primitive and undefined terms and premises, he contends, and to ignore this situation is to seek a fictional security. Meaning, like an eroding hillside, slowly dissolves until language and texts take on a configuration quite different from their original state. A reader in 1952 may have derived a different meaning from a phrase than does a reader of the same phrase in 2004. Meaning derived from research data or frames of reference cannot help but reflect the ideology and social contexts which surround them. Unexamined frames of reference lead to claims of scientific certainty which perpetuate privilege for the privileged and oppression for the oppressed (Cherryholmes, 1988; Carlson, 1997; Carlson and Apple, 1998).

Seeking Certainty in a World where Meanings Do Not Remain Constant

These ideas have important implications for teacher researchers when they attempt to make sense of existing educational research and when they begin to formulate the questions they wish to explore themselves. Teacher research and practice, for example, cannot be conceived as mere problem-solving, because a problem does not unambiguously present itself. A problem is, as we have already maintained, identified as a result of particular ideologies and social frames (Altrichter and Posch, 1989). This situation serves to illustrate the value of our notion of critical constructivism discussed in Chapter 3. Piagetian formal thinking with its emphasis on problem-solving is insufficient for the critical teacher researcher. Such thinking does not allow researchers to explore the origins of problems, the assumptions which move us to define some situations as problems and others as not problems, or the source of authority which guides us in our formulation of criteria for judging which problems merit our research time. This is where our critical constructivist notion of postformal thinking helps us understand the complexity of our role as teacher researchers. Employing such a thinking style, we begin to uncover the hidden ways ideology shapes the questions resting at the foundation of our research. Thus, we see far more clearly the shaky foundation, the lack of constancy of meaning on which the quest for certainty rests.

Consider for a moment how our faith in the constancy of meaning shapes our lives as teachers. The meanings researchers attribute to terms such as reading, teaching, and learning influence the forms our evaluations of teachers, students, and schools take. For example, think about a researcher seeking to determine whether a constructivist method of teaching science produces more learning than an inquiry method. The researcher begins the study by identifying what learning is and what behaviors should be examined to determine whether it has or has not taken place. There is nothing objective about such a process; absolute, certain knowledge does not emerge from such a study. The knowledge emerging is inherently conditional — dependent on an acceptance of a variety of assumptions about the goals of science education, the definition of a good student, the nature of learning, and so on. As Robert Donmoyer (1990a) argues, these research issues are always questions of meaning. As our perspective on research fashions our teacher evaluation strategies, the designation of who is a competent or who is an incompetent teacher is contingent on the system of meaning on which researchers operate (Hart, 2001).

Donmoyer (1990a) writes about a school district's attempt to evaluate a whole language teacher he knows. Everyone in the system, including individuals who do not embrace a whole language approach, regard him as an excellent teacher. However, when administrators attempted to evaluate him on the basis of a new evaluation instrument, a problem developed. The supervisor came to his classroom several times to evaluate the teacher but always left without doing so. The evaluator kept waiting for the teacher to 'teach' — teaching, according to the research on which the system of evaluation was based, involved standing in front of students and delivering information. The researchers who developed the instruments used by the supervisors assumed a constant, one-dimensional meaning of teaching and learning. Donmoyer concludes that researchers must consider questions of meaning, and diverse constructions of both learning and the teaching act. No research project, no curriculum, no evaluation instrument should be developed before different conceptions of what it means to teach are considered.

Once again we are confronted with the danger of the quest for certainty, the search for a universal knowledge applicable in all situations. The teacher evaluations, the curricula developed, the ability grouping which come out of this sacred educational science are clothed in the garb of technical expertise (Cherryholmes, 1988; Donmoyer, 1990b). The force field of certainty surrounds them, rendering them impenetrable to the misgivings of those directly affected: creative teachers with negative evaluations; individuals from low status cultures whose experiences, whose subjugated knowledges, are absent from school curricula; brilliant students with unique learning styles whose talents are not appreciated by the culture of the schools nor measured by standardized tests.

Contrary to the assumptions of the positivistic cult of certainty which too often shapes school practice, meanings are never constant and closed to interpretation but remain forever open — open to negotiation. Interpretations are never final because humans are incapable, thankfully, of a final perception. A student may be taught and evaluated by a gaggle of teachers, but only one may recognize genius previously overlooked. Knowledge doesn't age well; it often turns to vinegar. New facts come to light, fresh interpretations uncover new relationships which render traditional accounts *passé*. Albert Einstein as a student is viewed as a failure, but as a scientist, a genius. Yesterday's certainties are tomorrow's superstitions. Deliver me from the dreary universe where everything can be known (Reinharz, 1979, 1992; Lincoln and Guba, 1985; Slaughter, 1989; Denzin and Lincoln, 2000). Such is the world of the camp science fiction movie where a time traveler changes one event, and scientists in charge of the time travel project 'know' that if this particular event is changed then a particular set of consequences will result. Such cinematic depictions illustrate the simplicity and determinism of positivistic science's quest for certainty.

Recognizing Chaos: The Complex Web of Reality

The certainty of modernity has created a host of rigid dichotomies that affect the educational research act and educational practice: objective reality and subjective experience, fact and imagination, truth and opinion, neutrality and partisanship, logic and emotion, secular and sacred, and public and private. The cause–effect linearity of modernist positivism, with its emphasis on decontextualized problem-solving, sets the agenda for what we consider important about the educational process. From the perspective of Ilya Prigogine, the 1977 Nobel Prize winner in chemistry and proponent of postmodernist chaos theory, such linearity not only determines what we consider important about the world but distorts our view of the world in the process. Prigogine argues that unstable dissipative structures are far more common than structures that are stable. Such structures are highly complex wholes that emerge spontaneously in relation to their environmental context (Prigogine and Stengers, 1984; Capra, 1996). The recognition of these unstable dissipative structures is a major step in the human attempt to make sense of the physical and social world. We need to move beyond both modernity's simplistic linearity and its yearning for certainty and adopt more sophisticated tools of analysis.

A postmodern mode of analysis assumes that the world is complex, characterized by a web-like configuration of interacting forces. Scientists, like everyone else, are inside, not outside, the web. As we realized in

Chapter 3, the knower and the known are inseparable — they are both a part of the web of reality. No one in this web-like configuration of the universe can achieve a God-like perspective — no one can totally escape the web and look back at it from afar. We all must confess our subjectivity; we must recognize our limited vantage points. To recognize how our particular view of the web shapes our conception of educational reality, we need to understand our historicity (our place in space and time). Cause–effect educational research tends to ignore the way our historicity works to construct our consciousness; as a result, our concept of social activity and of the educational process is reduced to a static frame. Thus, the positivistic researcher feels empowered to make predictions, to settle questions, to ignore the dialectical process in which all social activity is grounded. From this perspective linear mathematics controls the variables, eliminates extraneous perturbations, and paints a Norman Rockwell portrait of the schoolhouse (Doll, 1989; Slaughter, 1989; Kincheloe, 2001; Raven and Stephenson, 2001).

Prigogine and postmodern analysts realize that such simplicity does not work. A so-called 'extraneous perturbation' falling into the complex interactions we have referred to as the web of reality, can produce an expanding, exponential effect. Inconsequential entities can have a profound effect in a non-linear universe. The shape of the physical and social world depends of the smallest part. The part in a sense is the whole, for via the action of any particular part, the whole in the form of transformative change may be seen. To exclude such considerations is to miss the nature of the interactions which constitute reality. The development of a postmodern, counter-Cartesian mode of educational research does not mean that we simplistically reject all empirical science — obviously there are questions in education which involve counting, figuring percentages, averages, correlations, and so on.

It does mean, however, that we conceive of such empirical questions as one part of the web, that is, the interactive configuration. A counter-Cartesian, complex rethinking of educational research means recognizing, as Dewey did, as feminist epistemology does, that the knower and the known are intimately connected, that a science which separates fact from value, purpose, and belief is a pseudo-science divorced from the *Lebenswelt*, the lived world of human consciousness. Such a reconceptualization reminds us as teacher researchers that we can display our findings and argue for their value, but always with one hesitation, a stutter, a tentativeness — never as the truth (Besag, 1986b; Briggs and Peat, 1989; Doll, 1989; O'Sullivan, 1999).

'So what?' many teachers interested in action research may ask, 'We just want to learn the five steps to classroom research,' they argue. Why all this talk about the postmodernist response to the quest for certainty? As with the other themes of this book, the reason that such explorations are important involves the way they shape our professional consciousness.

The models of teaching we are taught, the definitions of research which support our inquiry, the angles from which we view intelligence, the modes of learning which shape the way we think, all emerge from the certainty of modernism. And these dynamics take on a special importance when we realize that ways of seeing that come from particular social/political locations can create situations where individuals coming from different social/cultural/political locations are consistently harmed. Like reality itself, schools and classrooms are complex webs of interactions, codes, and signifiers in which both teachers and students are interlaced. Just as postmodernism asserts that there is no single, privileged way to see the world, there is no one way of seeing the classroom, seeing intelligence, seeing teacher or pupil success.

What's the Value of Research That Can't Produce Certainty?

Once teachers escape the entrapment of the positivistic way of seeing, they come to value and thus pursue new frames of reference in regard to their students, their classrooms, their workplaces. They begin to look at their lessons from the perspective of their students — their black students, their Latino students, their white students, their poor students, their middle- and upper-middle-class students, their traditionally successful students, their unsuccessful students. They examine their teaching from the vantage points of their colleagues or an outside lay observer from the community. Thus, they step out of their teacher bodies, looking down on themselves and their students as outsiders. As they hover above themselves they examine their teacher education with its emphasis on bulletin board construction, standards-test drill and recitation, behavioral objective writing, discussion skill development, and classroom management. They begin to see that such professional training reflects the certainty of modernity, as it assumes that professional actions are reducible to a set of skills applicable to all situations (Nixon, 1981; Benson, Glasberg, and Griffith, 1998).

But if science can't be certain, and if we come to realize that our particular location in the web influences what we see, how then can educational research be of any value? Many teachers become quite anxious upon such realizations and without reflection assert that research is a waste of time, capable only of yielding opinion. They have been educated in a culture of positivism which teaches that knowledge is universally applicable, always superior to the 'softness' of opinion. Critical qualitative researchers, of course, try to alleviate teacher anxiety with the observation that even though their educational inquiry has value dimensions, even though it is not absolute, it can be helpful. Critical action research, for example, can be viewed as a postmodern science of becoming. Certainty and prediction can be replaced with a notion of anticipation — the imaginative construction of the possible. Prediction is predicated on a positivistic body of empirical data and cause–effect relationships; anticipation takes empirical data into account but then moves into another dimension of the imagination. The quest for control of educational phenomena is abandoned, as is the search for a precise reflection of educational reality. Postmodern research is always tentative. It is nothing more than a temporary perspective on a particular segment of the educational world, concerned with the humble process of anticipation with all of its attendant qualifications (Lincoln and Guba, 1985; Noblit, 1985, 1999; Clough, 1998; Denzin and Lincoln, 2000).

When teachers as researchers gain the analytical ability to transcend this positivistic certainty, they begin to remake their world of practice in a way which reveals the deep structures which have determined their professional lives. Here again the notion of critical constructivism reenters our analysis, as teacher researchers gain what can be labeled reflexive awareness. Those trapped in the culture of positivism may find this reflection insignificant. The critical constructivist teacher researcher, however, uses this process to escape dominant power-inscribed constructions in order to see the ways our perception is constructed through linguistic codes, cultural signs, and embedded ideologies. This move constitutes a giant step in learning to research, to teach, indeed, to think. We are required to construct our perception of the world anew, not just in a random way but in a manner which questions what appears natural, which opens to question that which seems real.

We ask questions of how that which is came to be, whose interests do particular institutional arrangements serve, and from where do our own frames of reference come. In other words, we are engaging in a critical (re)construction of the world and our relation to it. In an educational context practitioners can, via their action research, critically construct, that is, remake, their professional lives around the asking and answering of such questions. Facts are no longer simply 'what they are'; the truth of beliefs is not simply testable by its correspondence to these facts. Professional knowledge does not rest on the foundation of the empirically proven. To engage in critical action research is to take part in a process of world-making. To remake, to rename our world we seek guidance from our system of meaning, our emancipatory, democratic source of authority (Schön, 1987; Slaughter, 1989; Pinar, 1994; Sumara, 1996; Hinchey, 1998).

Critical constructivist researchers will face many challenges as they pursue their research and pedagogy. Positivists will confront them with Cartesian–Newtonian-like generalizations about the act of teaching. The correlations that emerge from such positivistic research do not negate our critical system of meaning — human action is constructed not caused (Donmoyer, 1990b). For example, if scientists 'prove' via statistical techniques that one particular action results in one particular outcome, such a form of knowledge does not invalidate the larger principles, the ethical precepts which guide our actions. Educational researchers, for instance, determine a statistical correlation between ability grouping and the improvement of standardized test score averages in a set of schools. Are we to infer from this that ability grouping is a scientifically proven, effective educational technique? The answer is no, because of several issues of interpretation, ethics, and justice which emerge from our democratic system of meaning. Are standardized test score improvements valid indicators of student progress? What segments of the student population improved their test scores? The worst students? The average students? The best students? What strategies did teachers use to improve the scores? Did socio-economic class play a role in the way the ability groups were divided? We begin to see in this context that critical constructivist modes of teacher research valuing complexity possess a value that positivist research lacks — the capacity to ask sophisticated questions of meaning.

Thus, the way we interpret such a study depends on the way we construct our system of meaning. The empirical data derived from the study are not simple irrefutable facts — they do not constitute certainty. They represent hidden assumptions — assumptions the critical action researcher must dig out and expose to the light of day. Ability grouping, therefore, is not necessarily the proven way to bring about educational improvement. As Einstein and Heisenberg pointed out long ago, what we see is not what we see but what we perceive. The knowledge that the world yields has to be interpreted by men and women who are a part of that world. What we call information always involves an act of human judgment (Besag, 1986b). In the case of ability grouping, our perception of the proof of its success is quite dependent on what part of the web of reality in which we are entangled: From whose perspective do we see the effects of ability grouping? What constitutes an educational improvement? Are there facets of schooling that might be more important than fact accumulation? What happens to students placed in low ability groups? Such questions do not show up in many empirical studies. Without a critically constructed system of meaning, they will remain unasked.

Bidding Certainty Adieu: Research as a Cognitive Act

The quest for certainty, action research, and the way we think are intricately entwined. It might help us visualize our notion of a critical constructivist form of research if we look at it as the highest of three levels of research cognition: Level 1, puzzle-solving research; Level 2, self-monitoring, reflective research; Level 3, critical constructivist research.

First-level research revolves around the concept that puzzles are well-structured problems. All aspects necessary for a solution to a puzzle are knowable and there is a particular procedure for solving it. The role of the researcher is to learn this procedure and then to go about solving puzzles.

Educational problems, thus, are viewed as puzzles for which particular solutions may be inductively agreed upon after researchers have all been exposed to a common set of empirical observations. Certainty is deemed possible because puzzles push researchers into one way of thinking — a correct pathway to a solution exists, the goal of the research act is to find it. Research as puzzle-solving does not require the consideration of alternative strategies; such a view of research often blinds the inquirer to information which does not ostensibly relate to the solution of the puzzle. The attempt to verify or refute existing educational theories is a form of puzzle-solving — the rules are all established *a priori*. Indeed, puzzle-solving as a mode of research has little to do with the everyday world of schooling because educational decision-making rarely presents itself in the form of puzzles. It is far more complex.

Level 2 research involves a form of meta-cognition where researchers reflect on their Level 1 research activities. Such reflection may involve the identification of mistakes and the analysis of alternative strategies and data-gathering tools in the attempt to solve the puzzle. New variables may be found which make the research process more sophisticated, new forms of research which provide unique perspectives on the puzzle may be applied. The third level of research draws upon our notion of critical constructivism as it opens the door to epistemological considerations. Here, researchers examine the criteria of knowing, and the certainty of knowing, asking questions about the nature of problems themselves. An important difference between the levels of research cognition involves the Level 2 analysis of the problem-solving potential of a particular research strategy and the Level 3 questioning of whether or not particular research questions allow for a solution we know for certain to be correct.

Most research in educational situations involves ill-structured problems. Puzzles and ill-structured problems are different epistemologically, that is, in the ways they can be known. To argue that the act of teaching is a puzzle problem is to trivialize its multi-dimensional complexity. Cartesian teacher education too often treats it as such.

Differences in these epistemological assumptions become very important when teacher researchers begin to consider the types of questions they want to ask about their teaching. Here again we turn to our system of meaning to help us select our questions. We critically construct our epistemological compass which guides us through the morass of research convention and its Level 1 and Level 2 assumptions about the existence of an objective reality, a puzzle-filled universe that is absolutely knowable and known. Level 3 teacher research with its postmodern rejection of certainty transcends the conventional view of inquiry which accepts the universal applicability of the educational knowledge base. There is a correct way, conventionalists assume, to set up a fifth grade math class. The empirical research base does not support diverse ways of teaching this subject at this level; they are not just different, they are incorrect.

Each level of research is necessary to the understanding of the. Indeed, there are puzzle-like questions in education that lend themselves to empirical analysis. A form of meta-cognition is undoubtedly valuable to increasing the sophistication of such empirical questions. But such forms of research cognition do researchers little good when we begin to look at ill-defined questions such as 'What is the relationship between school performance and social class?' and 'How do definitions of intelligence affect that relationship?' To approach the problem, researchers must gather empirical evidence about school performance and its relationship to social class. Also important is empirical data on the ways that intelligence tends to be defined by particular groups. The gathering of such information is a Level 1 research activity. In the process of finding such evidence, researchers may gain a meta-awareness of problems in their samples and of better ways of understanding the complexity of the various relationships. To make sense of the data acquired we must move to a Level 3, critical constructivist form of research. Here we draw upon our critical sense of meaning to understand the significance of the evidence collected. What do we ask of it? For what purposes might we put it to use? Now that we understand certain aspects of the relationships between school performance, social class, and definitions of intelligence, what might we do in schools that we are not now doing? Our data seem to tell us that social class background influences students' perceptions of what role schools are supposed to play in their lives. Students from lower socio-economic class homes not only tend to make lower grades but hold different definitions of school success from middle- and upper-middle-class students. We have discovered that the definitions of intelligence used by school leaders better match the middle- and upper-middle-class students' definitions of intelligence than they do lower socio-economic class students.

With this information in hand, what do we do? We may seek to engage teachers in a dialogue about how different socio-economic groups come to define intelligence and what we as teachers have to learn from such conflicting definitions. In this process we have drawn on our critical system of meaning, which has reconceived the concept of justice, rendering it more than a legalistic notion. As a result, teachers may come to see intelligence in a context which enhances understanding of the inherent inability of educational psychologists and educational leaders to provide a universally applicable, certain answer to the question, 'What is intelligence?' What we define as intelligence often depends on where we are standing in the web of reality — from what socio-economic location? From what gender location? From what racial or ethnic location? Such analysis turns teachers' thoughts about intelligence inward, encouraging them to examine their own definitions and the impact such definitions make on the ways they approach students from different backgrounds. Such analysis induces teachers to consider how their approaches affect school performance of diverse students, their self-concepts, and their view of the role of schools in their lives. Thus, without this third level of analysis the research act ends before its meaning can be explored. This illustrates the power of a critical constructivist, complex, counter-Cartesian mode of practitioner research.

It is here at Level 3 that teacher researchers learn to think about their professional lives in a postformal way: What are the significant questions which come out of research data? What are the purposes of our professional lives? What does it mean to possess knowledge about educational activities? It is at Level 3 that we must consider the nature of the research problem and adopt a contextually appropriate type of thinking. In the example concerning school performance and socio-economic class, definitions of intelligence educational research as puzzle-solving are not very helpful. Although Level 1 and Level 2 questions are a part of our example and are certainly important, such questions hold implicit dimensions which might be examined at a critical constructivist level of research. These Level 3 questions yield unpredictable answers, often leading to higher stages of consciousness and awareness on the part of the researcher. At these higher stages of consciousness multiple answers of equal validity to research questions may coexist. By definition the higher state of consciousness which emerges from Level 3 analysis demands a loss of a certain degree of comfort and certainty (Kitchner, 1983; Altrichter and Posch, 1989; Slaughter, 1989; Lester, 2001).

Again referring to our example, we can never be sure of just what intelligence is. We can never rest comfortably with particular conceptions of school success. We can never assume that we hold a privileged perspective on such matters from outside the web of reality. We, too, are flies entangled in a particular part of the web. But if we are conscious of our position there is no reason for despair. We are human agents capable of much more than simply following rules to solve pre-defined problems. We are active interpreters and negotiators involved in an exciting process of cultural reconstruction and educational reconceptualization. If we hold the power to reconstruct our own consciousnesses, then we are capable of reinterpreting our traditions and reinventing our futures together in solidarity with other self-directed human agents.

Practitioner thinking, of course, is intricately connected to these levels of research cognition. The teacher researchers who operate at a critical constructivist level seem to be more tolerant, flexible, and adaptive, and employ a wider repertoire of teaching models. They tend to be more self-directed and better equipped to handle paradox, contradiction, and conceptual complexity. The teacher researcher operating at a critical constructivist level enters into a post-conventional world where certainty is sacrificed in the recognition of discrepancies between surface appearances and inner reality. Such a recognition allows a teacher researcher to use action inquiry as a vehicle to overcome bureaucratic definitions of his or her deskilled role in the workplace. Action research in this context transcends mere teacher monitoring of the implementation of administrative edicts; it involves the analysis of structural effects of schooling and the generation of new knowledge (Oja and Ham, 1984; Apple, 1999).

Level 3 teacher research adopts a progressive view of knowledge which assumes that even as data are being collected they are being subjected to critical analysis. A more positivistic view of knowledge assumes that only after one knows the facts is he or she ready to analyze. Such a view misses the important point that what we designate as the facts is an act of interpretation — in the case of positivistic research it is an unconscious act of interpretation (Ellis, 1998; Jardine, 1998; Smith, 1999; Mayers, 2001a, 2001b). Knowledge derived from research in a Level 3 critical constructivist orientation is not a static or inert entity — privileged groups with the authority to certify knowledge have often taken this viewpoint. Critical constructivist research proceeds tentatively, ever mindful of ambiguity and uncertainty. When we know for certain, little need exists to pursue alternative ways of knowing. 'Deviant ways of seeing' are dismissed as irrelevant — they are not viewed as an important source of new insight and socio-educational innovation (Romanish, 1986; Schön, 1987; Progler, 2001; Malewski, 2001a).

This view of research cognition in an interpretive context shaped by critical constructivism revolutionizes the way we view teaching and the education of teachers. The negative consequences of the quest for certainty are avoided, as teacher researchers and teacher educators begin to imagine and construct new ways of thinking about teaching and teacher education. If the act of teaching were known and constant, teachers could act on empirical generalizations and teacher educators would know exactly what teachers needed to know to perform successfully. But teaching is not constant and predictable — it always takes place in a microcosm of uncertainty. Teachers know, for example, that sure-fire teaching methods that worked last year may not work this year. Thus, what we call valuable practitioner knowledge is elusive. How to teach teachers what to do in conditions of uncertainty is even more elusive.

The positivism of professional schools of education in the early twentieth century used science to eliminate the uncertainty of professional practice and replace it with empirical knowledge about the teaching act. The cult of the expert in the educational sphere precluded an admission of uncertainty. The uniqueness of particular teaching situations was ignored by educational researchers/experts whose clients demanded official knowledge — a form of data which specified the scientifically-sanctioned 'right way' to proceed (Schön, 1987; Raven and Stephenson, 2001). In a culture which relies on the expert for guidance, uncertainty doesn't play well — indeed, the denial of complexity and the certainty this act makes possible are the accoutrements of strength, of positive, affirmative leadership. The higher our levels of research cognition, the weaker our perspectives often appear to a culture which has been conditioned to buy into a quest for certainty. This cruel irony tends to impede the attempt to teach sophisticated, critical thinking and to retard the movement to put teachers into positions of control over their workplaces.

Chapter 8

Verifiability and the Concept of Rigor in Qualitative Research

Positivistic social sciences are concerned with developing verifiable knowledge. The logical positivists of the Vienna Circle developed the verifiability principle of meaning which contended that something is meaningful only if it is verified through the senses (empirically). The verifiability principle necessitates the use of operational definitions to specify that which is under study (Popkewitz, 1981b; Phillips, 1983). An operational definition assigns meaning to an entity by enumerating the activities (operations) necessary to its measurement. The operational definition serves as a manual of instructions for a researcher, granting him or her a list of activities necessary to the research process. Fred Kerlinger gives an example of an operational definition of intelligence: 'Intelligence . . . is scores on X intelligence test, or intelligence is what X intelligence test measures' (Kerlinger, 1973: 31).

Distinguishing Truth from Fiction in a Complex World

The positivistic impulse and the behaviorist research traditions merge with Thorndike's argument that anything which exists, exists in some amount and can thus be measured. Such an idea when applied to education focuses research on statistical analysis of quantified variables. If the objects of positivistic research in education can always be quantified, then anti-positivists argue that quantifiability becomes an essential precondition for that which is to be studied. Thus, given enough time the truth or falsity of the findings of educational research can be established — that is, data can ultimately be verified in a quantifiable manner (Macmillan and Garrison, 1984; Donmoyer, 1985; Lather, 1991).

Denis Phillips (1983) claims that the verifiability principle of the logical positivists died long ago, choked to death under its own weight. It was never clear about how to verify scientific principles — using its own criteria for meaning, a principle was not verifiable through the senses. Instead of criticizing and misrepresenting positivism, Phillips argues, eclecticists such as Eisner and Giroux should begin devising methods of verifying knowledge and separating fact from belief.

Phillips represents a host of social science and education researchers who express great discomfort with eclectic qualitative research. If what counts as knowledge, he asks, is always shaped by power, values, and interests and if objectivity is always socially agreed upon, what is left to protect us from relativism? If individuals can invent their microcosms, how can researchers distinguish truth from fiction? We have gone far enough, Phillips and his supporters argue. In our rejection of positivism we have thrown out the baby with the bathwater and in the process, they argue, we have done away with the concept of a mistake. The attempt to verify data is complicated by the post-Kuhnian (Thomas Kuhn wrote on the nature of paradigmatic change in 1962) proliferation of research strategies. Positivists are horrified by the breakdown of knowledge; anti-positivists are heartened by the possibility of new forms of understanding.

A breakdown of knowledge? No way of determining a mistake? You must be kidding, research eclecticists taunt their critics. Proponents of pluralistic methods contend that different research methods produce different perspectives, that different theories couch their observations in divergent terms, that different world views lead to different conclusions. Th result of these contentions, they assert, does not lead to the conclusion that there is no way of knowing when someone has made a mistake. Positivists want a single way to validate a statement. In many ways, the eclecticists argue, positivists are like religious fundamentalists in their belief that there is only one way to heaven. And that one way, my dear friends and true believers, is the straight and narrow path of positivist validation (Eisner, 1983; Phillips, 1983; Smith, 1983; Carspecken, 1996, 1999).

Those of us who hold the validity of a variety of ways of approaching reality, eclecticists contend, have not abandoned rationality — logocentrism, yes, rationality, no. We must be aware of alternative paradigms and develop rational methods of selecting one as we contemplate our research. If empirical evidence, for example, is not appropriate for assessing the worth of information, then some other basis for validation or some critical reconceptualization of the notion of validation must be developed. Generally, researchers in education have not considered the question of alternative paradigms and the rational search for alternative methods of validation. Often educational researchers have found themselves unable to see beyond empirical validation of their research data. Mistakes are determined via empirical methods or not at all.

Transcending Positivist Methods of Validation: Analyzing Mistakes

In the attempt to transcend empirical methods of validation, researchers need guidance. One of the best ways to initiate thinking about a reconceptualization, a redefinition of validation might involve discussion of different orders of mistakes. First-order mistakes result when evidence cannot support conclusions that are arrived at through the use of a particular language. Examples of such mistakes would involve problems of researchers concerned with traditional experimental and correlational design, for example, inappropriate generalization and inadequate sample size. Second-order mistakes come about when language employed to state propositions is inappropriate for particular purposes. A good example of such a mistake would be Newtonian physics, as its language is inadequate when we travel at the speed of light. Third-order mistakes involve the inadequacy of the purposes of the research. An example of a concern with third-order mistakes is Henry Giroux's, Patti Lather's, and Gaile Cannella's critique of mainstream educational research. These critiques are not primarily concerned with methodology or language; their focus is on questions of overall purpose. The analysis of third-order mistakes helps researchers choose between competing paradigms (Eisner, 1983; Capra, 1996; O'Sullivan, 1999). Such orders of mistakes are similar to our concept of the levels of research cognition.

Positivists argue that the only way to avoid mistakes is through the application of a rigorous research methodology, that is, one that follows a strict set of objective procedures which separate the researcher from that being researched. In order to be meaningful, the argument goes, social inquiry must be rigorous. Indeed, positivists see the pursuit of rigor as the most effective means to validation. The basis of rigorous research is, of course, quantification. Unambiguous and precise, rigorous quantitative research reduces subjective influences and minimizes the ways in which information might be interpreted. It keeps humans and the distortions of their biased perspectives at bay.

Positivists have traditionally preferred quantitative to qualitative data because of the search for methodological rigor and thus freedom from the distortion of human subjectivity. Among most social science researchers quantitative research might at first glance appear to be a superior means to approach validation. Let us follow an argument presented by Kenneth R. Howe which raises some questions about this assumption.

'Mrs. Johnson's class contains 29 students' is an example of an observation sentence in which the data are low in fallibility. The phrase, low fallibility, means that there will be a high degree of agreement as to the accuracy of the data by observers regardless of their world views and backgrounds.

'Mrs. Johnson's class was more valuable than most middle school classes in that students, through Mrs. Johnson's assistance, began to understand their own personal histories and in the process made an important step toward self-direction.' Here the data are quite distanced from simple observation statements and have high fallibility, meaning that intersubjective agreement as to their accuracy will be low. Thus, it has been often stated that quantitative data are superior to qualitative data relative to the criterion of fallibility. Howe argues that this judgment cannot be generalized and just the opposite ordering of fallibility is often the case in social and educational research.

To prove his point, Howe offers the example of the testing of a research instrument designed to evaluate attitudes. Of course, the basic aim of such a research instrument is to gather quantitative data about attitudes. Experience teaches us over and over again that measurements of attitude are affected by problems of interpretation. These interpretive problems are often so severe that the validity of the data obtained from the instrument is questionable. Different researchers and respondents will assign different meanings to an instrument's questions because of the imprecision and multivocality of language. Different respondents will employ different criteria for marking the intensity of a response on a graduated scale: 1 strongly agree, 2 agree, 3 no opinion, 4 disagree, 5 strongly agree. Differing researchers will produce conflicting assessments of both the meaning of the respondents' replies and the social forces shaping them. It is not difficult to discern that such research tends to be highly fallible. At the very least, certainty is elusive.

Wishing It Were So: The Positivists' Faith in the Infallibility of Their Validation Procedures

The only way to lessen the fallibility, Howe argues, is to induce respondents to discuss the instrument. Researchers must ask for and listen to the opinions of the respondents about the meaning of their responses and how the instrument might be interpreted. Such opinions are, of course, qualitative data and are very distanced from simple observation statements. But this subjective data is being used in this case to reduce the fallibility of the quantitative data collected. Thus, in this situation the qualitative method is less fallible than the quantitative method (Howe, 1985).

Validation is thus rendered more problematic than many quantitative-empirical researchers would prefer. There is less certainty and more fallibility in survey data-gathering, correlational studies, and control treatment experiments than educational researchers would like to admit. Many philosophers of educational research wince when Fred Kerlinger (1973) argues that research methods are procedures on which beliefs have no effects. Techniques of inquiry, he maintains, are skills which exist independent of the predispositions, politics, and commitments of those people who do research.

Many philosophers of research not only doubt Kerlinger's protestations about the possibility of objectivity, but they even doubt that empirical researchers themselves really follow the rigorous methodological steps advocated by researchers like Kerlinger in their everyday research practices. Actual research, they argue, is often quite different from the so-called reconstructed logics that writers of textbooks on educational research espouse. Real-life field researchers use what is termed logic-in-use, which refers to the reasonable, flexible, and expedient means often employed when undertaking a project. The logic-in-use research process is often a capricious journey with side trips and lots of dead-end streets. These detours, however, are usually omitted when it comes time to write up and justify research findings. The intuitive leaps, the thinking which gave birth to the research question, the values which moved the researcher to pursue a particular question are usually not included in the reconstructed logics of educational research. The final reports, many analysts would argue, are idealized versions of what researchers believe pure scientific method and the most rational form of research should be (Donmoyer, 1985; Howe, 1985).

The Relationship between Validity and Significance: Variables in a Complex World

Research eclecticists do not want the search for empirical validation, methodological rigor, or data infallibility to sabotage the search for significance. To be rigorous in the positivistic sense is one thing; to focus on significant issues is something else. If the rigorous method is not suited to the subject matter, it contributes little to understanding. Methodology should not be criticized as ambiguous and vague, if the problems to which it is applied are ambiguous and vague. And this is the condition of educational research. The problems of the educational world are complex, not given to simple description, and rarely reducible to only a few variables. A research orientation's inability to produce infallible research outcomes is not a mark of failure. Such a complication reflects the inherent properties of the reality under scrutiny and the types of complex questions that the students of the discipline ask about the meaning of that complex reality (Kerlinger, 1973; Soltis, 1984; Steinberg and Kincheloe, 1998).

Consider the question of the control of variables in this context. Take, for example, the hundreds of studies conducted on classroom discipline in the past thirty years. In addition to problems of sample size, of the relationship between what is defined as good discipline and desirable educational achievements, and of cause and effect, the control of variables in discipline research presents special difficulties. Literally thousands of unmentioned factors have a significant influence on what happens in any classroom (Barrow, 1984; Shweder and Fiske, 1986; Arney, 2000). One student may respond to a specific teacher's disciplinary action in one manner, not because of the disciplinary action itself, but because he or she is accustomed to a certain type of disciplinary action at home. A Native American child, for example, raised in a permissive home may interpret a subtle, mildly coercive, non-corporal disciplinary act very differently from a black child raised in a strict home where the rod is not spared. To the

American Indian child, the disciplinary action is understandable and consistent with prior experience; to the black child it is a sign of the teacher's weakness.

Another child reacts differently to the subtle, mildly coercive disciplinary act because of the nature of his or her relationship with the teacher. A student whose parents are long-time acquaintances of the teacher, knows the teacher as a trusted friend. When confronted with corrective action of any kind, this student may feel very embarrassed because he or she is unaccustomed to conflict in his or her relationship with the teacher. What appears to the researcher as a mild admonishment elicits a great deal of embarrassment from the student. Another student is affected by the presence of an outside observer and reacts in a way that is inconsistent with prior behavior. There is no way that the observer can account for all of the possible variables affecting what is being observed (Barrow, 1984).

The various facets of a student's or a teacher's nature, of every individual's background, of every context, and of all the interrelationships and combinations of these factors, may be the key elements in helping explain what is going on in a classroom. The point is that the uniqueness of the combination of the factors may constitute the explanation for what is happening in Mr. King's tenth grade English class on March 30, 2005; if it is unique, then it cannot be used as a basis for generalization. If variables cannot be controlled, data certainly cannot be validated in any empirical sense.

Egan's Illustration of Analytic and Arbitrary Validation

Much research on teaching is validated, non-positivists argue, only by means of the analytic and the arbitrary. The analytic means of validation involves that which is true by definition; the arbitrary is that which is significant only in the particular case, and thus is arbitrary, not a constant which lends itself to generalization (Barrow, 1984). Kieran Egan illustrates the analytic and the arbitrary methods of validation using a couple of examples. He writes of a hypothesis set up for empirical validation: lists of facts presented in an ordered way are easier to learn than facts presented in an unordered way. The task of the empirical researcher is to validate or not validate this hypothesis.

Couched within the hypothesis, however, is an analytic element, that is, something that by necessity is already true. It is already true that a body of facts that is ordered in some manner is easier to learn than one which is not, because of the conceptual relationship between *learning* and *order*. It is a logical impossibility to learn a list of facts which possesses no pattern or order. The process of learning imposes an order on the list. Understanding, a corollary of learning, involves the shaping of that which is learned. Even rote learning involves the imposition of pattern, even if the pattern is only based on sound. One does not need to formulate an empirical study to discover that. Yet, study after educational study seeks to validate hypotheses such as the more time on task a student spends, the more he or she learns. Why bother?

Following Egan's examples, the important questions thus become: What do we mean by ordering? When does something become ordered? What types of ordering facilitate the learning process? Obviously, different configurations of facts may appear ordered to different people. Bob looks at a list of apparently random numbers; Martha looks at them and sees her telephone number. This is where Egan's conception of arbitrary validation appears. Empirical research finds that some children learn some lists better than others and vice versa. Researchers give some children ordered lists and others unordered lists, but, as we already understand, all learned lists are ordered in some way. Different children's learning of lists has to do with their divergent conceptions of what is and is not ordered.

The child who can learn list A more easily than list B apparently sees more order in list A than in list B. Empirical researchers have often missed this point as they observe the child. The investigators impute an ability of the child to learn an unordered list — it is a list unordered from the *researcher's* perspective. In other words, the child saw order where the researcher did not. There is nothing to be validated or generalized from such research. If researchers find that certain factual arrangements enhance student learning in one specific context in one specific study, it does not follow that another student will experience similar learning enhancement. His or her perception of order may be quite different.

Validating Correlations between Teaching Style and Student Performance

Another example of the problematic nature of empirical validation of research on teaching involves inquiries into the relationship connecting teaching style and student performance. Typically, researchers attempt to validate relationships between so-called styles of teaching and standardized test score improvement. In addition to questions such as the control of important variables and the reliability of standardized tests, the question of the validity of the categorization of teaching styles emerges. Critical researchers make the argument that the attempt to reduce teaching styles to, say, two or three categories is futile. In practice no teacher will clearly represent one category. In other words, no teacher will display only the characteristics of a formal teacher as opposed to an informal teacher. All teachers to some extent are formal in some regards and informal in others. When disagreements over the characteristics of the different styles appear, the validity of the categories is called into further question.

When observers classify the same teacher differently, the conclusions drawn from the data will, of course, be significantly affected. In order to manage the data of such studies, teaching styles must be reduced to a minimal number of categories. While it may be profitable to classify cars or hats in terms of styles, it is probably unwise to classify loving or teaching in such a manner — especially when we feel the necessity to lay out only two or three types. Empirical validation in such contexts is a pipe dream, logically impossible because of the complexity of the reality of human experience (Barrow, 1984).

Where does all of this leave validation? We must reconstruct our thinking about the meaning and applicability of the concept of validation in the context of educational research, eclecticists argue. Our goal in research is not merely to validate the statistical relationship of variables, but to understand, to make intelligible, and to preserve the cohesiveness of the phenomena being studied. This process may better be accomplished by portraying patterns rather than by discovering causes. As a result, a researcher may be more concerned with choosing a language where signification and the concern with meaning take precedence over statistical significance. Indeed, eclecticists may be more concerned with unique events than with repetitive ones that allow researchers to manipulate quantifiable variables. Proponents of research pluralism are less concerned with reducing the world to quantifiable atomistic parts than with the attempt to create a social synthesis which leads to a new level of understanding.

The level of understanding that can be obtained is limited only by the vision of the researcher (Frankel, 1986). Before we can reach those new levels of understanding, before we can attain Level 3 critical constructivist research cognition, we must reconceptualize the notion of verifiability. In the process of this rethinking we might draw insight from the limitations of the traditional positivistic definitions of verifiability. We have already discussed how setting influences human behavior. The 'place' (Kincheloe and Pinar, 1991) in which social activity, consciousness construction, and schooling occurs cannot be dismissed by the inquirer. When researchers attempt to remove human activity from its place, its natural setting, serious consequences result. Positivist researchers often set up contrived settings, typically laboratory situations. Such researchers frequently possess similar assumptions, ask similar questions, and look for similar outcome measurements. Is it surprising that such settings are perceived to generate regularities in individual behavior — regularities which form the basis for verified generalizations (Wilson, 1977)?

Validation and Significance in the Lived World

Such a system of verification, of truth claim for research findings, tells us little about how the world works, how consciousness is constructed, how schools operate. A process of verification conducted in a non-naturalistic, artificial venue attends only to particular, measurable, isolated variables. Such variables are sometimes so isolated, so insignificant in light of the multitude of other variables not explored, that the results of the inquiry are irrelevant. The validity claims of such research are, to say the least, questionable. Positivistic laboratory researchers present verified knowledge about how a particular technique produces success in teaching; understanding their process of verification, we may hold justifiable skepticism that such a technique will prove successful in a real school, in the everyday classroom that teachers inhabit. Remove this concept for a moment from the educational world and think of it in a zoological context. Ethnologists have written of similar insights into research on animals. Research conducted in animal labs or zoos produces data on wildlife that has little to do with how they behave in natural settings. Zoos, labs, and questionnaires in a sense become unique settings in their own right with their own dynamics and peculiar forces which help mold behavior (Wilson, 1977; Orteza Y Miranda, 1988; Kincheloe, 2001).

Positivistic researchers in their search for verifiable data fail to recognize that their controlled situations take on this Frankenstein life of their own. Such blindness precludes understanding of the often hidden processes by which settings shape behavior. Both the physical arrangements of the settings and the subjects' internalized expectations of what is allowable generate forces which fashion research findings. In natural settings such as schools participant behavior cannot be understood without careful attention to the participant's relationship to the traditions, norms, roles, and values which are inseparable from the lived world of the institutions. The inability of positivistic researchers to say very much that is meaningful about school life is due in part to their lack of regard for these often invisible, but foundational aspects of organizational life. Research removed from the natural setting cannot account for such aspects of organizational life because they are not present in the contrived laboratory situation — hence, the truth value of the knowledge produced is undermined (Wilson, 1977; Eisner, 1984; Carspecken, 1999; Paley and Jipson, 2000).

The Critical Qualitative Reworking of Validity

If the truth value of research is indeed undermined, positivistic researchers find themselves in a crisis of verification. Critical teacher research seeks a way out of this crisis; the way out involves our attempt to reconceptualize the notion of verifiability. One place to start is to distinguish traditional positivistic verifiability from a more critical, qualitative perspective. As we have already argued, traditional positivistic verifiability is rational, based on a mathematical set of assumptions; we might conceive of the critical, qualitative orientation in a more emotionally empathetic, artistic frame. Where positivistic verifiability rests on a rational proof built upon literal, intended meaning, a critical qualitative perspective always involves a less certain approach characterized by participant reflection and emotional involvement. With these general statements in mind, the central question emerges: How do we judge the quality of inquiry carried out by critical teacher researchers (Reinharz, 1979; Lincoln and Guba, 1985)?

The question is complex — validity is probably an inappropriate word in the non-positivistic context. We need to move beyond the attempt to develop critical qualitative research criteria that parallel those of the positivist paradigm. Qualitative researchers have sometimes failed to move research to a higher level of cognition when they have allowed the positivistic tradition to dictate their vocabulary, their grammar, and their criteria for research quality. To a critical constructivist teacher researcher, validity means much more than the traditional definitions of internal and external validity usually associated with the concept. Positivism has traditionally defined internal validity as the extent to which a researcher's observations and measurements are true descriptions of a particular reality; external validity has been defined as the degree to which such descriptions can be accurately compared to other groups. Is trustworthiness a more appropriate word to use in a critical constructivist research lexicon? Maybe such a word is helpful because it connotes and signifies a different set of assumptions about research purposes than does the term 'validity.' Let us consider what criteria might be used to assess the trustworthiness of critical constructivist teacher research.

Credibility of Portrayals of Constructed Realities

Critical teacher researchers reject the positivistic notion of internal validity which is based on the assumption that a tangible, knowable reality exists and research descriptions accurately portray that reality. Our reconceptualization of validity discards the concept of internal validity, replacing it with the notion of credibility of the researcher's portrayals of constructed realities. Such a category recognizes the complex postmodern concept that the world is not explicable in terms of simplistic cause–effect relationships.

The universe can be viewed from multiple perspectives which are constructions of the human mind. There is no absolute benchmark to which we can turn for certainty and comfort — we award credibility only when the constructions are plausible to those who constructed them. And even then there may be disagreement, for the researcher may see ideological distortions in the constructions of those researched — distortions which those researched may not see themselves. Indeed, the researched may argue that the word 'distortion' is entirely inappropriate when applied to them. Thus, no scale can measure the trustworthiness of critical constructivist research, no TQ ('trustworthiness quotient') can be developed.

Critical constructivist researchers reject the positivistic notion of external validity. The ability to apply pristine generalizations from one research study to another accepts a one-dimensional, cause–effect universe. In a positivistic context all that is needed to ensure transferability is to understand with a high level of internal validity something about a particular classroom and to know that the make-up of this classroom is representative of another classroom to which the generalization is being applied. The positivist would argue that the generalization derived from the first classroom is valid in all classrooms within that same population. Time or context factors are irrelevant in the positivistic context. Many qualitative researchers have argued that the positivistic concept of external validity is far too simplistic. Such researchers assert that if generalizations are to be made, if we are to be able to apply findings in context A to context B, we must make sure that the contexts being compared are empirically similar.

This is an important step (it moves us from Level 1 puzzle-solving to Level 2 reflective research cognition) for it alerts us to the misleading nature of what passes for positivistic, nomothetic (inquiry concerned with producing universal laws) generalization. But another step, maybe a leap, is necessary. Our notion of transferability of research findings from one context to another is still quite constricted by this Level 2 qualitative perspective. If we accept a Piagetian notion of cognitive constructivism, we begin to see that in everyday situations humans don't make generalizations in this positivistic way. Piaget's notion of accommodation seems appropriate in this context, as it asserts that humans reshape cognitive structures to accommodate unique aspects of what is being perceived in new contexts. In other words, through our knowledge of a variety of comparable contexts we begin to understand their similarities and differences — we learn from our comparisons of different contexts. Prediction, the goal of both Level 1 and Level 2 research, is not the desired outcome, that is, anticipatory accommodation. We will explore this concept (this criterion) in more detail later in this chapter when we analyze the nature of generalizability. With these two criteria of trustworthiness we begin our reconceptualization of validity at a critical constructivist level.

Validity in Practitioner Research: Deconstructing Generalizability

Positivists may argue that our reconceptualization of validity is little more than an attempt to destroy our ability to truly know anything. Expressed in such language, the charge may be true. But just because we may not be able to *truly* know anything (i.e., to know with certainty), this does not mean that we can't pursue knowledge and judge the quality of our pursuit within certain limits — limits that are a product of our theoretical base, our prior assumptions. From a critical action research perspective traditional efforts to achieve validated knowledge insofar as they seek to establish distance between the researcher and that which is researched actually impede our understanding and insight.

We *can* pursue knowledge by promoting a closeness between researcher and researched — a closeness based on a lengthy interaction which explores the etymology of the phenomenon and seeks to discover relationships between its history and present context. As we cultivate this closeness we make use of our most powerful ways of knowing — our subjectivities and intuitions. We use our images and symbols to help explain the phenomenon we have grown to know so intimately. Our intuition is more than an occasional flash of insight; it is a tool which allows us to see the forest, the trees, and the wood and the simultaneous, multidimensional relationships among them. Research which promotes such insight, which can be used to improve our practice, is of a higher quality than that which holds internal and external validity but tells us little that we didn't already know or could use in our professional lives.

The concept of generalizability provides a key to our attempt to redefine verifiability. If critical teacher researchers can derive insight into one educational context from the analysis of another, they have made an important start in their attempt to understand what reconceptualized verifiability might mean. The restricted concept of positivistic generalizability is inappropriate for the critical educational action researcher. Practitioner fields such as teaching, counselling, and social work are concerned with individuals, not aggregates, and as a result do not need empirically verified knowledge in the same way that a chemist would need it. Verified, statistically significant information from studies with large randomly selected samples, Robert Donmoyer (1990a) writes, says little to particular individuals in particular situations. Teacher researchers thinking in terms of critical constructivism with its anticipatory accommodation will always have to decide whether a research generalization is relevant to a particular student. They will have to decide whether the generalization needs to be fine tuned to accommodate the student's uniqueness, or whether the generalization is irrelevant to certain students in certain classrooms. Critical constructivist teacher researchers realize that verified generalizations can never tell teachers what to do; but research on teaching can help teachers raise questions and consider possibilities.

It is at this point that we can clearly see the value of action research, as it forces us as teachers to reconsider the notion of verifiability. It induces us to think about what knowledge in one context says to us about another situation. This concept of transferability involves more than a simple thought process. As critical teacher researchers we constantly confront the issue of the trustworthiness of our action research. What does it tell us about other situations in our own professional lives or in other teachers' professional lives? Does it help us expand our repertoire of social constructions and the complexity of our understanding of them? Does it help us accommodate new situations in our attempt to make sense of our professional microcosm? The value of critical action research begins to become apparent: in the spirit of critical constructivism it helps us formulate questions rather than providing answers to previously constructed puzzles.

Thus, the notion of external validity is transcended; the way we compare our action research to other groups is more in terms of a heuristic (a means of furthering investigation, questioning our practice) than in terms of mathematical probability. If we fail to reconsider the positivistic notion of external validity, teachers will continue to argue that research has little relevance for them, that researchers (those mysterious experts sitting in the ivory towers) hold a naïve and idealistic view of the real world of the classroom. Teachers intuitively know that classrooms with their many significant and peripheral variables, their complexity and chaos, are not good places to replicate (validate) research.

Such validation demands that the same conditions found in the original situation exist in the second situation — we can't cross the same river twice, teachers intuit. Consider what a naïve view of validation teacher researchers would hold if they, like positivist researchers, attempted to externally validate research in our classrooms. Teachers operating this way would attempt to teach a student to read using only validated general principles of reading pedagogy. Teacher spontaneity and creativity based on understandings of the unique experience of the student would be suppressed because it might not jibe with the generalized pedagogical principles (Lincoln and Guba, 1985; Orteza Y Miranda, 1988; Denzin and Lincoln, 2000).

To the positivist, generalizations are the *raison d'être* of research. All this talk about particularity (i.e., the unique experience of the learner) and anticipatory accommodation seems rather fatuous to the positivist who questions the worth of inquiry not seeking to validate generalizations. Our critical constructivist notion of anticipatory accommodation, of course, moves beyond a positivist concern with generalization. At the same time, however, it moves beyond a desire to know only the unique. We want to assimilate in the Piagetian sense — i.e., we want to understand the commonalities of particular categories. As we seek these commonalities we are searching in a way for valid generalizations. But assimilation without accommodation never moves beyond lower levels of research cognition — we must understand the unique, the particularistic aspects of our lived worlds, our classrooms, in order to make a difference in the lives of our students, to connect their particular experience to the world at large.

If we live in an instrumentally rational world of research for the purpose of prediction and control, our concern with the dialectic of particularity and generalization is certainly misguided. Uniqueness and particularity complicate the attempt to derive validated laws which can be applied to the effort to predict and thus control human behavior. The positivistic concept of validated generalizations reeks of determinism and totalitarian forms of government. Researchers become partners of the guardians, as they provide these lawgivers with the validated generalizations which make it unnecessary to consider the particulars of each case. What is good for one citizen is good for all — at least citizens in that particular classification or sampling. What is good for one student is good for all — at least students in that particular classification or sampling (Lincoln and Guba, 1985; Denzin and Lincoln, 2000). Orwellian images surround the positivistic view of validation.

If teachers take seriously the positivistic perspective toward the production and use of validated generalizations, they are rendered virtually helpless by unusual or unique situations. Teachers find themselves in much the same situation as Jack Nicholson did in the famous diner scene in *Five Easy Pieces*. The diner had devised a set of generalizations for all situations. When Nicholson placed a unique order, the waitress acting on the diner's established generalizations didn't know what to do. The particularity of Nicholson's unique order could not be *accommodated* by the 'positivistic' generalizations of the diner. In a bureaucratized world which operates on positivistic validated generalizations, we often face similar conflicts in everyday life.

Indeed, Burger King builds an entire advertising campaign around the concept of 'have it your way', meaning that they can perform the extraordinary feat of making a hamburger with pickles or without, with lettuce or without, and so on. This attention to particularity is so unusual in the contemporary era that it must be broadcast to all who will listen. Positivistic science has created a way of seeing which denies the researcher's and the researched's uniqueness to the point that they are replaceable and interchangeable with any other researcher or subject. Positivistic alienation conquers, depersonalization ensues.

Yes, Virginia, There Will Always Be a Jack Nicholson: Particularity, Generalization, and Validity

There will always be a Jack Nicholson requesting the unexpected, the chicken salad sandwich without the chicken salad; there will always be contingencies, fissures, disjunctions, and disruptions. But in the quest for certainty, the search for validated knowledge, researchers study groups of things, not single things (Reinharz, 1979; Lincoln and Guba, 1985; Kincheloe and Steinberg, 1993; Pinar, 1994). The essence of the particular is missed when it is treated as a sample of a species or a type — it is not itself, it is a representative. Viewed in this way the particularistic, the individualistic has no proper name; it is alienated and anonymous.

A child is interesting to the positivistic researcher only as he or she represents something other than himself or herself. A theory of place as a category of particularity fights this reductionist tendency of positivistic generalization, of external validation. Place is the entity which brings the particularistic into focus; a sense of place sharpens our understanding of the individual and the psychic and social forces which direct him or her. Without place our appreciation of such particularistic forces is ever fuzzy and depersonalized. Place with its attention to local conditions renders positivistic external validation impossible.

There are always differences in context from place to place, and even a single place differs over time (Kincheloe and Pinar, 1991). The notion of positivistic validation exerts a direct effect on our attempt to promote teachers as self-directed researchers. Teachers as researchers are taught to distrust the generalizability of their work. How could it be applicable to other situations when it is unscientific? It does not lend itself to statistical aggregation and thus falls short of the demands of external validity. Because such research falls short of the rigor of positivistic generalizability, teachers must turn to the authority of the traditional school hierarchy with its top-down flow of power.

The *status quo* is thus legitimized as teachers are unable to validate their own research — they must follow the edicts derived from 'truly' scientific studies of the experts. Expert research is replicable in the positivistic sense; the personal insight of anticipatory accommodation is not (Besag, 1986a; Elliott, 1989a). The culture of positivism exalts validation that is rationalistic, propositional, and law-like. The trustworthiness criterion, anticipatory accommodation, is suspect in the positivistic culture because its foundation rests upon intuition, direct experience, and vicarious experience. What good is an educational insight derived from anticipatory accommodation, positivists ask, when it represents merely a time- and context-bound working hypothesis? Give us validated facts, the positivists demand (Lincoln and Guba, 1985; Aronowitz, 1988, 1996; Giroux, 1997; Clough, 1998).

When we think of how we learn from experience, we realize the limitations of the positivist quest for validated generalizations. In this context diversity between settings becomes a liability, not an asset — the opposite should be the case. Critical constructivist researchers see diversity between settings as an opportunity for cognitive growth. Novelty of setting can sophisticate our research cognition, as it forces us to accommodate new situations. The teacher researcher, in the language of Piagetian schema theory, through accommodation begins to integrate his or her understanding of a concept to account for more and more diversity and to differentiate those understandings in a way that highlights distinctions in the meaning and application of the concept. A teacher researcher attempting to explore the meaning of intelligence, for example, would assimilate an understanding of the concept based on his or her experience.

The teacher would accommodate the concept as he or she began to examine students who were labeled unintelligent but upon a second look exhibited unconventional characteristics which were sophisticated nonetheless. The teacher would then integrate this recognition of exception (accommodation) into a broader definition of intelligence. The process of differentiation in this context would involve the teacher's ability to discover new kinds of intelligence among his or her students and to categorize these different forms of intelligence for future use. In a sense, this process of assimilating, accommodating, integrating, and differentiating is the operation that Howard Gardner (1983) followed in developing his theory of multiple intelligences. Such a process would not be constrained by a positivistic notion of verifiability, but would unleash the researcher's creative powers (Flavell, 1977; Reinharz, 1979; Donmoyer, 1990a; Steiner, Krank, McLaren, and Bahruth, 2000; Berry, 2000, 2001).

Validity and Power: Critical Constructivist Insights

Once again our system of meaning helps us conceptualize the purposes and processes of our research. In this context we value:

- the insight gained from the recognition of the dialectic of particularity and generalization;

- the attempt to move beyond our assimilated experience;

- the struggle to expose the way ideology constrains our desire for self-direction; and

- the effort to confront the way power reproduces itself in the construction of human consciousness.

We ask questions about validation that those unacquainted with our system of meaning might never consider. Instead of allowing ourselves to be controlled by a positivistic concern with external validity, we seek, through a comparison of our own action research to the research of others, an integration which provides us with a higher level of understanding of particular aspects of our classrooms, of education in general. In the process of constructing a new integration we begin to rethink our purposes as teachers. Thus, teacher researchers don't need to seek positivistic validation because they have to live with their findings. The professional activity of critical action researchers is shaped and grounded by their inquiry — theirs is applied research. Traditional positivistic researchers are satisfied with tests of statistical significance, often ignoring the test of lived experience. Validated information from a positivistic perspective tells us 'about' something, shunning the attempt to construct a system of meaning which helps us conceptualize the purposes that research might serve and the nature of the relationship of knowledge to the construction of a teacher's or a student's consciousness (Reinharz, 1979).

Positivistic research does not worry about validating knowledge in a way in which people usually experience it — the thought processes of positivism are in many ways a perversion of how humans validate information and make judgments in everyday life. Such an unnatural mode of thinking, of validation, does not work to extend, to integrate our understandings. When we simply validate knowledge 'about' something we fail to ask questions related to our system of meaning. In other words, such a positivistic form of validation serves to keep us on a level of research assimilation (much like Level 1 puzzle-solving research cognition), where we validate information merely in terms of familiar cognitive techniques. Without help from our system of meaning, researchers may never ask the questions which move us to a level of research accommodation.

This is where we begin to redefine validation, where we recognize that our assimilations are sometimes constructed not so much by ourselves but by dominant ideological and discursive forces within the society (Lemke, 1995; Courts, 1997). This is how power is reproduced; dominant ideology blocks our recognitions of exceptions, our attempt to modify our assimilated understanding of the world of education. At this point we progress to Level 2, self-monitoring, reflective research and then on to Level 3, critical constructivist research. Here validation takes on a new meaning as we gain awareness of the relationships connecting our system of meaning, our research findings, and our everyday experiences as teachers (Lincoln and Guba, 1985; Donmoyer, 1990a; Denzin and Lincoln, 2000; Kincheloe and McLaren, 2000).

Connecting Critical Constructivist Validity to More Rigorous Research and Pedagogy

As critical constructivist teacher researchers use these insights on validity to move past the positivistic correspondence theory of truth — true research most accurately reflects reality — they begin to call into question unproblematized curricular content and psychometric claims indicating correspondence between I.Q. and the capacity of measured minds. Such teacher researchers do not seek Level 3 critical constructivist modes of validation to recover the real truth as they expose the failure of the positivist epistemology of correspondence. The point of such insight involves a more complex insight into the socially constructed nature of what passes as the unchallengeable validity of mainstream modes of research. Positivistic metaphors of knowledge as the map of true reality and validity as the correspondence of the chart with actuality crumble in the critical context. When this happens, the defenders of positivism use the process as one more manifestation of the decline of rigorous research and scholarship in the scholarly cosmos.

Critical knowledge workers, however, are caught in a bind here. Because of the high level of their scholarly work, their understandings of how research methods always mediate reality in philosophical, political, epistemological, ideological, discursive, and linguistic ways, they cannot simply dismiss these understandings and retreat to a more socially acceptable mode of reductionistic, unproblematized research and validation. Critical constructivists have traveled too far to abandon their deep insights into the political and textual construction of ways of knowing the world. Such abandonment would in an early modernist context be like asking Galileo to destroy his telescope because the knowledge it engaged was offensive to particular Church leaders. Positivist epistemology and the research it supports provide little help in the effort to analyze the construction of knowledge, the historicity of the knower, and the important relationship between them (Leshan and Margenau, 1982; Kvale, 1995). These factors have nothing to do with validity in the positivist world.

Critical constructivists are particularly interested in exploring and understanding the consciousness of the researchers and how it shapes the knowledge he or she produces. The positivist view of consciousness assumes that it emerged in the world late on the scene of history and found the world already established and organized. Consciousness then improved the senses of humans in a way that helped them get a better sense of what existed. Validity emerged in this context as a measurement of how good a job the senses were doing in comprehending reality. Critical constructivists reject this historical view, arguing that the classification and organization of 'reality' are human constructions. What humans perceive about reality reflects our own way of making sense of it. Consciousness is always an integral aspect of reality. Indeed, reality without consciousness is a foggy if not unimaginable concept. This understanding modifies the way we validate knowledge about the world.

What we are dealing with here is an attempt to understand the complexity of the knowledge production act. As we previously put it: the relationship between the knower and the known. In this complex context both the development of research methods and processes of validation demand new modes of scholarly rigor. Such modes might include diverse forms of reason and different types of interpretive judgments. The new scholarly rigor in the validation process advocated by critical constructivists involves contextual insights and multiple ways of considering evidence and argumentation (Leshan and Margenau, 1982; Fischer, 1998). Old positivist rules delineating formal procedures of knowledge production and step-by-step modes of logic are no longer sufficient for the task in light of critical constructivists' concerns with researcher consciousness and the connection between knower and known.

How can validation be a simple act when we know that the researcher's location in the web of reality profoundly shapes the act of knowledge production? When we understand the interconnection of things-in-the-world — for example, students, cultural contexts, curricula, socio-economic factors, *ad infinitum* — we begin to recognize the reductionism of positivist validity. Indeed, it doesn't take into account the distortions engendered by studying educational acts outside their contexts and relationships. Positivism is guilty of reductionism when it researches things-in-the-world as merely things-in-themselves (Karunaratne, 1997). Critical constructivists as well as postformalists and critical qualitative researchers in general are interested in overcoming this positivist reductionism and fragmentation in the name of both rigorous scholarship and ethical concerns with human connection with the natural world and one another.

This connectivity is a central concern in the validation process and teacher research in general. When we pursue the fragmenting research of positivism, the quality of knowledge produced is undermined and all human beings are cognitively, intellectually, ethically, and even spiritually diminished. In this context we lose our connection to the web of reality and the interrelationship of living processes. In Latin, the term *religio*, from which 'religion' derives, means 'reconnecting'. Critical constructivists take a lesson from Einstein and his General Theory of Relativity in this context, arguing that there is no such thing as empty space in the cosmos. With this understanding in mind we come to realize that any rigorous mode of validation must take the connections between entities into account when judging the quality of data. What positivists have traditionally perceived as boundaries between objects, critical constructivists see as webs of interconnections. Consciousness itself is a part of this web and a key aspect of critical complex research involves the nature of these connections, their effects and their evolution into systems (Grof, 1993; Capra, 1996).

Rethinking Validity in a Critical and More Complex Manner

In its most basic sense, validity involves questioning and theorizing. The modes of validation that critical constructivists employ are contingent on the research questions asked and questioning always reflects particular modes of theorizing. Numerous theoretical assumptions are implicit in all observational processes leading to the construction of information. There is no way around it: the data of all research acts are intersubjective constructions of individuals in particular disciplines. Indeed, observation is saturated by interpretative strategies themselves soaked by theory. With these insights at the forefront of their consciousness, critical constuctivists seek not to validate 'certain knowledge' but work with a concept better expressed by the phrase 'compelling knowledge claims.' The 'valid truth' is replaced by the 'quality of researcher accomplishment.' The worth of these knowledge claims is debated in the context of conflicting interpretations. In action research the implications of research for particular actions are always a matter of negotiation by practitioners.

A basic principle of a democratic education involves the free, participatory process of making meaning and creating values. This ethic is central to a critical constructivist form of validity in practitioner research. Whenever this process is undermined or obstructed — in the case of positivism by the domineering claim of expertise — it must concern friends of democracy. This is why all aspects of knowledge production and pedagogy must in a democratic society be grounded on this democratic ethic. If schools are based on democratic principles and a commitment to engaging students in an authentic quest for understanding, then they must become centers for research — research conducted by teachers, administrators, and students with criteria for worthiness a constant source of dialogue and analysis. Such an orientation leads to not only a new embrace of democracy and a new access to subjugated knowledges from around the planet but also a new level of quality and rigor (defined in the non-positivist way) in education (Apple, 1993, 1999; Kvale, 1995; Novick, 1996; Gergen and Gergen, 2000).

In this context we are walking through the valley of the shadow of postmodernism where knowledge as a reflection of reality is traded for knowledge as a discursive and social construction of the world. Issues of trustworthiness or validity and interpretative negotiation take on a new importance on this new epistemological terrain. Knowledge in this land of uncertainty is not reduced to a confrontation with inanimate things-in-themselves but becomes a more complex interaction with consciousness construction and interaction with other human beings. New forms of researcher reflection are demanded, as issues of validity become entangled with the historical, cultural, and linguistic situatedness of the inquirer and with the nature of the relationship between researcher and researched.

Critical constructivists place great emphasis on the nature of these and other forms of relationships. The trustworthiness of research is undermined when analysts fail to identify and attend to various forms of relationships connecting researcher, researched, data, contexts, and the discursive field on which all of this activity takes place. This complexity cannot be dismissed on the qualitative path to empowerment. In high-quality critical democratic teacher research, inquirers must possess knowledge of these issues in order to produce worthy knowledge. The empowerment in question involves not only political and pedagogical dynamics but cognitive aspects as well. Critical constructivists are terrifically excited about rigorous research as an 'intellectual technology.' In the context of these new research strategies and methods of validation, we can begin in the spirit of postformalism to push the boundaries of human cognition. This initiates a quantum leap in the worthiness of research and the future of all human beings.

We all become smarter, we all push the envelope of our collective intelligence as we rethink validity in a more complex manner. Patti Lather (1991, 1993) creatively provides a set of transgressive forms of reconceptualized validity including:

- ironic validity — focuses on linguistic difficulties in describing concepts in question;

- paralogical validity — accounts for the limits of language in the research act;

- rhizomatic validity — analyzes the processes by which dominant paradigmatic research practices are subverted and how new local norms emerge;

- voluptuous validity — questions the inseparability of ethical and epistemological questions.

In the cognitive realm of becoming smarter maybe we could add cognitive validity to Lather's list. Such validity might ask whether the knowledge produced in our research makes us more insightful and wise. When we take into account new information technologies with their combination of text and image, how is our conception of validity affected? How do technologies of information that connect us instantaneously to libraries of information via hypertextual links change notions of validity and expertise? These are questions critical researchers must deal with in the electronic hyperreality of the twenty-first century (Kerckhove, 1995; Lee, 1997; Murphie, 1998; Levy, 1999).

Hermeneutic Validity: The Dialogue between Parts and Wholes

The data that teacher researchers collect may involve observed behavior, documents, conversations, and artifacts, but these sources can never be separated from the meanings granted to them by past, present, and future human agents. The hermeneutic dimension of research attempts to appreciate this question of meaning by focusing on the interpretive aspects of the act of knowledge production. In the Cartesian cosmos of research, hermeneutics is deemed irrelevant. Understanding that all knowledge is an interpretation, critical constructivist researchers devote much attention to the interpretive world of hermeneutics. No rethinking of validity can take place outside of a context informed by hermeneutics.

Informed by hermeneutics, teacher researchers recognize the historic dichotomy between objectivism and relativism in Western thinking.

Objectivism posits that a fixed, transhistorical, transcultural framework exists which researchers must use to determine validity. Relativism maintains that all concepts of truth and reality are contingent on a particular cultural or theoretical matrix. Hermeneutics attempts to avoid these bi-polar extremes of epistemology, as it promotes a dialogical notion of knowledge production. The hermeneutic dialogue cannot be objective and universal; it is always shaped by tacit forces making a complicated process even more complex. But this is the hand humans are dealt, and, consequently, we must deal with it.

In this context hermeneutics forces us into a complex dialogue between whole and parts, the so-called hermeneutic circle. No final, valid interpretation is sought in this context, since the activity of the circle proceeds with no need for closure (Gallagher, 1992; Peters and Lankshear, 1994; Pinar, Reynolds, Slattery, and Taubman, 1995; Mayers, 2001a, 2001b). This movement of whole to parts is combined with an analytic flow between abstract and concrete. Such dynamics often tie interpretation to the interplay of larger social forces (the general) with the everyday lives of individuals (the particular). A critical hermeneutics brings the concrete, the parts, the particular, into focus, but in a manner that grounds them contextually in a larger understanding of the forces, the whole, the abstract (the general). Focus on the parts is the dynamic that brings the particular into focus, sharpening our understanding of the individual in light of the social, discursive, and psychological forces that shape him or her. The parts, and the unique places they occupy, ground hermeneutic ways of seeing by providing the contextualization of the particular, a perspective often erased in traditional inquiry's search for abstract generalizations, external validity (Kellner, 1995; Miller and Hodge, 1998).

The give-and-take of the hermeneutic circle provokes analysts to review existing concepts in light of new understandings. Here the researchers reconsider preconceptions so as to provide a new way of exploring a situation. Making use of insights hermeneutically does not mean replicating authors' responses to their original questions. In the hermeneutic process an interpretation or an 'answer' is valuable only if it catalyzes the production of a new question for our consideration in the effort to make sense of the world that confronts us. This might be viewed as one dimension of hermeneutic validity. Another dimension of hermeneutic validity might involve the notion of construct validity. A construct of a concept such as intelligence often finds validation when it is convincing to a group of inquirers. The process of persuasion of this group of inquirers to accept a particular construct may have nothing to do with positivistic modes of empirical proof. Validity in this context is much more a hermeneutical process in which collaborative investigation leads to more compelling interpretations of our observations of the world (Kvale, 1995; Jardine, 1998; Smith, 1999).

Validity in a World of Diverse Knowledges and Textual Readings

In a multivocal world with diverse forms of epistemology and knowledge production, validity becomes an even more complex concept. If a researcher's purpose involves revealing the multiple truths circulating in a particular cultural or educational setting, what are the implications for validity? If critical constructivists question the notion of universal truth, how do they deal with local, personal, indigenous, and community forms of truth? When teacher researchers seek multiple knowledges constructed from diverse vantage points and differing assumptions about knowledge, they move into a new dimension of research where traditional rules no longer operate. They experience some of the same dislocations as quantum theorists when they realized that the physical laws of the universe were no longer applicable at the sub-atomic level. Does the term, validity, need to be used in this new dimension? If we do use the term, should it be removed from the domain of truth claims (Gergen and Gergen, 2000; Jones, 2001)?

Move this entire discussion of validity into the realm of cyberspace. In the first decade of the twenty-first century we are witnessing the development of virtual domains providing expressions of a wide variety of global knowledges (Levy, 1999). As such knowledges circulate, are interpreted, and are rearticulated, *ad hoc* modes of validation are taking place. Such validation-in-action lends even another layer of complexity to our original concerns. Critical constructivist researchers have to deal with these new cyberrealities — young people and students have already developed practical modes of addressing them. Critical researchers must begin this process by using their abilities as textual analysts who historicize and contextualize all knowledges, all forms of informational assessment. In the context of cyber-informational bombardment we have no choice: we must read, interpret, and criticize. In this process critical researchers work to expose the cultural and discursive inscriptions that shape any knowledge.

Here we gain insight into how students' Internet-based validation-in-action takes place. Students and other individuals tossed into cyberreality employ particular ways of reading and reproducing knowledge that operate within the cosmos of the text and textual form in question. Teacher researchers conversant with our critical conversation about validity and modes of analysis can move such students to new insights about their use of Internet data. In the context of hermeneutical validity, teacher researchers can reintroduce the triad of read, interpret, and criticize. The interpretive process here involves connecting a textual reading to discursive and ideological networks that signal from what place in the web of reality a particular cybertext might originate. The hermeneutical focus on these connective aspects of the texts opens the world of knowledge production to students. In the process it helps them assess their relationship to it, criticize it, and generate alternative knowledge (Scholes, 1985; Lemke, 1995; Travis, 1998; Cornis-Pope, 2001).

In a world where power wielders are more powerful because of the centralized control of knowledge production, such validation and assessment processes become democratic survival skills. Teacher researchers help students struggle with and disrupt texts so that dominant readings do not immobilize them. In this context teachers and students reveal 'what is not said' in particular texts, step outside the house of detention constructed by unstated assumptions, and view from a critical distance the impact these cybertexts might have on particular individuals. These dynamics raise merely a few concerns about the process of information consumption, production, and validation in a so-called 'knowledge society.' While the phrase is kicked around promiscuously in the first decade of the twenty-first century, it is true that our capacity as knowledge workers must be more sophisticated now than ever before. Indeed, we must confront these complexities of knowledge work at a time that the changes in knowledge production are becoming more unpredictable. What the world of diverse knowledges and textual readings will morph into is not clear (Scholes, 1985; Fontana and Frey, 2000; Mayers, 2001a; Bereiter, 2002).

Connecting Validity to Higher Orders of Thinking and Deeper Levels of Analysis

From a pedagogical perspective these concerns with validity in relation to cyberspace, reading, interpreting, criticizing, diverse knowledge production, and textual analysis are inseparable from good teaching. One of the central concerns of this book reveals itself: teachers who are adept researchers are better prepared to be teachers. To teach research, teachers must be researchers. To be an excellent researcher, one must be a higher-order thinker. While understanding the complexities of the validation and knowledge production processes cannot provide precise procedures for turning out 'correct data,' it does help construct modes of thinking that contribute to critical and ethical decision-making. Teacher researchers who are aware of the complexity of validation can develop legitimate and diverse justifications for particular actions and for believing that certain decisions are better than others.

Such assertions are connected to numerous issues involving many different domains. Focusing on the validation process, these concerns with higher-order thinking and deeper levels of analysis bring us back to the skills and abilities of the researcher. Making sense of a situation is always in part an act of self-understanding on the part of the researcher. How one chooses to approach a research situation is shaped by the researcher's subjectivity, his or her place in the web of reality. In this context students of research have raised issues of voice, historicity, frames of reference, and other dimensions of 'perspective' (Madison, 1988; Gergen and Gergen, 2000).

These scholars have been concerned with the ways that researchers situate their voices in their narratives. Such modes of thinking and analysis are central to critical constructivist research, but must not be embraced to the exclusion of larger social concerns and macro-social/political issues. Without this social dimension, concerns with subjectivity may devolve into the *angst* of the privileged. Validity in this context may degenerate into facile comparisons of decontextualized personal experiences. Make no mistake, critical constructivist notions of research and validity are not complete without the inclusion of evidence of deep levels of analysis and relevance for changing important social, political, and educational practices in a just manner (Jones, 2001).

Teacher researchers are better prepared to become higher-order thinkers who tie classroom activities to profound pedagogical, social, historical, and philosophical purposes. Teachers who operate in this way study the multiple contexts in which education takes place and adjust their teaching accordingly. They identify the inadequacies of their own and their students' conceptual structures and engage students in activities where they reflect on how and why they constructed such ideas as they did (Davidovic, 1996). These teachers are critical thinkers in the critical theoretical sense (Weil, 1998; Weil and Anderson, 2000) in that their understandings translate directly into forms of critical action. They possess a critical x-ray vision that allows them to see through the walls of the conventional, the curtains of commonsense. Such thinking and the vision that accompanies it provide such teachers with the confidence to transcend the limitations of extant institutions. Their interpretations are validated by the concrete actions they catalyze — thus, they reflect Lather's (1991, 1993) catalytic validity.

In this context the higher order critical thinking of teacher researchers cannot be separated from hermeneutics. As an historically grounded mode of thinking and producing knowledge, it always seeks to engage communication and dialogue — it works to create living hermeneutical circles. Such circles of analysis uncover the scars of positivism and the political economic structures propped up by instrumental rationality. The critical hermeneutic at work in this context is ever concerned with the power of ideology and discourse and the way they function in the classroom to subvert deeper levels of analysis and democratic functioning (Giroux, 1997; Hinchey, 1998).

Teacher researchers in this context are future-oriented as they seek catalytical validation in light of the democratic actions they motivate. In this future orientation, however, they refuse to be enchanted by the technical virtuosity of new technologies. As critical interpreters, they subject such innovations to the same forms of analysis they would apply to any concept — technology being a concept. In this context they delve into the ideological dynamics surrounding new technologies and other futuristic innovations. They seek the non-positivistic rigor of hermeneutics and a form of constructivist validity where compelling and convincing interpretations of various phenomena are pursued. A form of pedagogical validity emerges as students gain the ability to understand particular domains and to act critically on the basis of their understandings. These are the foundations of powerful pedagogies.

The Complexity of Pragmatic Validity: Catalytic Validation through Successful Action

Most observers agree: the issue of validity in a post-positivistic world is very complex and even disarming. Historically, we have just begun the conversation about what it may mean. To state the matter as directly as possible, qualitative researchers are attempting to move beyond the correspondence notion of validity (research texts reflect true reality) to a more complex understanding of the ways that social, political, cultural, and philosophical constructions of the world complicate the process. Those with a more pragmatic orientation maintain in this context that knowledge produced by research may be best validated via its role in practice — thus, the notion of pragmatic validity. Here knowledge earns its stripes in its confrontation with the lived world, in its ability to perform worthwhile actions. As previously mentioned, Patti Lather (1991, 1993) was operating in this conceptual parlor when she conceived catalytic validity as the degree to which research engages its subjects to better conceptualize the world and the forces that construct it so they can transform it.

Pragmatic/catalytic validation is appealing to critical constructivists as we struggle to deal with the issue of validity. Critical teacher research and pedagogical action in this context proceed simultaneously. A key element of the complexity of this pragmatic approach involves deciding what values and assumptions support the actions we take. These are questions of intellect and ethical reasoning where researchers struggle with issues of interpretation within a socio-educational context. No simple task, such an interpretative ability rests at the heart of a rigorous critical education. As Paulo Freire (1970a) argued decades ago, we have to account for social, political, and economic contradictions in our pedagogical efforts to confront and change the world, to become transformative teachers. The complex task of discerning the implications of research for action is part hermeneutics, part self-awareness, part consciousness-raising, and part development of ethical radar. Here we move toward a greater good that is connected to but outside of the self and self-interest. Such movement implies action in the world (Kvale, 1995; de Oliveira and Montecinos, 1998; Zeno, 1998).

If pragmatic validation were not already sufficiently complex, add another layer to the conceptual wedding cake. In our efforts to collect and interpret information leading to informed action (praxis), critical teacher researchers must not simply collect multiple perspectives on an object of study. While this process is necessary, it is also essential that such perspectives be scrutinized in relation to the social, linguistic, cultural, and ideological forces that shape them. Critical researchers must ask what is the relationship between these diverse voices and the social systems in which they emerge. Where do they fit in various complex systems (Carspecken, 1996, 1999; Boje, 2000; Janesick, 2000)? So often researchers fail to obtain authentic responses from interviewees out of their fear of reprisal from hierarchical superiors, avoidance of disapproval, concern with appearing stupid, distrust of the researchers, discomfort with the situation, and many other factors. In a recent research project on McDonald's (Kincheloe, 2002) I found that many interviewees didn't respond to my queries until I unintentionally provoked them to anger with a critical observation of the company. At this point many respondents offered valuable information concerning their ideological relationship with McDonald's.

In this context a notion of configurational validity (trustworthiness enhanced by multiple viewpoints) brings together 'the discordant and the harmonious' (Goldman-Segall, 1995), 'mimesis and alterity' (Taussig, 1993), 'the raw and the cooked' (Lévi-Strauss, 1966). Understanding the necessity for multiple viewpoints analyzed in relation to social, linguistic, cultural, and ideological forces, teacher researchers begin to take control of their professional lives as knowledge-producing scholars. They are empowered to enter into the discourse about validity with experts who would challenge the veracity of their knowledge production. Using their appreciation of configurational validity *vis-à-vis* pragmatic validity, they begin to appreciate the insights of parents, community members, and students traditionally excluded from the conversation about education.

Buoyed by a rigorous and critical engagement with these issues of validation, teacher researchers are becoming scholars with a critical consciousness. Such individuals possess the ability to become not only exemplary teachers but organic intellectuals, agents of change who can help reshape their communities in democratic ways. They can work to escape the forces that dominate us and subvert our understanding of the ways the world operates as well as developing new and exciting visions of the future. Such actions cannot be separated from our notion of pragmatic validity, when research is evaluated in light of its ability to enable sophisticated understanding and to help individuals gain the power to take control of their lives. In this context pragmatic validity intersects with the critical theoretical notion of 'imminent critique.' Imminent critique is a way of thinking about research grounded on the questions: how does it help us consider what could be in relation to what is?, and where do we go from here? Such concerns have been consistently neglected by the culture of positivism.

Pushing the Limits of Critical Pragmatic Validity:
Enter Imminent Critique

The achievement of a critical pragmatic validity is not a simple task learned in a few classroom lessons. It is a lifelong pursuit marked by theoretical understanding and practical experience marked by success and failure. The action that one takes as a result of teacher research is never self-evident. Teachers involved in such a process must always be reflective, self-monitoring scholars who quickly perceive when something is not working, or is not consistent with a critical system of meaning. Such teacher researchers will find that they need outside help to alert them to unnoticed features of their cultural and pedagogical landscape. They must be open to the distanced analysis of others who perceive recurrent patterns of unproductive behavior that the teachers themselves don't see. Such critics can help the teacher researcher contemplate actions that transcend solutions of facile, surface-level problems and move their analysis and practice to a confrontation with tacit and more powerful distortions (Kvale, 1995; Lester, 2001).

Pragmatic validity *vis-à-vis* imminent critique pushes us to new levels of cognition and pedagogical practice, as it challenges our capacities as researchers. Engaging in this process, we come to see the specters of action embedded in our data. With these images in mind we develop new sets of pedagogical alternatives from which to choose, new purposes for social and educational organization, new ways to conceptualize justice, and new and better ways of being human. Attention to the intersection of pragmatic validity and imminent critique helps create new conditions under which knowledge is produced and learning takes place (Newland, 1997).

With this emphasis on what could be and forms of action to take us there, teacher research and the pedagogies emanating from it evolve into ways of exploring the production of meanings and values. This act involves everyone, not just 'expert researchers' and the guardians of the Cartesian–Newtonian–Baconian canon. In the critical context, deliberations of these kinds always study the impediments to widespread participation in such sophisticated conversation (Apple, 1996, 1999). The unequal distribution of power and the ways it privileges the privileged and silences the disprivileged is a cardinal feature of the conversation. As Phil Carspecken (1996, 1999) contends, these critical dynamics are central to the act of knowledge production. Critical researchers who take pragmatic validity *vis-à-vis* imminent critique seriously do not make vague gestures toward social justice, they carefully study the omnipresent but often invisible structures of power which squash concerns with justice.

Pragmatic validity *vis-à-vis* imminent critique demands that critical teacher researchers become rigorous scholars of power. In such a context teacher researchers explore the ways that they themselves, their students, their administrators, members of the community, and human beings in general are positioned by power in particular places in the web of reality. Within this web they come into contact with signifiers, ideologies, hegemonic practices, and material dynamics produced by power. They act upon power, they receive power, they exert power, they change in relation to power. Many times they are dominated by power, other times they engage with a productive form of power that helps them produce intelligence and wisdom. The study of power is complex, ambiguous, and even contradictory. Critical teacher researchers have to diligently work to distinguish between its positive and its regulatory effects (Macedo, 1994; Giroux, 1997; McLaren, 2000; Kincheloe, 2002).

While some would argue that poststructuralism's semiotic concern with signs and discursive practices moves critical analysts away from the study of consciousness, critical constructivist researchers disagree. There is no contradiction between a concern for the impact of signification and the nature of consciousness construction. In fact, I would argue that the two processes are intimately connected. Indeed, each can better be understood in relation to the other. With these ideas in mind, the intersection of pragmatic validity with imminent critique moves teacher researchers to ponder the evolution of their consciousness, the production and transformation of their subjectivity, and the nature of this process in general. As we explore validity in the pragmatic and imminent context, we come to realize that focusing on what could be makes possible new forms of consciousness (Grof, 1993; Kincheloe, Steinberg, and Tippins, 1999; Shoham, 2000). We become aware that behind the positivist curtain reside exciting forms of consciousness, ways of thinking that are being squashed by the Western scientific obsession with one narrow form of rationality. A fantastic intellectual journey into this domain awaits us.

Chapter 9

The Value of the Qualitative Dimension

Ever since positivists applied physical science methods to social science research there has been a struggle to address those aspects of the human condition that need not just counting but understanding. Social scientists produce data but what is not generally understood is that this information demands interpretation — its meaning is not self-evident. Taking a lesson from hermeneutics, critical teacher researchers understand that the meaning of data is inseparable from human inscription and socio-cultural context. Qualitative research is dedicated to the study of this process of human meaning making. As long as educational researchers base their inquiries on concepts with such diverse meanings as, say, intelligence, qualitative judgment will (or at least *should*) remain a central concern of educational research (Holland and Mansell, 1983; Howe, 1985; Denzin and Lincoln, 2000).

Basic Features of Qualitative and Quantitative Research

Qualitative research is distinguished from quantitative research in that quantitative research is concerned with frequency while qualitative research is concerned with abstract characteristics of events. Qualitative researchers maintain that many natural properties cannot be expressed in quantitative terms — indeed, they will lose their reality if expressed simply in terms of frequency. Knowledge of human beings involves the understanding of qualities which cannot be described through the exclusive use of numbers. As qualitative researchers direct their attention to the meanings given to events by participants, they come to understand more than what a list of descriptions or a table of statistics could support. When positivistic researchers focus inquiry exclusively on a quantitative dimension, research in the social sciences is narrowed to those aspects which lend themselves to numerical expression. Instead of focusing on a student's disposition toward learning, her creativity, or hard-to-measure dimensions of genius, positivistic educational research will instead direct its energy to achievement — an operationally defined achievement based on standardized tests at that (Popkewitz, 1981a; Willers, 1987; Kincheloe and Weil, 2001).

Qualitative researchers are not attempting to argue that there is no need for quantitative research in education. Quantitative research is obviously important in a variety of educational contexts, for it often serves as a check on qualitative data. Well-executed quantitative research with an understanding of context and a concern with purpose can provide important insights into certain human affairs. Quantitative methods allow us to focus on variables of interest, and the use of mathematical symbols permits an economical summary of information.

This economy is illustrated by the attempt to perform arithmetic functions in English without the help of mathematical symbols. Many questions in education are dependent upon comparisons of specific variables. Using quantification, such comparisons are rendered manageable and degrees of difference can be determined. All of these benefits and more can be derived from quantitative methods, as long as quantitative researchers are aware of the qualitative dimensions to all quantitative research. All quantitative research grows out of a qualitative context, that is, it is shaped by paradigms, values, political tendencies, and ideologies. The problem with quantitative research in education is that it is not always aware of this qualitative dimension. Thus, to improve their 'trade,' quantitative researchers must address three essential questions before, during, and after the inquiry process: (1) What is the relationship of the investigator to the investigated?; (2) What is the relationship between facts and values?; and (3) What is the goal of the investigation? (J. Smith, 1983; Sherman, Webb, and Andrews, 1984; Howe, 1985; Janesick, 2000).

Philosophers of research have found the attempt to describe the universal concerns of qualitative research to be quite difficult. Because of its abstract nature, different qualitative researchers will promote different goals for their research. Typically holding an eclectic position, the qualitative researcher will purposely seek divergent research strategies and goals. Recognizing this diversity as a part of the qualitative culture, Robert Sherman, Rodman Webb, and Sam Andrews (1984) set out on the difficult quest to identify the general characteristics of qualitative research. They conclude that certain characteristics can indeed be identified in most qualitative research.

One of the most important aspects of qualitative research is its concern with context. 'Context stripping' is an unfortunate feature of positivistic science. Scientific methods distort the reality they attempt to portray when they do not consciously work to avoid this stripping. Human experience is shaped in particular contexts and cannot be understood if removed from those contexts. Thus, qualitative research attempts to be as naturalistic as possible, meaning that contexts must not be constructed or modified. Research must take place in the normal, everyday context of the researched. Ethnography, for example, is a quintessential form of qualitative research, as it studies events as they evolve in natural settings.

Qualitative research views experience holistically, as researchers explore all aspects of an experience. As individuals explore human situations, they must attend to the variety of factors which shape them. Critical constructivist qualitative researchers address the underlying complexities of school experience, so often missed by quantitative researchers. This is a key aspect of their larger quest for holism in knowledge production. The connections which tie experiences together and provide their significance in human affairs are essential features of holistic qualitative research.

One of the most important characteristics of qualitative inquiry is the belief that methods of inquiry must be appropriate to the aims of inquiry. Qualitative researchers take seriously Aristotle's point that each 'science' has relevant methods which are uncovered when inquiry takes place in the discipline's unique subject matter. This does not mean that qualitative researchers do not borrow or share different methods — they are typically eclectic in their approaches. The research methods that they employ may be diverse, but they will be consistent with the general aims of qualitative inquiry. Instead of intervening in experience by removing it from its natural setting or by structuring the 'important' aspects of the experience quantitatively, qualitative research looks for social and cultural patterns of experience, relationships among various occurrences, and the significance of such events as they affect specific human endeavors.

Qualitative research, Sherman, Webb, and Andrews argue, is concerned with experience as it is 'lived', 'felt' or 'undergone.' This concern with phenomenological consciousness is an essential aspect of qualitative research. Qualitative thinking involves the feeling and appreciation dimension of human activity which, of course, borders on the aesthetic dimension. Thus, qualitative research attempts to appreciate human experience in a manner empathetic to the human actors who feel it or live it. Ethnography as a mode of qualitative research succeeds on one level to the degree that it enables one to understand what goes on in a society or a social circumstance as well as the participants. The readers of high-quality ethnography should feel that if they were to find themselves in the school described they would have a keen understanding of the forces moving, say, the principal to act in a certain way.

Another common aspect of qualitative research involves the idea of making judgments. The function of this appraising aspect of qualitative research is to describe the qualities of events, to interpret meanings and relationships among those events, and to appraise the significance of these events in the larger picture of social and educational concerns. In making these types of judgments, qualitative research must be explicit about the social values and human interests on which its appraisals are grounded. Without such explicit delineation of this grounding, qualitative research falls prey to the same demons it criticizes in much quantitative research (Sherman, Webb, and Andrews, 1983: 25–8).

The Unique Benefits of the Qualitative Dimension

With such concerns paramount in the minds of qualitative researchers, common problems of educational research can be addressed. Awareness of context, holism, aims, consciousness, and appraisal can prevent educational researchers from simplistically transforming value-laden policy issues into technical questions with empirical answers. It can free researchers from the futile search for empirical answers to non-empirical questions. It can release researchers from slavish adherence to unanswerable questions of truth and falsity so that they might focus more on both the desirability of the purposes that their research promotes and the methods of appraising the value and credibility of research purposes in general (Donmoyer, 1985; Carspecken, 1996, 1999).

Teacher researchers use qualitative research perspectives to enrich their own unavoidably subjective view of the lived world of education. After involving ourselves in action research, do we possess new and better ways of seeing educational events? Are we better able to conceptualize educational questions in general and questions about our practice in particular? Do we gain the ability to discern the unseen forces at work in all educational contexts? Can we better transcend the empty rhetoric and the clichés dominating education-talk, for example, 'we're here for the children,' 'we believe in quality education for everyone,' 'our school system seeks to provide educational excellence,' 'standards must be raised'? Does our qualitative teacher research equip us, in the spirit of anticipatory accommodation, to apply insight gained from one context to another?

The purposes of qualitative research are multidimensional, as the inquiry attempts to engender understanding on three levels simultaneously: the issue being researched, the research process itself, and the researcher. When qualitative research is framed by our notion of critical constructivism and is aware of pragmatic validity *vis-à-vis* imminent critique, important things happen. Our research becomes practice-based in the sense that it seeks to change for the better (within the context provided by our system of meaning) the issue being researched, the research process, and the researcher. It moves them in an emancipatory, democratic direction (Reinharz, 1979; Donmoyer, 1987; Smyth, 2001; Kincheloe, 2002).

Such a critical constructivist perspective on the purposes of qualitative inquiry values teacher empowerment, believes in human agency (i.e., the capacity of individuals to change their own lives), and trusts that teacher workplaces can become growth-inducing, humane environments. Qualitative research teaches action researchers to heighten their consciousnesses of themselves as players on the educational stage, to take themselves less for granted, and to view themselves as objects of study. By providing techniques which allow us to see from new perspectives what schools and the contexts in which they operate are like and why they have come to be that way, critical constructivist research catalyzes this inquiry into the production of teacher subjectivity.

As teachers watch themselves be educators, they ask questions such as: Who do I call on in class? Who do I criticize and from whom do I withhold criticism? Where in the school do I hang out? Where do I stand when I'm teaching? How do I arrange my room? Do I respond differently to the misbehavior of different students? Teachers here gain a dialectic of distance, that is, a closeness to students marked by an awareness of who they are, their concerns, their interests, their experiences, their socio-economic backgrounds, and their diverse forms of intelligence. Concurrently, they also view students from a metaphorical distance which allows them to step back and watch from afar how their backgrounds affect their daily lives at school, their self-definitions, the perceptions of them held by other teachers, and their educational successes (Bogdan and Biklen, 1983; Mayers, 2001b).

The Insights of the Qualitative Dimension: Understanding the Social Construction of the World

The insights and benefits of the qualitative dimension are profound in the domains of both knowledge production and pedagogy. In this analysis I will work to illustrate the synergistic connections between these two processes. The qualitative realm is intensely concerned with studying the holistic experience of consciousness and its relationship to social, political, linguistic, cultural, and economic practices in the world. In this domain we come to learn about the social construction of the world. Such an effort is often difficult, as it runs counter to the Cartesian–Newtonian–Baconian assumptions implicit in the process of acculturation in Western societies. But learn it we must, qualitative advocates maintain, because humans inevitably view the cosmos from a point resting within themselves. Indeed, they converse about the world in a language shaped by human experience. The positivistic effort to remove human perspectives from our knowledge of the world is a one-way street to an epistemological abyss. In this situation we pass the event horizon of the black hole of positivism from which the light of insight cannot escape.

In the qualitative analysis of the process of social construction our critical orientation never allows us to dismiss the reality of power-produced human suffering. This moral concern is always connected with the pursuit of rigorous scholarly work producing a mode of research that is meticulous but not inflexible, visionary but not dogmatic. As critical constructivists study the social construction of the world, we are radically humble because we know that we too are socially constructed. Located in a particular place in the web of reality and informed by a specific set of relationships, critical qualitative researchers have nothing more than a partial perspective on the educational and social phenomena we explore. Just as we understand that the world is socially constructed, we understand that research of any stripe creates a world — it does not reflect a world. The interrelationships of living beings and their environments are cognitive interactions; the process of living itself is a process of world-making (Madison, 1988; Capra, 1996; Giroux, 1997; O'Sullivan, 1999).

If knowledge is socially constructed, then critical qualitative researchers understand that the debate over what knowledge is of the most worth is never ending. This is why critical qualitative researchers understand the importance of paradigmatic debate. Teachers as researchers must possess a rigorous understanding of the way paradigms compete for validation of the knowledge they produce. Depending on what paradigm in which one learns to conduct research, different constructions of the educational, social, and psychological worlds may be produced. Researchers who understand these paradigmatic dynamics can discern their effects in different research studies. With these dynamics in mind, teacher researchers can never passively accept the knowledge of experts without questioning the paradigmatic frames that helped construct it.

Contemporary education in general and education of researchers in particular do not devote sufficient attention to the existence of different processes of knowledge production and thus world-making. When diverse cultural and indigenous knowledge production is added to paradigmatic concerns, the heterogeneity of ways of seeing, understanding, and constructing the world is daunting. How dare the advocates of a national curriculum in England and top-down content standards in the U.S. propose to teach only one small portion of these diverse knowledge traditions. What an insufficient education this epistemological narrowness produces. A curriculum of any type that does not acknowledge the social construction of the knowledge it promotes and the modes of research it teaches, or is not ironical and self-reflective, will not produce thoughtful, transformative scholars (Apple, 1993, 1999; Carlson, 1997; Carlson and Apple, 1998; Lester, 2001).

In this qualitative domain of social construction, teacher researchers clearly understand that the decisions they make as knowledge producers and teachers are not neutral. Once this dynamic is appreciated, a new level of cognition is achieved, a mode of thinking that helps such teachers discern dimensions of propositions and policies previously unrecognized. Awareness of the social construction of knowledge about the world moves teachers to new levels of reasoning about other people's reasoning. In this cognitive domain they may discern insight into other people's knowledge production and concurrent weaknesses in their own conclusions (Harrington and Quinn-Leering, 1995). They may engage in paradigmatic and social theoretical reflections previously unimagined. This is the strength of a democratic mode of knowledge production and pedagogy. In avoiding a tyrannical 'one and only way' of producing truth and then inculcating

:o a captive group of students, such a democratic process opens
vorld of understandings and cognitive and ethical growth emer-
___ ___ such new experiences.

With these democratic concepts in mind, an appreciation of the
social construction of knowledge enables teachers, students, and citizens
to monitor the politics of knowledge production and consumption in their
lives. When schools are critical democratic spheres, educational leaders do
not fear individuals being aware of the social construction of knowledge.
In totalitarian, anti-democratic schools such awareness is viewed as
dangerous. The danger results from the power of such insight to help
individuals challenge particular constructions of the world, especially
those that support the interests of power wielders. Also, as individuals
gain awareness of their own location in history and culture, they begin to
develop a sense of personal empowerment that refuses attempts to adapt
them to the *status quo*. Democracy in Western societies in the twenty-first
century is still, unfortunately, a dangerous practice.

The Qualitative Domain and the Development of a Critical Consciousness

It is not easy to come to terms with the notion that consciousness and
perceived reality are mutually constructed. The notion from the perspective
of many Westerners seems to defy commonsense. In this context critical
constructivists use the qualitative dimension to produce a critical form
of consciousness. As individuals grasp the way power operates to shape
both their perceptions of the world and their sense of self, they become far
more attuned to asymmetries surrounding particular social, cultural, psychological, and educational norms. Such asymmetries may involve forms
of knowledge produced and broadcast around issues of race, class, gender,
sexuality, environmental issues, and so on. Individuals sensitive to issues
of racial justice, for example, may tune in to the knowledge produced in
psychology about the cognitive inferiority of non-Whites (see Herrnstein
and Murray, 1994 and Kincheloe, Steinberg, and Gresson, 1996). In this
context the disjunction between their lived experience and the official
knowledge of positivist psychometrics may open a new consciousness of
the relationship between power and knowledge (O'Sullivan, 1999).

In this way critical qualitative researchers bring criticality together
with Afrocentrism, feminism, indigenous knowledges, post-colonial perspectives. Such syntheses help unite the interests of marginalized groups
and, just as importantly, grant critical qualitative researchers profound
new insights from subjugated and historically silenced perspectives. Such
valuable insight contributes profoundly to the development of new forms
of consciousness. Such a 'critical' consciousness not only becomes more
sensitive to often 'officially dismissed' forms of human suffering and

exploitation. A critical consciousness involves both cognitive and ethical understandings and is engaged in a struggle against inequality. Such a struggle engages the lived suffering that comes out of inequality and its consequences in the realm of knowledge production. Indeed, this struggle takes subjugated knowledges very seriously.

Critical constructivists in the qualitative context value and make use of subjugated and marginalized views of the world. Critical qualitative researchers point out that what has been promoted as Western rationality has been used to legitimate the domination of particular marginalized peoples — 'they are not a rational people, they cannot govern themselves.' Particular forms of Cartesian–Newtonian–Baconian rationality may not be valuable for certain questions used in specific cultural situations. In the postmodern, postcolonial world of the twenty-first century, analysts working in the qualitative domain have come to realize that the world is not a monological system that can be described and interpreted by the same methods and a universal rationality. The point of such analyses is not to eliminate Cartesian rationality, as has so often been charged. The purpose is to use paradigmatic, social theoretical, discursive, and cultural frames of reference in the qualitative domain to grasp the limits of Cartesian rationality in the lived world.

Researchers fall into a rationalistic trap when they fail to grasp the limits of Cartesian rationality. In attempting to make sense of the convolutions of everyday life in social and educational spheres, they overlook the significance of the non-rational and the irrational. The straight road of rationality, the superhighways of positivism, miss the cultural and geographic detail of the crooked path. The qualitative domain allows us to walk the crooked path, to explore particularity, intuition, emotion, rage, cognition, desire, interpretation, experience, positionality, passion, social theory, and knowledge in relationship to one another. As researchers bring these features together, they create a whole greater than the sum of the separate parts.

The critical feature of critical consciousness picks up on the qualitative dimension and uses it to associate 'reason' with a particular time and place. The notion of progress associated with such forms of 'white reason' is deconstructed in this context and shown to be a Eurocentric dream of rational development for those who are capable. The possibility of other non-Western forms of progress is negated in this context. Western reason, monoculturalists maintain, must remain pure and unpolluted by intercultural intercourse (Steinberg, 2001). Infused with a critical consciousness, the qualitative dimension knows there has to be more than this. There are numerous ways of knowing, making meaning, and producing knowledge in the world and critical researchers must learn from all of them (Degenaar, 1995; Thomas, 1998; Lester, 2001). Teacher researchers can change the structure of schooling as they understand and implement these complex notions.

Interpretive Insight and the Qualitative Dimension

Simply put, a key value of the qualitative dimension involves developing good judgment in analyzing the social, cultural, psychological, political, economic, and educational realms of human activity. In the critical constructivist domain in which we operate, an important distinction is made between good judgment and correct judgment. While critical teacher research does not pursue correct judgment, it does value well-argued, compelling judgments that are not constructed arbitrarily or on a whim. Such compelling judgments are based on specific reasons and particular concepts. A critical teacher researcher can justify his or her judgments by referring to particular criteria, relationships, and precepts. The relationship between the qualitative judgment and these criteria, relationships, and precepts is very complex. Criteria, relationships, and precepts cannot be simply 'put to use' in a concrete research situation where a judgment is demanded to provide us with truth. Such application in no way tells us what the situation means or how to construct our description of it.

The ambiguous and complex relationship noted by researchers in this context reminds us of why we are not positivists — there is too much going on to 'surrender' to reductionistic, simple answers. The criteria, relationships, and precepts that critical qualitative researchers employ are merely guiding concepts in developing interpretations of the situation and deciding what action might improve it. Putting them to use in a particular setting is never an exact, procedural scientific process — it is more an art, the art of interpretation. In critical qualitative research there are no rules for such application. Within the qualitative dimension we practice applying our criteria, relationships, and precepts (our critical system of meaning), so as to energize our interpretive insight. The more we do it, the better we understand our system of meaning, the more exposure we gain to brilliant researchers who engage in this process adeptly, the better researchers/ interpreters we become (Madison, 1988; Ellis, 1998; Barone, 2000; Mayers, 2001a; Smyth, 2001)

In this qualitative context it is important to assert that these researchers/ interpreters become better teachers. As they learn to make sense of lived situations and reflect on their own beliefs and behaviors, they are better prepared to teach for rigorous levels of understanding. Teachers with interpretive insight are more attuned to rationales, modes of analysis and synthesis, guiding values, epistemological assumptions — the nuts and bolts of scholarly activity (Gordon, 2001). Interpretive insight in the qualitative dimension moves teacher researchers to attend to context. We simply cannot appreciate a lived situation until we appreciate its embeddedness in a variety of settings. A live situation takes place in a particular historical period and a specific culture or collision of cultures. These factors help shape the situation, individuals' perceptions of it, its meaning to observers, the way it is described to others, its effects, its relationship to other situations. When we concern ourselves with improving research skills, these dynamics must be taken into account (Haggerson, 2000; Thayer-Bacon, 2001).

Teacher researchers with interpretive insight focus on complexities and asymmetries in specific lived situations. As they study such circumstances in relation to their criteria, relationships, and precepts, they focus on their contextual embeddedness. They take these data and consider what knowledge emerges from their interaction. They study how they fit together in ways that result in compelling judgments and practical actions. The knowledge that emerges from this critical qualitative research helps students construct better lives as they produce a more just and happy world. Producing such knowledge and sharing the process of its construction with students lay the foundation for preparing students to operate in a knowledge society.

Many speak of such a society and our need to train students for it, but few delineate the pedagogical demands of such a situation. Teachers as researchers who develop interpretive insight constantly grapple with what the concept, knowledge society, means, how knowledge work might be conceptualized, and how students might be best prepared for it. Western education, education in the U.S. in particular, has not cultivated knowledge work among teachers, students, or its citizens. This has precipitated negative consequences in a variety of socio-cultural and political locales. Both primary and secondary research skills are weak and the neo-positivistic standards movement has only made the situation worse. The interpretive insights of teacher researchers have never been more needed (Ohanian, 1999; Schubert and Thomas, 2001; Bereiter, 2002).

Thinking about the Criteria for Interpretation in the Qualitative Domain

As critical constructivist teacher researchers flee the inferno of reductionistic positivist rule-following, they do not find sanctuary in some nihilistic, relativistic realm. Critical constructivists do not trade positivist objectivity for relativism. In such circumstances the process of interpretation must involve an analysis of the criteria it employs to produce and evaluate the meaning it makes. An interpretation is an argument and an argument always appeals to a set of principles. A collection of these principles makes up a set of criteria to which we refer in the meaning-making process. These interpretive criteria help us argue and defend particular interpretations of the lived world; they help us decide which interpretations are better and which are worse. Of course, we can argue the value and viability of particular criteria; this is, of course, another aspect of the larger interpretive process.

G. B. Madison provides some examples of criteria that might be used in this process:

- Comprehensiveness — involves whether or not the interpretation provides a cohesive picture of a phenomenon. Asks if the interpretation contradicts itself.

- Penetration — involves the interpretation's abiltity to make sense of a phenomenon by pointing out the intention of those involved with it. Raises questions about the concerns that guided these agents.

- Throughness — asks whether the interpretation deals with all of the questions it asks about a phenomenon and whether it addresses the questions the phenomenon brings up concerning its own interpretation.

- Appropriateness — asks if the questions answered by an interpretation are the ones raised by the phenomenon under study.

- Contextuality — asks if the interpretation has accounted for the historical and cultural context in which the phenomenon exists.

- Agreement — asks whether the interpretation accounts for previous interpretations of the phenomenon. For example, does it point out their deficiencies?

- Suggestiveness — wants to know whether the interpretation is fertile in raising new questions and evoking new research about the phenomenon.

- Potential — involves the ability of the interpretation to lend itself to the construction of future interpretations. Asks whether it can be extended in a way as to generate new insights.

(Madison, 1988, 29–30)

Obviously, these interpretive criteria are not exacting and rigidly defined. They are always open to diverse interpretations. Ultimately, they are concerned with what it means to make judgments in the qualitative domain. The conversation about such criteria tells us where we are standing historically. It is a conversation that could take place only at this particular historical moment and this cultural place. In the larger context of the history of intellect and ideas we have just begun to question over the last few decades (a short wink in the larger expanse of history) what type of information science has provided us about the world. Science has not provided us with an objective reflection of the world, but a culturally, historically, linguistically, and paradigmatically specific view. As we have learned, the *modus operandi* the scientist uses shapes the world that he or she sees. Thus, when a paradigmatic change takes place, it is not simply the *modus operandi* of science that changes, but the world itself is transformed. Indeed, what we know of the world is grounded on the questions about it we can imagine — the basis of constructivism.

With this knowledge and the epistemological crisis it pro struggle to figure out what to do. This discussion of the qualitative doman interpretive criteria is a manifestation of that struggle, of human beings trying to find a light in the darkness or at least attempting not to be afraid of the dark. Amidst the crisis and the development of these criteria, we rediscover the brilliance of the Oracle at Delphi and the provision of ambiguous answers to the questions of the ancient Greeks. Affirmation and denial are complex when we come from different backgrounds and are forced to operate in the medium of language. In this complexity we understand that the knowledge we produce is dependent on our questions and our questions are dependent on the formation of our subjectivities. As we feel our way through this epistemological darkness, we try to avoid the stumbling blocks of intractable norms and arbitrary interpretations. At the same time we seek a place where we can make justifiable qualitative distinctions between interpretations.

Power in the Qualitative Dimension: Critical Interpretation

As we stumble in the epistemological darkness, we may find insights into this situation that were not accessible in the artificial light of positivism. Many argue that particular meanings of events may reveal themselves only to the one who tells stories about them — the historian, the ethnographer, the psychoanalyst, the semiotician. We realize that there is a profoundly complex relationship between the stories of the human actors in particular situations and the narrators'/researchers' stories about them. There is no doubt that there are dynamics understood by the actors that are not understood by the storytellers; and that there are concepts appreciated by the storytellers that are not appreciated by the actors. In light of such complexity what does qualitative research have to tell us in these circumstances? A trustworthy account of the actor's words, intentions, and motivations? A true presentation of the meanings actors are making? In the context of critical constructivism and critical interpretation, is the role of power as it relates to the lived world of the actors better understood by the storytellers than the actors themselves? These are complex concerns that complicate critical analysis and knowledge production in the qualitative domain.

Critical constructivists set out with these difficult questions in mind to gain insight into the power dimensions of the interpretive process. Interpretations offered by those situated at different locations in the web of reality will reflect the effects of these inscriptions of power. Issues of race, class, gender, sexuality, religion, and geographical place all contribute to these inscriptions and must always be taken into account. In this context the critical analyst examines the relationship between linguistic and textual influences and the ontological (having to do with being, what it means to be human) reality of human suffering, terror, and domination. The failure to account for both dimensions leads to interpretive distortions.

On one hand observers identify a *naïveté* about how linguistic and textual influences insidiously shape what we perceive and don't perceive about the world. On the other hand they point out how an interpretation operating exclusively at the theoretical level separates us from and renders us insensitive to the emotion and lived nature of human pain and suffering and the forces that shape them. Both this *naïveté* and insensitivity are unacceptable to the critical constuctivist researcher struggling with power in relation to the act of interpretation. As researchers come to appreciate the interacting insights of the theoretical and the lived domains, the catalytic value of their work increases. With such appreciations informing their interpretations they begin to produce knowledge that can be used to promote rigorous scholarship, justice, and egalitarianism (Madison, 1988; Giroux, 1997; Hicks, 1999; Barone, 2000).

With these notions in mind, critical teacher researchers may come to see things about the world, and discern the covert workings of power in specific situations that typically sneak past. The power-sniffing abilities of feminist theory, poststructuralism, discourse analysis, and postcolonialism are invaluable to critical interpreters in these processes. Here critical constructivists are able to produce interpretations that combine the wide lenses of historical contextualization with the microscope of particularity. In the interplay of these perspectives we begin to see the intricacies of the historical and social construction of everyday life and classroom practice. In this context we become power literate and use our new literacy to take on responsibility for our social/political/educational practices as they relate to the demands of democracy. In this manner the interpretive act in the qualitative dimension becomes more than an act of knowledge production — it morphs into history-making (Grossberg, 1995; Kellner, 1995; Giroux, 1997). It breaks down the blinders of 'what is' and 'what is possible.' It grants us a voice in struggles where the concept of power is excluded. Very importantly, it provides this society with the possibility of self-reflection.

The power of interpretive insight to promote historicization and self-reflection — like so many other aspects of the qualitative dimension — moves us to become great researchers and great scholars. By understanding the impact of power in a larger historical context and in the micro socio-educational domain, researchers gain the ability to approach the most pressing, demanding, confusing, and distressing issues facing a society in the most compelling academic manner possible. This central feature of this book emerges yet again: teachers as researchers lead the way to a rigorous educational reform. The focus on what can be learned in the qualitative dimension, the struggle for a rigorous high-quality education, and the political goals of inclusivity and social justice converge at this point.

The type of interpretive insight discussed here grants us a much thicker understanding of the ways the powers of racism, class bias, sexism, and heterosexism operate to undermine the promise of democracy. With these knowledges, teacher researchers can take action on challenges to the struggle for democracy (Giroux, 1997; Kincheloe, Steinberg, Rodriguez, and Chennault, 1998; Rodriguez and Villaverde, 2000; Weil, 2001a). Teaching in this scholarly, insightful, and democratic context can no longer be conceptualized as merely the process of knowledge transmission. Instead, it becomes a sophisticated form of knowledge work that is an inseparable aspect of the democratic process, as it raises questions about the complex ways that knowledge, curricula, and consciousness are produced. These questions rest at the core of teacher research and the benefits of the qualitative dimension.

Historical Analysis in the Qualitative Dimension

Although it is rarely discussed in the literature of teacher action research, the conceptual grounding of rigorous teacher inquiry and a fundamental feature of the qualitative dimension involve historical analysis. In a hermeneutical, interpretive context the world can no longer be viewed as a fixed, static, non-temporal entity but as one that is historically constructed and thus always in process. In constructing a critical qualitative view of the world, therefore, immutability gives way to complex change and universal history surrenders to cultural genealogies. This insight changes the way we study, for example, schooling. We know that it has been constructed at a particular place and time and that it reflects power-shaped values, assumptions, social relationships, and ways of seeing. Thus, via the historical analysis of the qualitative domain, teacher researchers begin to see how human beings have made the world in particular, culturally specific ways. Armed with such knowledge they can more clearly understand that such a world and all its institutions can be changed by human beings (Madison, 1988; D. Smith, 1999; Horn, 2000; Fleischer, 2001; Kincheloe, 2001).

Such grounding deflects rationalistic efforts to divert teacher research into dutifully examining solvable, well-structured problems devised by school administrators. Such distortions cannot stand the scrutiny of the historical analysis of the development of organizational purpose. Is the purpose of education just? ethical? conceptually cohesive? What are the goals of teacher research in relationship to differing pedagogical purposes? What epistemologies, values, ideologies, discourses are shaping the nature and purposes of teacher inquiry? How do we rethink the purposes and the means of executing our research in light of these historical inquiries? With such questions and the historical research they promote, teachers begin to understand the complex ways that power contributes to the shaping of educational purpose.

What critical analysts have learned over the last three decades is that socio-economic and political power does not simply dictate educational purpose and socialize passive teachers into robotic hegemonic agents. Humans are more savvy than this 'Stepford wife model' of human agency would indicate. But power is so insidious, so ingrained in every dimension of our everyday lives that none of us escape it. I may be a confident analyst of power who warns my fellow scholars and teachers about its surreptitious effects. But I would be shamefully dishonest if I did not admit that power gets me too — right when I least expect it. Historical contextualization by no means guarantees that we won't periodically be duped by power. It does, however, make us less vulnerable as it exhibits numerous examples of the political features of culture and education. It helps teachers and students understand that history has inscribed the consciousness they bring with them to the schoolhouse.

Here they begin to analyze the relationships, the conflicts, and the affinities between that consciousness and the social and political assumptions undergirding the culture of schooling. Thus, they come to realize what types of academic skills may help them grasp what power has done via social and educational institutions to construct and subvert their dreams, vocational ambitions, and interpersonal ways of being. With these profound understandings they can begin the process of gaining self-direction, redefining their relationships with the school and the world. Such insight may be the best form of 'remedial' education that could be developed. First, it doesn't view marginalized students as deficient and in need of remediation; and second, it addresses the ways that power shapes school in general and student subjectivity in particular. Such constructions exert a profound impact on marginalized dispositions toward school and learning (Theobold and Mills, 1995; Apple, 1999; Agnello, 2001; Gordon, 2001; Lester, 2001).

This historical awareness provides marginalized students with a new sense of purpose, a new perspective on how to approach learning. The point here is not to adjust students to the hegemonic aspects of schooling and manipulate them into developing a 'good attitude' toward learning. The critical goal is much more complex; such students come to recognize the hegemonic aspects of schooling for what they are — forms of manipulative power. What teacher researchers are attempting to teach students in the context of helping them develop a historical consciousness involves the disposition to teach themselves, to develop research skills, to become aware of how they can use counter-hegemonic forms of learning to fight the forces that disempower themselves and their communities.

Since its inception, critical theory has stressed historical consciousness as a necessary part of studying the way power has shaped identity and consciousness. Teachers and students with a historical consciousness possess an analytical basis from which to begin their research. They quickly understand the hegemonic and ideological implications of interpretive schema and curricula that stress social harmony and fail to question prevailing socio-political and cultural assumptions. Without the self-reflection promoted by this historical consciousness, critical social change and the attainment of more authentic democratic institutions are not possible. In this context teacher researchers gain the ability to identify social contradictions. In these asymmetries they find the abrasive grains of sand that generate their research projects. In these all-important contradictions they find the necessity of immanent critique as they compare what is to what should be.

As teacher researchers with a consciousness of history study the ways power has shaped identity and consciousness, they become more and more aware of the relationship that connects power in its guises of ideology, hegemony, and discourse to the unconsciousness. Here is where critical teacher researchers move to a reconceptualized psychoanalysis (a post-structuralist psychoanalysis) that has rid traditional psychoanalysis of its patriarchal, heterosexist, and Eurocentric inscriptions. In this context teacher researchers study the ways power constructs human needs and desires. Such constructions often reveal themselves in irrational behaviors that provide us with insights into the relationships between power and self not to be found via other methodologies. Here teacher researchers operating with historical consciousness may identify power-generated unconscious processes that construct resistance to progressive change and induce self-destructive behaviors.

Poststructuralist psychoanalysis offers hope to teacher researchers concerned with producing knowledge that helps them motivate marginalized students, as it gains new insights into human potential. New understandings of the constructed nature of human needs and desires emerge in this complex process. In this context heightened sensitivities to expressions of racism, sexism, and homophobia may be developed, moving the discourse of multi-culturalism away from the study of race as only a black and non-white conundrum to a new locale where it involves the enigma of whiteness as well. Teacher researchers may find data on these dynamics in previously unexpected places: popular culture and reactions to it, expressions of pleasure, sexual fantasies, the 'banalities' of everyday life. The insights gained here are cardinal features of the critical qualitative domain (Alford, 1993, Russell, 1993; Block, 1995; Giroux, 1997; Kincheloe, Steinberg, Rodriguez, and Chennault, 1998; Hicks, 1999; Rodriguez and Villaverde, 2000).

The Power of the Qualitative Dimension in Improving Educational Quality

A central goal in this discussion of the value of the qualitative domain is apparent to many readers: the integration of the processes of teacher research, social change, student learning, and the improvement of educational quality so that it's hard to tell where one ends and the others begin.

Teachers as researchers are not frightened by the complexity of such a task. As they avoid the facile answers of positivism, they embrace the analytical, social constructivist, interpretive, power-literate, and historicized complexity and sophistication of the qualitative dimension. As mentioned earlier, curriculum developers and teachers who possess these qualitative abilities are significantly better prepared to produce a rigorous pedagogy than those who do not. They understand where knowledge comes from, who produced it, under what circumstances it was produced, and the hidden assumptions that guided its production. They possess a capacity for reflection, criticism, and higher orders of cognition made possible by these understandings.

Such teacher researchers know that school knowledges as well as media knowledges cannot be passed off as objective bodies of information. Teachers as researchers who use knowledge derived from the qualitative dimension are committed to producing a meta-awareness of any curriculum that engages a rigorous understanding of its (in the postformal lexicon) etymology. This etymology is the story of its historical origins, its ideological dimensions, and the power interests it serves. In the power-saturated world of schooling in the twenty-first century, however, these are the precise features of curriculum and instruction that are repressed. The effort to make this conceptual rigor a part of the mainstream curriculum will not be easy. Even in sophisticated higher educational settings, these concerns are not appreciated. Teaching in many English, philosophy, psychology, sociology, history, physical science, and communications departments, for example, is still seen as the unproblematic transmission of certified data. Critical teacher researchers at all educational levels from elementary to doctoral programs insist on problematizing the curriculum, the purpose of education, and the conditions under which all knowledge is produced and received (Apple, 1993, 1999; Giroux, 1997; Perry, 2001).

Critical teacher researchers understand that pedagogy is always a cultural act where power is produced and received around dynamics of consciousness, unconsciousness, ethics, values, and lived experiences. To remove teaching from this context is to be guilty of a crass act of reductionism. When such a removal takes place, pedagogical authority is positioned in a socio-political location that is beyond questioning. Critical teacher researchers are always focused on the relationship between knowledge and power and conduct their research and formulate their pedagogy in ways that open this relationship to the sunlight of analysis. In an era of free market fundamentalism (Aronowitz and DiFazio, 1994; Kincheloe, 1999) where the power of the market to dominate is outside the realm of questioning, this critical qualitative form of research and analysis becomes even more important. The power of the market and its elite promoters to produce popular culture, media, and school knowledges has never been so unchallenged. It is a frightening time for advocates of democratic research and education.

The squashing of an educational conversation and a public discourse about these pedagogical problems makes democracy even more fragile than it already is. In this context we clearly perceive the necessity for education for critical knowledge work in the contemporary landscape. Educational reform and understanding of the contemporary socio-political moment are inseparable. Indeed, educational reform cannot be conceptualized outside of a deep appreciation of the social, cultural, political, economic forces that shape contemporary Western societies and their educational institutions. Critical teacher researchers, therefore, develop a detailed understanding of these social dynamics and their relationship to the role and purposes of schooling. Comprehending these complex relationships, they are better equipped to understand what operating on the grounding of a critical system of meaning might look like in present conditions. In this context their research abilities enable them not simply to be better teachers but to conceptualize the socio-political landscape in relationship to what it means to be an educated person in the first decade of the twenty-first century (Giroux, 1997; Ellis, 1998; Fischer, 1998).

With these insights in place, teacher researchers are well equipped to study the communities in which their students live and the ways they shaped their relationships to pedagogies being employed. Such macro- and micro-inquiries provide teachers with the intellectual power to construct the conditions of their professional practice, to use their knowledges to make everyday decisions about the nature of their teaching. In this context they find they need to develop specific curricula for unique circumstances, to formulate special programs for particular problems that emerge. It is in these ways that teachers use the qualitative dimension as a path to empowerment for themselves, their colleagues, and their students. This is the heart and soul of a democratic pedagogy: creating the conditions that allow for the production of critical citizens who develop an articulate voice in the public conversation.

It is in this research context, in this domain of politics and citizenship that we gain the ability to change educational practice. Here is where the argumentation, interpretation, problem-identification and problem-solving abilities of the qualitative dimension emerge and find pedagogical application. The power of the qualitative dimension can help us create new educational dimensions, new ways of knowing, learning, and being that will create better individual and collective lives. These types of changes are simply not possible without scholarly teacher researchers who engage in forms of knowledge work now required in the twenty-first century. Teachers are hungry for these abilities and the empowerment that they bestow.

Chapter 10

Values, Objectivity and Ideology

If we adopt a critical constructivist epistemology, we reject the positivistic notion that facts and values are separate. From this perspective values are seen as a basic dimension of the research process from the selection of what is to be investigated, to the methods employed, to the definitions given to terms encountered during the investigation. This is quite a contrast to the traditional positivist belief that values play no role in the research process unless to undermine its validity.

Critical Constructivist Research and the Exposé of Values

A point which critical qualitative research has made repeatedly is that underlying all social research are specific assumptions about society — value-laden assumptions which refer to the way we view social control, order, and responsibility. Critical qualitative researchers have accepted the fact that inquiry is anything but a neutral activity, as it draws upon our values, our hopes, and the mysteries emerging from our social worlds. We are constantly confronted with value questions dealing with morality, critical constructivist researchers maintain, since the subjects and objects of social science are humans. Social and educational research finds it impossible to remove itself from value assumptions about social relationships. Indeed, many philosophers of research argue that educational research is meaningful only to the extent that it has a value orientation (Popkewitz, 1981a; J. Smith, 1983; Brennan and Noffke, 1997; Carson and Sumara, 1997; Brosio, 2000).

Critical constructivists, of course, reject the possibility of value-free research into social and educational phenomena and see attempts to argue the case for value freedom as a form of ideological mystification — that is, an attempt to hide the political interests of educational practice and the research about it. If researchers fail to keep the normative or value dimension of educational research in mind, the research they produce and the ends to which it is applied will simply serve to reproduce hegemonic social relations. Thus, from the critical perspective an awareness of the value orientation of research is essential, as it brings to consciousness the fundamental embodiments of power which move social and educational events (Soltis, 1984; McLaren, 2000).

Thomas Popkewitz (1981a) maintains that social and educational research expresses the researcher's value orientation in at least two important ways: (1) The research we undertake reflects our view of socio-political values. Our research allows us to reconcile what we see as social contradiction and to ponder the consequences of the actions of institutions. For example, we may see a class-stratified society beset by problems resulting from the existence of a so-called permanent underclass. We want to know how the arrangement of educational institutions affects this situation. (2) Our value orientations shape both our research questions and the manner in which we approach our study. And since social research (especially empirical social research) holds such a high status in the society, many individuals promote the belief that educational problems can only be solved through the application of rigorous science. Thus, solutions that emerge from community participation and democratic negotiation are dismissed — society has come to rely on the cult of the expert, those social scientists with precise, dispassionate answers to technical problems.

When researchers fail to note the existence of this omnipresent value dimension, Kenneth Howe (1985) contends that unpleasant outcomes typically result: (1) The research will be useless as information which informs practical action. Value judgments are inseparable from educational descriptions because of the relationship between educational research and educational practice. If researchers do not allow values to serve as a link between research and practice, educational inquiry will be irrelevant to what teachers and administrators actually do. In other words, the relationship between what we know and how we act upon the knowledge is problematic. Values not only inform what we claim to know but the actions that we take as a result of the knowledge. (2) Value-free research will be inefficient. If research in the field is not grounded upon explicitly stated values that are open to evaluation, little benefit will ever be derived from such research. Thus, energy and resources will have been wasted. (3) Value-free research holds the potential to produce harmful results (Howe, 1985: 17). When research purports to be value-free but covertly promotes specific values, various groups and individuals are rendered quite vulnerable. Students who are culturally different may be labeled emotionally disturbed; young girls and boys who attempt to transcend gender restrictions may be seen as maladjusted; or thoughtful young people with intelligent questions about social convention may be labeled as troublemakers.

Obviously, values in research affect human beings in very concrete ways. If the values of research are typically hidden, then the justifications for the educational policies based on them are also concealed. When such restrictions are out of sight, teachers have only a restricted view of why they do the things that they do. An analysis of the historical forces which have structured values is an integral part of critical constructivist action research. As we know, research is never a neutral means to a particular end. Research and its methodology grow out of the values of a particular world view. This particular world view, this paradigm, determines what constitutes legitimate research or an acceptable way of thinking. Even though positivistic, instrumentally rational research models have been challenged in many academic settings, they still dominate the mind-set of many elementary and secondary schools. They are even attempting to reestablish control in numerous academic settings in the first decade of the twenty-first century. Emerging from business and military (remember Alice Rivlin) sources, modernist manifestations of positivistic research inject the values of business management and the military into the life of the school. Here is where the importance of our phenomenological, historical, semiotic, and ethnographic forms of qualitative research become so important to the teacher researcher. They provide the tools with which we reveal the forces which make schools what they are, which tacitly construct the goals of education in an industrial society (Cherryholmes, 1988; Orteza Y Miranda, 1988; Carson, 1997).

Power, Values, and Specific Research Practices

Why do educational researchers use particular words, metaphors, and models when they design their inquiry, interpret it, and suggest policies based on it? Their research language reflects the effects of the influence of power in the larger society. Power, as Foucault has argued, has served to censor, exclude, block, and repress like a great superego; but, he continues, it also serves to produce knowledge, creating effects at the level of desire (Britzman and Pitt, 1997). As a censor in educational research, power serves to limit what constitutes a legitimate question, excluding 'dangerous' investigations such as explorations of how class factors affect student performances in school. As a producer in educational research, power serves to reward particular ways of seeing and particular activities. For example, educational researchers follow particular research norms to achieve conventional definitions of success in their fields. Such success allows them the rewards of funded grants and promotions based on scholarly productivity. The ways that different research orientations draw boundaries between what is acceptable and what is not constitute an ideological dimension of the act of inquiry (Cherryholmes, 1988). Here, power is at work, promoting particular views of educational excellence and educational failure.

As critical constructivist teacher researchers we make a mistake when we assume that a cabal of conspirators exercise this power, as they consciously seek to control the educational world. Much of the time the ideological construction of consciousness emanating from sources of power does not take place at the level of conscious intention. For example, positivistic educational researchers do not simply seek to design research resulting in the perpetuation of business and military values in school practices. School administrators do not simply seek to use educational research which represses ethical considerations and questions of justice in their efforts to run their schools. And most teachers do not consciously attempt to suppress their students' ability to think at a more critical level nor do they try to punish the underprivileged or reward the privileged. But all of these unfortunate things happen and most of the time we have no clue why. We don't catch on because we don't understand the subtle semiotic dimensions of power reproduction, that is, how codes, symbols, and signs subtlety construct our world views. As critical constructivist action researchers we begin to see how educational research produced by such subtle forces legitimizes particular values and delegitimizes others (Purpel, 1999).

For example, in terms of concrete research practices, who is legitimate to interview, to use as a reliable source, and who is not? As a high school social studies teacher I often watched social studies teachers bring experts to their economics classes to speak and to answer student questions. In my high school these experts were usually successful *businessmen* who delivered a remarkably standardized ideological package for student consumption. The idea of inviting individuals from other social classes or other ideological traditions (e.g., labor leaders, social workers, welfare rights leaders, etc.) was never considered. Dominant values and ideology were thus reproduced, not at a level of conscious intent on the part of the teachers, but at a tacit, unconscious stratum (Kincheloe, 2001). On this same stratum the records of any historical era favor those who direct public events or produce the records; the masses, the common voices of working people, are excluded from the picture. Critical constructivist teacher researchers, aware of these hegemonic dimensions of power in inquiry, take special pains to collect testimonies of individuals outside of power (Reinharz, 1979; Glasberg, 1998; Semali and Kincheloe, 1999; Horn, 2000).

Expert researchers from academic settings like to believe that the university, because it is called 'academic,' is removed from these historical realities, value dimensions, and ideological forces which shape the form their research takes. Our research, no matter who we are, is never as independent of outside influences as we would like to think. We are all caught at a particular point in the web of reality. Our project, of course, is to understand what our particular vantage point is and how it limits our vision. This process involves our awareness of our own historicity, or place in history (Grimmett, 1997; Quinn, 2001). We become conscious of our own ideological inheritance and its relationship to our belief and value structures, our interests, our questions about our professional lives (Hart, 2001). In his studies of the eugenicists and their influence on the way educators came to view intelligence and school performance, Steven Selden traces how social visions shaped eugenicist research design. Ideological conceptions of what

d civilization, human progress, and a good society could not be
from the formulation of eugenicist research. What is ironic in
this case, is that many of the instruments devised by eugenicist researchers
to measure learning, intelligence, and ability are still employed in contemporary education. Thus, at an unseen level the value assumptions of the
eugenicist movement are embedded in contemporary educational practices
(Selden, 1984; Cherryholmes, 1988; Owen and Doerr, 1999).

Mainstream researchers have ridiculed such claims, arguing that no
one in modern educational research is a eugenicist. Indeed, they are correct in their assertion that eugenics is out of fashion and that educational
researchers from almost any ideological perspective would vigorously
reject association with the tradition. Even the work of Richard Herrnstein
and Charles Murray (1994) in *The Bell Curve*, perceived by many as neo-
eugenicist (Kincheloe, Steinberg, and Gresson, 1996), was promoted as
anti-eugenicist. Research, however, derives its meaning and its importance from the purposes for which it was designed. Much of the time the
purposes are not known by those educators who consume the research.
Unfortunately, educators and political leaders too often only notice that
research serves particular ideological intentions when those purposes
confront some aspect of the *status quo* (Bogdan and Biklen, 1982; Denzin
and Lincoln, 2000).

The *status quo* is challenged, for example, when an educational
researcher contends that business sponsorship of excellence programs in
particular schools is saturated by power. When critical constructivists point
out that such research serves to produce unquestioning attitudes toward
the positive role of business in the local community and a one-dimensional
perspective on the virtues of a Chamber of Commerce-view of unregulated
free enterprise economics, feathers are ruffled. It is at this point that cries
of bias and politicized research make their way into the popular media as
well as teacher, parent, and community awareness. Power has its ways;
research emerging from a system of meaning, like ours, that challenges dominant ideology will typically be viewed as politicized and biased. Research
which does not will often be deemed neutral and value-free (Macedo,
1994).

Intelligence Testing as Positivist Research:
Power Tracks in the Snow

It may sound trite on one level, but the analysis of values in educational
inquiry must remind teacher researchers that they need to consider the
desirability of what we do (Sumara and Davis, 1997; Butler, 1998; Steinberg
and Kincheloe, 1998; Purpel, 1999). Critical researchers have repeatedly
broached this question in a variety of contexts. If self-direction and emancipation are possible, they remind us, we must become aware of hidden

values in *how* and *what* we come to know. Human institutions and the various forms of work which go on within them must always be examined with these value questions in mind.

Inquiry failing to acknowledge this value dimension of educational research introduces, rather than eliminates, the possibility of bias and deception. Once again let us use the example of intelligence testing in this society to illustrate the point. Such tests measure qualities that are tacitly valued as important or good. Many societies in different times and places would value abilities quite different from those that are often identified by this society as manifestations of intelligence. Thus, the emotions that are elicited by the attempts to generate standardized measurements of intelligence across ethnic, cultural, and racial lines are not surprising (Soltis, 1984; Howe, 1985; Rodriguez and Villaverde, 2000). What is surprising is our inability to catch on to the value dimension (typically unstated) which must be understood to make sense of the intelligence debate. Let us extend our discussion of values and research with a more detailed example of the intelligence question.

David Owen and Marilyn Doerr (1999), in their exposé of the Educational Testing Service (ETS), devote much attention to uncovering the values which have contributed to the testing institution's definition and thus the society's definition of intelligence. Tracing the history of the ETS back to the days of Carl Brigham and the College Board, Owen and Doerr describe the value assumptions of those who developed the SAT, LSAT, MCAT, and many other instruments designed to measure aptitude, achievement, developed ability, higher-order reasoning abilities, or whatever term substituted for intelligence that had not yet developed pejorative connotations. If one wants to know the next synonym for intelligence employed by the ETS, Owen and Doerr advise the reader to consult the thesaurus.

In 1961, Henry Chauncey inherited from Brigham the scepter of leadership of the testing company. It is interesting to note that Brigham, the developer of the SAT, was an avowed eugenicist who believed that the 'dilution of the master race had been a direct consequence of the abolition of slavery.' Owen and Doerr are quick to point out that Brigham did not create the SAT simply to promote his eugenicist views and keep blacks out of college. His purpose was to use the SAT as a basic tool in the creation of a new social order. He foresaw that a meritocratic society would reduce the potential for disappointment and frustration by quickly pointing out to those of inferior capabilities, aptitudes, or intelligences (often non-Anglo-Saxons) that their quest for high-level, demanding positions was ill-advised. The efficient new society would appropriately place the less able in suitable slots.

Chauncey was a man very much after Brigham's heart, and as such carried on the traditions laid down by Brigham. Chauncey believed that intelligence was 'a hard, smooth nut' (i.e., discrete and easily measured) embedded deep in the brain. Standardized tests could measure the nut and in the process remake the society. Reflecting the spirit of Brigham, Chauncey believed in a meritocratic social order, where the intelligence testing establishment served as the troll at the bridge who regulated access to schools, professions and jobs. Chauncey's political and social values shaped his view of the essential role of intelligence measurement in determining one's ultimate rung on the social ladder. Not only did one's values determine the definition of intelligence, they also determined one's view of the *status quo*. Intelligence tests, Owen and Doerr argue, have bequeathed the nation's well-to-do with a conscience-soothing, scientifically grounded rationalization for the benefits they have enjoyed. The wealthy lived well because they were smart; the poor lived in squalor because they were dumb. There was a just rationality to the *status quo*.

Chauncey believed that test scores were the equivalent of money in the pocket in the meritocratic marketplace. Since testing was based on value-free definitions of intelligence, the new society could be organized objectively and efficiently. Chauncey argued at length that the responsibility for ordering society rests with the test-makers, the scientifically trained experts. If the results of the test become the basis for the structuring of society, then the test becomes the schema for society. Under the banner of fairness and objectivity, Owen and Doerr maintain, merit is defined as what the most powerful interests within a society value as meritorious. In a perverse way 'society's rewards become their own justification.' If the meritocratic society is supposed to honor the deserving by paying them lots of money, then the wealthy must be worthy. Thus, our values come to determine our strategies for determining aptitude, our definitions of merit, our educational objectives, and our socio-political policies. The claim of value freedom rings quite hollow, Owen and Doerr maintain. Far from being value-free, the 'objective' system, they conclude, serves to perpetuate old injustices by portraying them as neutral workings of a system based upon the hard scientific research of dispassionate experts.

Integrating Value Analysis into the Everyday Practices of Qualitative Research

If value judgments in inquiry are deemed to have little to do with cognition, or if they are biased, or if they are viewed as beyond the realm which requires logical justification, then social and educational research will always be flawed. This outcome is not inevitable. If social and educational researchers approach value judgments as an essential thread in the fabric of their investigations, they will come to see that such judgments require defense and criticism just like any other form of assessment. Indeed, there are two kinds of value judgments: the well supported and the poorly supported. To distinguish the two types of judgments, philosophers of research argue, researchers must transcend the conventional discourse which focuses exclusively on the reliability and validity of research procedures (Howe, 1985; Berry, 1998; Griffith and Paul, 1998).

Analysis of reliability and validity procedures is important, but its traditional modes of operation are unable to illuminate the social, cultural, and political values embedded in the research procedures. If we accept the post-Kuhnian axiom that science is a socio-cultural activity, then scientific inquiry must be examined for its cultural definitions and its value assumptions. A routine portion of the research procedure should involve the consideration of questions which expose value orientations toward social and political affairs embedded in the various dimensions of the inquiry. Such value-appraising activities, many analysts argue, are especially important when educational researchers extend their work to the evaluation and the development of school programs.

Educational scholars who wish to incorporate the insights of value analysis into their work need to consider three principles: (1) educational researchers embrace a self-reflective and critical orientation; (2) the notion of research adequacy must be extended; and (3) the design of curriculum must be reconsidered in light of the knowledge we have gleaned from the analysis of the value dimension of research. Let us briefly explain each of these principles.

Educational researchers embrace a self-reflective and critical orientation. Research methods and the theories derived from them are not neutral. As this survey of the debates in modern educational research attests, numerous philosophers of science have reconsidered the traditions of objectivity, detachment, and scientific disinterest. Even in the first decade of the twenty-first century too little of this intellectual activity has found its way into the everyday conversations of educational practice.

The notion of research adequacy needs to be extended. Scientific research is not adequate simply because it is valid and reliable in the positivistic sense. Adequacy must take into account moral considerations, purposes, and ethical premises. Educational research will succeed to the degree that it encourages a public conversation about the ways schools and educational agencies contribute to a just and ethical society. Educational research must expose the pretensions and deceptions which make unjust educational structures seem benevolent.

The design of curriculum must be reconsidered in light of the knowledge we have gleaned from the analysis of the value dimension of research (Pinar, 1994; Pinar, Reynolds, Slattery, and Taubman, 1995; Sumara, 1996). When formulating educational policy, we are in essence applying research outcomes to practice. Without the benefits derived from understanding the value-dimension, confusions about educational purpose are bound to arise. The inability of many educational leaders to discuss the social role of school or to have a clear view of the conflicts implicit in diverse plans for educational reform may be evidence of researchers' neglect of the value dimension (Popkewitz, 1981b; Agnello, 2001).

The Critical Confrontation with Objectivism

The debate over the value dimension in educational research has grown more intense in recent years as critical analysts have raised serious objections to what they describe as a misleading use of the term 'objectivity.' Henry Giroux (1981, 1997) asserts that the positivistic culture rationalizes its advocacy of value-free inquiry on the basis of an ill-conceived notion of objectivity. To produce worthwhile knowledge, researchers must engage in value-free inquiry, far away from the messy world of beliefs and presuppositions. That this belief in pseudo-objectivity could last so long, science educator John Head (1979) contends, is amazing when we consider how scientific research actually takes place. The idea of a science patiently and objectively recording a series of observations and then arranging them in a logical pattern reflecting the nature of reality depicts a process much in conflict with the psychology of human perception. Human beings are quite selective about what they attend to and very subjective in ascribing meaning to their observations. This denial of the subjective nature of the process is frightening, for, as Robert N. Bellah (1983) reminds us, it is precisely a social science that sees itself uninvolved in the social world. It is an objective social science that considers itself free from all ethical norms other than the dispassionate pursuit of knowledge and that creates engines of manipulation and human control for anyone who finds it possible to put them into practice (Barton and Osborne, 2001).

Giroux continues the argument, claiming that when knowledge and research are separated from values, more is hidden than uncovered. The notion of objectivity in any field reflects the values and assumptions of the scholars working in the field. In the name of objectivity these values and assumptions are hidden. It is impossible, he says, to separate values from facts and inquiry from ethics. The effects, Giroux (1981, 1997) tells us, of a pseudo-objective, value-free research methodology are numerous. The most obvious effect is the inaccurate picture we get of social phenomena. Cursed with a distorted picture of reality, we find it difficult to recognize problems which exist in our political and educational lives. For all the assumptions that the pseudo-objective culture of positivism makes, it fails to base its view of the world on the pretext that humans should be free to direct their own lives.

Filling the vacuum left by this failure to embrace human emancipation is an insidious form of social engineering. It is insidious in the sense that it does not admit its true nature. It is social engineering in the sense that it views humans as entities to be manipulated. The positivistic culture consistently denies the possibility that it begins with specific presuppositions. Examined thoughtfully, Giroux asserts, the failure to assume that the extension of human freedom is basic to any truly humane view of the world or any research question is a frightening assumption. The critical inquirer, he maintains, may begin his or her research with a set of assumptions; but at least they are openly stated assumptions.

Worshipping the god of objectivity, Giroux claims, the culture of positivism succumbs to what has been called the 'fallacy of objectivism.' This fallacy occurs when a research methodology is self-limiting to the point that it cannot reflect on its own presuppositions. It cannot reflect on presuppositions because it claims they do not exist. Trapped by its adulation of empirical fact, the culture of positivism fails to acknowledge the historical and social context which gave birth to it. Devoid of such context, it fails to see itself clearly — it cannot perform self-analysis. Thus, it renews with a vengeance its focus on 'what is.' Typically, the result of the analysis of 'what is' is that the *status quo* is basically sound. Teaching that is based on this culture uncritically passes 'facts' along to students outside social or historical contexts.

Giroux argues that all human activity must be fragmented to meet the requirements of empirical investigation. Schools steeped in the culture of positivism teach the outcomes of such empirical fragmentation — isolated facts. The attempt to comprehend the world as a network of interconnections is lost. Students are taught to attack problems as if they emerged in isolation, detached from the dynamic social and political forces which bestow meaning. Researchers and students of education in general can break the culture of positivism by exposing the pseudo-objectivity on which it is grounded. Such an unmasking, Giroux contends, will best be accomplished by a detailed analysis of the process which produces knowledge. In this way we will come to understand the logic behind the knowledge, its context and significance, and the implications of such understandings as we undertake new research. The process, critical researchers contend, will provide multi-dimensional educational benefits. By studying the process by which knowledge is produced, students learn about the nature of learning. It is in this way that an individual student accomplishes that important goal of education — learning to teach himself or herself. An individual who learns to teach himself or herself has engaged in one of the most basic acts of human emancipation. Because it is unconcerned with the attempt of men and women to control their own destiny, Giroux concludes that the culture of positivism is indifferent to learning which attempts to move beyond the acquisition of second-hand, authorized, ready-made facts.

Research and Ideological Analysis

One of the main points of the critical perspective as argued by Giroux, Habermas, Marcuse, Macedo, McLaren and many others is that this so-called culture of positivism is ideological. It is an ideology which induces us to focus our attention on technical questions — that is, on the search for efficient means to educational ends that we take for granted. It is an ideology, critical analysts have argued, which accepts the common-sense viewpoint that the social world is exactly as it appears. Such a viewpoint is a manifestation of a consciousness constructed by positivist ideology. As such beliefs dominate the minds of those who study and administer schools, educators fail to ask what kind of social and human life our schools produce and reproduce (Smart, 1976; Soltis, 1984; Luce-Kapler, 1997; Willinsky, 1997, 2001a; Knobel, 1999).

Research, therefore, must be subjected to ideological analysis. Habermas writes of a dialogical process of ideological analysis where participants (the scholarly community) continuously take part in an examination of the social and psychological basis of their attitudes. This continual dialogue allows researchers to frame their ideas in a manner whereby the effects of the ideological orientation, the milieu, and the historical period in which they have arisen are considered. Habermas is comfortable with the uncertainty of such a situation and admits that such a method provides no certainty for those in search of it (Holland and Mansell, 1983).

Peter McLaren (1989a) picks up on Habermas's concern with ideological analysis and frames it in an educational context. Teachers as researchers have much to learn from McLaren's explanation of why an understanding of ideology, power, and consciousness construction is so important to teachers seeking to build democratic workplaces and to provide emancipatory experiences for students. McLaren explains in his preface to *Life in Schools* how as a teacher in the poverty-stricken Jane-Finch Corridor of Toronto, he survived the classroom by drawing upon practical knowledge and untutored pedagogical instinct. But survival was not enough. McLaren was increasingly troubled by the feeling that he had not made a difference, that he had not helped his students in their pursuit of a hopeful future. Thwarted by a lack of acquaintance with social theory, qualitative research, and ideological analysis, McLaren could not see the connection between the schooling process and larger socio-economic realities. Without such understandings, McLaren concluded that he missed an important opportunity to develop an educational perspective that would work to empower students and transform inequities in the local community.

To draw attention to the social conditions of the students he taught, the young McLaren published the journal he kept during his years in Jane-Finch. As the years passed, he grew increasingly dissatisfied with the journal's attempt to understand and communicate his classroom experiences. Advised by a prominent journalist to let the vignettes speak for themselves, McLaren's journal consisted basically of raw material, uninterpreted stories about schooling. Observations of events, McLaren learned, never speak for themselves — every story is ideologically loaded, full of signifiers and subtle reflections of power relations. No aspect of school-ing is ideologically innocent; no thoughts, theories, or pedagogies are completely autonomous. Ideas, perspectives, research orientations and the teaching practices that come out of them are always connected to power and value interests. To 'know,' McLaren came to argue, is to deconstruct power/value/knowledge configurations. 'By failing to set my classroom journal within a critical theoretical context,' McLaren concluded, 'I could not reveal how power and knowledge work in the interests of certain groups over others' (p. ix).

McLaren's reconceptualization of his journal and his experience in Jane-Finch are very helpful in our attempt to understand the need for teacher researchers to grasp the value and ideological dimensions of action research. After teaching in Jane-Finch, McLaren worked to construct a system of meaning, a critical means of interpreting his experience. Like our efforts in this book, he turned to social theory to facilitate his ability to make sense of his teaching, his students, and the world they inhabited. To accomplish such a task we must transcend the traditional confines of action research both conceptually and geographically. We must move beyond the confines conceptually in the same sense that we have discussed throughout this book: we must construct a critical system of meaning to help us ask new questions, to see from new angles. We must surpass traditional action research geographically in the sense that we do not allow our inquiry to be confined only to the school. If teacher researchers are to act on McLaren's ideological reconceptualization of teaching experience, we must analyze inter-institutional relationships and the ways that such connections shape school life.

Not only do critical teacher researchers need to study sites outside school to understand power and ideological relationships, but they must understand that in the last three or four decades schools have been replaced as the primary educational institutions within Western societies. If edu-cation is defined as consciousness construction and not simply as what occurs inside schools, then our attention as critical constructivist teacher researchers by necessity must focus not only on schools but on mass dis-course and popular culture as well. Many educational analysts have under-stood this dynamic and acted on it. The forces of consciousness production involve the intersection of mass communications, youth culture, schooling, and countless other cultural entities. At this historical juncture the process of consciousness construction and the ideological production of self becomes more complex than ever before (Wexler, 1987; Anderson, 1989; Grossberg, 1992, 1995; Aronowitz, 1993; Steinberg and Kincheloe, 1997; Weinstein, 1998; Pinar, 2001; Kincheloe, 2002). Teacher researchers cannot allow them-selves to be stuck in antiquated notions of theory implementation, valida-tion, or invalidation; they must ask new questions of education in this age of mass discourse as pedagogical agent.

Employing Genealogy to Explore Values, Objectivity, and Ideology

In Foucault's sense of the term 'genealogy,' critical constructivist teacher researchers must be self-critical genealogists who trace the formation of their own subjectivities. What are the ideological bases of our claims to truth in our research? By recognizing the many contradictions in the construction of our own consciousnesses, teacher researchers can understand not only the complexity of their students' *Lebenswelt*s but also avoid the trap of the belief in the possibility of a transcendental view of the social world outside the web of reality. In other words, we come to recognize that there are no value-free, privileged knowers who ask ideologically unfettered questions about the methods they will employ in their studies. Drawing upon the early work of Alvin Gouldner, critical constructivist teacher researchers come to recognize that research methodology is not simply a logic but a morality in the sense that it represses or liberates particular moral questions about social and educational reality. Teachers, researchers, and teacher researchers are moral agents, rejecting or accepting the moral obligations of moral imperatives (Goodlad, 1988; McLaren, Hammer, Reilly, and Sholle 1995; McLaren, 2000).

As we engage in our self-critical genealogy, draw on our critical system of meaning, employ our phenomenological, semiotic, ethnographic, and historiographical techniques, our action research becomes 'immoral' from the perspective of those positivists who wag their fingers at our lack of research piety, that is, rigor. Our self-critical genealogy and the critical action research which grows out of it, constitute an emancipatory right of passage as we leave behind our research 'adolescence.' Exercising our new maturity, we come to formulate more penetrating questions about our professional practice, see new levels of activity and meaning in our classrooms, decipher connections between socio-cultural meanings and the everyday life of school, and reconceptualize what we already 'know.' As we grow to understand the race, class, gender, and sexual locations of the students and others that we study, we come to appreciate our own location and the social relationships such locations produce (Reinharz, 1982; Briton, 1997; Salvio, 1997; Perry, 2001).

Without this ideological self-criticism we cannot find the path to the *Lebenswelt*. As Hans-Georg Gadamer (1975) argued, the critique of both the prevalent notions of objectivity and the way these ideas have shaped us, allow us to get behind the objectivity of inquiry so that we might discover the life-world. Standing at the intersection of his or her own subjectivity and that which is being observed, the researcher discovers a crack in time and space through which he or she might crawl (Smits, 1997). From the other side of this temporal and spatial fissure, the world can be seen afresh — the trivial becomes the profound, comfortable assumptions are turned inside out. This genealogical self-criticism has become an epic reconstruction of consciousness; indeed, we have stumbled on the process of not only how researchers make new discoveries but how fields of inquiry are transformed (Utke, 1998). Major advances in how we see social and educational phenomena do not emerge from a linear accumulation or extension within the matrix of previous discoveries. Major reconceptualizations come out of a meta-analysis of the ideological assumptions on which the framework underlying the accumulation of extant knowledge is grounded. Critical knowledge is produced not so much by asking questions *within* the framework as it is by asking questions *about* the framework (Reinharz, 1979; Brent, 1998).

The very notion of critical constructivist action research is an example of how fields advance. Its existence is predicated on a set of inquiries about the framework of traditional educational research — about the ideological assumptions on which it rests. Advocates of critical action research have questioned the following:

- the viability of propositional knowledge in a particular field;

- the ethics of employing educational research in the attempt to predict and thus control the effects of technical process-product reasoning on how teachers conduct their professional lives; and

- the trustworthiness of linear cause–effect research designs in socio-educational settings.

Such questions are value-laden in that they promote action research in education as a form of ethical reflection within the domain of practice. Action research would never have existed if consciousness of the ideological malformations of the workplace had not existed. Advocates of action research based their ideas on the assumption that the established way of doing research did not benefit practitioners as it produced a series of top-down rules for directing the professional lives of teachers. In the name of scientific objectivity, very specific ideological assumptions about knowledge, and the organization of the workplace, and the role of teachers *vis-à-vis* administrators, were being promoted (Elliott, 1989a).

Research, Objectivity, and the Lessons of Vietnam and Manufactured Consent

Critical constructivist teacher researchers see objectivity from another angle — a vantage point which advances our understanding of practitioner knowledge. Let us use some non-schooling examples to illustrate the critical constructivist attempt to demystify uncritical notions of objectivity. Until the Vietnam War journalists (with significant exceptions) conceived of objectivity as 'official-source journalism'. Tom Wicker (1975) writes that journalists who did not rely on governmental and corporate official sources were considered subjective, if not subversive. But their front-line experience in the South-east Asian jungles changed the minds of many in the profession as they began to uncover the lack of truth in the information provided by official governmental sources. As reporters spent time with Vietnamese people, low-ranking U.S. officials in the hinterland, and soldiers and nurses, they began to uncover a very different picture of how the war was going. These reporters surrendered their official source objectivity, and in the manner of action researchers began seeing for themselves and analyzing for themselves, often at the risk of physical harm and governmental wrath. From the perspective of those who fought the war and cared for its victims, the claims of the Pentagon spokespeople, the generals, and the ambassadors began to appear fatuous and hollow. The reporters had taken a dangerous and subversive step: they had abandoned their official source objectivity for a phenomenological first-hand engagement with the lived world of the war. It was at this very point that they were accused of bias; the dominant view of proper reporter behavior was able to persuade a large portion of the American public of their 'misguided, pro-Communist' motives (Bogdan and Biklen, 1982: 218).

The critical constructivist action research attempt to demystify objectivity can be informed by an acquaintance with Edward Herman's and Noam Chomsky's (1988) analysis of how dominant ideology insidiously works to construct consciousness in contemporary life. Their analysis of what they call 'manufactured consent' can be applied to any institution, education in particular, and can help us transcend positivistic notions of objectivity. Herman and Chomsky's analysis forces action researchers to rethink our notions of source evaluation, how we designate a source as credible. Typically, perspectives, such as critical constructivism, which focus our attention on domination are dismissed by mainstream researchers as conspiracy theories. Herman and Chomsky's analysis of manufactured consent or the process of domination is *not*, they zealously contend, a conspiracy theory. In the modern media, for example, most ideological domination comes from the pre-selection of innocent people, internalized perceptions, and the influences of ownership, organization, market, and political power on reporters and editors. Censorship is usually self-censorship, by researchers and commentators who have internalized the constraints imposed by sources, media organizations, market considerations, and governmental power.

Herman and Chomsky direct their attention to how money and power work to filter out news unfavorable to their interests, to marginalize dissent, and to grant access to government and dominant private interests to get their messages across to the public. These so-called news filters include four headings with important implications for action researchers attempting to analyze consciousness construction. The first filter involves the size, ownership, and profit orientation of the mass media. Since the industrial revolution, ownership of media has been limited to the required large investment — in the contemporary era only twenty-nine media systems account for more than half of the output of newspapers and most of the magazines, broadcasting, books, and movies. These media systems are large profit-seeking organizations which have been fully integrated into the culture of the economic marketplace. Thus, they face pressures of stock-holders, directors, and bankers to direct their attention to the bottom line. Because of their profitability, media systems constantly face the threat of takeovers, prompting their managers to focus even more exclusively on profitability. Thus, content and coverage decisions fall increasingly in the hands of finance directors, bankers, and investors. Market objectives thus take precedence over traditional journalistic goals.

The second filter involves advertising as the primary income source for the mass media. An examination of the history of newspapers seems to indicate the power of advertisers to influence content and perspective. Papers that could attract ads could sell copies well below production costs. Papers that could not, by necessity had to keep copy prices high and price of packaging (format, features, promotion) low. Thus, advertising-supported papers drove out of existence or marginalized papers that depended on sales alone. In the newspaper business papers which were typically driven out of business or marginalized were those with perspect-ives critical of business and other potential advertisers. Modern broadcast media are affected by similar forces but take the process one step farther: TV networks labor to assure their stockholders that they are not interested in appealing to audiences *per se* but to audiences with buying power. When combined with TV network competition for advertisers' patronage — networks hire and train special staffs to assure advertisers how their programs serve advertisers' needs — the effect on the content of TV pro-grams becomes clear. Examples abound: when public station WNET aired *Hungry for Profit*, a documentary containing material critical of multina-tional corporate activities in the Third World, the Gulf and Western corporation withdrew its funding. The message to other broadcasters was clear.

The third filter involves the reliance of media on information sup-plied by government, business, and experts (educational and otherwise) funded or approved by these power sources. To survive, to meet their news schedules, mass media need a steady flow of raw material of news. Practical economics dictates that they concentrate their resources where pre-packaged news emanates in the form of carefully planned leaks and formal press conferences: the White House, the Pentagon, the State Department, the Department of Education are all such venues. On the local level, city hall, the police department, business corporations, trade organizations, and the central office of a local school district provide analogous settings. These bureaucracies can be trusted consistently to turn out the volume necessary to media needs. Such bureaucracies also have the merit of credibility granted by status and prestige. Falling prey to the cult of the expert, newsworkers treat bureaucratic accounts as factual because they refuse to question the order of authorized knowers in the society. In this context a bureaucracy's claim to knowledge is viewed not as a claim but as a validated piece of knowledge. When one examines the resources allocated by these bureaucracies to get the word out, the scope of their control over information is staggering.

The fourth filter involves 'flak' as a means of disciplining the media. Flak refers to negative reactions to a media statement or media programming, often taking the form of letters, telegrams, phone calls, petitions, lawsuits, boycotts, and so on. If flak is large-scale it can prove to be very costly to the media, as positions have to be defended and advertisers withdraw patronage. During the McCarthy period TV and radio stations were routinely subdued by flak from determined 'Red hunters.' In the first decade of the twenty-first century advertisers and media systems are very careful not to offend certain constituencies that are potential flak producers. Certain topics or types of programming are consistently avoided in hopes of avoiding flak. The ability of an interest group to produce flak which is effective is related to power. In the 1970s, 1980s, and 1990s numerous organizations were funded by business and industrial groups for the express purpose of producing flak. Such efforts have proved very successful in filtering what topics are covered and how they are covered in newspapers and on TV. Herman and Chomsky grant action researchers insight into the alleged innocence of the information which shapes the consciousness of students, teachers, administrators, and community members. As they destroy the myth of an ideology-free consciousness, they teach a lesson on the insidious, unintended process by which consciousness is shaped (Herman and Chomsky, 1988: 2–28). No longer can action researchers explore the educational world outside of a cultural frame; no longer can they fail to see the impact of power relationships on everyday life in school and society. Such awareness sets the stage for critical constructivist teacher research as a form of political action.

Working Our Way through the Ideological Swamp: Teacher Research as Praxis

Before action research can become a form of praxis (i.e., action informed by reflection with an emancipatory intent), teacher inquirers must understand that many aspects of the research process inhibit political actions. The relationship, for example, between researcher and researched is shaped, of course, by dominant ideological perspectives on the goals and methods of inquiry. Dominant research orientations preclude researchers from pointing out forms of domination to the researched; such orientations obstruct attempts to encourage emancipatory social change for the betterment of the individuals, groups, and communities being studied. An understanding of the hierarchical relationships between researcher–researched alerts teacher researchers to the dynamics of the emancipatory relationships they hope to establish with the students, other teachers, administrators, and community members they research. Drawing upon our understanding of subjugated knowledge, we examine the hierarchical relations between qualititative researchers and minority groups, for example, Blacks, Latinos, and Native Americans. Because they often understand the researchers' hierarchical view of them (listen to Sioux tribal member Floyd Westerman's insightful song, 'Here Come the Anthros,' as an example of the perspective of the researched), the subjugated objects of research view inquirers with distrust and often refuse to let them into their lives. As researchers fail to understand many of the unique and subtle characteristics of the informants' world, their research distorts the lived conditions and the potentials of the researched. Such misrepresentations limit the possibility of the inquiry to serve as a basis for improving the life chances of the people being studied. The researchers just report what they see; and what they see may be severely limited by the ideological construction of their own psyche (Gordon, Miller, and Rollock, 1990; McLaren, 2000).

There is a lot more to the act of research, critical constructivist researchers argue, if it is to be praxis-based, if it is to make a difference in the lives of the researchers and the researched. Since the social perceptions of the researched are ideologically constructed either by way of traditional forces such as religion in preindustrial cultures or by Herman and Chomsky's media filters in late industrial societies, then an important aspect of the research act involves unmasking these social constructions. In late industrial societies the praxis-based unmasking of informant constructions of reality is important because such constructions perpetuate powerlessness. Beginning with a phenomenological understanding of the consciousness of the researched, critical constructivist researchers interrogate the forces which contribute to the shaping of that consciousness. Thus, critical constructivist action researchers unmask the consciousness of educational actors, deconstructing the ways that ideology constructs concepts such as giftedness, intelligence, success, effective schools, quality education, and so on. Questioning such concepts in the context of their critical system of meaning, critical teachers as researchers are able to identify the sources of power which define the concepts and the interests that benefit from the perpetuation of prevailing definitions. Having identified power sources and privileged interests, critical researchers and their informants can move to the praxis-based dimension; they can transform the distorted situation, emancipating the informants and themselves from the repression, the hegemony. As discussed in Chapter 8, Patti Lather (1991, 1993) argues that educational research is valid only if it moves to this level of praxis. Eschewing traditional notions of the term, Lather contends that research has achieved 'catalytic validity' if it enlightens and energizes the researcher and researched and moves them in the direction of self-determination of their own consciousness construction (Anderson, 1989).

The subjugated, as critical researchers such as Patti Lather, Bill Pinar, Valerie Janesick, Michele Fine, Marjory Mayers, Peter McLaren, and Gary Anderson would argue, have the right to name their reality. Critical action researchers have much to learn from this principle, as they take seriously the experiences of our students and the others we might research. Not only do we attend closely to the way our informants construe their realities, but we assist by encouraging them to break out of the culture of silence and apply their constructions to the shaping of their own lives. For example, empowered students and parents from a subjugated class or racial culture who were able to reconstruct a view of intelligence which was more sensitive to the talents that they already possessed, could help reshape both curricula and modes of evaluation, which typically valued only dominant forms of intelligence. In a sense, critical action research becomes pedagogical, as it teaches researcher and informant empowerment. Teachers as researchers through their understandings empower both themselves as professional agents in schools and their students and other informants as they expose ideological restrictions on their own lives and the lived experience of others (Besag, 1986b).

Thus, action research as praxis involves three basic steps:

1   phenomenological empathy — researchers develop an interpretive appreciation of the intersubjectivities, the values, and the motives held by participants in a particular venue;
2   genealogical disclosure — researchers employ historical research to reveal the origins and present forms of the ideologies, the social conditions, and the linguistic, political, and economic structures that limit the aspirations of informants and construct their world views and self-images;
3   transformative self-production — researchers in close consultation with the researched formulate strategies of resistance to those impediments to self-direction which were identified in the previous steps of the research. Aware of ideological malformations such as definitions of intelligence and success that favor privileged groups, critical researchers challenge such hegemonic constructions by helping to form networks of resistance. Such groups are composed of victims of the constructions and individuals who are willing to act on their recognition of the injustices which result from them.

As critical constructivist teacher researchers move through these three steps, they can employ a variety of research techniques to move their inquiry to the praxis-based dimension. Oral history and informant narratives from ethnography can be used to reveal ideological consciousness construction and to lay the foundation for emancipatory action. Most research interviews tend to examine the responses of the researched as if they existed in isolation from the social contexts that produced them. Critical action researchers listen carefully to an informant's construction of his or her own life history. They carefully analyze the stories, the anecdotes, the digressions important to the researched. The teacher researcher as semiotician views these stories and the ways that they were told as texts full of signs and codes. He or she then helps the respondent restructure them in a narrative form — a form comfortable to the respondent, a form which encourages the respondent to discover and then speak in his or her own voice (Anderson, 1989). In this non-hierarchical collaboration between researcher and researched rests a central feature of teacher research as praxis. Critical teacher research not only serves to expose ideological malformations existing in the school and the community that surrounds it, but the act of collaboration itself is counter-hegemonic as it redefines the way that knowledge about schooling is produced. No longer can educational researchers view the objects of their inquiry as characters on television. Critical constructivist action researchers are more than voyeurs; they are agents, participants in the praxis of the research act.

Chapter 11

The Foundations of Teacher Research:
A Sample Syllabus

The following syllabus might be useful for educators contemplating a course in teacher research or action research. I put it together not only to provide help for such a course but to construct a conceptual overview of ways to approach the study of teachers as researchers. The course takes teachers through a variety of rigorous intellectual experiences that are all formulated to help them construct a rigorous, democratic, just, inclusive, and self-directed professional practice. It puts them in touch with some of the great debates shaping twenty-first-century intellectual life. It assumes that they are capable of the most demanding forms of academic scholarship and that they will be able to develop the capacity to creatively apply the insights derived from such work in their professional practice. A key dimension of the course involves an understanding of the complexities of the social theoretical dimensions of disciplinarity and interdisciplinarity in relation to the subject matter of the humanities, social sciences, and pedagogical analysis. In this context the course engages in the study of the research bricolage and its efforts to create the most compelling approach to research that is currently possible. Because of space limitations this description focuses exclusively on the themes of the course.

COURSE THEMES

Theoretical Grounding of Teacher Research

Analyzing Theoretical Perspectives

On one level this is an interdisciplinary social science, humanities, and pedagogy course that analyzes different theoretical perspectives involving the ways teachers as researchers come to know the world. Participants will be asked to focus these theoretical frames on the educational act. In this context the course will examine the process of theory-building and the theoretical frameworks employed by scholars in the social sciences, the humanities, and pedagogy. As the course attempts to delineate, assess, and improve these theoretical frames, it focuses attention on the application of social theory to the effort to act in and on social and educational reality. Inseparable from this dynamic is the effort to understand the various disciplines in the social sciences and humanities including specific disciplines:

- Humanities: history, philosophy, literary studies.
- Social Sciences: sociology, anthropology, cultural studies, geography, economics, and political science.

Building Theoretical Frameworks

Students too often emerge from the social sciences, humanities, and professional education classes uncomfortable with the complex and ambiguous nature of meaning-making in these fields. In this context they frequently lack a map or framework for assessing the knowledge with which they come into contact. Over the last few decades a dynamic conversation about social theory has developed that has provided numerous analytical tools within the social sciences, humanities, and pedagogical domain. Many of these tools have led to a more sophisticated understanding of the ways that social, cultural, political, and educational practices are inscribed on educational institutions *vis-à-vis* relations of power. Such theoretical tools have been used to better understand everyday life in general and daily practices in classrooms and other educational venues. The course will analyze these dynamics and help participants construct theoretical frames on which to ground their knowledge work, research, and pedagogies.

Examples of Theory Work in Teacher Research

A few examples of the type of study in which teacher researchers might engage in this theoretical grounding of the disciplines might involve analyzing the theoretical imprints in language and literacy pedagogy. Though not explicitly referenced in school practice, teacher researchers might explore the functionalist theoretical assumptions in a pedagogy of reading and writing that certifies, preserves, and inculcates a body of literature revered by a particular cultural group. Or they might examine a more critical constructivist theoretical imprint in a pedagogy of reading and writing that views these acts as social practices where meaning is negotiated and constructed among speakers, listeners, readers, and writers.

Paradigms in Teacher Research

Paradigms as Models of Making Sense of a Discipline

In the last four decades many scholars in the humanities, social sciences, and pedagogy have come to understand that scientific and humanities practices are shaped not so much by procedures and rules as they are by paradigms or models of making sense of a discipline. In this context students take their theoretical insights and view them within the context of the development of different paradigms. Students begin to appreciate the emergence of 'scientific crises' and the ways they are resolved in relation to conceptions of 'progress' within these disciplines. Here students discern the existence of diverse paradigms and the ways they shape both knowledge production within the domain and the professional lives of those who work in the area.

The appearance of diverse paradigms has been catalyzed by the perceived breakdown of particular dominant cultural narratives over the last few decades. Numerous scholars have debated the existence of a 'postmodern condition' characterized by a cultural logic that is uncomfortable with dominant cultural narratives. Because of these differing paradigmatic perspectives, scholars coming from different theoretical domains have found it increasingly difficult to communicate with one another. In education this situation exerts a profound effect on curriculum development and goal-setting, as different educational leaders may subscribe to conflicting paradigms. Conflicts over educational policy and practice result from these divergent perspectives.

Paradigms and the Cultural Significance of Science

In this paradigmatic context a student comes to question whether science is a universal practice driven by objective rules and procedures or a culturally constructed practice shaped by the particular world views of people living in a particular place and time. If one becomes aware of different cultures and different historical periods and the models for viewing domains covered by the arts, humanities, and the social sciences employed therein, what impact does this awareness of diversity have on the 'normal science' of the disciplines? Could such cultural diversity be extended by awareness in the realms of gender, socio-economic class, religion, sexuality, and so on? In light of these questions students explore the impact of the cultural legitimation on disciplinary, epistemological, research, and pedagogical practices.

Paradigms, Power and Diversity

Students of teacher research learn about debates over disciplinary conventions, ideological orientations, and the relationships between disciplines of knowledge and external reality. As they explore these features, students explore the work of the social sciences, humanities, and pedagogy in light of social power. They learn that in relation to these paradigmatic issues the Western conversation about philosophy has changed profoundly over the last quarter of a century. German and French philosophers such as Theodor Adorno, Hans-Georg Gadamer, Martin Heidegger, Jürgen Habermas, Jean-François Lyotard, Hélène Cixous, Jacques Derrida, and Michel Foucault became very influential in social science and humanities in the 1970s and 1980s and brought about significant change in what was considered canonical.

Feminist critics such as Sandra Harding, Meaghan Morris, Donna Haraway, bell hooks, Susan Bordo, and many others issued powerful critiques of the social sciences and humanities, calling into question power relationships and gendered practices long accepted in the domain. Around gender and other axes of diversity, critics of traditional scholarly work in the social sciences, humanities, and pedagogy pointed out problematic practices. Raising questions of power and privilege as they related to these disciplines and the knowledge they produced, critical analysts explored issues of race, socio-economic class, sexuality, human relationships, norms of beauty, and spirituality. Such studies induced many educators to conclude that questions of learning must always consider issues of power, diversity, access, and opportunity. Students learn that such insights profoundly change the way teachers approach the educational process.

Paradigms and Complexity

In their study of social theory and paradigms, students gain insight to the complexity of research and scholarship in the humanities, social sciences, and pedagogy in the twenty-first century. The questions raised and the insights garnered over the last several decades demand a more rigorous and complex form of scholarship than ever before. While many of the questions raised possess no one correct answer, just any answer will not suffice. As students ponder this dynamic, they understand that this complexity demands that they come to terms with the presence of ambiguity and uncertainty. Learning to act in a socially responsible, just, and courageous way in light of complexity becomes an important dimension of the course.

Indeed, social action in the face of complexity is a difficult task that in many ways runs counter to dominant social science and humanities traditions. Prior to the theoretical/paradigmatic challenges mentioned here, the dominant impulse in research involved the pursuit of certainty in the production of universal generalizations. Students in this course analyze not only these dynamics but study their personal relationships to them as knowledge producers in this domain. In this context students analyze the push for interdisciplinarity in light of the concern with complexity. They explore the assertion that educational phenomena are influenced by social, political, geographical, cultural, and philosophical factors acting in concert and that simplistic single-course descriptions are not sufficient in delineating the process of social and educational phenomena.

Everyday life, cognition, and the pedagogical process are much more complex, many assert, than previously imagined. In this complex paradigmatic context language emerges not merely as a conduit through which meaning can be unproblematically transmitted, but as a culturally inscribed social construction that shapes meaning, conveys values and assumptions, and constructs subjectivity without anyone noticing. Cities seen in this paradigm become complex systems that must be viewed from a plethora of angles and disciplinary perspectives. Students quickly learn that becoming a teacher researcher is a challenging, life-long task.

Producing Knowledge in Teacher Research

Knowledge Needs: Acquiring and Using Knowledge

Well-grounded with a knowledge of the paradigmatic aspects and theoretical structures of social scientific, humanities-based and pedagogical research, students focus their attention on the knowledge production process. In this context students study the knowledge and information needs of teachers, researchers, and the public. With such needs in mind students examine the complexities of what is involved in the acquisition and use of knowledge in contemporary education. What principles might be used, they ask, in the selection, acquisition, interpretation, organization and use of artistic, humanities, and social scientific knowledge? Extending these concerns, they ask what current issues and future trends shape and will shape the collection and dissemination of these knowledges? In light of such questions students explore digital, oral, graphic, semiotic, musical, and video-based modes of knowledge. In this context they analyze the ways knowledge needs and knowledge forms are changing in the twenty-first century.

One of the biggest mistakes of existing systems of education, many argue, involves the assumption that educators don't need these types of knowledge work skills. Teachers according to particular reductionistic conceptions of pedagogy are low-skill workers who simply transfer data provided to them to students. In this articulation of pedagogy, teacher knowledge of where such information came from or how it was produced is irrelevant. The role of such knowledge work abilities in pedagogy raises basic questions about the objectives of intellectual activity and learning in a democratic society. Teachers operating with an appreciation of complexity in knowledge production move beyond reductionistic conceptions of

educational purpose that involve transmitting a simple body of information to students and then testing them to see how well the data have been
committed to memory. The knowledge to be mastered in this conception
is isolated from the socio-cultural context and the paradigms that produced
it as well as from the experiences of the students who are expected to
learn it.

Epistemology

As the branch of philosophy that studies knowledge, epistemology addresses questions that surround the process of knowing. Students are
expected to understand the epistemological dimensions of how professionals in the field authorize and certify the knowledge they produce. These
understandings are essential in an era where the belief in objectivity and
a value-free, non-rhetorical language of science has been shattered. In such
a situation epistemological insight becomes a basic skill in the effort to
educate sophisticated practitioner knowledge producers who understand
the complex relationship between knowledge production and the pedagogical process. Epistemological insight in this domain is based on the
understanding that the knowledge certification process is always grounded
on culture. In this context students appreciate the impact of, say, dominant
Western modes of thinking on the knowledge produced in such a context.
They understand what it might mean to discuss gendered ways of knowing. Such insights are possible only by studying diverse historical and
cultural modes of knowing and learning.

With such epistemological dynamics in mind, students are asked to
explore the social epistemological construction of their own consciousness.
Here they trace the effects of their cultural value systems upon their frames
of reference and perception of the world around them. Along lines of race,
class, gender, geographic place, national origin, sexuality, generation,
and other factors, students gain personal epistemological insights and an
understanding of how similar dynamics construct the epistemological
orientations of others. Such awareness holds profound pedagogical consequences, as teachers who are aware of the epistemological influences of
diverse social and cultural backgrounds gain deep insight into invisible
forces that shape student performance in school.

Such insights are grounded on an understanding of the importance of
context in epistemology and knowledge production. Any aspect of knowledge work can be better understood and undertaken when the influence
of context is appreciated. Temporal issues, geographical place, politics,
and language all shape epistemology and the research process. Within paradigmatic debates, of course, there are many knowledge producers who
dismiss the centrality of context. In lieu of such concerns they maintain
that authentic truth exists independent of context. In its singularity and

substance, such epistemologists argue, truth is universal and never dependent on cultural factors.

In contrast to this universalist approach, the complex epistemological awareness cultivated here makes students more sensitive to different ways of seeing and producing knowledge. Such sensitivity allows all of us to make use of numerous perspectives in an effort to gain a deeper understanding of a social or educational phenomenon, to change our minds about something we thought we understood. Thus, students and everyone involved in this process are more disposed to examine the diverse epistemologies that ground voices of dissent, ways of seeing that challenge prevailing assumptions. Indeed, such epistemological awareness allows students to discern a collision of civilizations that was previously hidden from the sight of many individuals operating within the cultural and epistemological borders of Western societies and the educational system they support. Instead of viewing this cultural collision as a disaster to be contained, teacher researchers operating with a complex epistemological consciousness use it to seek new ways of producing knowledge, more rigorous modes of pedagogy, and better ways of being human.

Research Methods and the Interpretation of Data

In the study of knowledge production, of course, a central feature of the process involves gaining awareness of diverse methods of conducting research. In this context students become familiar with ethnography, phenomenology, *currere* (to be defined and discussed on pp. 234–36), semiotics, social psychoanalysis, historiography, and hermeneutics.

Ethnography

Ethnography is often described as the most basic form of social research: the study of events as they evolve in their natural setting. It makes an effort to place human events within a richer, thicker, fuller context. Many ethnographers assert that ethnography involves not merely the production of knowledge but also the way that data collected in the field are resituated into a written format. In this context ethnography produces culturally situated accounts of human activities. Ethnography attempts to gain knowledge about a particular culture, to identify patterns of social interaction, and to develop holistic interpretations of societies and social institutions.

Thus, ethnography in education attempts to understand the nature of schools, other educational agencies, and cultural pedagogies in these ways, seeking to appreciate the social processes that move educational events. Ethnography attempts to make explicit the assumptions one takes for granted as a culture member. The culture could be as broad as Japanese culture or as narrow as the upper-middle-class student culture of George Washington High School. The critical ethnographer of education seeks to describe the concrete experiences of everyday school/educational life and the social patterns, the deep structures that construct it. One of the most basic tools of the critical constructivist teacher researcher involves the research orientation derived from the ethnographic tradition (Hammersley and Atkinson, 1983; Smith, 1989; Clough, 1998; Tedlock, 2000).

Forms of ethnography attentive to complexity have focused on the discontinuities, contradictions, and inconsistencies of cultural expression and human action. As opposed to reductionistic forms of ethnography, more complex methods refuse the attempt to reconcile the differences once and for all. The poststructuralist critique of classical ethnography, for example, highlights the tendency of the tradition to privilege a dominant narrative and a unitary, privileged vantage point. In the effort to conflate knower and known, the poststructuralist ethnographer proposes a dialogue between researcher and researched that attempts to undermine traditional hierarchical relations between them (Atkinson and Hammersley, 1994). In the process, the notion of ethnography as an instrument of enlightenment and civilization of the 'native' objects of study dies an overdue death. Complex ethnographies are texts to be argued over, texts whose meanings are never 'natural' but are constructed by circumstance (Aronowitz, 1993).

Phenomenology

There is no discrete boundary line that separates ethnography from phenomenology. Ethnography can, for example, be phenomenological in its orientation. Phenomenologists have argued that consciousness is an essential aspect of humanness and should be studied if we are ever to gain significant insight into the affairs of human beings. However, the study of consciousness, phenomenologists warn, is limited by two important factors: (1) consciousness is not an object that is similar to the other objects of nature; and (2) there are aspects of consciousness which cannot be studied via traditional empirical methods of science. Ever fascinated with the content of elusive consciousness, therefore, phenomenologists cannot be concerned with the empirical question of what is or is not real. They simply begin with the nature of consciousness — whatever that nature might be — as significant data to be studied.

Phenomenology attempts to render problematic all presuppositions about the nature of its own activity, the object being investigated, and the method appropriate to this kind of inquiry (Husserl, 1970). The attempt to rid oneself of as many presuppositions as possible grants phenomenology the possibility of unmasking hidden assumptions about the nature of reality. Phenomenologists also attempt to view consciousness as intentional, meaning that it is directed toward a specific object. Another way of expressing this thought is that consciousness is consciousness of something.

Thus, phenomenologists think that it is absurd to divide reality (or the research process) into subjects and objects. The two cannot be separated, and the attempt to do so distorts reality (Stewart and Mickunas, 1974; Gubrium and Holstein, 2000).

Employing the concept of *Verstehen*, phenomenology attempts to grasp a sense of the meaning that others ascribe to their own lived world. This form of understanding involves putting oneself in place of the other person and attempting to recreate his or her feelings. It is easy to see the impact of phenomenology on modes of research such as ethnography. When researchers ask not about the absolute meaning of a work of art but ask instead what is its meaning for a certain individual or a group, they move research in new directions. The qualitative knowledge which emerges when researchers ask about and attempt to interpret the meanings that particular persons give to particular phenomena allows us new understandings and unique perspectives on social events and the human beings who participate in them. The human realm of intersubjective meaning becomes accessible in a way never imagined by empirical researchers, as scholars interrogate the conventions, forms, and codes of everyday social life (Smith, 1983; Soltis, 1984; Donmoyer, 1985).

Phenomonologically produced understanding of the way individuals construe their world and their place in it is one way in which intersubjective knowledge leads us to new dimensions of seeing social experience. In educational inquiry such ways of seeing allow researchers to understand how teachers and students give meaning to their lived worlds in light of the social and cultural forms they reflect and help produce. Indeed, such forms of inquiry facilitate our understanding of the often hidden and always ambiguous process by which education initiates us into our culture (Gubrium and Holstein, 2000).

Currere

Over the last quarter of a century scholars of curriculum theory have drawn upon these phenomenological themes in an attempt to better understand educational experience and reform undemocratic and repressive educational practice. Much of the focus of this work has been directed at apprehending the nature of the interior experience of the individual, especially within a broadly defined educational context. This interior experience is essential to social understanding in that: (1) it is affected by the external (social) world; and (2) it provides the basis for the understandings and actions which help shape the external (social) world. This reflexive purpose illustrates the importance of interior experience to scholarly analysis and educational research: it is the habitat of what we call human consciousness and the territory where meaning is produced; and it is the headquarters for a body of connections between human beings and their lived worlds. To understand the rich complexity of political and social forces, researchers must understand interior experience (Willis, 1978; Pinar, Reynolds, Slattery, and Taubman, 1995).

What we are talking about here involves the attempt to heighten individual awareness. Husserl delineated methodologies designed to facilitate understanding of the structure of consciousness and therefore the way meaning is attained. This method, which he called 'bracketing,' involves consciously setting aside accepted assumptions about one's immediate apprehensions (Chamberlin, 1974). Once this bracketing of assumptions has taken place, the individual examines and makes explicit all the meanings which were tacitly grounded within these immediate apprehensions. In this way individual awareness is heightened as previously hidden assumptions are revealed. The individual thus finds himself or herself more in touch with the values, fears, and associations which unconsciously direct his or her actions.

Continued analysis of such factors may uncover their social, cultural, and ideological origins, thus contributing to a more contextualized self-understanding and self-knowledge. Admittedly, in explaining this conception of phenomenological understanding and bracketing, I have emphasized the idea of self-knowledge. This results not from a tendency toward self-absorption but from a practical necessity. The foundations of the phenomenological method must rest on a self-knowledge that, once gained, allows an individual or a researcher to turn his or her focus outward to more textured understandings of the interior experiences of others. Thus, the researcher approaches that new dimension of understanding which phenomenology claims to offer (Willis, 1978).

In his attempt to develop a practical method of analyzing the educational experience of the individual, William Pinar takes this phenomenological orientation and fuses it with psychoanalysis and aesthetics. He calls his analytical form, *currere* (the Latin root of the word 'curriculum,' meaning the investigation of the nature of the individual experience of the public). We are returned once again to the inner world, the *Lebenswelt*, and to its relationship with the educational experience. A traditional criticism of much of the theoretical work in education is that it is not connected with the everyday experiences of teachers and students. Pinar's use of the concept of *currere* helps bring about the synthesis of theorizing and *Lebenswelt* with all the benefits that are to be accrued from such a fusion (Pinar, 1975, 1994, 1998).

Pinar claims that in curriculum research, meaning is typically derived from the analysis of the relationship between signs and experience. Taking his cue from Maxine Greene (1975), Pinar contends that the quest for an understanding of experience impels researchers to tap their own subjectivity so that common sense may be transcended — that is, we must go beyond what we take for granted. As researchers we must ask questions such as: What is involved in moving beyond the common-sense world? How does one initiate the process? What possible benefits are to be derived? Are there examples of other individuals who have accomplished such a transcendence and what did they gain? How do such attempts affect what we know in education? It is through such questions that we approach the *Lebenswelt* or, in Pinar's words, 'that realm of the *Lebenswelt* associated with currere' (Pinar, 1975: 396–403).

As we engage in this phenomenological bracketing of experience in our own lives, Pinar argues that we are better prepared as scholars to understand the nature and contents of consciousness as they appear to us in social and educational contexts. The social insight and personal empowerment that results involve a freedom from cultural conditioning and social regulation. In this analytical process we 'loosen' our identification with the contents of consciousness, in order to gain some distance from them — a distance that results in a form of existential freedom. From our new vantage point we may be able to view those psychic realms formed by conditioning and unreflective adherence to socio-political convention. Many analysts might refer to this as the demystification of the ideological construction of our consciousness.

Once we have embarked on our quest to understand *currere*, Pinar tells us, we will uncover a great diversity of formats and sources. The educational *Lebenswelt* comes in a variety of packages — one package may contain historical information, another the insights of free association, another the contemplations of specific literary passages, and still another may hold ostensibly insignificant slices of school life. Both cognitive and intuitive insights (or a creative synthesis of the two) will inform our perceptions of *currere*.

At first, Pinar concludes, the information derived from our attempt to examine *currere* may be idiosyncratic. Eventually, however, our examinations will uncover aspects of a collective or transpersonal realm of educational experience. In other words, once we transcend the unique details of an individual's biography we may gain greater insight into hidden social, cultural, discursive, and ideological structures and the way they shape human subjectivity. Such structures may, as phenomenologists have anticipated (Merleau-Ponty, 1962), appear very different when viewed at the stratum of individual perception but may be similar when analyzed at the level of their roots. The understanding of these structuring dynamics and their relationship to the socio-political world and thus their impact on the world of education may be one of the most important outcomes of phenomenological analysis and Pinar's method of *currere*.

Semiotics

Another basic tool of knowledge production in qualitative research is semiotics. Semiotics involves the study of signs (it derives from a Greek word meaning 'sign') and codes. Semiotic researchers decode the systems of symbols and signs that enable human beings to derive meaning from their surroundings. Television wouldn't make sense to a Martian, for example, even if the alien could speak the language TV employed — too many signs and codes exist which could be deciphered only by an acquaintance with the cultural experience that TV represents. This is why individuals from one culture, even though they speak fluently the language of another culture, might completely fail to catch the humor of a situation — it is contextualized in a culture in which they are aliens.

Each language, each system of codes and signs is peculiar to a particular historically grounded culture. Semiotics views everything in a culture as a form of communication arranged in ways similar to that of verbal language. Researchers who employ semiotics attempt to study culture as a communication phenomenon — they study it as a whole, always exploring interrelationships, never looking only at decontextualized bits and pieces. They search for these relationships between phenomena in the context of an examination of the structures of institutions and individual consciousness. In the process they uncover previously unnoticed manifestations of how power is reproduced and how consciousness is constructed (Scholes, 1982; Hodge and Kress, 1988; Britzman, 1991; Manning and Cullum-Swan, 1994).

In unexpected places semioticians uncover new insights into social and psychological processes — for example, the forms of what people call courtesy, the packaging of fast food, the facial expressions of an employee while talking to his or her boss, the points at which movie-goers laugh during a film, and so on. The school is a diamond mine for semiological study, for it abounds with codes and signs, in conventions that call for unique insight. The ways teachers, students, and administrators dress, pupils' language when speaking to teachers as compared to conversations with classmates, graffiti in a middle school rest-room, systems of rewards and punishments for students, the use of bells in school, memos sent to parents, the nature of the local community's conversation about school athletics, are only a few of the many school topics that semioticians could study.

Teacher inquirers employing semiotics in their repertoire of qualitative research strategies might pay especially close attention to the ostensibly insignificant, off-hand comments of students, for it is here in what is typically dismissed as noise that semiological significance is revealed. An adolescent's observation that 'You [the teacher] always pick on me,' may be far more revealing when pursued than an expert's questionnaire. A pupil's excited attempt to interject a description of a Snoop Doggy Dogg rap into a class discussion of *Sister Carrie* may provide unique and multi-dimensional insight when analyzed semiotically. James Anthony Whitson (1991) provides excellent examples of techniques of semiotic analysis and how such techniques can be used to open new vistas on the meaning of schooling which can be adapted by educators as teacher researchers (Gibson, 1984).

ιe semiotician a text is not simply printed material. It is far more
υιοαωιy υefined, involving any aspect of culture that contains encoded
meaning. For example, the text of a homecoming queen pageant holds
multiple levels of meaning that can be read to reveal cultural insights and
gender constructions. In the same way a child's lunch is a map to a child's
home culture: for example, a Mexican student in South Texas who packs
a single tortilla in a paper bag; the suburban student whose single parent
picks up lunch at McDonald's on the way to school. A basic characteristic
of semiotics involves its assumption that the interpretation of a text is not
tied to the author's conscious understanding of its meaning. It thus follows
that the socio-educational and political importance of a school practice
may have little to do with what those who devised and implemented it
had in mind. Certain disciplinary classroom management practices may have
been formulated in the minds of school leaders simply as mechanisms to
keep order. The assumptions about the values, interests, and motivations
of children, the purposes of schools, the meaning of democracy, the role
of gender, definitions of good behavior, and so on embedded in such
policies never entered into the consciousness of the school administrators
as they conceived their discipline policy.

The meaning of such practices is never static to the semiotician —
meanings continue to reveal themselves as long as semioticians devise new
questions of them. Thus, semiotics is a subversive form of research that
teaches us to read the lived world in a new way. It is a form of reading
that desocializes us from the official interpretations of the dominant codes;
it frees us from the authorial interpretations of social texts that exploit
those less equipped to question such impositions. What does the flag mean?
What does school spirit mean? What does maturity mean? What does
popularity in school mean? Semiotic researchers uncover their dominant
meanings as well as a variety of subjugated, uncertified oppositional meanings. As a result, semioticians cannot help but involve themselves in the
study of ideology, how it expresses itself and shapes consciousness in a
variety of ways in a number of different places (Scholes, 1982; Whitson,
1991; Manning and Cullum-Swan, 1994).

Teacher scholars who employ semiotics begin to understand the
school as a terrain of contestation, of competing power interests where
rival groups struggle over the meaning of semiotic representations. Few
forms of inquiry are better equipped to reveal the hidden divisions within
the social fabric, the mystified and often unconscious struggle between the
dominant and the dominated. To sustain their privilege, the dominant
must control representation — they must encode the world in forms that
support their own interests, their own power. But such an attempt is
not so easy as some analysts have tried to portray it. V. N. Voloshinov
(1973) writing in the first three decades of the twentieth century argued
that we misconstruct reality when we assume that power groups simply
impose their meanings on the symbols and codes of a culture. Voloshinov

maintained that symbols and language systems were always 'multi-accentual,' meaning that lodged within cultural codes were oppositional interpretations. Therefore, while dominant groups certainly attempt to impose their meanings on, say, the signification of school symbols, they are not necessarily successful (Hodge and Kress, 1988).

The study of this struggle to define cultural and educational codes and signs is one of the most important aspects of semiotic research. When the dominated are seen as merely the blind victims of the dominator's encoding of the world, a one-dimensional, deterministic view of the social world has been constructed. Marginalized groups are often aware of efforts of power blocs to define social symbols — and when they are, they resist them. An awareness of these forms of semiotic power dynamics is extremely important for scholars and researchers in educational and other social contexts.

Social psychoanalysis

Psychoanalysis adds a dimension of insight typically ignored by many forms of inquiry and research methods. Freud's concerns with the unconscious, irrationality, repression, feeling, and sexuality and their important relations to social, cultural, and political affairs are still central to the efforts of qualitative scholars to develop a complex understanding of everyday life. An ethnographer or semiotician who understands psychoanalysis is better equipped to analyze social behavior and cultural expression, especially the way the irrational operates in these domains. Social psychoanalysis signifies an application of the insights of psychoanalysis to the study of the social, cultural, political, psychological, and economic domains.

Any force that shapes agency (our ability to act in the world) in a manner that is contradictory to the ways in which we ourselves think of an experience is important — even if the notion of self is not as stable and knowable as early psychoanalysts assumed. Indeed, it is psychoanalysis that allows us to view the formation of identity, subjectivity, and consciousness from unique vantage points not attainable via other methodologies. In such a procedure, analysts often discern the unconscious processes that create resistance to progressive change and induce self-destructive behavior. Psychoanalysis offers hope to qualitative scholars concerned with social analysis and the exploration of the possibilities of human potential. When psychoanalysis takes into account the Deweyan, the Vygotskian (the work of Russian psychologist Lev Vygotsky and his cognitive theories) and more recently the rejection of Freud's separation of the psychic from the social realm, it becomes a powerful tool in the qualitative scholars' tool kit (Alford, 1993; Henriques *et al.*, 1984; Russell, 1993).

In connection with psychoanalysis I use the term 'depth psychology', an admittedly old-fashioned term to emphasize the political aspect of the arts, humanities, and social sciences. Depth psychology with its implication of getting beneath the illusion of surface appearances focuses directly on the nature of 'personality' development and its relation to creativity, artistic/ aesthetic endeavor, and morality. No cognitive/psychological theory, for example, worthy of inclusion in a rigorous research curriculum can ignore these issues and their relationship to learning, motivation, school performance, and the nature of the teaching process. In addition, a depth psychology aware of the wisdom gleaned from an epistemology of complexity can motivate interest and insight into the ways an individual subjectively experiences social, cultural, political, and educational structures. In this context public issues can be viewed at the private level and the modernist separation of the political (external) and personal (internal) can be addressed. Social theory's concerns with identity, difference, and power can be directed to the broad notion of psychological studies by way of the interests of depth psychology (Samuels, 1993). In this reconceptualized context the democratic work of teacher researchers can never be the same.

In the name of a complex notion of psychoanalysis, analysts of pedagogy call for an examination of such issues in relation to educational practice. As we begin to grasp the importance of a socially situated unconsciousness in the production of identity and in the learning process connected to it, practitioners gain vital insights into the ways education might be reconfigured. In this context scholar educators are quick to note that their appreciations of psychoanalysis and depth psychology are cautious and very selective. Following the lead of many feminist psychoanalysts, they employ only those aspects of the tradition that are conscious of the problematic nature of defining psychic health as conformity to dominant cultural norms. Taking their cue from feminist theory, such scholars understand the patriarchal inscriptions of traditional psychoanalysis and struggle to avoid the repressive landmines hidden in the field. Psychoanalysis and depth psychology possess progressive features that can be used by critical constructivist teacher researchers to create a more democratic and better-educated world, a resacralized society where human beings are studied and appreciated in terms of their unique individual and social abilities and hard-to-quantify talents (Henriques *et al.*, 1984; Elliot, 1994; Ventura, 1994).

The epistemologically complex vision of psychoanalysis is a poststructuralist psychoanalysis — poststructuralist in the sense that it reveals the problems embedded in the sciences emerging from reductionistic 'universal structures' (Block, 1995). As poststructuralist psychoanalysis makes use of the democratic aspects of the psychoanalytical tradition, it presents a view of humans quite different from the reductionistic psychological portrait. In the process it challenges the erasure of feeling, valuing, and caring in contemporary Western societies and attempts to rethink such features in light of power and its construction of consciousness. In this context the poststructuralist impulse challenges Freud's positioning of the pleasure principle in opposition to the reality principle. In many ways, poststructuralist psychoanalysts argue, such an oppositional construction places Freudianism squarely within the boundaries of reductionism and hyperrationality with their structures of rationality over irrationality, masculinity over femininity, civilization over primitivism, logic over emotion, and play as separate from work.

From the poststructuralist perspective, therefore, the psychoanalytic tradition is complicit in the regulatory objectives of positivism. In its effort to produce a healthy (read conformist) population, traditional psychoanalysis sets out to repress desire. Poststructuralist psychoanalysis has often embraced unconscious desire as a positive feature with the social potential to unfasten the hegemonic straitjacket of reductionistic scholarship. For example, in this configuration play and work are not incompatible activities. Poststructuralism admonishes the discipline of traditional pedagogy to accept the undesirability of regulatory agenda (Henriques *et al.*, 1984; Eliot, 1994). Regulatory education must also understand that its rationalistic view of being and its faith in an unexamined rationality are ill-suited for everyday life in contemporary electronic 'hyperreality' riddled and destabilized by affective intensities and powerful forces of libidinal desire. Humbled by the poststructuralist critique, traditional psychoanalysis timidly looks into the mirror of self-reflection and begins to discern the relationship between suppressed desire and political power, the affiliation between the fear of passion and cultural reproduction. These understandings hold profound consequences for students of teacher research.

Obviously, in this context, any use of the psychoanalytical tradition in critical scholarship must be highly selective. I am highly sensitive to traditional Freudianism's privileging of the familial positioning of the father and the notion of penis envy. I reject traditional psychoanalysis's attribution of psychological differences between men and women to biological causation with such a position's accompanying assumption that women's subordination is inevitable. This so-called Anglo-Saxon interpretation of Freudian psychoanalysis has long connected the unconscious to the biological needs of men and women. Such interpreters employed behavioristic and positivistic science to prove their deterministic assertions (Henriques *et al.*, 1984). In addition the poststructuralist psychoanalysis used here also understands and refuses to participate in the hierarchical power relations that characterize the relationship between analyst and analysand (the individual being analyzed). The material produced by psychoanalysis is not the property of analysts but is accessible to all parties (Young, 1990).

Too rapid a dismissal of psychoanalysis for the reasons delineated here will miss the democratic and scholarly possibilities still offered by a reconceptualized psychoanalysis. Poststructuralist psychoanalysis provides teacher scholars with an unparalleled insight into the hidden content of symbolic expression — repressed life history. The meaning or significance of a patient's actions can be better understood in terms of the latent and unconscious content that move him or her. Successful interpretations that lead to therapy can be formulated only by uncovering the salient unconscious factors. Therapy proceeds by making these unconscious factors known to the patient *and* understood by the patient. These understandings inform both critical constructivist scholarship and pedagogy. Such complex insights help move the study of the humanities, social sciences, pedagogy and psychoanalysis itself beyond their tendencies to be used as methods of adjusting individuals to existing power structures.

Poststructuralist psychoanalysis with its concern with semiotics, signification, and the construction of interpretation lays a framework for a complex form of social research and pedagogical practice. Psychoanalysis has traveled from the *individual* analysand to a *social* psychoanalysis concerned with the analysis of both the individual and the society-at-large. Interpretations in the psychoanalysis of individuals can be developed only within the framework provided by a general theory of neurosis. Similarly the teacher researcher employing a psychoanalytic theoretical structure generates interpretations in the context of a general theory of social pathology — for example, racism, sexism, and class bias. Indeed, social psychoanalysis refuses to isolate the individual from the social domain, as it provides unique ways of discerning the complex relationship between them.

Historiography

History is the part of the 'bricolage' of qualitative modes of inquiry that often gets ignored. Such a reality is unfortunate, for any qualitative form of analysis needs to be historicized. Consciousness itself is impossible without such historicizations, without the use of history as a force for demystification that sheds light on the hidden contradictions of societies. In concert with its demystifying function, many analysts believe that history can illustrate that something else is possible, that rational change is conceivable (Zinn, 1984).

Paulo Freire (1985) creatively clarifies this point by observing the differences between animals and humans. Unlike humans, animals are simply *in* the universe, unable to objectify either themselves or nature. Thus, animals live a life outside of time, they have no chance of confronting reality or stepping outside of it. Humans, on the other hand, possess the capacity for a historical sense. They can go beyond reality and transcend mere being in the world. They can, Freire argues, 'add to the life they have the existence which they make' (p. 68). Because of their temporal understanding and the transcendence it allows, men and women can transform, decide, and create. They can reflect on the domains of their existence and question their relationship to the world — they can experience the dialectic between determinism and freedom. Only creatures who can ponder the fact that they are socially constructed are empowered to free themselves.

Historical consciousness extends this type of reflection and thus serves as human beings' most accessible force of self-determination.

Rigorous analysis, according to Freire, desires a deeper reading of the word and, for that matter, the world. Historical consciousness serves as a force that allows for this deeper reading, for this ability to distinguish essence from appearance. As he puts it, 'there is no "here" relative to "there" that is not connected to a "now," a "before," and an "after"' (1985: 70–1). Thus, humans must understand what came before in order to comprehend the here and now. To understand themselves, men and women must grasp their own biographies. To change, to educate themselves and/or the world, humans must connect past injustice to present suffering; they must fathom the mind-set of their ancestors in order to expose the forces that have created present conditions.

Henry Giroux (1988) writes of historical inquiry as a model for constituting the potential of memory. Maxine Greene (1984) argues that educational history, for example, addresses the sometimes desperate efforts of humans to select and maintain that which they deem a proper human way of life. Educational history considers that which is worthy of conservation in a sea of change, as it determines what is worthy of note in ages past. The historian may find that what he or she considers worthy of note in the past is precisely the opposite of that which educators of the past found worthy of conservation. Indeed, Greene concludes, that which educational historians find to be inappropriate may be the very values and attitudes that have been frozen into our heritage. The historian is unavoidably rendered an interpreter, with all the value choices that accompany the role. Care must be taken to seek those epistemological organizing principles, social values, and ideas that form the framework of our historical interpretations. As we seek a democratic way of life through our historical investigations, the pedagogical potential of memory moves toward fulfillment.

Simply put, teacher researchers in pursuit of rigorous modes of analysis, ways of producing knowledge, and forms of pedagogy cannot afford to view themselves outside of history. History in this rigorous context becomes an analysis of the relationship of the particularity of private experience *vis-à-vis* the generalizations of socio-economic, cultural, political, and psychological patterns. Critical teacher scholars working as historical analysts attend to both the particularistic and the general, and the complexity of the various levels of interaction between them. In this context, history is not viewed as a simple linear story of social, economic, and political forces; nor is it a collection of particularistic anecdotes. Instead, a complex history accounts for the interplay between the particularistic and the general that informs our understanding of the production of subjectivity, the construction of consciousness, the forces that shape professional lives and student perspectives.

What we are referring to here is using history to develop a sense of historicity — an awareness of our placement in history. This concept is central to rigorous scholarly work in any domain. A complex sense of historicity is derived from the intersection of a historical consciousness with the ability to produce knowledges via multiple methodologies. The knowledges produced in these contexts are analyzed, interpreted, probed for implications, applied in different contexts, and used to initiate social and educational change. How these processes are carried out always involves a rigorous analysis of their relationship to historical context. We are always better equipped as educational analysts when we bring this historical facility to our scholarly deliberations. In this context we come to appreciate our own historicity and the historicity of the knowledges we produce.

This historical consciousness, this appreciation of historicity, involves the act of placing oneself and one's scholarly work in the web of reality. The historiographical aspect of a complex epistemology induces teacher scholars to become more aware of where they stand in the web of reality and how it shapes views of self, world, and knowledge production. These historiographical and epistemological concepts lay the foundation for the concept of positionality. Positionality involves the notion that since our understanding of the world and ourselves is socially constructed, we must devote special attention to the differing ways individuals from diverse social backgrounds construct knowledge and make meaning.

Thus, depending on our location in the web with its diverse axes of power, we will designate what constitutes the most important information in a research act very differently. For example, when in the 1980s, I read E. D. Hirsch's construction of what essential knowledge citizens should know, I was amazed at how his location as a white, upper-middle-class, American male shaped his choice of knowledge — it was predominantly made up of data about white, upper/upper-middle-class males from a Western heritage. I want Hirsch (and myself) to understand the ways his location in the web of reality, his historicity, shapes his perspectives about it.

An epistemology of complexity teaches us about the social world's complicated web-like configuration of interacting forces. Knowledge producers, like all of us, are entangled in, not disengaged from the web. The complexity principle asserts that knower and known are inseparable — both part of the web of reality. No one in this web-like configuration of the universe can achieve a god-like perspective — no one can totally escape the web and look back at it from afar. We all must confess our subjectivity; we must recognize our limited vantage point. These are the lessons of historicity for teacher analysts and researchers — a keen awareness of our positioning in time and space. Reductionism and the knowledge production it supports tend to ignore the way our historicity shapes our consciousness; as a result our concept of the social world is stripped of its complexity and reduced to a static, one-dimensional frame. Thus released from the complexities of historicity, reductionistic knowledge producers feel confident that they can make precise predictions, settle controversial questions, and ignore the complex, interactive process in which all social activity is grounded (Doll, 1989; Slaughter, 1989).

Teacher scholars with a historical consciousness refuse to accept or reject validity claims of any body of information without considering its discursive nature, that is, where the information comes from in the web of reality, what can be officially transmitted and what cannot, and who translates it and who listens. Without such reflection, individuals travel through life imprisoned by the prejudices derived from everyday existence or by what is often labeled common sense. The habitual beliefs of an individual's historical age become tyrants to a mind unable to reflect on its genesis. We often emerge from sixteen to twenty years of schooling without having been asked to think about our own thinking. In this situation we are unprepared to meet the demands of being a rigorous scholar or an engaged citizen.

Hermeneutics

The hermeneutic dimension of critical constructivist teacher research permeates and informs every mode of inquiry delineated here. Hermeneutics is an essential aspect of the research process, as it raises questions of meaning by focusing on the interpretive dimensions of knowledge production. How do we make sense of this finding? What do these data mean? How do we begin an examination of such inquires? These are all hermeneutic questions. In a reductionistic academic universe this hermeneutic dimension is often dismissed. Understanding that all knowledge is an interpretation, a rigorous complex notion of teacher research places great emphasis on hermeneutics.

Indeed, an epistemology of complexity appreciates that in critical knowledge production — no matter how much reductionistic experts may argue that the facts speak for themselves — interpretation is always at work. Sometimes it is a conscious process; many times it is unconscious. Nevertheless, it is always there (Rosen, 1987; Grondin, 1994; Vattimo, 1994; Gross and Keith, 1997). The hermeneutic act of interpretation involves in its most elementary articulation making sense of what has been observed in a way that communicates understanding. Not only is all knowledge production merely an act of interpretation, but, hermeneutics contends, perception itself is an act of interpretation. The quest for understanding is a fundamental feature of human existence, as encounter with the unfamiliar always demands the attempt to make meaning, to make sense. The same, however, is also the case with the familiar. Indeed, as in the study of commonly known texts, we come to find that sometimes the familiar may be seen as the most strange. It should not be surprising that even the so-called objective writings about the social domain are interpretations, not value-free descriptions (Gallagher, 1992; Denzin, 1994; Jardine, 1998; D. Smith, 1999).

Learning from the hermeneutic tradition and an epistemology of complexity, teacher scholars begin to reexamine textual claims to authority. No pristine interpretation exists — indeed, no methodology, social or educational theory, or discursive form can claim a privileged position that enables the production of authoritative knowledge. Knowledge producers must always speak/write about the world in terms of something else in the world, 'in relation to . . .' As creatures of the world, we are oriented to it in a way that prevents us from grounding our theories and perspectives outside of it. Thus, whether we like it or not, we are all destined as interpreters to analyze from within its boundaries and blinders. Within these limitations, however, the interpretations emerging from the hermeneutic process can still move us to new levels of understanding, appreciations that allow us to 'live our way' into an experience described to us.

Despite the impediments of context, hermeneutically informed analysts of the humanities, social sciences, and pedagogy can transcend the inadequacies of thin descriptions of decontextualized facts. In this informed context they gain the ability to produce thick descriptions of social texts characterized by the contexts of their production, the intentions of their producers, and the meanings mobilized in the processes of their construction. The production of such thick descriptions/interpretations follows no step-by-step blueprint or mechanical formula. As with any art form, hermeneutical analysis can be learned only in the Deweyan sense — by doing it. Researchers into the context practice the art by grappling with the text to be understood, telling its story in relation to its historical and other contextual dynamics and other texts first to themselves and then to a public audience (Madison, 1988; Gallagher, 1992; Denzin, 1994; Carson and Sumara, 1997; Ellis, 1998; Jardine, 1998).

These concerns with the nature of hermeneutical interpretation come under the category of philosophical hermeneutics. Working in this domain, hermeneutical scholars attempt to think through and clarify the conditions under which interpretation and understanding take place. The complex hermeneutics that grounds thick knowledge production moves more in the direction of normative hermeneutics in that it raises questions about the purposes and procedures of interpretation. In this complex context the purpose of hermeneutical analysis is to develop a form of sociocultural analysis revealing power dynamics within diverse texts. Educators familiar with this complex hermeneutics build bridges between reader and text, text and its producer, historical context and present, and one particular social circumstance and another. Accomplishing such interpretive tasks is difficult, and researchers situated in normative hermeneutics push ethnographers, historians, social psychoanalysts, psychologists, semioticians, literary critics, and content analysts to trace the bridge-building processes employed by successful interpretations of knowledge production and culture (Gallagher, 1992; Kellner, 1995; Kogler, 1996; Rapko, 1998).

Grounded by the hermeneutical bridge-building, educators in a hermeneutical circle (a process of analysis in which interpreters seek the historical and social dynamics that shape textual interpretation) engage in the back-and-forth of studying parts in relation to the whole and the whole in relation to parts. No final interpretation is sought in this context, as the activity of the circle proceeds with no need for closure (Gallagher, 1992; Peters and Lankshear, 1994; Pinar, Reynolds, Slattery, and Taubman, 1995). This movement of whole to parts is combined with an analytic flow between abstract and concrete. Such dynamics often tie interpretation to the interplay of larger social forces (the general) to the everyday lives of individuals (the particular). A complex hermeneutics brings the concrete, the parts, the particular into focus, but in a manner that grounds them contextually in a larger understanding of the social forces, the whole, the abstract (the general). In this way hermeneutics contributes to our understanding of historicity and its effects.

Disciplinarity in Teacher Research

Foundations of Disciplines in the Humanities, Social Sciences, and Pedagogy

The humanities, social sciences, and pedagogy are grounded in a divergent but shared heritage. In concert they provide understanding into political concerns, social, cultural, and economic relationships, mind, human behavior, the nature of human beings, and the educational act. The foundations of these disciplines involve the development of theories, the employment of methods, and the interpretation of information. In all of the disciplines a phenomenon is identified and justified as being consequential, definitions are provided for key terms, and particular methods are chosen for the purpose of gathering evidence. A body of literature is identified and opened to diverse interpretations and reviews and the usefulness of particular claims and conceptual frameworks is defended.

Discursive Analysis of the Disciplines

As students gain a working knowledge of the humanities, social sciences, and pedagogical studies, their literature, and research methods, they historicize the disciplines and study them as discourses. In this context students study specific discursive practices within the disciplines, who has and had not had the power to shape their practices, what can be done in the name of the disciplines and what cannot be done. In such a discursive analysis students examine the multiple ways that conventional mechanisms of textual construction shape disciplinary practices. In this context rhetorical modes of study are used to delineate the forces that have constructed the disciplines historically.

Problems of Disciplines

The foundations of a teacher research course carefully examine the limitations of disciplinarity and the problems that result from the use of disciplinary perspectives. Understanding these aspects of disciplinarity, the course induces students to analyze the connections between different humanities, social sciences, and pedagogical subject matters that have traditionally been isolated from one another. Complexity of insight increases as these diverse interrelations are brought to light. In this context a key concept of the seminar emerges: pedagogy is often viewed from the perspective of one or two disciplines and much to its scholarly detriment is not viewed from multidisciplinary perspectives. By the nature of the course arrangement, education students are encouraged to transcend uni-disciplinary approaches and gain a deep understanding of the dynamic interdependence that connects the various subject matters and research orientations. As they gain sophistication in this process, teacher scholars are encouraged to make their own cross-disciplinary connections in their personal research and pedagogy. Such activities can produce far more rigorous, democratic, and transformative knowledge work and educational practice.

Interdisciplinarity in Teacher Research

Transcending Single-discipline Scholarship

In recent years many scholars have posited that we have a much better opportunity to produce rigorous and complex scholarship if we employ the lenses of the various disciplines and research methods that comprise the humanities, social sciences, and pedagogy. In this context students learn not only disciplinary perspectives and research methods emanating from them but also the diverse theoretical expressions and paradigmatic orientations that intersect with them. Sensing the problems with single-discipline perspectives previously discussed in the course, scholars have watched disciplinary boundaries in the humanities, social sciences, and pedagogical studies begin to fade away. In this emerging transdisciplinary context concerns with self/subjectivity, society, and history are addressed more rigorously via the dynamic structure of an interdisciplinary curriculum. Here scholars gain the benefits of multiple perspectives and multiple theoretical frames so crucial to the analysis and criticisms of culture, pedagogy, and education.

As teacher scholars explore educational phenomena from an interdisciplinary perspective, one observes the juxtapositioning of historical, cognitive, philosophical, social, cultural, economic, and geographical lenses in relation to the scholarly and pedagogical task at hand. In this context the textured understandings produced justify the journey into unknown territory required by the transcendence of single-discipline scholarship. With these concepts in mind students are prepared to grapple with the theoretical, paradigmatic, epistemological, disciplinary, and knowledge production dimensions of the concept of bricolage.

Bricolage in Teacher Research

Our notion of interdisciplinarity is extended by the concept of the research bricolage. As Claude Lévi-Strauss put it, the bricoleur is an individual who employs the 'means at hand,' the tools he or she finds in close proximity that were originally conceived for another purpose. The knowledge worker teacher research uses tools in a trial and error manner, not insecure in altering them whenever the necessity arises in the particular circumstance in which he or she is operating. The teacher bricoleur views research methods actively rather than passively, meaning that researchers actively construct their methods from the tools available rather than passively receiving the 'correct, universally applicable' methodologies.

Avoiding modes of knowledge production and reasoning that come from certified processes of research and analysis, bricoleurs also steer clear of preexisting guidelines and checklists developed outside the specific demands of the inquiry at hand. In its embrace of complexity, the research bricolage constructs a far more active role for humans both in shaping reality and in creating the research processes and narratives of social reality that assume the effects of particular social, political, economic, and educational processes. At the same time and in the same conceptual context this belief in active human agency refuses standardized modes of knowledge production.

Seeking Multiple Perspectives on the World: The Bricolage and Complexity

Avoiding the reductionistic knowledge of externally imposed methods, the bricoleur pursues complexity by sidestepping monological forms of knowledge. Monological knowledge is produced in the rationalistic quest for order and certainty. In such a trek, a solitary individual abstracted from the cultural, discursive, ideological, and epistemological contexts that have shaped him or her and the research methods and interpretive strategies he or she employs, seeks an objective knowledge of unconnected things in themselves. Not only does monological knowledge reduce human life to its objectifiable dimensions, that is, what can be expressed numerically,

but it is also incapable of moving beyond one individual's unilateral experience of the world. At its core the bricoleur struggles to find and develop
numerous strategies for getting beyond this one-dimensionality. In this
monological context thick descriptions are lost to the forces of order and
certainty who are satisfied with right and wrong answers that preclude
the need for other perspectives. Thus, monological knowledge is a smug
knowledge that is content with quick resolutions to the problems that
confront researchers (Madison, 1988; Thomas, 1998).

Bricoleurs understand a basic flaw within the nature and production
of monological knowledge — unilateral perspectives on the world fail to
account for the complex relationship between material reality and human
perception. When this relationship is ignored, knowledge producers have
hell to pay. Such a failure includes the costs of not taking into account that
our perceptions are shaped by a panoply of factors. Mistaking perception
for truth not only reduces our ability to make sense of the world around
us but also harms those with the least power to pronounce what is true
(Karunaratne, 1998). In his initial speculations on the nature of the bricolage,
Lévi-Strauss (1966) emphasized this point. A knowledge producer, he
argued, never carries on a simple dialogue with the world but, instead,
interacts 'with a particular relationship between nature and culture definable
in terms of his particular period and civilization and the material means at
his disposal' (p. 19).

Lévi-Strauss, of course, was delineating bricolage's concern with
an understanding of the dialectical relationship between knowledge and
reality. In the decades since his pronouncements, social analysts have argued
that in the complexity of this relationship, knowledge and reality change
both continuously and interdependently. In the recognition of this complexity many researchers have come to the conclusion that the description
of what really exists may be far more difficult than originally thought. In
this context bricoleurs seek multiple perspectives not to provide the truth
about reality but to avoid the monological knowledge that emerges from
unquestioned frames of reference and the dismissal of the numerous relationships and connections that link various forms of knowledge together.

Here rests a central epistemological and ontological assumption of the
bricoleur: the domains of the physical, the social, the cultural, the psychological, and the educational consist of the interplay of a wide variety of
entities — thus, the complexity and the need for multiple ways of seeing
advocated by bricoleurs. As part of a larger process that is ever changing,
the reality that brocoleurs engage is not a fixed entity. In its impermanence
the lived world presents special problems for researchers that demand
attention to the nature of its changes and the processes of its movements.
In this dynamic and impermanent nature of the world, bricoleurs propose
compelling insights into their engagement with reality and the unresolved
contradictions that characterize such interactions (Young and Yarbrough,
1993; Lomax and Parker, 1996; Karunaratne, 1998).

Teacher Researchers as Problem-posers and Problem-solvers

Social and Educational Improvement via Rigorous Scholarship

Throughout the term students are reminded that the purpose of the course is to gain interdisciplinary insight in teacher research in order to use the various ways of seeing in the struggle for social and educational improvement. With such an objective in mind, the course is constantly attuned to the relation of this scholarship to the political, cultural, social, and economic processes through which education is shaped. How does the bricolage help students gain insight into the ways that political coalitions are constructed to push particular social and educational policies in urban settings? Using their multiple perspectives, teacher researchers study the diverse interests and the different players who work to promote or impede social and educational transformation. Again, teacher scholars employ their rigorous knowledge work abilities to gain complex insights into the formulation of public political policy and educational policy as well as the way such politics shape classroom activities and non-formal educational experiences — in other words, cultural pedagogies.

Teacher Scholars as Problem-posers

At the conceptual basis of the course rests the notion that teachers become scholars to help explain and engage in a larger democratic historical struggle. Such a quest seeks to free humans from the social, cultural, political, economic problems that plague them and undermine their efforts to produce an effective, just, and challenging system of education. In this context teacher scholars use their knowledge and skills to highlight and 'pose' problems for analysis and solution. In the course students explore causes and effects of problems such as poverty, drug addiction, homelessness and inadequate housing, violence, racism, sexism, class bias, and homophobia. Understanding that such problems do not take place in a contextual vacuum, students use knowledge work skills to analyze the ways that global and regional dynamics are linked to the problems of specific educational venues.

Grounding Problem-solving on Visions of Social Justice

As teacher scholars study and pose problems in the broad context of urban education, they ground their analysis on a vision of social justice. In such a context concerns with equality, inclusivity, access, self-determination, and democratic participation are always foregrounded in both the development of teacher scholarship and its application to the various educational contexts. Often those who are socially and culturally privileged are blind to the suffering of marginalized peoples. Problem-solving grounded on a vision of social justice extends students' ability to render the powerless visible. The effects of marginalization are tragic, as capable individuals are denied useful social and economic participation. Educators often operate as cultural brokers for power blocs that perpetuate these exploitative conditions. Teachers in this course are prepared to study and produce knowledge about these unjust dynamics as a central feature of their understanding of a rigorous pedagogy.

Developing a Rigorous Pedagogy Grounded on Teacher Knowledge Work

The Reflective Educator as Scholar Researcher

This part of the course helps teacher scholars tie their disciplinary, interdisciplinary, theoretical, paradigmatic, and knowledge work understandings directly to pedagogy. Using a model of teaching as reflective inquiry, teacher scholars appreciate the numerous ways that scholarship is connected to teacher education, curriculum development, and the teaching act itself. Teachers can use these understandings to make informed decisions about life in the classroom. Such a process helps them create a climate where students can develop into active, curious, researcher citizens of a diverse globalized society. Such pedagogical decisions are grounded on teachers' insights into consciousness construction in the experience of both themselves and their students, the intersection of the social and the cognitive, diversity, social and educational theory, and instructional strategies.

At the basis of this pedagogical orientation rests the ability of teachers and subsequently their students to conduct research and engage in knowledge work. Throughout the learning process the teachers cultivate their insights via systematic research that problematizes the taken-for-granted, problem-poses the official curriculum, analyzes the historical processes that shaped contemporary conditions, and explores diverse educational purposes. In this research context teachers and students continuously reflect on their scholarly work and contemplate ways to improve it. Together teachers and students gain a sophisticated view of educational purposes and the power interests particular purposes serve. Such informed teaching creates unprecedented levels of awareness and higher forms of cognitive activity.

The pedagogical context described here uses knowledge work abilities to raise questions and explore the ways society works and how it should work — immanent critique. Teachers and students research the forces that shape our efforts to ask and answer these questions. Using research-based, theoretically informed reflection, teachers as researchers come to see dimensions of schooling that had been previously unseen and engage in actions that raise the conceptual and ethical quality of professional practice. A new world of education is created.

Pedagogy and the Production of Subjectivity

A key feature of pedagogical concerns in this critical reflective context involves the production of subjectivity or the construction of identity. Informed by the bricolage, students in the course explore the ways both formal and non-formal pedagogical processes contribute to this process. A deep understanding of subjectivity production is necessary not only to pedagogical practice but to knowledge work in general. Indeed, central to any scholarly and educational activity is the analysis of forces that engage the individual in socio-cultural context. With these dynamics in mind, teacher researchers gain new insights into the complexities of everyday life in contemporary society and in educational venues.

The problem of subjectivity is studied and taught via the dynamism of an interdisciplinary curriculum. Contemplating these issues in a curriculum context, as teachers frame language and literacy, for example, in a social, cultural, historical, racial, political, and ethnic context they would cultivate a rigorous awareness of the roles of language and literacy in the shaping of identity. In a social studies curriculum teachers might explore subjectivity in terms of the political enculturation of young people into adulthood, the social forces that subvert or encourage political participation, the diverse ways history and economics are implicated in the production of civic apathy, political activism, and philosophical belief structures, and the effect of a pedagogy of social justice on the values and perspectives of students (Zevin, 2001).

Pedagogy and Cognition

As teacher researchers learn to use their understandings of the disciplines, interdisciplinarity, and the bricolage to gain insight into the pedagogical process, they inevitably turn their attention to concerns with producing higher orders of cognition. Just as they study the forces that produce subjectivity, teacher scholars develop the ability to gain a meta-awareness of the cognitive processes involved in the acts of teaching and learning. Such an awareness allows teachers and their students to monitor the cognitive, cultural, affective, discursive, and political dynamics operating in classrooms and the ways they affect particular individuals at particular times. In this context teachers and students become researchers who explore the reasons why some individuals are operating at more complex cognitive levels than others. They ask the following questions:

- Is the distinction separating those operating at higher and lower levels constructed around cultural lines?

- Are students' facilities with the skills being taught based on cognitive or dispositional/affective dynamics?

- How might students' familiarity with the discursive aspects of school culture shape their responses to classroom activities?

- What are the political and ideological implications of the material being investigated?

- Do student performances reflect power relations in the existing society?

- How can the classroom and its pedagogical activities be rearranged to disrupt the reproduction of those extant power relations in democratic and just ways?

When teacher scholars ask, research, and answer such questions, they gain the power to change dominant and unsuccessful pedagogies; they gain the ability to transform the ways teachers approach their classrooms and students. Educators who have studied such socio-cognitive phenomena can never again simply pass along a body of unexamined information for memorization by a group of students whose cultural and class backgrounds are irrelevant. Pedagogy in this context moves beyond 'adjustment procedures,' efforts to simply enculturate students into existing cognitive schemes and unexamined approaches to political, cultural, and vocational life. Instead, pedagogy becomes a more complex process whereby teachers and students develop the complex cognitive skills involved with exploring bodies of knowledge and developing thinking skills that put them in contact with the reality of their existence and its meaning. Such a pedagogical process involves teachers confronting students with the ways by which all human beings have been socially constructed, the ways such construction works to limit self-determination and agency. Education and the world change as a result of these activities.

References

ADORNO, T. *et al.* (1950) *The Authoritarian Personality*, New York, Harper and Row.

AGNELLO, M. (2001) *A Postmodern Literacy Policy Analysis*, New York, Peter Lang.

ALFORD, C. (1993) 'Introduction to the special issue on political psychology and political theory,' *Political Psychology*, 14, 2, pp. 199–208.

ALLEN, M. (2000) 'The Voice of Reason,' <http://www.curtin.edu.au/learn/unit/10846/arrow/vorall.htm>.

ALLISON, C. (1995) *Present and Past: Essays for Teachers in the History of Education*, New York, Peter Lang.

ALTRICHTER, H. and POSCH, P. (1989) 'Does the "grounded theory" approach offer a guiding paradigm for teacher research?,' *Cambridge Journal of Education*, 19, 1, pp. 21–31.

ANDERSON, G. (1989) 'Critical ethnography in education: Origins, current status, and new directions,' *Review of Educational Research*, 59, 3, pp. 249–70.

APPLE, M. (1993) 'The politics of official knowledge: Does a national curriculum make sense?,' *Teachers College Record*, 95, 2, pp. 222–41.

APPLE, M. (1996) 'Dominance and dependency: Situating *The Bell Curve* within the conservative restoration,' in J. Kincheloe, S. Steinberg, and A. Gresson (Eds) *Measured Lies: The Bell Curve Examined*, New York, St. Martin's.

APPLE, M. (1999) *Power, Meaning and Identity: Essays in Critical Educational Studies*, New York, Peter Lang.

ARLIN, P. (1975) 'Cognitive development in adulthood: A fifth stage?,' *Developmental Psychology*, 11, 5, pp. 602–6.

ARMSTRONG, M. (1981) 'The case of Louise and the painting of landscapes,' in J. Nixon (Ed.) *A Teachers' Guide to Action Research*, London, Grant McIntyre.

ARNEY, W. (2000) *Thoughts Out of School*, New York, Peter Lang.

ARONOWITZ, S. (1973) *False Promises*, New York, McGraw-Hill.

ARONOWITZ, S. (1983) 'The relativity of theory,' *The Village Voice*, December 27, p. 60.

ARONOWITZ, S. (1988) *Science as Power: Discourse and Ideology in Modern Society*, Minneapolis, University of Minnesota Press.

ARONOWITZ, S. (1993) *Roll over Beethoven: The Return of Cultural Strife*, Hanover, NH, Wesleyan University Press.

ARONOWITZ, S. (1996) 'The politics of science wars,' in A. Ross (Ed.) *Science Wars*, Durham, NC, Duke University Press.

ARONOWITZ, S. and DiFAZIO, W. (1994) *The Jobless Future: Sci-tech and the Dogma of Work*, Minneapolis, University of Wisconsin Press.

ASTMAN, J. (1984) 'Special education as a moral enterprise,' *Learning Disability Quarterly*, 7, 4, pp. 299–308.

ATKINSON, P. and HAMMERSLEY, M. (1994) 'Ethnography and participant observation,' in N. Denzin and Y. Lincoln (Eds), *Handbook of Qualitative Research*, Thousand Oaks, CA, Sage.

BALDWIN, E. (1987) 'Theory vs. ideology in the practice of teacher education,' *Journal of Teacher Education*, 38, pp. 16–19.

BARONE, T. (2000) *Aesthetics, Politics and Educational Inquiry: Essays and Examples*, New York, Peter Lang.

BARROW, R. (1984) *Giving Teaching Back to Teachers*, Totowa, NJ, Barnes and Noble Books.

BARTOLOME, L. (1998) *The Misteaching of Academic Discourses: The Politics of Language in the Classroom*, Boulder, CO, Westview.

BARTON, A. and M. OSBORNE (Eds) (2001) *Teaching Science in Diverse Settings: Marginalized Discourses and Classroom Practices*, New York, Peter Lang.

BELENKY, M., CLINCHY, B., GOLDBERGER, N., and TARULE, J. (1986) *Women's Ways of Knowing: The Development of Self, Voice, and Mind*, New York, Basic Books.

BELLAH, R. (1983) 'Social science as practical reason,' in D. Callahan and B. Jennings (Eds) *Ethics, the Social Sciences, and Policy Analysis*, New York, Plenum Press.

BENSON, G., GLASBERG, R., and GRIFFITH, B. (Eds) (1998) *Perspectives on the Unity and Integration of Knowledge*, New York, Peter Lang.

BEREITER, C. (2002) *Education and the Mind in the Knowledge Age*, Mahwah, NJ, Lawrence Erlbaum.

BERRY, K. (1998) 'Nurturing the imagination of resistance: Young adults as creators of knowledge,' in J. Kincheloe and S. Steinberg (Eds) *Unauthorized Methods: Strategies for Critical Teaching*, New York, Routledge.

BERRY, K. (2000) *The Dramatic Arts and Cultural Studies: Acting Against the Grain*, New York, Falmer.

BERRY, K. (2001) 'Democracy — Standards of complexity in a postmodern democracy,' in J. Kincheloe and D. Weil (Eds) *Standards and Schooling in the United States: An Encyclopedia*, Santa Barbara, CA, ABC-Clio.

BESAG, F. (1986a) 'Reality and research,' *American Behavioral Scientist*, 30, 1, pp. 6–14.

BESAG, F. (1986b) 'Striving after the wind,' *American Behavioral Scientist*, 30, 1, pp. 15–22.

BEYER, L. (2000) *The Arts, Popular Culture, and Social Change*, New York, Peter Lang.

BEYER, L. and LISTON, D. (Eds) (1996) *Creating Democratic Classrooms: The Struggles to Integrate Theory and Practice*, New York, Teachers College Press.

BLOCK, A. (1995) *Occupied Reading: Critical Foundations for an Ecological Theory*, New York, Garland.

BODNER, G. (1986) 'Constructivism: A theory of knowledge,' *Journal of Chemical Education*, 63, 10, pp. 873–8.

BOGDAN, R. and BIKLEN, S. (1982) *Qualitative Research for Education: An Introduction to Theory and Methods*, Boston, Allyn and Bacon.

BOJE, D. (2000) 'Issues of validity and reliability for academics studying Nike,' <http://abae.nmsu.edu/~dboje/nike.html>.

BOOKS, S. (2001) 'Saying poverty doesn't matter doesn't make it so,' in J. Kincheloe and D. Weil (Eds) *Standards and Schooling in the United States: An Encyclopedia*, Santa Barbara, CA, ABC-Clio.

BOURRICAUD, F. (1979) 'Individualistic mobilization and the crisis of professional authority,' *Daedalus*, 108, 2, pp. 1–20.

BOWERS, C. (2001) *Educating for Eco-Justice and Community*, Athens, GA, University of Georgia Press.

BRACY, G. (1987) 'Measurement-driven instruction: Catchy phrase, dangerous practice,' *Phi Delta Kappan*, 68, 9, pp. 683–6.

BRENNAN, M. and NOFFKE, S. (1997) 'Uses of data in action research,' in T. Carson and D. Sumara (Eds) *Action Research as a Living Practice*, New York, Peter Lang.

BRENT, D. (1998) 'Information technology and the breakdown of places of knowledge,' in G. Benson, R. Galsberg, and B. Griffith (Eds) *Perspectives on the Unity and Integration of Knowledge*, New York, Peter Lang.

BRIGGS, J. and PEAT, F. (1989) *Turbulent Mirror*, New York, Harper and Row.

BRITON, D. (1997) 'Psychoanalysis and pedagogy as living practices,' in T. Carson and D. Sumara (Eds) *Action Research as a Living Practice*, New York, Peter Lang.

BRITZMAN, D. (1991) *Practice Makes Practice: A Critical Study of Learning to Teach*, Albany, NY, State University of New York Press.

BRITZMAN, D. and PITT, A. (1997) 'Pedagogy in transferential time: Casting the past of learning into the presence of teaching,' in T. Carson and D. Sumara (Eds) *Action Research as a Living Practice*, New York, Peter Lang.

BROSIO, R. (1994) *The Radical Democratic Critique of Capitalist Education*, New York, Peter Lang.

BROSIO, R. (2000) *Philosophical Scaffolding for the Construction of Critical Democratic Education*, New York, Peter Lang.

BROWN, C. and DAVIS, J. (2000) *Black Sons to Mothers: Compliments, Critiques, and Challenges for Cultural Workers in Education*, New York, Peter Lang.

BROWN, S. (2001) *Reconstructing School Mathematics: Problems with Problems and the Real World*, New York, Peter Lang.

BULLOUGH, R. and GITLIN, A. (1995) *Becoming Students of Teaching: Methodologies for Exploring Self and School Context*, New York, Garland.

BUTLER, M. (1998) 'Negotiating place: The importance of children's realities,' in J. Kincheloe and S. Steinberg (Eds) *Students as Researchers: Creating Classrooms that Matter*, London, Falmer Press.

CALLAHAN, R. (1962) *Education and the Cult of Efficiency*, Chicago, University of Chicago Press.

CANNELLA, G. (1997) *Deconstructing Early Childhood Education: Social Justice and Revolution*, New York, Peter Lang.

CAPRA, F. (1996) *The Web of Life: A New Scientific Understanding of Living Systems*, New York, Anchor Books.

CARLSON, D. (1997) *Making Progress: Education and Culture in New Times*, New York, Teachers College Press.

CARLSON, D. and APPLE, M. (Eds) (1998) *Power/Knowledge/Pedagogy: The Meaning of Democratic Education in Unsettling Times*, Boulder, CO, Westview.

CARR, W. and KEMMIS, S. (1986) *Becoming Critical*, Basingstoke, The Falmer Press.

CARSON, T. (1997) 'Reflection and its resistances: Teacher and education as living practice,' in T. Carson and D. Sumara (Eds) *Action Research as a Living Practice*, New York, Peter Lang.

CARSON, T. and SUMARA, D. (Eds) (1997) *Action Research as a Living Practice*, New York, Peter Lang.

CARSPECKEN, P. (1996) *Critical Ethnography in Educational Research: A Theoretical and Practical Guide*, New York, Routledge.

CARSPECKEN, P. (1999) *Four Scenes for Posing the Question of Meaning and Other Essays in Critical Philosophy and Critical Methodology*, New York, Peter Lang.

CARY, R. (1998) *Critical Art Pedagogy: Foundations for Postmodern Art Education*, New York, Garland.

CHAMBERLIN, G. (1974) 'Phenomenological methodology and understanding education,' in D. Denton (Ed.) *Existentialism and Phenomenology in Education*, New York, Teachers College Press.

CHATTIN-MCNICHOLS, J. and LOEFFLER, M. (1989) 'Teachers as researchers: The first cycle of the teachers' research network,' *Young Children*, 44, 5, pp. 20–7.

CHERRYHOLMES, C. (1988) *Power and Criticism: Poststructural Investigations in Education*, New York, Teachers College Press.

CHURCH, R. and SEDLAK, M. (1976) *Education in the United States*, New York, Macmillan.

CLANDININ, D. and CONNELLY, F. (1995) 'Teachers' professional knowledge landscapes: Secret, sacred, and cover stories,' in F. Connelly and D. Clandinin (Eds) *Teachers' Professional Knowledge Landscapes*, New York, Teachers College Press.

CLATTERBAUGH, K. (1997) *Contemporary Perspectives on Masculinity: Men, Women, and Politics in Modern Society*, Boulder, CO, Westview.

CLOUGH, P. (1998) *The Ends of Ethnography: From Realism to Social Criticism*, New York, Peter Lang.

COBEN, D. (1998) *Radical Heroes: Gramsci, Freire and the Politics of Adult Education*, New York, Garland.

COCHRAN-SMITH, M. and LYTLE, S. (1993) *Inside/Outside: Teacher Research and Knowledge*, New York, Teachers College Press.

COCHRAN-SMITH, M. and LYTLE, S. (1998) 'Teacher research: The question that persists,' *International Journal of Leadership in Education*, 10, pp. 19–36.

CONNELL, R. (1989) 'Curriculum politics, hegemony, and strategies of social change,' in H. Giroux and R. Simon, *Popular Culture: Schooling and Everyday Life*, Granby, MA, Bergin and Garvey Publishers.

CONNELLY, F. and BEN-PERETZ, M. (1980) 'Teachers' roles in the using and doing of research and curriculum development?,' *Journal of Curriculum Studies*, 12, 2, pp. 95–107.

CORNIS-POPE, M. (2001) 'Literary education in the age of hypertextual and networked communication: strategies for an interactive critical pedagogy,' <http://www.liternet.revolta.com/iser/pope1.htm>.

COURTS, P. (1997) *Multicultural Literacies: Dialect, Discourse, and Diversity*, New York, Peter Lang.

CULBERTSON, J. (1981) 'Antecedents of the theory movement,' *Educational Administration Quarterly*, 17, pp. 25–47.

DAVID, J. (1988) 'The use of indicators by school districts: Aid or threat to improvement,' *Phi Delta Kappan*, 69, 7, pp. 499–503.

DAVIDOVIC, M. (1996) 'Rethinking reflection: Critical and creative,' <http://sol.aston.ac.uk/lsu/lsub10md.html>.

DEGENAAR, J. (1995) 'Myth and the collision of cultures,' *Myth and Symbol*, 2.

DENZIN, N. (1994) 'The art and politics of interpretation,' in N. Denzin and Y. Lincoln (Eds) *Handbook of Qualitative Research*, Thousand Oaks, CA, Sage Publications.

DENZIN, N. and LINCOLN, Y. (Eds) (2000) *Handbook of Qualitative Research*, Thousand Oaks, CA.

DE OLIVEIRA, W. and MONTECINOS, C. (1998) 'Social pedagogy: Presence, commitment, indentification, and availability,' *Teaching Education*, 9, 2.

DEWEY, J. (1908) *Ethics*, New York, Henry Holt and Company.

DEWEY, J. (1916) *Democracy and Education*, New York, The Free Press.

DEWEY, J. (1929) *The Sources of a Science of Education*, New York, Horace Liveright.

DIAMOND, P. and MULLIN, C. (Eds) (1999) *The Postmodern Educator: Arts-based Inquiries and Teacher Development*, New York, Peter Lang.

DOBSON, R., DOBSON, J. and KOETTING, R. (1987) 'Problematic aspects of school reform,' *Capstone Journal of Education*, 7, 2, pp. 3–13.

DOLL, W. (1989) 'Foundations for a post-modern curriculum,' *Journal of Curriculum Studies*, 21, 3, pp. 243–53.

DONMOYER, R. (1985) 'The rescue from relativism: Two failed attempts and an alternative strategy,' *Educational Researcher*, 14, pp. 13–20.

DONMOYER, R. (1990a) 'Curriculum evaluation and the negotiation of meaning,' *Language Arts*, 67, 3, pp. 274–86.

DONMOYER, R. (1990b) 'Generalizability and the single case study,' in A. Peshkin and E. Eisner (Eds) *Qualitative Research in Education*, New York, Teachers College Press.

DOYLE, W. (1977) 'Paradigms for research on teacher effectiveness,' *Review of Research in Education*, 5, pp. 163–98.

DU BOIS-RAYMOND, M., SÜNKER, H., and KRÜGER, H. (2001) (Eds) *Childhood in Europe*, New York, Peter Lang.

DUCKWORTH, E. (1987) *'The Having of Wonderful Ideas' and Other Essays on Teaching and Learning*, New York, Teachers College Press.

DUKE, D. (1977) 'Debriefing: A tool for curriculum research and course improvement,' *Journal of Currulum Studies*, 9, 2, pp. 157–63.

DUKE, D. (1985) 'What is the nature of educational excellence and should we try to measure it?,' *Phi Delta Kappan*, 66, 10, pp. 671–4.

EGAN, K. (1997) *The Educated Mind: How Cognitive Tools Shape Our Understanding*, Chicago, University of Chicago Press.

EISNER, E. (1983) 'Anastasia might still be alive, but the monarchy is dead,' *Educational Researcher*, 12, pp. 13–14, 23–4.

EISNER, E. (1984) 'Can educational research inform educational practice?,' *Phi Delta Kappan*, 65, 7, pp. 447–52.

ELLIOT, A. (1994) *Psychoanalytic Theory: An Introduction*, Cambridge, MA, Blackwell.

ELLIOTT, J. (1981) 'Introduction,' in J. Nixon (Ed.) *A Teachers' Guide to Action Research*, London, Grant McIntyre.

ELLIOTT, J. (1989a) 'Studying the school curriculum through insider research,' Paper presented to the International Conference on School Based Innovations: Looking Forward to the 1990s, Hong Kong.

ELLIOTT, J. (1989b) 'Action-research and the emergence of teacher appraisal in the United Kingdom,' Paper presented to the American Educational Research Association, San Francisco.

ELLIS, J. (1998) 'Interpretive inquiry as student research,' in S. Steinberg and J. Kincheloe (Eds) *Students as Researchers: Creating Classrooms that Matter*, London, Falmer.

EMERY, F. and THORSRUD, E. (1976) *Democracy at Work*, Leiden, Martinus Nijhoff.

Fay, B. (1975) *Social Theory and Political Practice*, London, George Allen and Unwin.

Fee, E. (1982) 'Is feminism a threat to scientific objectivity?,' *International Journal of Women's Studies*, 4, 4, pp. 378–92.

Fenimore-Smith, T.K. and Pailliotet, A. (2001) 'Teacher education — Teaching standards of complexity in preservice education,' in J. Kincheloe and D. Weil (Eds) *Standards and Schooling in the United States: An Encyclopedia*, 3 vols, Santa Barbara, CA, ABC-Clio.

Fenstermacher, G. (1994) 'The knower and the known: The nature of knowledge in research on teaching,' in L. Darling-Hammond (Ed.) *Review of Research in Education*, vol. 20, Washington, DC, American Educational Research Association.

Finn, C. (1982) 'A call for quality education,' *American Education*, 108, pp. 28–34.

Fischer, F. (1998) 'Beyond empiricism: Policy inquiry in postpositivist perspective,' *Policy Studies Journal*, 26, 1, pp. 129–46.

Fiske, D. (1986) 'Specificity of method and knowledge in social science,' in D. Fiske and R. Shweder, *Metatheory in Social Science: Pluralisms and Subjectivities*, Chicago, University of Chicago Press.

Flavell, J. (1977) *Cognitive Development*, Englewood Cliffs, NJ, Prentice-Hall.

Fleischer, L. (2001) 'Approaching a paradigm for critical educational theorizing: Penetrating the macro/micro divide — Reflections on teaching a core course,' *Taboo: The Journal of Culture and Education*, 5, 1, pp. 122–37.

Fontana, A. and Frey, J. (2000) 'The interview: From structured questions to negotiated text,' in N. Denzin and Y. Lincoln (Eds) *Handbook of Qualitative Research*, 2nd Ed., Thousand Oaks, CA, Sage.

Foote, M. and Goodson, I. (2001) 'Regulating teachers — A sword over their heads: The standards movement as a disciplinary device,' in J. Kincheloe and D. Weil (Eds) *Standards and Schooling in the United States: An Encyclopedia*, Santa Barbara, CA, ABC-Clio.

Foucault, M. (1980) *Power/Knowledge: Selected Interviews and Other Writings*, Ed. C. Gordon, New York, Pantheon.

Frankel, B. (1986) 'Two extremes on the commitment continuum,' in D. Fiske and R. Shweder, *Metatheory in Social Science: Pluralisms and Subjectivities*, Chicago, University of Chicago Press.

Freire, P. (1970a) *Pedagogy of the Oppressed*, New York, Herder and Herder.

Freire, P. (1970b) 'Research methods,' Paper presented to a seminar entitled Studies in Adult Education, Dar-es-Salaam, Tanzania.

Freire, P. (1985) *The Politics of Education: Culture, Power, and Liberation*, South Hadley, MA, Bergin and Garvey.

Gadamer, H. (1975) *Truth and Method*, G. Barden, and J. Cumming (trans. and Eds) New York, Seabury Press.

GALLAGHER, S. (1992) *Hermeneutics and Education*, Albany, NY, SUNY Press.

GARDNER, H. (1983) *Frames of Mind: The Theory of Multiple Intelligences*, New York, Basic Books.

GARMAN, N. and HAZI, H. (1988) 'Teachers ask: Is there life after Madeline Hunter?,' *Phi Delta Kappan*, 69, pp. 670–2.

GEE, J., HULL, G., and LANKSHEAR, C. (1996) *The New Work Order: Behind the Language of the New Capitalism*, Boulder, CO, Westview.

GERGEN, M. and GERGEN, K. (2000) 'Qualitative inquiry: tensions and transformations,' in N. Denzin and Y. Lincoln (Eds) *Handbook of Qualitative Research*, 2nd Ed., Thousand Oaks, CA, Sage.

GIARELLI, J. and CHAMBLISS, J. (1984) 'Philosophy of education as qualitative inquiry,' *Journal of Thought*, 19, pp. 34–46.

GIBSON, R. (1984) *Structuralism and Education*, London, Hodder and Stoughton.

GIBSON, R. (1986) *Critical Theory and Education*, London, Hodder and Stoughton.

GIROUX, H. (1981) *Ideology, Culture, and the Process of Schooling*, Philadelphia, Temple University Press.

GIROUX, H. (1983) *Theory and Resistance in Education*, South Hadley, MA, Bergin and Garvey.

GIROUX, H. (1986) 'Critical theory and the politics of culture and voice: Rethinking the discourse of educational research,' *Journal of Thought*, 21, pp. 84–105.

GIROUX, H. (1988) *Schooling and the Struggle for Public Life*, Minneapolis, University of Minnesota Press.

GIROUX, H. (1997) *Pedagogy and the Politics of Hope: Theory, Culture, and Schooling*, Boulder, CO, Westview.

GIROUX, H. and ARONOWITZ, S. (1985) *Education Under Siege*, South Hadley, MA, Bergin and Garvey.

GIROUX, H. and SIMON, R. (1989) 'Popular culture as a pedagogy of pleasure and meaning,' in H. Giroux and R. Simon (Eds) *Popular Culture: Schooling and Everyday Life*, Granby, MA, Bergin and Garvey.

GIROUX, H. and SIMON, R. (Eds) (1989) *Popular Culture: Schooling and Everyday Life*, Granby, MA, Bergin and Garvey.

GLASBERG, R. (1998) 'Objective science as the subjective projection of culture on to nature: Rethinking the problem of Enlightenment,' in G. Benson, R. Glasberg, and B. Griffith (Eds) *Perspectives on the Unity and Integration of Knowledge*, New York, Peter Lang.

GOLDMAN-SEGALL, R. (1995) 'Configurational validity: A proposal for analyzing multimedia ethnographic narratives,' *Journal for Educational Multimedia and Hypermedia*, 4, 2, pp. 163–82.

GOODLAD, J. (1988) 'Studying the education of educators: Values-driven inquiry,' *Phi Delta Kappan*, 70, 2, pp. 105–11.

GOODSON, I. (1997) *The Changing Curriculum: Studies in Social Construction*, New York, Peter Lang.

GOODSON, I. (1999) 'The educational researcher as public intellectual,' *British Educational Research Journal*, 25, 3, pp. 277–97.

GORDON, E., MILLER, F., and ROLLOCK, D. (1990) 'Coping with communicentric bias in knowledge production in the social sciences,' *Educational Researcher*, 19, 3, pp. 14–19.

GORDON, M. (2001) 'Philosophical and analytical standards,' in J. Kincheloe and D. Weil (Eds), *Standards and Schooling in the United States: An Encyclopedia*, Santa Barbara, CA, ABC-Clio.

GRADY, H. and WELLS, S. (1985–86) 'Toward a rhetoric of intersubjectivity: Introducing Jürgen Habermas,' *Journal of Advanced Composition*, 6, pp. 33–47.

GRAMSCI, A. (1988) *An Antonio Gramsci Reader*, ed. D. Forgacs, New York, Schocken Books.

GREENE, M. (1975) Curriculum and consciousness,' in W. Pinar, *Curriculum Theorizing; The Reconceptualist*, Berkeley, McCutchan.

GREENE, M. (1985) 'A philosophic look at merit and mastery in teaching,' *Elementary School Journal*, 86, pp. 17–23.

GRIFFITH, B. and PAUL, J. (1998) 'Constructing, deconstructing, and synthesizing knowledge narratives,' in G. Benson, R. Glasberg, and B. Griffith (Eds) *Perspectives on the Unity and Interpretation of Knowledge*, New York, Peter Lang.

GRIMMETT, P. (1997) 'Breaking the mold: Transforming a didatic professor into a learner-focused teacher educator,' in T. Carson and D. Sumara (Eds) *Action Researcher as a Living Practice*, New York, Peter Lang.

GROF, S. (1993) *The Holotropic Mind*, New York, HarperCollins.

GRONDIN, J. (1994) *Introduction to Philosophical Hermeneutics*, New Haven, CT, Yale University Press.

GROSS, A. and KEITH, W. (Eds) (1997) *Rhetorical Hermeneutics: Invention and Interpretation in the Age of Science*, Albany, NY, State University of New York Press.

GROSSBERG, L. (1992) *We Gotta Get out of this Place*, New York, Routledge.

GROSSBERG, L. (1995) 'What's in a name (one more time)?,' *Taboo: The Journal of Culture and Education*, 1, pp. 1–37.

GRUMET, M. (1988) *Bitter Milk: Women and Teaching*, Amherst, MA, University of Massachusetts Press.

GUBRIUM, J. and HOLSTEIN, J. (2000) 'Analyzing interpretive practice,' in N. Denzin and Y. Lincoln (Eds) *Handbook of Qualitative Research*, 2nd ed., Thousand Oakes, CA, Sage.

HABERMAS, J. (1970) *Knowledge and Human Interests*, trans by Jeremy Shapiro, London, Heinemann.

HABERMAS, J. (1971) *Knowledge and Human Interests*, trans. J. Shapiro, Boston, Beacon Press.

HABERMAS, J. (1973) *Theory and Practice*, trans. J. Viertel, Boston, Beacon Press.

Teachers as Researchers

HAGGERSON, N. (2000) *Expanding Curriculum Research and Understanding: A Mythopoetic Perspective*, New York, Peter Lang.

HAMMERSLEY, M. and ATKINSON, P. (1983) *Ethnography: Principle in Practice*, New York, Tavistock.

HANEY, W. and MADAUS, G. (1989) 'Searching for alternatives to standardized tests: Whys, whats, and whithers,' *Phi Delta Kappan*, 70, 9, pp. 683–7.

HANKINS, K. (1998) 'Cacophony to symphony: Memoirs in teacher research,' *Harvard Educational Review*, 68, 1, pp. 80–95.

HARAWAY, D. (1991) *Simians, Cyborgs, and Women*, New York, Routledge.

HARRINGTON, H. and QUINN-LEERING, K. (1995) 'Reflection, dialogue, and computer conferencing,' Paper presented at the American Educational Research Association, San Francisco.

HARRIS, M. (1981) *America Now*, New York, Simon and Schuster.

HART, T. (2001) *From Information to Transformation: Education for the Evolution of Consciousness*, New York, Peter Lang.

HEAD, J. (1979) 'Personality and pursuit of science,' *Studies in Science Education*, 6, pp. 35–45.

HELD, D. (1980) *Introduction to Critical Theory: Horkheimer to Habermas*, Berkeley, CA, University of California Press.

HENRIQUES, J., HOLLWAY, W., URWIN, C., VENN, C., and WALKERDINE, V. (1984) *Changing the Subject*, New York, Methuen.

HERMAN, E. and CHOMSKY, N. (1988) *Manufacturing Consent: The Political Economy of the Mass Media*, New York, Pantheon Books.

HERRNSTEIN, R. and MURRAY, C. (1994) *The Bell Curve: Intelligence and Class Structure in American Life*, New York, The Free Press.

HICKS, E. (1999) *Ninety-five Languages and Seven Forms of Intelligence*, New York, Peter Lang.

HIRSCH, E. D. (1987) *Cultural Literacy*, Boston, Houghlin Mifflin.

HINCHEY, P. (1998) *Finding Freedom in the Classroom: A Practical Introduction to Critical Theory*, New York, Peter Lang.

HINCHEY, P. (2001) 'Purposes of education — Educational standards: For whose purpose? For whose children?,' in J. Kincheloe and D. Weil (Eds), *Standards and Schooling in the United States: An Encyclopedia*, Santa Barbara, CA, ABC-Clio.

HODGE, R. and KRESS, G. (1988) *Social Semiotics*, Ithaca, NY, Cornell University Press.

HOLLAND, R. and MANSELL, T. (1983) 'Meanings and their interpretations in science education research,' *Studies in Science Education*, 10, pp. 100–7.

HORKHEIMER, M. (1974) *Critique of Instrumental Reason*, New York, Seabury Press.

HORN, R. (2000) *Teacher Talk: A Post-formal Inquiry into Education Change*, New York, Peter Lang.

HORN, R. (2001) 'Texas — A postformal conversation about standardization and accountability in Texas,' in J. Kincheloe and D. Weil (Eds),

Standards and Schooling in the United States: An Encyclopedia, Santa Barbara, CA, ABC-Clio.

HORN, R. and KINCHELOE, J. (Eds) (2001) *American Standards: Quality Education in a Complex World*, New York, Peter Lang.

HOUSE, E. (1978) 'Evaluation as scientific management in U.S. School reform,' *Comparative Education Review*, 22, 3, pp. 388–401.

HOWE, K. (1985) 'Two dogmas of educational research,' *Educational Researcher*, 14, pp. 10–18.

HOWLEY, A., PENDARVIS, E. and HOWLEY, C. (1993) 'Anti-intellectualism in U.S. Schools,' *Education Policy Analysis Archives*, 1, 6.

HURSH, D. (1997) 'Critical, collaborative action research in politically contested times,' in S. Hollingsworth (Ed.), *International Action Research: A Case for Educational Reform*, New York, Falmer.

HURSH, D. and ROSS, E. (2000) *Democratic Social Education: Social Studies for Social Change*, New York, Falmer Press.

HUSSERL, E. (1970) *The Crisis of European Sciences and Transcendental Phenomenology: An Introduction to Phenomenology*, Evanston, IL, Northwestern University Press.

JACOBY, R. (1975) *Social Amnesia*, Boston, Beacon Press.

JAGGAR, A. (1983) *Feminist Politics and Human Nature*, Totowa, NJ, Rowman and Ailanheld.

JAMES, M. and EBBUTT, D. (1981) 'Problems and potential,' in J. Nixon (Ed.) *A Teachers' Guide to Action Research*, London, Grant McIntyre.

JAMES, W. (1956) *The Will to Believe and Other Popular Essays in Popular Philosophy*, New York, Dover Publications.

JANESICK, V. (2000) 'The choreography of qualitative research design: Minuets, improvisations, and crystallization,' in N. Denzin and Y. Lincoln (Eds) *Handbook of Qualitative Research*, 2nd ed., Thousand Oaks, CA, Sage.

JARDINE, D. (1998) *To Dwell with a Boundless Heart: Essays in Curriculum Theory, Hermeneutics, and the Ecological Imagination*, New York, Peter Lang.

JAYARATNE, T. (1982) 'The value of quantitative methodology for feminist research,' in G. Bowles and R. Klein (Eds) *Theories of Women's Studies*, Boston, Routledge and Kegan Paul.

JAYNES, J. (1976) *The Origin of Consciousness in the Breakdown of the Bicameral Mind*, Boston, Houghton Mifflin.

JIPSON, J. and PALEY, N. (1997) *Daredevil Research: Recreating Analytic Practice*, New York, Peter Lang.

JONES, S. (2001) 'In defense of rogue scholarship: performing the scholar in qualitative work,' http://www.roguecom.com/roguescholar/sholman.html.

KARUNARATNE, V. (1997) 'Buddhism, science, and dialectics,' http://humanism.org/opinions/articles.html.

KEAT, R. (1981) *Politics of Social Theory: Habermas, Freud, and the Critique of Positivism*, Chicago, University of Chicago Press.

KEGAN, R. (1982) *The Evolving Self: Problem and Process in Human Development*, Cambridge, MA, Harvard University Press.

KELLNER, D. (1995) *Media Culture: Cultural Studies, Identity and Politics between the Modern and the Postmodern*, New York, Routledge.

KEMMIS, S. *et al.* (Eds) (1982) *The Action Research Reader*, Geelong, Victoria, Deakin University Press.

KERCKHOVE, D. (1995) 'Practicing collective intelligence,' <http://www.cfd. rmit.edu.au/ws/ws95/papers/kerckhove.html>.

KERLINGER, F. (1973) *Foundations of Behavioral Research*, New York, Holt, Rinehart and Winston.

KICKBUSCH, K. (1985) 'Ideological innocence and dialogue: A critical perspective on discourse in the social studies,' *Theory and Research in the Social Studies*, 13, 3, pp. 45–56.

KINCHELOE, J. (1993) *Toward a Critical Politics of Teacher Thinking: Mapping the Postmodern*, Westport, CT, Bergin and Garvey.

KINCHELOE, J. (1995) *Toil and Trouble: Good Work, Smart Workers, and the Integration of Academic and Vocational Education*, New York, Peter Lang.

KINCHELOE, J. (1999) *How Do we Tell the Workers? The Socio-economic Foundations of Work and Vocational Education*, Boulder, CO, Westview.

KINCHELOE, J. (2001) *Getting Beyond the Facts: Teaching Social Studies/Social Science in the Twenty-First Century*, 2nd edn, New York, Peter Lang.

KINCHELOE, J. (2002) *The Sign of the Burger: McDonald's and the Culture of Power*, Philadelphia, Temple University Press.

KINCHELOE, J. and McLAREN, P. (2000) 'Rethinking critical theory and qualitative research,' in N. Denzin and Y. Lincoln (Eds) *Handbook of Qualitative Research*, Thousand Oaks, CA, Sage.

KINCHELOE, J. and PINAR, W. (1991) 'Introduction,' in J. Kincheloe and W. Pinar (Eds) *Curriculum as Social Psychoanalysis: Essays on the Significance of Place*, Albany, NY, State University of New York Press.

KINCHELOE, J. and STEINBERG, S. (1993) 'A tentative description of postformal thinking: The critical confrontation with cognitive theory,' *Harvard Educational Review*, 63, 3, pp. 296–320.

KINCHELOE, J. and STEINBERG, S. (1997) *Changing Multiculturalism*, London, Open University Press.

KINCHELOE, J. and STEINBERG, S. (1998) *Unauthorized Methods: Strategies for Critical Teaching*, New York, Routledge.

KINCHELOE, J., STEINBERG, S., and GRESSON, A. (Eds) (1996) *Measured Lies: The Bell Curve Examined*, New York, St. Martin's Press.

KINCHELOE, J., STEINBERG, S., and HINCHEY, P. (1999) *The Postformal Reader: Cognition and Education*, New York, Falmer.

KINCHELOE, J., STEINBERG, S., RODRIGUEZ, N., and CHENNAULT, R. (1998) *White Reign: Deploying Whiteness in America*, New York, St. Martin's Press.

KINCHELOE, J., STEINBERG, S., and TIPPINS, D. (1999) *The Stigma of Genius: Einstein, Consciousness, and Education*, New York, Peter Lang.

KINCHELOE, J., STEINBERG, S., and VILLAVERDE, L. (1999) *Rethinking Intelligence: Confronting Psychological Assumptions about Teaching and Learning*, New York, Routledge.

KINCHELOE, J., and WEIL, D. (Eds) (2001) *Standards and Schooling in the United States: An Encyclopedia*, Santa Barbara, CA, ABC-Clio.

KINCHELOE, J. *et al.* (1987) 'From Jaynesian consciousness to critical consciousness,' Paper presented to the Louisiana Philosophy of Education Society, New Orleans, Louisiana.

KING, J. and MITCHELL, C. (1996) *Black Mothers to Sons*, New York, Peter Lang.

KITCHNER, K. (1983) 'Cognition, metacognition, and epistemic cognition,' *Human Development*, 26, pp. 222–32.

KLEIN, R. (1982) 'How to do what we want to do: Thoughts about feminist methodology,' in G. Bowles and R. Klein (Eds) *Theories of Women's Studies*, Boston, Routledge and Kegan Paul.

KNELLER, G. (1984) *Movements of Thought in Modern Education*, 2nd edn, New York, John Wiley and Sons.

KNOBEL, M. (1999) *Everyday Literacies: Students, Discourse, and Social Practice*, New York, Peter Lang.

KOGLER, H. (1996) *The Power of Dialogue: Critical Hermeneutics after Gadamer and Foucault*, Cambridge, MA, MIT Press.

KOHLI, W. (2000) 'Teaching in the danger zone: Democracy and difference,' in D. Hursh and E. Ross (Eds) *Democratic Social Education: Social Studies for Social Change*, New York, Falmer.

KOLLER, A. (1981) *An Unknown Woman: A Journey to Self-Discovery*, New York, Bantam Books.

KOVEL, J. (1981) *The Age of Desire*, New York, Pantheon Books.

KRAFT, N. (2001) 'Certification of teachers — A critical analysis of standards in teacher education programs,' in J. Kincheloe and D. Weil (Eds) *Standards and Schooling in the United States: An Encyclopedia*, Santa Barbara, CA, ABC-Clio.

KRAMER, D. (1983) 'Post-formal operations? A need for further conceptualization,' *Human Development*, 26, pp. 91–105.

KROATH, F. (1989) 'How do teachers change their practical theories?,' *Cambridge Journal of Education*, 19, 1, pp. 59–69.

KVALE, S. (1995) 'The social construction of validity,' *Qualitative Inquiry*, 1, 1, pp. 19–40.

LAKES, R. (1994a) 'Critical education for work,' in R. Lakes (Ed.), *Critical Education for Work*, Norwood, NJ, Ablex.

LAKES, R. (1994b) 'Is this workplace democracy?: Education and labor in postindustrial America,' in R. Lakes (Ed.) *Critical Education for Work: Multidisciplinary Approaches*, Norwood, NJ, Ablex.

LASCH, C. (1979) *The Culture of Narcissism*, New York, W. W. Norton.

LATHER, P. (1986) 'Research as praxis,' *Harvard Educational Review*, 56, pp. 257–77.

LATHER, P. (1991) *Getting Smart: Feminist Research and Pedagogy with/in the Postmodern*, New York, Routledge.

LATHER, P. (1993) 'Fertile obsession: Validity after poststructuralism,' *Sociological Quarterly*, 34, pp. 673–93.

LAVINE, T. (1984) *From Socrates to Sartre: The Philosophic Quest*, New York, Bantam Books.

LEE, A. (1997) 'What is MIS?,' in R. Galliers and W. Currie (Eds) *Rethinking MIS*, London, Oxford University Press.

LEISTYNA, P., WOODRUM, A., and SHERBLOM, S. (1996) *Breaking Free: The Transformative Power of Critical Pedagogy*, Cambridge, MA, Harvard Educational Review.

LEMKE, J. (1995) *Textual Politics: Discourse and Social Dynamics*, London, Taylor and Francis.

LESHAN, L. and MARGENAU, H. (1982) *Einstein's Space and Van Gogh's Sky: Physical Reality and Beyond*, New York, Macmillan.

LESTER, S. (2001) 'Working with knowledge — Learning for the twenty-first century: Raising the level,' in J. Kincheloe and D. Weil (Eds) *Standards and Schooling in the United States: An Encyclopedia*, Santa Barbara, CA, ABC-Clio.

LÉVI-STRAUSS, C. (1966) *The Savage Mind*, Chicago, University of Chicago Press.

LEVY, P. (1999) 'Toward super language,' <http://www.hnet.uci.edu/mposter/syllabi/readings/levy.html>.

LEWIN, K. (1946) 'Action research and minority problems,' *Journal of Social Issues*, 2, pp. 34–6.

LINCOLN, Y. and GUBA, E. (1985) *Naturalistic Inquiry*, Beverly Hills, CA, Sage.

LINNE, R. (2001) 'Urban education — teacher perspectives on standards and high-states testing: from the urban to the suburban,' in J. Kincheloe and D. Weil (Eds) *Standards and Schooling in the United States: An Encyclopedia*. Santa Barbara, CA, ABC-Clio.

LOMAX, P. and PARKER, Z. (1996) 'Representing a dialectical form of knowledge within a new epistemology for teaching and teacher education,' Paper presented at the American Educational Research Association, New York.

LONGSTREET, W. (1982) 'Action research: A paradigm,' *Educational Forum*, 46, 2, pp. 136–49.

LOWE, D. (1982) *History of Bourgeois Perception*, Chicago, University of Chicago Press.

LUCE-KAPLER, R. (1997) 'Reverberating the action research text,' in T. Carson and D. Sumara (Eds) *Action Research as a Living Practice*, New York, Peter Lang.

LYND, S. (1987) 'Foreword,' in D. Wells (Ed.) *Empty Promises*, New York, Monthly Review Press.

LYTLE, S. and COCHRAN-SMITH, M. (1992) 'Teacher research as a way of knowing,' *Harvard Educational Review*, 62, 4, pp. 93–109.

MACEDO, D. (1994) *Literacies of Power: What Americans are Not Allowed to Know*, Boulder, CO, Westview Press.

MCCUTCHEON, G. (1981) 'The impact of the insider,' in J. Nixon (Ed.) *A Teachers' Guide to Action Research*, London, Grant McIntyre.

MACDONALD, J. (1975) 'Curriculum and human interests,' in W. Pinar, *Curriculum Theorizing: The Reconceptualists*, Berkeley, CA, McCutchan.

MCGINTY, S. (Ed.) (2001) *The Politics and Machinations of Educational Research: International Case Studies*, New York, Peter Lang.

MCKERNAN, J. (1988) 'Teacher as researcher: Paradigm and praxis,' *Contemporary Education*, 59, 3, pp. 154–8.

MCLAREN, P. (1985) 'The ritual dimensions of resistance: Clowning and symbolic inversion,' *Journal of Education*, 168, 2, pp. 84–97.

MCLAREN, P. (1986) *Schooling as Ritual Performance: Toward a Political Economy of Educational Symbols and Gestures*, London, Routledge and Kegan Paul.

MCLAREN, P. (1989a) *Life in Schools*, New York, Longman.

MCLAREN, P. (1989b) 'On ideology and education: Critical pedagogy and the cultural politics of resistance,' in H. Giroux and P. McLaren (Eds) *Critical Pedagogy, The State, and Cultural Struggles*, Albany, NY, SUNY Press.

MCLAREN, P. (1995) *Critical Pedagogy and Predatory Culture: Oppositional Politics in a Postmodern Culture*, New York, Routledge.

MCLAREN, P. (2000) *Che Guervara, Paulo Freire, and the Pedagogy of Revolution*, Lanham, MD, Rowan and Littlefield.

MCLAREN, P., HAMMER, R., REILLY, S., and SHOLLE, D. (1995) *Rethinking Media Literacy: A Critical Pedagogy of Representation*, New York, Peter Lang.

MACMILLAN, C. and GARRISON, J. (1984) 'Using the "new philosophy of science" in criticizing current research traditions in education,' *Educational Researcher*, 13, pp. 15–21.

MCMAHON, M. (1970) 'Positivism and the public schools,' *Phi Delta Kappan*, 51, pp. 515–17.

MCNAY, M. (1988) 'Educational research and the nature of science,' *Educational Forum*, 52, 4, pp. 353–62.

MCNEIL, L. (1988) 'Contradictions of reform,' *Phi Delta Kappan*, 69, 7, pp. 478–86.

MADAUS, G. (1985) 'Test scores as administrative mechanisms in educational policy,' *Phi Delta Kappan*, 66, 9, pp. 611–17.

MADISON, G. (1988) *The Hermeneutics of Postmodernity: Figures and Themes*, Bloomington, Indiana University Press.

MAEROFF, G. (1988) 'A blueprint for empowering teachers,' *Phi Delta Kappan*, 69, 7, pp. 472–7.

MAHONEY, M. and LYDDON, W. (1988) 'Recent developments in cognitive approaches to counseling and psychotherapy,' *Counseling Psychologist*, 16, 2, pp. 190–234.

MALEWSKI, E. (2001a) 'Administration — Administrative leadership and public consciousness: Discourse matters in the struggle for new standards,' in J. Kincheloe and D. Weil (Eds) *Standards and Schooling in the United States*, Santa Barbara, CA, ABC-Clio.

MALEWSKI, E. (2001b) 'Queer sexuality — The trouble with knowing: Standards of complexity and sexual orientations,' in J. Kincheloe and D. Weil (Eds) *Standards and Schooling in the United States: An Encyclopedia*, Santa Barbara, CA, ABC-Clio.

MANNING, P. and CULLUM-SWAN, B. (1994) 'Narrative, content, and semiotic analysis,' in N. Denzin and Y. Lincoln (Eds) *Handbook of Qualitative Research*, Thousand Oaks, CA, Sage.

MARCUSE, H. (1955) *Eros and Civilization*, Boston, Beacon Press.

MARCUSE, H. (1964) *One Dimensional Man*, Boston, Beacon Press.

MARZANO, R. and KENDALL, J. (1999) 'The fall and rise of standards-based education,' <http://www.mcrel.org/standards/articles/fall-and-rise-one.dsp>.

MAYERS, M. (2001a) *Street Kids and Streetscapes: Panhandling, Politics, and Prophecies*, New York, Peter Lang.

MAYERS, M. (2001b) 'Interpretation — Hermeneutics invitation to meaning making: The ecology of a complexity of standards, educational research, policy, and praxis,' in J. Kincheloe and D. Weil (Eds) *Standards and Schooling in the United States: An Encyclopedia*, Santa Barbara, CA, ABC-Clio.

MERLEAU-PONTY, M. (1962) *Phenomenology of Perception*, London, Routledge and Kegan Paul.

MIES, M. (1982) 'Toward a methodology for feminist research,' in G. Bowles and R. Klein, *Theories of Women's Studies*, Boston, Routledge and Kegan Paul.

MILLER, S. and HODGE, J. (1998) 'Phenomenology, hermeneutics, and narrative analysis: Some unfinished methodological business,' unpublished paper.

MORRIS, M., DOLL, M., and PINAR, W. (1999) *How We Work*, New York, Peter Lang.

MOSHA, R. (2000) *The Heartbeat of Indigenous Africa: A Study of the Chagga Educational System*, New York, Garland.

MUNDAY, L. and DAVIS, J. (1974) *Varieties of Accomplishment After College: Perspectives on the Meaning of Academic Talent*, Iowa City, IO, ACT Publications.

MURPHIE, A. (1998) 'Cyberfictions and hypertext: what is happening to text?,' <http://wwwmcs.elm.mq.edu.au/staff/Andrew/307/hypeprt.html>.

MYERS, L. (1987) 'The deep structure of culture: Relevance of traditional African culture in contemporary Life,' *Journal of Black Studies*, 18, 1, pp. 72–85.

NELSON, W. (1998) 'The naked truth about school reform in Minnesota,' *Phi Delta Kappan*, 79, 9, pp. 679–85.

NEWLAND, P. (1997) 'Logical types of learning,' <http://www.envf.port.ac.uk/newmedia/lecturenotes/EMMA/at2n.htm>.

NIXON, J. (1981) 'Postscript,' in J. Nixon (Ed.) *A Teachers' Guide to Action Research*, London, Grant McIntyre.

NOBLIT, G. (1984) 'The prospects of an applied ethnography for education: A sociology of knowledge interpretation,' *Educational Evaluation and Policy Analysis*, 6, 1, pp. 95–101.

NOBLIT, G. (1999) *Particularities: Collected Essays on Ethnography and Education*, New York, Peter Lang.

NOBLIT, G. and EAKER, D. (1987) 'Evaluation designs as political strategies,' Paper presented to the American Educational Research Association, Washington, DC.

NOFFKE, S. and STEVENSON, R. (1995) *Educational Action Research: Becoming Practically Critical*, New York, Teachers College Press.

NORRIS, N. (1998) 'Curriculum evaluation revisited,' *Cambridge Journal of Education*, 28, 2.

NOVICK, R. (1996) 'Actual schools, possible practices: New directions in professional development,' *Education Policy Analysis Archives*, 4, 14.

NYANG, S. and VANDI, A. (1980) 'Pan Africanism in world history,' in M. Asante and A. Vandi, *Contemporary Black Thought: Alternative Analyses in Social and Behavioral Science*, Beverly Hills, CA, Sage.

ODI, A. (1981) 'The process of theory construction,' *Journal of Research and Development in Education*, 15, 2, pp. 53–8.

OHANIAN, S. (1999) *One Size Fits Few: The Folly of Educational Standards*, Portsmouth, NH, Heinemann.

OJA, S. and HAM, M. (1984) 'A cognitive developmental approach to collaborative action research with teachers,' *Teachers College Record*, 86, 1, pp. 171–92.

OLDROYD, D. (1985) 'Indigenous action research for individual and system development,' *Educational Management and Administration*, 13, pp. 113–18.

OLDROYD, D. and TILLER, T. (1987) 'Change from within: An account of school-based collaborative action research in an English secondary school,' *Journal of Education for Teaching*, 12, 3, pp. 13–27.

ORTEZA Y. MIRANDA, E. (1988) 'Broadening the focus of research in education,' *Journal of Research and Development in Education*, 22, 1, pp. 23–8.

O'SULLIVAN, E. (1999) *Transformative Learning: Educational Vision for the Twenty-first Century*, New York, Zed.

OWEN, D. (1985) *None of the Above: Behind the Myth of Scholastic Aptitude*, Boston, Houghton Mifflin.

OWEN, D. and DOERR, M. (1999) *None of the Above: The Truth behind the SATs*, Lanham, MD, Rowman and Littlefield.

OXTOBY, M. and SMITH, B. (1970) 'Students entering Sussex and Essex Universities in 1966: Some similarities and differences,' *Research in Education*, 3, pp. 87–100.

PALEY, N. and JIPSON, J. (2000) *Questions of You and the Struggle of Collaborative Life*, New York, Peter Lang.

PERRY, P. (2001) *A Composition of Consciousness: Roads of Reflection from Freire to Elbow*, New York, Peter Lang.

PETERS, M. and LANKSHEAR, C. (1994) 'Education and hermeneutics: A Freirean interpretation,' in P. McLaren and C. Lankshear (Eds) *Politics of Liberation: Paths from Freire*, New York, Routledge.

PHILLIPS, D. (1983) 'After the wake: Postpositivistic educational thought,' *Educational Researcher*, 12, pp. 4–12.

PIAGET, J. (1973) *To Understand is to Invent: The Future of Education*, New York, Grossman.

PINAR, W. (Ed.) (1975) *Curriculum Theorizing: The Reconceptualists*, Berkeley, CA, McCutchan.

PINAR, W. (1994) *Autobiography, Politics, and Sexuality: Essays in Curriculum Theory, 1972–1992*, New York, Peter Lang.

PINAR, W. (Ed.) (1998) *Curriculum: Toward New Identities*, New York, Garland.

PINAR, W. (1999) *Contemporary Curriculum Discourses: Twenty Years of JCT*, 2nd edn, New York, Peter Lang.

PINAR, W. (2001) *The Gender of Racial Politics and Violence in America: Lynching, Prison Rape, and the Crisis of Masculinity*, New York, Peter Lang.

PINAR, W. and GRUMET, M. (1988) 'Socratic Caesura and the theory practice relationship,' in W. Pinar (Ed.) *Contemporary Curriculum Discourses*, Scottsdale, AZ, Gorsuch Scarisbrick.

PINAR, W., REYNOLDS, W., SLATTERY, P., and TAUBMAN, P. (1995) *Understanding Curriculum*, New York, Peter Lang.

PONZIO, R. (1985) 'Can we change content without changing context?,' *Teacher Education Quarterly*, 12, 3, pp. 39–43.

POPKEWITZ, T. (1981a) 'The study of schooling: Paradigms and field-based methodologies in education research and evaluation,' in T. Popkewitz and B. Tabachnick (Eds) *The Study of Schooling*, New York, Praeger.

POPKEWITZ, T. (1981b) 'Education research: Values and visions of social order,' in H. Giroux, A. Penna, and W. Pinar (Eds) *Curriculum and Instruction*, Berkeley, CA, McCutchan.

PORTER, A. (1988) 'Indicators: Objective data or political tool?,' *Phi Delta Kappan*, 69, 7, pp. 503–8.

POSNER, G. (1982) 'Cognitive science and a conceptual change epistemology: A new approach to curricular research,' *Journal of Curriculum Theorizing*, 4, pp. 106–26.

POSTER, M. (1989) *Critical Theory and Poststructuralism: In Search of a Context*, Ithaca, NY, Cornell University Press.

POWELL, R. (2001) *Straight Talk: Growing as Multicultural Educators*, New York, Peter Lang.

PRIGOGINE, I. and STENGERS, I. (1984) *Order Out of Chaos*, New York, Basic Books.

PROGLER, Y. (2001) 'Social studies — Social studies standards: Diversity, conformity, complexity,' in J. Kincheloe and D. Weil (Eds) *Standards and Schooling in the United States: An Encyclopedia*, Santa Barbara, CA, ABC-Clio.

PURPEL, D. (1999) *Moral Outrage in Education*, New York, Peter Lang.

PUSHKIN, D. (2001) 'Science — To standardize, or too standardized? What becomes of our curriculum?,' in J. Kincheloe and D. Weil (Eds) *Standards and Schooling in the United States: An Encyclopedia*, Santa Barbara, CA, ABC-Clio.

QUINN, M. (2001) *Going Out, Not Knowing Whither: Education, the Upward Journey, and the Faith of Reason*, New York, Peter Lang.

RAPKO, J. (1998) 'Review of *The Power of Dialogue: Critical Hermeneutics after Gadamer and Foucault* (Herbert, H.),' *Criticism*, 40, 1, pp. 133–8.

RASBERRY, G. (2001) *Writing Research/Researching Writing: Through a Poet's I*, New York, Peter Lang.

RAVEN, J. and STEPHENSON, J. (2001) *Competence in the Learning Society*, New York, Peter Lang.

REINHARZ, S. (1979) *On Becoming a Social Scientist*, San Francisco, Jossey-Bass.

REINHARZ, S. (1982) 'Experimental analysis: A contribution to feminist research,' in G. Bowles and R. Klein (Eds) *Theories of Women's Studies*, Boston, Routledge and Kegan Paul.

RICHARDS, C. (1988) 'Indicators and three types of educational monitoring systems: Implications for design,' *Phi Delta Kappan*, 69, 7, pp. 495–9.

RICHARDSON, V. (1994) 'Conducting research on practice,' *Educational Researcher*, 23, 5, pp. 5–10.

RIVLIN, A. (1971) *Systematic Thinking for Social Action*, Washington, DC, The Brookings Institution.

RODRIGUEZ, N. and VILLAVERDE, L. (2000) *Dismantling White Privilege*, New York, Peter Lang.

ROMANISH, B. (1986) 'Critical thinking and the curriculum: A critique,' *Educational Forum*, 51, 1, pp. 45–56.

ROMANO, R. (2000) *Forging an Educative Community: The Wisdom of Love, the Power of Understanding, and the Terror of It All*, New York, Peter Lang.

ROSEN, S. (1987) *Hermeneutics as Politics*, New York, Oxford University Press.

ROSENAU, P. (1992) *Postmodernism and the Social Sciences: Insights, Inroads, and Intrusion*, Princeton, NJ, Princeton University Press.

ROSENHOLTZ, S. (1987) 'Education reform strategies: Will they increase teacher commitment?,' 37, pp. 534–62.

ROSS, D. (1984) 'A practical model for conducting action research in public school settings,' *Contemporary Education*, 55, 2, pp. 113–17.

ROTH, W., TOBIN, K., and RITCHIE, S. (2001) *Re/constructing Elementary Science*, New York, Peter Lang.

RUDDICK, J. (1989) 'Critical thinking and practitioner research: Have they a place in initial teacher training?,' Paper presented to the American Educational Research Association, San Francisco.

RUDDICK, S. (1980) 'Material thinking,' *Feminist Studies*, 6, 2, pp. 342–67.

RUSSELL, D. (1993) 'Vygotsky, Dewey, and externalism: Beyond the student/discipline dichotomy,' *Journal of Advanced Composition*, 13, 1, pp. 173–97.

SALGANIK, L. (1985) 'Why testing reforms are so popular and how they are changing education,' *Phi Delta Kappan*, 66, 9, pp. 607–10.

SALVIO, P. (1997) 'On keying pedagogy as an interpretive event,' in T. Carson and D. Sumara (Eds) *Action Research as a Living Practice*, New York, Peter Lang.

SAMUELS, A. (1993) *The Political Psyche*, New York, Routledge.

SCHNEIDER, J. and LAIHUA, W. (2000) *Giving Care, Writing Self: A "New" Ethnography*, New York, Peter Lang.

SCHOLES, R. (1982) *Semiotics and Interpretation*, New Haven, CT, Yale University Press.

SCHOLES, R. (1985) *Textual Power: Literary Theory and the Teaching of English*, New Haven, CT, Yale University Press.

SCHÖN, D. (1987) *Educating the Reflective Practitioner*, San Francisco, Jossey-Bass.

SCHÖN, D. (1995) 'The new scholarship requires a new epistemology,' *Change*, 27, 6.

SCHUBERT, W. and THOMAS, T. (2001) 'History — Responding to standards: The professor of education's legacy and responsibility,' in J. Kincheloe and D. Weil (Eds) *Standards and Schooling in the United States: An Encyclopedia*, Santa Barbara, CA, ABC-Clio.

SELDEN, S. (1984) 'Objectivity and ideology in educational research,' *Phi Delta Kappan*, 66, 4, pp. 281–3.

SEMALI, L. and KINCHELOE, J. (1999) *What is Indigenous Knowledge? Voices from the Academy*, New York, Garland.

SHERMAN, R. (1985) 'The trial and error of merit pay,' Paper presented to the Southeast Philosophy of Education Society, Tuscaloosa, Alabama.

SHERMAN, R., WEBB, R. and ANDREWS, S. (1984) 'Qualitative inquiry: An introduction,' *Journal of Thought*, 19, pp. 22–33.

SHOHAM, S. (2000) *God as the Shadow of Man*, New York, Peter Lang.

SHOR, I. (1987) *Critical Teaching and Everyday Life*, Chicago, University of Chicago Press.

SHOR, I. and FREIRE, P. (1987) *A Pedagogy for Liberation*, South Hadley, MA, Bergin and Garvey.

SHOTTER, J. (1993) *Cultural Politics of Everyday Life*, Toronto, University of Toronto Press.

SHOTTER, J. (1998) 'Action research as history making,' *Concepts and Transformations: International Journal of Action Research and Organizational Renewal*, 2, 3, pp. 279–86.

SHWEDER, R. and FISKE, D. (1986) 'Introduction: Uneasy social science,' in D. Fiske and R. Shweder, *Metatheory in Social Science: Pluralisms and Subjectivities*, Chicago, University of Chicago Press.

SIMPSON, D. and JACKSON, M. (1997) *Educational Reform: A Deweyan Perspective*, New York, Garland.

SLAUGHTER, R. (1989) 'Cultural reconstruction in the postmodern world,' *Journal of Curriculum Studies*, 3, pp. 255–70.

SMART, B. (1976) *Sociology, Phenomenology, and Marxian Analysis*, London, Routledge and Kegan Paul.

SMITH, D. (1974) 'Women's perspective as a radical critique of sociology,' *Sociological Inquiry*, 44, 1, pp. 7–13.

SMITH, D. (1999) *Pedagon: Interdisciplinary Essays in the Human Sciences, Pedagogy, and Culture*, New York, Peter Lang.

SMITH, J. (1983) 'Quantitative versus qualitative research: An attempt to clarify the issue,' *Educational Researcher*, 12, pp. 6–13.

SMITH, P. (1989) 'Pedagogy and the popular-cultural-commodity text,' in H. Giroux and R. Simon (Eds) *Popular Culture: Schooling and Everyday Life*, Granby, MA: Bergin and Gavey.

SMITS, H. (1997) 'Living within the space of practice: Action research inspired by hermeneutics,' in T. Carson and D. Sumara (Eds) *Action Research as a Living Practice*, New York, Peter Lang.

SMYTH, J. (2001) *Critical Politics of Teachers' Work*, New York, Peter Lang.

SOLTIS, J. (1984) 'On the nature of educational research,' *Educational Researcher*, 13, pp. 5–10.

SOTO, L. (1997) 'Bilingual education in America: In search of equity and justice,' in J. Kincheloe and S. Steinberg (Eds) *Unauthorized Methods: Strategies for Critical Teaching*, New York, Routledge.

SOTO, L. (Ed.) (2000) *The Politics of Early Childhood Education*, New York, Peter Lang.

STANLEY, L. and WISE, S. (1982) '"Back to the personal" or our attempt to construct "feminist research",' in G. Bowles and R. Klein (Eds) *Theories of Women's Studies*, Boston, Routledge and Kegan Paul.

STEINBERG, S. (2000) 'The new civics: Teaching for critical empowerment,' in D. Hursh and E. Ross (Eds) *Democratic Social Education: Social Studies for Social Change*, New York, Falmer.

STEINBERG, S. (Ed.) (2001) *Multi/Intercultural Conversations*, New York, Peter Lang.

STEINBERG, S. and KINCHELOE, J. (1997) *Kinderculture: Corporate Constructions of Childhood*, Boulder, CO, Westview.

STEINBERG, S. and KINCHELOE, J. (1998) *Students as Researchers: Creating Classrooms that Matter*, London, Falmer Press.

STEINER, S., KRANK, M., McLAREN, P., and BAHRUTH, R. (Eds) (2000) *Freirean Pedagogy, Praxis, and Possibilities: Projects for the New Millennium*, New York, Garland.

STERNBERG, R. (1985) *Beyond I.Q.*, New York, Cambridge University Press.

STEWART, D. and MICKUNAS, A. (1974) *Exploring Phenomenology*, Chicago, American Library Association.

STRICKLAND, D. (1988) 'The teacher as researcher: Toward the extended professional,' *Language Arts*, 65, 8, pp. 754–64.

SUMARA, D. (1996) *Private Readings in Public: Schooling the Literary Imagination*, New York, Peter Lang.

SUMARA, D. and DAVIS, B. (1997) 'Enlarging the space of the possible: Complexity, complicity, and action research practices,' in T. Carson and D. Sumara (Eds) *Action Research as a Living Practice*, New York, Peter Lang.

SYMES, C. and MEADMORE, D. (1999) *The Extra-Ordinary School: Parergonality and the Pedagogy*, New York, Peter Lang.

TAUSSIG, M. (1993) *Mimesis and Alterity: A Particular History of the Senses*, London, Routledge.

TEDLOCK, B. (2000) 'Ethnography and ethnographic representation,' in N. Denzin and Y. Lincoln (Eds) *Handbook of Qualitative Research*, 2nd edn, Thousand Oaks, CA, Sage.

THAYER-BACON, B. (2001) 'Epistemology — An examination and redescription of epistemology,' in J. Kincheloe and D. Weil (Eds) *Standards and Schooling in the United States: An Encyclopedia*, Santa Barbara, CA, ABC-Clio.

THEOBOLD, P. and MILLS, E. (1995) 'Accountability and the struggle over what counts,' *Phi Delta Kappan*, 76, 6.

THOMAS, G. (1998) 'The myth of rational research,' *British Educational Research Journal*, 24, 2.

THOMAS, T. and SCHUBERT, W. (2001) 'Certification of teachers — Reinterpreting teacher certification standards: Locating limitations and expanding possibilities,' in J. Kincheloe and D. Weil (Eds) *Standards and Schooling in the United States: An Encyclopedia*, Santa Barbara, CA, ABC-Clio.

TOLSTOY, L. (1981) 'Anna Karenina,' in *Letters from the Country*, C. Bly (Ed.), New York, Penguin Books.

TORNEY-PURTA, J. (1985) 'Linking faculties of education with classroom teachers through collaborative research,' *Journal of Educational Thought*, 19, 1, pp. 71–7.

TRAVIS, M. (1998) *Reading Cultures: The Construction of Readers in the Twentieth Century*, Carbondale, IL, Southern Illinois University Press.

TRIPP, D. (1988) 'Teacher journals in collaborative classroom research,' Paper presented at the American Educational Research Association, New Orleans.

TUTHILL, D. and ASHTON, P. (1983) 'Improving educational research through the development of educational paradigms,' *Educational Researcher*, 12, pp. 6–14.

UTKE, A. (1998) 'Introduction: The (re) unification of knowledge: Why? How? Where? When?,' in G. Benson, R. Glasberg, and B. Griffith, (Eds) *Perspectives on the Unity and Interpretation of Knowledge*, New York, Peter Lang.

VAN DEN BERG, O. and NICHOLSON, S. (1989) 'Teacher transformation in the South African context: An action research approach,' Paper presented to the International Conference on School Based Innovations: Looking Forward to the 1990s, Hong Kong.

VAN HESTERAN, F. (1986) 'Counselling research in a different key: The promise of human science perspective,' *Canadian Journal of Counselling*, 20, 4, pp. 200–34.

VAN MANEN, M. (1978) 'Objective inquiry into structures of subjectivity,' *Journal of Curriculum Theorizing*, 1, pp. 44–64.

VATTIMO, G. (1994) *Beyond Interpretation: The Meaning of Hermeneutics for Philosophy*, Stanford, CA, Stanford University Press.

VENTURA, M. (1994) 'The age of endarkenment,' *Utne Reader*, 64, July/ August, pp. 63–6.

VINSON, K. and ROSS, E. (2001) 'Social studies — Social education and standards-based reform: A critique,' in J. Kincheloe and D. Weil (Eds) *Standards and Schooling in the United States: An Encyclopedia*, Santa Barbara, CA, ABC-Clio.

VOLOSHINOV, V. (1973) *Marxism and the Philosophy of Language*, New York, Seminar Press.

VON GLASERSFELD, E. (forthcoming) 'An exposition of constructivism: Why some like it radical,' in R. Davis, C. Maher, and N. Noddings (Eds) *Constructivist Views on the Teaching and Learning of Mathematics*.

WALLACE, M. (1987) 'A historical review of action research: Some implications for the education of teachers in the managerial role,' *Journal of Education for Teaching*, 13, 2, pp. 97–115.

WAX, R. (1971) *Doing Fieldwork: Warnings and Advice*, Chicago, University of Chicago Press.

WEIL, D. (1998) *Towards a Critical Multicultural Literacy: Theory and Practice for Education for Liberation*, New York, Peter Lang.

WEIL, D. (2001a) 'Functionalism — From functionalism to neofunctionalism and neoliberalism: Developing a dialectical understanding of the standards debate through historical awareness,' in J. Kincheloe and

D. Weil (Eds) *Schooling and Standards in the United States: An Encyclopedia*, Santa Barbara, CA, ABC-Clio.

WEIL, D. (2001b) 'Goals of standards — World class standards: Whose world, which economic classes, and what standards?,' in J. Kincheloe and D. Weil (Eds) *Schooling and Standards in the United States: An Encyclopedia*, Santa Barbara, CA, ABC-Clio.

WEIL, D. (2001c) 'Florida's advanced academic standards for the assessment of critical and creative thinking,' in J. Kincheloe and D. Weil (Eds) *Schooling and Standards in the United States: An Encyclopedia*, Santa Barbara, CA, ABC-Clio.

WEIL, D. and ANDERSON, H. (Eds) (2000) *Perspectives in Critical Thinking: Essays by Teachers in Theory and Practice*, New York, Peter Lang.

WEINSTEIN, M. (1998) *Robot World: Education, Popular Culture, and Science*, New York, Peter Lang.

WELCH, S. (1985) *Communities of Resistance and Solidarity*, Maryknoll, NY, Orbis Books.

WELLS, D. (1987) *Empty Promises*, New York, Monthly Review Press.

WESSON, L. and WEAVER, J. (2001) 'Administration — Educational standards: Using the lens of postmodern thinking to examine the role of the school administrators,' in J. Kincheloe and D. Weil (Eds) *Schooling and Standards in the United States: An Encyclopedia*, Santa Barbara, CA, ABC-Clio.

WESTKOFF, M. (1982) 'Women's studies as a strategy for change: Between criticism and vision,' in G. Bowles and R. Klein (Eds) *Theories of Women's Studies*, Boston, Routledge and Kegan Paul.

WEXLER, P. (1987) *Social Analysis of Education: After the New Sociology*, London, Routledge and Kegan Paul.

WHITE, H. (1978) *Topics of Discourse*, Baltimore, Johns Hopkins University Press.

WHITSON, J. (1986) 'Interpreting "the freedom of speech": Some First Amendment education cases,' in J. Deely (Ed.) *Semiotics: 1985*, New York, University Press of America.

WHITSON, J. (1991) *Constitution and Curriculum*, New York, Falmer.

WICKER, T. (1975) *On Press*, New York, Viking Press.

WIENER, J. (2000) 'Hard to muzzle: The return of Lynne Cheney,' *The Nation*, October 2, <http://past.thenation.com/cgi-bin/framizer.cgi>.

WIGGINS, G. (1989) 'A true test: Toward a more authentic and equitable assessment,' *Phi Delta Kappan*, 70, 9, pp. 703–13.

WILLERS, J. (1987) 'Interpretive social inquiry as future educational history,' Paper presented to the Southern History of Education Society, Knoxville, Tennessee.

WILLINSKY, J. (1997) 'Accountability in action,' in T. Carson and D. Sumara (Eds) *Action Research as a Living Practice*, New York, Peter Lang.

WILLINSKY, J. (1999) *Technologies of Knowing: A Proposal for the Human Sciences*, Boston, Beacon Press.

WILLINSKY, J. (2001a) 'Knowledge — Raising the standards for democratic education: Research and evaluation as public knowledge,' in J. Kincheloe and D. Weil (Eds) *Schooling and Standards in the United States: An Encyclopedia*, Santa Barbara, CA, ABC-Clio.

WILLINSKY, J. (2001b) *After Literacy: Essays*, New York, Peter Lang.

WILLIS, G. (1978) 'Phenomenological methodologies in curriculum,' *Journal of Curriculum Theorizing*, 1, pp. 65–79.

WILSON, S. (1977) 'The use of ethnographic techniques in educational research,' *Review of Educational Research*, 47, 1, pp. 245–65.

WIRTH, A. (1983) *Productive Work — In Industry and Schools*, Lanham, MD, University Press of America.

WOOD, P. (1988) 'Action research: A field perspective,' *Journal of Education for Teaching*, 14, 2, pp. 135–50.

YEAKEY, C. (1987) 'Critical thought and administrative theory: Conceptual approaches to the study of decision-making,' *Planning and Changing*, 18, 1, pp. 23–32.

YOUNG, M. (1971) *Knowledge and Control: New Directions for the Sociology of Education*, London, Macmillan.

YOUNG, R. (1990) *A Critical Theory of Education: Habermas and Our Children's Future*, New York, Teachers College Press.

YOUNG, S. (1986) 'Guba as a vanguard of naturalistic inquiry: A harbinger of the future?,' Paper presented to the Bergamo Conference on Curriculum Theory and Practice, Dayton, Ohio.

YOUNG, T. and YARBROUGH, J. (1993) 'Reinventing sociology: Mission and methods for postmodern sociologists,' *Red Feather Institute*, Transforming Sociology Series, 154.

ZAPPULLA, C. (1997) *Suffering in Silence: Teachers with AIDS and the Moral School Community*, New York, Peter Lang.

ZENO, G. (1998) 'A cultural critique of the use of networked electronic discourse in a liberatory composition pedagogy,' http://ocbbs.odessa.edu/public/oc/staff_dept/mjorday/index.htm.

ZEVIN, J. (2001) Personal correspondence.

ZINN, H. (1984) 'What is radical history?,' in R. Sherman (Ed.) *Understanding History of Education*, 2nd edn, Cambridge, MA, Schenkman.

ZUSS, M. (1999) *Subject Present: Life-Writings and Strategies of Representation*, New York, Peter Lang.

Name Index

Subject Index